W9-DCC-449

Developmental Editors

THE POLITICS OF TERRORISM

edited by
Michael Stohl
Department of Political Science
Purdue University
West Lafayette, Indiana

MARCEL DEKKER, INC.   New York and Basel

Library of Congress Cataloging in Publication Data

Main entry under title:

The Politics of terrorism.

    (Political science ; 9)
    Includes bibliographical references and index.
    1. Terrorism—Political aspects—Addresses, essays,
lectures. I. Stohl, Michael [Date]   II. Series:
Political science (New York) ; 9.
HV6431.P64   322.4'2   78-21088
ISBN 0-8247-6764-0

MARCEL DEKKER, INC.
270 Madison Avenue, New York, New York 10016

Current printing (last digit):
10 9 8 7 6 5 4 3 2 1

PRINTED IN THE UNITED STATES OF AMERICA

for Cynthia

Preface

The collection of essays that follows introduces students to the concept and practice of terrorism in the process of politics. The assembled authors explore the major theories, concepts, strategies, ideologies, practices, and implications of contemporary terrorism. From these explorations of political terrorism, students should become cognizant of the importance of the historical and situational constraints relevant to an analysis of terrorism. Hopefully, they will also gain some of the necessary tools to perform their own analysis of new situations as they arise.

In the process of assembling this collection, I have received the assistance of a number of persons to whom this preface acknowledges and expresses thanks. Kenneth Friedman and Dr. Maurits Dekker first encouraged and expressed interest in the project. Primary thanks go to the contributors whose original essays are, of course, the principal merit of the collection. To those prompt and cooperative contributors who patiently waited for their, shall we say kindly, not so prompt and cooperative contributors, I extend my appreciation. To the not so prompt, who resisted my early attempts to terrorize them into submission, thank you for finally finishing. Special thanks to Peter Grabosky, who constantly appraised me of information and materials that would be of use in developing the collection and the introductory essay.

The transformation of a collection of essays from manuscript to book was made possible by the efforts of the production staff at Marcel Dekker. The reader should be aware that some of the chapters were not edited for sexism, and as a result, masculine forms were used where actual gender is indefinite.

Finally, I extend my love and appreciation to Cynthia, Rachel, and Ilene for providing an atmosphere within which it is a pleasure to both work and play.

Michael Stohl

Contents

Contributors

Vaughn F. Bishop is Assistant Professor of Political Science at Emory University in Atlanta.

Raymond R. Corrado has taught comparative politics at the University of Pittsburgh and been a staff member of the Department of Political Science at Simon Fraser University in British Columbia. While a Canada Council Fellow and member of the Peace and Conflict Programme of the University of Lancaster, he conducted research on ethnic nationalism in Great Britain, resulting in a number of articles and a forthcoming book.

P. N. Grabosky is Director of the South Australian Office of Crime Statistics in Adelaide. He has been a Research Associate at the Center for Urban Affairs, Northwestern University; Russell Sage Fellow in Law and Social Science at Yale Law School; and Associate Professor of Political Science at the University of Vermont. In addition to articles on criminal policy and legal systems, he is co-author of *The Politics of Crime and Conflict: A Comparative History of Four Cities* and author of *Sydney in Ferment: Crime, Dissent and Official Reaction 1788-1973.*

Ted Robert Gurr is Payson S. Wild Professor of Political Science and Chairman of the department at Northwestern University. His books on civil conflict include *Why Men Rebel,* which received the Woodrow Wilson Prize as best book of 1970 in political science, and the widely publicized report *Violence in America: Historical and Comparative Perspectives,* prepared for the National Commission on the Causes and Prevention of Violence. He is also author or editor of a dozen other books and monographs, the most recent of which are *Patterns of Authority* (with Harry Eckstein) and *The Politics of Crime and Conflict: A Comparative History of Four Cities* (with P. N. Grabosky and Richard C. Hula). His current interests are historical processes of political conflict and change.

Frederic D. Homer is an Associate Professor of Sociology at the University of Wyoming and Director of the Administration of Justice Program. He is the author of published essays on crime and violence and of *Guns and Garlic: Myths and Realities of Organized Crime,* which was listed among the outstanding books published by university presses during 1973 and early 1974 by *American Scholar,* the publication of Phi Beta Kappa.

Richard C. Hula is Assistant Professor of Political Economy and Political Science at the University of Texas at Dallas. He is the coauthor of *The Politics of Crime and Conflict.*

Peter R. Knauss is Assistant Professor of Political Science at the University of Illinois at Chicago Circle. He has written several articles on political development in Kenya and Algeria which have appeared in the *Journal of Modern African Studies* and the *African Studies Review.* Research for his chapter was conducted during a Fulbright-Hays Professorship in Algeria.

Edward Mickolus is a Political Analyst with the International Issues Division, Office of Regional and Political Analysis, of the Central Intelligence Agency. He is completing a book entitled *Transnational Terrorism: Analysis of Terrorists, Events, and Environments,* which will also serve as his doctoral dissertation at Yale University. He has written on political psychology, revolutionary movements, African affairs, international organizations, and simulation methods for such journals as *Orbis, International Journal of Group Tensions, Terrorism, Social Studies,* the *Journal of the John Hay Society,* and the *Journal of Irreproducible Results.*

John W. Sloan is Associate Professor of Political Science at the University of Houston. He has published essays on Guatemalan politics, European integration, The Latin American Free Trade Association, Colombian politics, and U.S. policy toward Latin America.

Michael Stohl is Associate Professor of Political Science at Purdue University and Research Associate at the Richardson Institute for Conflict and Peace Research, Lancaster, England. He has published a number of articles on the relationship between foreign and domestic politics with special emphasis on the role of violence in politics. His book on this subject, *War and Domestic Political Violence: The American Capacity for Repression and Reaction,* appeared in 1976.

D. A. Strickland has taught political theory at Northwestern University and the University of New Mexico in recent years and is an editor of the forthcoming journal *Social Practice.* Research for his chapter was conducted during a Fulbright-Hays Professorship in Algeria.

Harry R. Targ is Associate Professor of Political Science and a member of the American Studies Committee, Purdue University. He is the author of numerous articles on childhood political socialization, peace education and world order studies, alternative futures, and theories of dominance and dependency. He is the coauthor of *Constructing Alternative World Futures* and coeditor of *Planning*

Alternative World Futures (both with Louis R. Beres) and is coeditor of *Global Dominance and Dependence: Readings in Theory and Research* (with Lawrence V. Gould).

Mary B. Welfling is a Research Scientist with the Minnesota Crime Control Planning Board. She has been an Assistant Professor of Political Science at Virginia Polytechnic Institute and State University and at Yale University. Her articles on comparative politics, African politics, and methodology appear in the *American Political Science Review, Comparative Political Studies,* and *Journal of Conflict Resolution.*

THE POLITICS OF
TERRORISM

Introduction

Myths and Realities of Political Terrorism

Michael Stohl*
Department of Political Science
Purdue University
West Lafayette, Indiana

> *Yet the most terrible of terrors*
> *Is man in his delusions.* (Schiller)

Introduction

Political terrorism, while not a recent addition to the catalog of humankind's problems, has achieved a position of notoriety rivaled by few contemporary global crises. Media fascination and the undeniable fact that terrorism provides a riveting spectacle, coupled with the honest concern of governments and their populations, have catapulted terrorism into a priority area for study. The burgeoning journalistic and scholarly literature that has resulted from this increased awareness has unfortunately not been accompanied by a commensurate increase in the understanding of the phenomenon.

The collection of essays that follows illuminates the process of political terrorism. The authors, as students of terrorism, do not have the capability to eliminate the causes of terrorism, nor even the symptoms. However, it is hoped that the analytic and historical examinations of the processes of political terrorism presented here will help to eliminate the problem of delusion as humankind confronts terrorism in the future.

*The author is also affiliated with the Richardson Institute for Conflict and Peace Research, Lancaster, England, where he is spending the academic year, 1978-1979.

Myths of Contemporary Political Terrorism

We begin the process of reducing the possibility of delusion by examining in this introductory essay eight pervasive myths regarding contemporary political terrorism. Next, we briefly explore some persistent realities of the purposes and processes of terrorism and conclude with an overview of the chapters of this volume. The eight myths discussed below are the following:

1. Political terrorism is the exclusive province of antigovernmental forces.
2. The purpose of political terrorism is the production of chaos.
3. Political terrorism is the province of madmen.
4. Terrorism is criminal, not political, activity.
5. All insurgent violence is political terrorism.
6. Governments always oppose nongovernmental terrorism.
7. Terrorism is exclusively a problem relating to internal political conditions.
8. Political terrorism is a strategy of futility.

A note of caution and explanation prior to the discussion of these myths is appropriate here. Although each of the myths presented is widely accepted, it is doubtful that the set of myths as a whole is accepted by any individual. The discussion of the myths provides a vehicle to introduce the reader to the complexities of terrorism.

Myth 1:   Political Terrorism Is the Exclusive
Province of Antigovernmental Forces

Perhaps the most important place to begin our survey of the myths of contemporary terrorism is with the myth that terrorism is the exclusive province of insurgents, dissidents, or antigovernmental forces. Although scholars and diplomats continue to debate the precise definition of the term "terrorism," a quite typical approach to the meaning of the term may be found in the statement of William Hannay (1974, p. 268) that

> recent contemporary usage tends to restrict its [terrorism] meaning to either
> random or extortionate violence, aimed ultimately at the target state of a
> guerrilla, resistance or liberation movement but which strikes at unarmed
> civilians, diplomats or non combatants. [See also Butler, 1976; Feary,
> 1976; Laqueur, 1976; Mallin, 1971, among many others.]

The particular irony of this myth is that the first usage of the term "terror" developed in response to the systematic employment of violence and the guillotine by the Jacobin and Thermidorian regimes in France.

> Etymologists claim that the English terms *terrorism, terrorist terrorise* did not come into use until the equivalent French words *terrorisme, terroriste, terroriser* had developed in the revolutionary period between 1793 and 1798. [Wilkinson, 1975, p. 9; see also Lefebvre, 1964, pp. 6-11]

The singular exception to this myth that is proposed by most liberal Western authors is the recognition that nondemocratic, totalitarian, fascist, or communist states practice terrorism or are able to remain in power only because of their utilization of terrorist practices.[1] The implicit conclusion of these writers is that terrorism is not something that is practiced by the governments of liberal Western democracies. However, it has become clear that in the past 15 years, a number of U.S. governmental agencies and employees have engaged in actions against internal dissidents, which Western liberal authors would have labeled as terrorism if these actions had occurred in the Soviet Union or Spain. (See Blackstock, 1976; Halperin et al., 1976; Wise, 1976 for an analysis of these activities.)

Yet the myth persists. Its persistence in the scholarly literature is all the more peculiar in that the finest analytical work on the nature of terrorism has been conducted by scholars who were primarily interested in the use of terrorism by governments. I refer here to the outstanding contributions of Arendt (1966), Moore (1966), Walter (1969), and Dallin and Breslauer (1970). In an interesting speculative work on the problem of ruling new nations, Howard Wriggins (1969) in a style reminiscent of Machiavelli, entitles one of his chapters "Intimidate the Opponent and the Wavering Ally" and proceeds to examine different techniques rulers have employed in retaining their power. The important point to be considered before leaving this myth is that the Reign of Terror, which characterized the Jacobin period in France, was not an isolated phenomenon. There have been, are, and most likely will continue to be regimes that are dependent upon or employ terror as a basic component ot their rule.

Myth 2: The Purpose of Political Terrorism
Is the Production of Chaos

A second myth, intimately related to the first, is that terrorism both in purpose and in practice produces chaos. In fact, a primary purpose of terrorism, as practiced by challengers of governmental authority, is the production of chaos to accelerate social disintegration, to demonstrate the inability of the regime to govern, and to challenge the legitimacy of attempts by such regimes to impose order. That insurgent terrorists are often quite successful, at least in the short term, at producing chaos is not often disputed. However, the most persistent and successful use of terror both in the past and in the modern era has been demonstrated by governments and authorities for the purpose of creating, maintaining, and imposing order.

> Mass terror has been used many times to consolidate and maintain power, and by various institutions and groups to achieve various ends. Spanish Inquisition was an instrument of this kind wielded by the Catholic Church, Calvin also used the stake as a means of terror against the Unitarians; and the Jacobins of the French Revolution resorted to the guillotine against the non-Jacobins. After the fall of the Paris Commune in 1871, mass terror was directed by the reactionary "versailles" French forces against the French workers. [Gross, 1957, p. 113]

The justification and necessity of state terror in postrevolutionary societies for the purpose of establishing and protecting the revolutionary society has nowhere been more vigorously presented than in Leon Trotsky's *Terrorism and Communism,* which was a reply to the criticism of the methods of the new Soviet regime by Karl Kautsky. Trotsky discusses the origin of the terror in the revolutionary struggle and takeover:

> The degree of ferocity of the struggle depends on a series of internal and international circumstances. The more ferocious and dangerous is the resistance of the class enemy who have been overthrown, the more inevitably does the system of repression take the form of a system of terror. [Trotsky, 1961, p. 55]

Terrorism thus becomes the weapon of the new regime in the takeover stage as it attempts to consolidate and protect its position. Dallin and Breslauer (1970, p. 13), in addition to Trotsky, remind us that use of terror at this stage is characteristic of revolutionary regimes in general, not simply a characteristic of communist takeovers.

This is not to say, however, that the official communist position is one of support for terrorism at all stages of revolutionary action. Quite the contrary is the case. "The classic and official communist formulation has not changed since Lenin characterized terrorism as a form of 'infantilism'" (Thompson, 1976, p. 1284). Current Soviet thinking can be ascertained from the following:

> Marxism-Leninism rejects individual terror as a method of revolutionary action since it weakens the revolutionary movement by diverting the working people away from the mass struggle. "The first and chief lesson," V. I.

Lenin wrote, "is that only the revolutionary struggle of the masses is capable of achieving any serious improvements in the life of the workers. . . ." International terrorism is radically different from the revolutionary movement of the people's masses, whose aim is to effect fundamental changes in society and which alone is capable of so doing. The terrorist act, however, even if its main point is to awaken public opinion and force it to pay attention to a particular political situation, can only have limited consequences: say, lead to the release of a group of prisoners, increase the financial assets of an organization. [Terekhov, 1974, pp. 20-22]

Myth 3: Political Terrorism is the Province of Madmen

A third myth, one that finds a particularly warm reception in the American media and in governmental statements concerning terrorism, is that terrorists are mentally unbalanced. The position taken in such statements and commentaries takes the form that only madmen would resort to many of the actions that terrorists have undertaken. Gerald McKnight, an English journalist, points out that "the comfortably accepted notion is that they are people lost to love and affection, twisted by hates and frustrations: perhaps no better than dangerous psychopaths" (1974, p. 13). This comfortably accepted notion would be the reasonable conclusion of many casual observers as they peruse their evening newspapers or sit watching the evening news and learn of the latest exploits of individual terrorist groups or actors, each treated as an isolated event, devoid of any political meaning except what the audience can decipher from the presentation of the immediate terrorist demands or messages. Rarely are actions of terrorists presented as part of an ongoing political struggle, related to any particular goals, and rarely are these goals presented as reasonable or even meaningful.

A corollary to this myth is found in the penchant of American observers to psychologize, to reduce structural and political problems to ones of individual pathologies and personal problems. In a recent series of hearings before Representative Ichord's now defunct Committee on Internal Security, Dr. F. Gentry Harris found the committee receptive to his assertion that

if we want an understanding of the really effective or driving forces or motives in terrorism we have to look deep. Such motives are not worn on the sleeve. In terrorism there are four of special interest. When we examine an individual terrorist this set can be looked for. We can call these (1) the assertion of masculinity (or femininity in the case of women); (2) desire for depersonalization, that is, to get outside or away from oneself, as a result of chronic low self-esteem; (3) desire for intimacy; and (4) belief in the magic of violence or blood. [1974, p. 4429]

If the perpetrators of terrorism have such severe psychological hangups, why look for any particular political source for their acts?

In addition to the theoretical difficulties that this approach to terrorism entails, there is a very immediate and practical shortcoming in accepting this myth. There are direct and unfortunately too obvious policy implications in accepting the myth of terrorists as madmen. When confronted by an insurgent terrorist action in progress, whether it be a hijacking, kidnapping, or other "hostage-barricade" situation where innocent civilians are directly involved, a policy maker accepting this myth might very well assume that negotiations and bargaining with the terrorists could not proceed on a rational basis. Thus, the only avenue left open to the policy maker is the use of force in an attempt to overpower the perpetrators with all the added risk that such behavior entails for the hostages (witness the unfortunate results at Munich in 1972).

However, the evidence is overwhelming, at least in the case of criminal hostage-barricade situations, that negotiations conducted by trained police personnel will most likely produce a nonviolent conclusion to the situation. In over eighty such situations in the past 3 years, the hostage team of the New York Police Department, using principles expounded by Harvey Schlossberg in *Psychologist with a Gun* (1974), have neither lost a hostage or a hostage taker (see Gelb, 1977, and Miller, 1977). The single clearly political hostage-barricade situation that occurred in the United States took place in March 1977 in Washington, D.C. The District of Columbia police employed a negotiating strategy in their confrontation with the Hanafi Muslims, which, from the standpoint of saving of lives, had quite successful results.

There is much criticism of such a strategy. Walter Laqueur (1976, p. 105) suggests that if governments did not give in to terrorist demands, there would be no further terror or it would be much reduced in scale. Laqueur also asserts that the media who broadcast the terrorist's exploits and the psychologists who advocate negotiation are among the best friends that the terrorists have. Laqueur is not alone in his objections to negotiations with terrorists or to submission to terrorist demands. The official policy of the U.S. Department of State (in contradistinction to the policy of most domestic American law enforcement agencies) during the Nixon-Kissinger-Ford tutelage was one of no negotiation, no ransom or yielding of any kind to terrorist demands (see Feary, 1976).

The official Israeli government position also disavows any possibility of negotiation. The Israeli case provides both counterfactual evidence to the Laqueur thesis and an excellent example of the problem of discussing terrorism without reference to the actual political situation. After 7 years of a clearly stated and consistent policy of no negotiations with, and no concessions to, terrorists that confront them, and furthermore delivering swift and brutal reprisals for any such confrontations, the problem of political terrorism in Israel has not by any means been alleviated. It has in fact been argued (see Miller, 1977) that the nonnegotiation policy may be viewed as a challenge to the Palestinian terrorists to escalate the level and horror of their attacks. Miller suggests that the transfer to children as the targets of terror that took place at Maalot in 1974 may well have occurred because the terrorists were trying to discover some act that would compel negotiations by the Israelis. The Israelis did not alter their position. The Israelis feel that any such negotiation would provide the Palestinians the forum they were seeking and in an important political sense "legitimate" their existence as far as "official" Israeli actions were concerned. Thus, the Israelis refused to sacrifice the long-term policy on nonrecognition (as much as it obviously pained them to do so) to the short-term possibility of saving lives.

The path out of the maze constructed by terrorists is not simple or inexpensive to travel. The important point is that if policy makers and the public refuse to recognize that terrorists are not universally psychopathic but are quite often serious political actors, the options for dealing with terrorists will be foreclosed. It is obvious that it is the policy maker's responsibility to balance the costs of the terrorists achieving their aim with the investment in lives that may or may not be saved now and in the future. It is also clear that a simple strategy of nonnegotiation, while obviously evidence of firm resolution, does not have any evidence on its side that it will prevent future terrorism. It is equally clear that a policy of negotiation with terrorists does not prevent future terrorism, but it does have a remarkable record of success in saving lives in the present.

Myth 4: Political Terrorism Is Criminal Activity

A myth directly related to the myth that all terrorists are psychopaths is one that is subscribed to, and promoted by, virtually all governments—that is, that terrorism is the activity of criminals. The purpose of this myth is to deny insurgents any possible legitimacy with the population they are trying to influence by their terrorist actions. Most modern systems of jurisprudence do not recognize "political" crimes as distinct from "purely" criminal acts, and thus governments consistently portray acts that terrorists conceive of as acts against the state for political ends as criminal activities with purely individual motives.

The waters of this myth become particularly murky, however, when governments that are engaging in terrorist activities themselves are caught not only consorting with organized crime operatives but also perpetrating "political" acts that surely appear "criminal" to their populations (see Halperin et al., 1976, and Wise, 1976 for discussions of the lawless American state). The government, of course, justifies its behavior in the name of national security, but a population would certainly have difficulty in discovering what makes governmental behavior in this instance political when the same act, if perpetrated by antigovernment "terrorists," would surely be condemned as a wanton criminal act.

> The concept of "political crime" has played no significant part in American legal history and hardly a greater role in American political history. Except in one important legal area, the United States, along with most other nations in the Anglo-American legal tradition, recognizes no concept of political crime that identifies a category of offenses possessing distinctive doctrinal significance or requiring application of distinctive modes of treatment to convicted offenders. [Allen, 1974, p. 25]

To illustrate the process whereby terrorists' acts are simply treated as criminal, let us briefly look at one of the more widely used tactics available to terrorists—kidnapping. It is a technique widely used in Argentina and in the past by the Tupamaros of Uruguay. Most of the kidnappings are treated as simple criminal acts and are isolated by law enforcement agencies as evidence of the base motives of extortion and blackmail. Richard Clutterback, author of a manual designed for elites and governments, illustrates the manner in which the political is collapsed into the criminal in the United States:

> Though the United States has a high score of criminal kidnappings there have been virtually no political kidnappings. The Symbionese Liberation Army (SLA) tried to put a political gloss on the kidnapping of Patricia Hearst, by making an initial demand for food for the poor, but it soon emerged that it was a straightforward criminal gang at work, with nothing more political in mind than a hatred of the rich. [1975, p. 42]

Whatever limited sympathies one might have for the political position of the SLA, surely the trivializing of their motives and objectives leads to a rather convenient solution to the problem of political terrorism in the United States—there is none! This solution, although useful for the purpose of propaganda, does not contribute much to the understanding of terrorist action.

Myth 5: All Insurgent Violence Is Political Terrorism

A fifth myth is that all insurgent violence and attacks are terrorist in nature. It is a commonplace for commentators as well as governments to portray regime opponents as terrorists because, as David Fromkin points out, "terrorism is so much more evil than other strategies of violence that public opinion sometimes can be rallied against it" (1975, p. 695). Walter Laqueur, an expert on guerrilla war, collapses the tactic of terrorism within the strategy of guerrilla warfare, effectively treating them as one phenomenon. Laqueur next attempts to demonstrate that in only one noncolonial, peacetime case has guerrilla war (read "terrorism") been successful in bringing the guerrillas to power (Laqueur, 1976, p. 103; for the same collapsing of concepts see also E. Halperin, 1976). That victory by guerrillas was

Castro's. The significant point, however, is that Castro's leading theorist of guerrilla war, Che Guevara, disavowed the use of terrorism. Guevara contended that

> terrorism, a measure that is generally ineffective and indiscriminate in its effects, since it often makes victims of innocent people and destroys a large number of lives that would be valuable to the revolution . . . hinders all more or less legal or semi-clandestine contact with the masses and makes impossible unification for actions that will be necessary at a critical moment. [1969, p. 26]

The important point to be kept in mind is that while some guerrillas, for example, the Vietcong, and FLN, may resort to terrorist tactics for tactical and strategic reasons they do not terrorize the populations within which they operate so they may, following Mao's dictim, "swim like fish in water" (for an extended discussion of this point see Wilkinson, 1975, pp. 79-107).

Myth 6: Governments Always Oppose Nongovernmental Terrorism

Contemporary research on violence and politics has traditionally considered government as society's neutral conflict manager, interested primarily in creating the conditions within which a healthy society may function and enforcing the maintenance of political order. However, as indicated elsewhere (Stohl, 1976; see Nardin, 1971, for a more extended discussion), the state may more usefully be considered as a party to conflict and as such not necessarily a neutral one. The myth that governments view all nongovernmental terrorism as disruptive and therefore are against nongovernmental terrorism occurring within their own borders arises from this misunderstanding of the role of government.

It is quite clear that vigilantism, whether from the right or the left, often employing terrorist tactics, which seeks to assist the established government in the performance of the maintenance of order, is often tolerated and too often encouraged by governments. Two of the most notorious contemporary illustrations of this phenomenon are found in Brazil and Argentina. The Esquadrao da Morte ("death squad") in Brazil, thought to consist mainly of off-duty policemen, has executed an estimated 500 to 1200 persons. According to persons claiming to be Esquadrao members, the death squads have been taking these actions because of the inefficiency of Brazil's established judicial institutions. (Rosenbaum and Wederberg, 1976, p. 10). In Argentina, the Anti-Communist Alliance (the Triple A) is believed to have been established by Jose Rega, the chief advisor to Isabel Peron and minister of social welfare in her regime. Within a 10-month period in 1974 and 1975, the Triple A is believed to have assassinated over 200 persons (see Clutterback, 1975, p. 50).

Government tolerance of vigilantism is not, by any means, confined to the

South American continent nor to the present. The activities of the Ku Klux Klan in the American South during and following Reconstruction and in the South and Midwest following World War I were intended to terrorize blacks and others. "It was always vaguely apparent that police and other law enforcement agencies were either employing Klan members, or that the local sheriff, for example, was working in a kind of tacit agreement with the Klan" (Kreml, 1976, p. 62; see also Chalmers, 1965). In Northern Ireland the Protestant establishment tolerated and encouraged what Rosenbaum and Sederberg (1976, p. 12) describe as social-group-control vigilantism to maintain the status quo. The silence of the government of the United Kingdom in Westminster was viewed as tacit approval of the policy by Northern Irish politicians. Countless other examples are available (see the collection of essays compiled by Rosenbaum and Sederberg, 1976). The important point for our consideration is the recognition that just as governments employ their own terrorism to impose or maintain internal order, they will sometimes tolerate and perhaps even encourage terrorism by nongovernmental groups.

Myth 7: Terrorism Is Exclusively a Problem
Relating to Internal Political Conditions

There is yet another myth about the role of government and the practice of terrorism that needs exploration. This is the myth that terrorism is primarily a problem for governments threatened with insurgency. That is, we tend to think of terrorism as something having to do with the revolutionary overthrow of regimes or, as in our previous examples, with the prevention of that overthrow by governments and their supporters. However, to complicate the picture, in addition to revolutionary terrorism and repressive terrorism, there is government terror that is exported. All types of governments export terror. Colonel Quadaffi of Libya has been reported to have suported the IRA (Provisional Branch), the Baader-Meinhof "Red Army Faction," and factions of the Palestine Liberation Organization. The Israelis, in addition to their widely publicized commando raids into Lebanon in retaliation for Palestinian terrorist actions, have conducted, through the Mossad (The Hebrew acronym for Central Institute for Intelligence and Security), a clandestine campaign of assassination against Palestinian and Arab agents (see Smith, 1977, p. 4). The covert operations of the American CIA through its dirty tricks, and the harassment and assassination of Soviet defectors also illustrate the covert export of governmental terror.

But, in addition to the covert use of terror by governments outside their own borders, there is the overt employment of terror to coerce other governments to capitulate or submit to the wishes of the dominant. Thomas Schelling (1966) refers to this use of terror as the "Diplomacy of Violence," and Alexander George et al. (1971) label it coercive diplomacy. Its most recent notorious use was the U.S. Christmas bombings of North Vietnam in 1972. The idea of this tactic is to make the possibility of noncapitulation "terrible beyond endurance" (Schelling, 1966, p. 15). It is not because governments are weak that they employ this tactic but rather because another tactic might be costlier in time, lives, or material. Consider the following passage by Schelling and its implications:

> These [the two atomic bombs dropped on Hiroshima and Nagasaki] were weapons of terror and shock. They hurt, and promised more hurt, and that was their purpose. The few small weapons we had were undoubtedly of some direct military value, but their enormous advantage was in pure violence. In a military sense the United States could gain a little by destruction of two Japanese industrial cities; in a civilian sense, the Japanese could lose much. The bomb that hit Hiroshima was a threat aimed at all of Japan. The political target of the bomb was not the dead of Hiroshima or the factories they worked in, but the survivors in Tokyo. The two bombs were in the tradition of Sheridan against the Comanches and Sherman in Georgia. Whether in the end those two bombs saved lives or wasted them, Japanese lives or American lives; whether punitive coercive violence is uglier than straightforward military force or more civilized; whether terror is more or less humane than military destruction; we can at least perceive that the bombs on Hiroshima and Nagasaki represented violence against the country itself and not mainly an attack on Japan's material strength. The effect of the bombs, and their purpose, were not mainly the military destruction they accomplished but the pain and the shock and the promise of more. [1966, pp. 16-17]

Within this single paragraph Schelling has amply demonstrated how and why, as a policy, terror may be effective.

Myth 8: Political Terrorism Is a Strategy of Futility

This brings us to the last myth that we shall discuss—the myth of the futility of terrorism. Walter Laqueur writes: "Terrorism creates tremendous noise. It will continue to cause destruction and the loss of human life. It will always attract more publicity, but politically it tends to be ineffective" (1976, p. 105). We may easily refute Laqueur's argument by reference to the above Schelling passage, the Stalinist terror of the 1930s (see Conquest, 1968), Robespierre and the Thermidorians (see Lefebvre, 1964), and numerous other examples of the successful employment of terror by governments (see Dallin and Breslauer, 1970; Walter, 1969; and Arendt, 1968). However, because Laqueur is, of course, referring only to insurgent terror, his argument should be confronted on his own ground.

Although it is true, as Laqueur has argued, that terrorism and terrorists by themselves have probably not been militarily responsible for a revolutionary victory or the end of colonial rule, is this the proper measure to judge the success or failure of terrorist actions? Let us briefly consider the case of the Palestinians. It is clear that the various terrorist groups have not accomplished their major purpose of dislodging the Israelis from any portion of the territory that they consider their homeland, nor have they achieved any significant military victories. Moreover, a direct consequence of their campaign of terror has been the alienation of a significant portion of the one-fifth of the world's population that Laqueur (1976, p. 105) prefers to call "civilized" and loss of many commandos and their own innocents. However, despite the continuing military failure and the human cost, can it be denied that the terrible price in lives and fear has been in large part responsible for the elevation of the "Palestinian situation" into the "Palestinian question" or the "Palestinian problem"? Can it be denied that Western leaders, the Israelis, and the Arab states have developed a much greater interest in providing a solution to the Palestinian question in the Middle East because the Palestinians have made it prohibitively costly to ignore them in considerations of the Middle East?

The Process and Purposes of Political Terrorism: Victims and Targets

> Terroristic activity, consisting in destroying the most harmful person in the government, in defending the party against espionage, in punishing the perpetrators of the notable cases of violence and arbitrariness on the part of the government and the administration, aims to undermine the prestige of the government's power, to demonstrate steadily the possibility of struggle against the government, to arouse in this manner the revolutionary spirit of the people and their confidence in the success of the cause, and finally, to give shape and direction to the forces fit and trained to carry on the fight. [Program of the Executive Committee, *Narodnaya Volya* ("Peoples Will") 1879[2]]

> If the attribute of popular government in peace is virtue, the attribute of popular government in revolution is at one and the same time *virtue and terror,* virtue without which terror is fatal, terror without which virtue is impotent. The terror is nothing but justice, prompt, severe, inflexible; it is thus an emanation of virtue. [Robespierre, *Discours et Rapports de Robespierre*[3]]

The process of political terrorism has, in its most succinct form, been characterized by Walter (1969) as consisting of three component parts: (1) the act or threat of violence, (2) the emotional reaction to such an act or threat, and (3) the social effects resultant from the acts and reaction. The initiation of the process of terrorism, as may be seen from the two passages just cited, arises for a number of quite different specific purposes, purposes that are dependent upon both the position of the agents and targets of terror.

An important key to the understanding of terrorism is to recognize that whereas each of the component parts of the process is important, the emotional impact of the terrorist act and the social effects are more important than the particular action itself. In other words, the targets of the terror are far more important for the process than are the victims of the immediate act. The act or threat of violence is but the first step. As Fromkin suggests in his analysis of the French misunderstanding of the Algerian situation in the 1950s:

> They the French thought that when the FLN planted a bomb in a public bus, it was in order to blow up the bus; whereas the real FLN purpose in planting the bomb was not to blow up the bus, but to lure authorities into reacting by arresting all the non-Europeans in the area as suspects. [1975, p. 694]

The victims of the terrorist act were the relatively limited number of passengers and bystanders in the area of the bombing. The targets of the bombing were many and varied. The French *colons* in Algeria perceived the attack as aimed at them, became fearful, and demanded greater protection and an increase in security measures. Many began to question the ability of the French government to provide that most basic of governmental services—security. Some formed vigilante groups to engage in activity that they perceived the government as unwilling or incapable of performing. A campaign of terror aimed at the native Algerian population was initiated. The campaign, of course, only further undermined the legitimacy and authority of the French regime. The Algerian population, having been singled out by the regime as a group distinct from "normal" Frenchmen and having become the object of terror by the *colons,* began to question the legitimacy of the regime and became more receptive to the message of the FLN. In addition to these two primary targets, the population and government of continental France began to see the Algerian colony as an economic, military, and political liability and sought a way out of the dilemma. The initial reaction of increased force, while providing a temporary halt to the Algerian revolution, in the end created severe strains within continental France.

In Algeria, as a result of the campaign of terror and the reaction of the French government and the *colons,* victory came to the FLN "less through its own brave and desperate struggle during seven and one-half years of war than through the strains which the war had produced in the foundations of the French polity" (Wolf, 1969, p. 242).

Although the ultimate purposes of terrorism are either to maintain a regime or create the conditions for a new one, there are a number of more immediate purposes for which regimes and insurgents employ terror. The first (and according to Bell [1975, p. 94] the principal) purpose of terrorism is the advertising of the cause. Terrorists by their actions intend not to destroy but to be heard, to be heard by both regimes and possible supporters. A second purpose of terrorism is the winning of specific concessions through coercive bargaining (see our earlier discussion concerning Schelling). The terrorist might be seeking anything from ransom money and/or the release of prisoners to surrender and capitulation. A third purpose of the terrorist is to create or enforce obedience either of the population at large or within the ruling party or insurgent organization (see Horowitz, 1972, p. 198). A fourth purpose, illustrated in the case of the Algerian FLN, would be to provoke indiscriminate reactions or repression. A fifth purpose is the punishment of activity that the terrorist views as illegitimate, and a sixth purpose is the deterrence of activity that the terrorist seeks to prevent.

The techniques for the implementation of these purposes are as unlimited as the terrorist's imagination, but there are a number that have been employed consistently. Terrorists have resorted to each of the following measures: public executions, kidnappings, bombings, hijackings, assassinations, arson, armed attacks, barricade and hostage situations, reprisals, and publishing of "death lists" and other threats to persons and property. Although it is possible for governments and populations to defend themselves against some of these techniques, at some time, or in some cases even prevent a particular behavior, there is no possibility of eliminating all such behavior. The success of each of these measures as terrorist techniques is ultimately dependent upon the reaction of the targets of terrorism.

Overview of the Essays

The chapters that follow explore more fully the purposes, techniques, and processes of political terrorism. The readings are divided into two parts. In Part I the characteristics and components of terrorism are explored across time and space with an emphasis on hypothesis generation and theory building. In Part II the characteristics and processes of terrorism are examined with reference to particular geopolitical regions. These essays examine in greater depth the terrorism of the particular region in question.

The essential characteristics of terrorist activities by nongovernmental groups in the 1960s is the subject of Chapter 1 by Ted Robert Gurr. Utilizing a cross-national data set, Gurr explores the identity and motives of participants, their numbers and organization, their targets and the duration of action, the casualties and the response of governments. The empirical findings challenge a number of widely held propositions of the conventional wisdom about political terrorism, views held by most officials and citizens of Western societies and by revolutionaries on the Left.

In Chapter 2, Peter Grabosky addresses two major questions: (1) Why is contemporary terrorist activity predominately urban? (2) How does the structure of cities condition terrorist organization and practice, repressive and revolutionary? Grabosky explores the utility of various strategies and their particular employment within the urban environment. Relying on evidence from urban settings around the globe, he concludes that the urban environment provides a quite favorable setting for covert and overt operations for both governments and dissidents.

In Chapter 3, Peter Knauss and Donald Strickland, relying on field research in a number of diverse settings, present a series of short case studies of urban riots in the United States, bombings in London, the civil wars in Lebanon and Cyprus, and a longer analysis of regime terrorism in Algeria through which they explore the connection between terrorism and the fear of anarchy. Their analysis challenges the conventional view of violence, terrorism, and politics in modern political theory.

The impact that the sociostructural context has on revolutionary political terrorism is the subject of Chapter 4. Harry Targ examines the characteristics of preindustrial, industrial, and postindustrial societies and discusses the sociostructural context in which revolutionary acts of political terrorism are most likely to occur. Targ concludes that acts of terrorism by revolutionaries are manifestations of the lack of a vibrant revolutionary movement and are thus more likely in preindustrial and postindustrial societies than in industrial ones.

Part II commences with an analysis of the tactics, targets, identity, and motivation of transnational terrorists and governmental responses in the period 1968-1975. Edward Mickolus draws upon the ITERATE (International Terrorism: Attributes of Terrorist Events) data bank that he developed for the Office of Political Research of the Central Intelligence Agency. Mickolus discusses this recent terrorist activity and points to possible future trends.

The character of political terrorism in Western Europe is Raymond Corrado's subject in Chapter 6. Focusing on the phenomena of ethnic terrorism and student-ideological terrorism, Corrado provides historical in-depth analysis of terrorist activity in Northern Ireland with particular reference to the IRA and discusses the foundations and relationship of the German student movements in the nineteenth century and the recent activities of the Baader-Meinhof Group. The major theme of the chapter is that the favorable conditions for terrorist activity in Western Europe are waning.

Mary Welfling in Chapter 7 investigates the use of terrorism in black Africa in three different sociopolitical contexts: (1) colonialism, (2) independent black African regimes, and (3) white minority regimes. Welfling finds that terrorism in Africa is much less pervasive than in many Western societies and hypothesizes that the vulnerability of African regimes to military coups may help to explain the general absence of terrorism in independent black Africa.

The use of terror by regimes and insurgents in Latin America is the subject of Chapter 8 by John Sloan. With particular reference to Argentina, Brazil, and Uruguay, Sloan finds that the fragmentation of the Left probably prevents terrorists and revolutionaries from overthrowing regimes. On the other side, despite the fact that Sloan finds that enforcement terror currently prevails, he suggests that the fragmentation of the Latin American regimes will allow for the continuation of insurgent terror in the future.

Chapter 9 by Vaughn Bishop describes the use of terror as a political tactic by the Palestinians in the Middle East in the period from June 1967 to October 1973. Bishop provides an analysis of the general development of the Palestinian resistance and of the relationship among the Palestinian movement, Israel, the Arab states, and the international community. Bishop stresses that terrorism rarely has a life of its own and is normally viewed by its perpetrators as a tactic for achieving a goal.

Moving a few thousand miles east, Richard Hula, in Chapter 10, provides a general overview of the role of political violence and terrorism in the politics of Bengal and the changing structure of violence and terror in terms of frequency, actors, and motivation in three historical periods: the traditional (1750-1900), the nationalist (1900-1947), and the postindependence (1947-). Hula explores the role of ideology, the roots of leaders and participants, and the specific grievances in each of the periods that led to violence and terror. He provides interesting insight to the surprising degree of stability of elites in Bengal despite the extraordinary level of political violence that has characterized life in the region for centuries.

Finally, Frederic Homer, in Chapter 11, examines the normative and empirical consequences of terror in the United States. Homer identifies three quite different perspectives within which one may evaluate political terrorism. He assesses the impact that these three perspectives have on scholars and governments as they attempt to create response strategies for confronting the problem of terrorism. Finally, he discusses the possibilities and implications of the development of an antiterror establishment for democracy in the United States.

Acknowledgments

The author expresses his appreciation to Irene Diamond, Harry Targ, and Cynthia Stohl for their comments on an earlier draft of this essay.

Notes

1. However, sometimes even this is challenged by contemporary scholars. Cassinelli (1976, p. 47) suggests that in Hitler's Germany, terrorism was not widespread or even that important to the regime and further that a majority of Germans did not feel the terror of the Nazi state but rather merely some repression and unpleasantness. Cassinelli's comments thus also illustrate the difficulty of clearly differentiating terrorism from repression and intimidation by governments.
2. Cited in Hardman (1934, p. 578).
3. Cited in Carr (1966, p. 163).

References

Allen, Francis A. 1974. *The Crimes of Politics.* Cambridge, Mass.: Harvard University Press.

Arendt, Hannah. 1968. *The Origins of Totalitarianism.* New York: Harcourt Brace & World.

Bell, David V. J. 1975. *Resistance and Revolution.* Boston: Houghton Mifflin.

Blackstock, Nelson. 1976. *Cointelpro.* New York: Vintage.

Butler, R. E. 1976. "Terrorism in Latin America." In *International Terrorism: National, Regional and Global Perspectives,* ed. Yonah Alexander, pp. 46-61. New York: Praeger Publishers.

Carr, E. H. 1966. *The Bolshevik Revolution 1917-23,* vol. 1. Harmondsworth, England: Penguin.

Cassinelli, C. W. 1976. *Total Revolution.* Santa Barbara, Calif.: Clio Press.

Chalmers, David. 1965. *Hooded Americanism.* New York: Doubleday.

Clutterback, Richard. 1975. *Living with Terrorism.* New Rochelle, N.Y.: Arlington House Publishers.

Conquest, Robert. 1968. *The Great Terror.* London: MacMillan.

Dallin, Alexander, and Breslauer, George. 1970. *Political Terror in Communist Systems.* Stanford, Calif.: Stanford University Press.

Feary, R. A. 1976. "International Terrorism." *Department of State Bulletin* 74, no. 1918 (March):394-403.

Fromkin, David. 1975. "The Strategy of Terrorism." *Foreign Affairs* 53, no. 4 (July):638-698.

Gelb, Barbara. 1977. "A Cool-Headed Cop Who Saves Hostages." *New York Times Magazine,* April 17, pp. 30-33, 39-91.

George, Alexander, Lall, David, and Simons, William. 1971. *The Limits of Coercive Diplomacy.* Boston: Little, Brown.

Gross, Feliks. 1957. *The Seizure of Political Power.* New York: Philosophical Library.

Guevara, Che. 1969. *Guerrilla Warfare.* Harmondsworth, England: Penguin.

Halperin, Ernst. 1976. *Terrorism in Latin America.* The Washington Papers 55, no. 33. Beverly Hills, Calif., and London: Sage Publications.

Halperin, Morton, Berman, Jerry J., Borosage, Robert L., and Marwick, Christine M. 1976. *The Lawless State.* New York: Penguin.

Hannay, William A. 1974. "International Terrorism: The Need for a Fresh Perspective" *International Lawyer* 8, no. 2 (April).

Hardman, J. B. S. 1934. "Terrorism." In *Encyclopedia of the Social Sciences,* vol. 14, pp. 575-580. New York: Macmillan.

Harris, F. Gentry. 1974. Letter Transmitted to House Committee on Internal Security. *Terrorism.* Hearings, Part 4, 93rd Cong., 2nd sess. Washington, D.C.: U.S. Government Printing Office.

Horowitz, Irving Louis. 1972. *Foundations of Political Sociology.* New York: Harper & Row.

Kreml, William P. 1976. "The Vigilante Personality." In *Vigilante Politics,* ed. H. Jon Rosenbaum and Peter C. Sederberg, pp. 45-63. Philadelphia: University of Pennsylvania Press.

Laqueur, Walter. 1976. "The Futility of Terrorism." *Harper's* 252, no. 1510 (March):99-105.

Lefebvre, George. 1964. *The Thermidorians and the Directory.* New York: Random House.

McKnight, Gerald. 1974. *The Terrorist Mind.* Indianapolis: Bobbs-Merrill.

Mallin, J. 1971. *Terror and Urban Guerrillas.* Coral Gables, Fla.: University of Miami Press.

Miller, Abraham. 1977. "Negotiations for Hostages." Paper presented at the Annual Meeting of the International Studies Association, St. Louis, March 16-20.

Moore, Barrington. 1966. *Terror and Progress-USSR.* Cambridge: Harvard University Press.

Nardin, Terry. 1971. *Violence and the State.* Beverly Hills, Calif.: Sage Publications.

Rosenbaum, H. Jon, and Sederberg, Peter C., eds. 1976. *Vigilante Politics.* Philadelphia: University of Pennsylvania Press.

Schelling, Thomas. 1966. *Arms and Influence.* New Haven, Conn.: Yale University Press.

Schlossberg, Harvey, and Freeman, Lucy. 1974. *Psychologist with a Gun.* New York: Conard.

Smith, Terence. 1977. "Israeli and Arab Agents Go On Killing—Each Other." *New York Times,* January 16, IV,4.

Stohl, Michael. 1976. *War and Domestic Political Violence.* Beverly Hills, Calif.: Sage Publications.

Terekhov, V. 1974. "International Terrorism and the Struggle Against It." *Novoye Vremya,* March 15, pp. 20-22.

Thompson, W. Scott. 1976. "Political Violence and the Correlation of Forces." *ORBIS* 19, no. 4 (Winter).

Trotsky, Leon. 1961. *Terrorism and Communism.* Ann Arbor: University of Michigan Press.

Walter, Eugene V. 1969. *Terror and Resistance.* New York: Oxford University Press.

Wilkinson, Paul. 1975. *Political Terrorism.* New York: Halsted Press.

Wise, David. 1976. *The American Police State.* New York: Random House.

Wriggins, Howard. 1969. *The Rulers Imperative.* New York: Columbia University Press.

part **I**

Theoretical Approaches to the Study
of Political Terrorism

1

Some Characteristics of Political Terrorism in the 1960s

Ted Robert Gurr
Department of Political Science
Northwestern University
Evanston, Illinois

Political terrorism is a distinctive revolutionary strategy in which sustained campaigns of violent action are directed against highly visible public targets. It is a relatively new strategy, one that has been resorted to especially by alienated, youthful members of the middle classes, and it has been increasing rapidly throughout the world. It is a particularly threatening form of political violence, both because of its destructiveness and its potential revolutionary consequences. It has a pronounced international dimension as well, whereby revolutionary terrorists rely on substantial support from similarly disposed groups and nations elsewhere.

The statements in the preceding paragraph are part of conventional wisdom about political terrorism. Most officials and ordinary people in Western societies would agree to them, and quite a few experts as well. So would most writers who have advocated political terrorism as a revolutionary strategy. Almost all the assertions can be found in Carlos Marighella's widely read "Minimanual of the Urban Guerrilla," for example. The only difficulty with this catechism is that not one of its elements is supported by the empirical evidence of the recent past. Some of the assertions are true of specific movements; as generalizations, however, all are false. The irony is that this particular fantasy of the revolutionary Left has been accepted as an ominous political reality by everyone else.

The mythic proportions of political terrorism have a substructure of reality. Political bombings, kidnappings, and assassinations are real and frequent occurrences. We can plot their incidence over time and among countries, categorize their targets, identify the kinds of groups that perpetrate them, and say something about their motives. But when this is done systematically, as I have for eighty-seven countries in the decade from 1961 to 1970, a rather different picture of "terrorist activity" emerges. The typical terrorist campaign was conducted by tiny groups and was short-lived. Their public motives were not notably different from those of groups using other unconventional methods of political action. More specifically, the perpetrators of terrorist activities seemed more often motivated by hostility toward particular policies and political figures than by revolutionary aspirations. Their actions were more often a social nuisance than a serious threat to life and property, more often a security problem than an imminent revolution. In fact one cannot identify even one unambiguous instance in the last 18 years of a campaign of political terrorism that led directly or indirectly to revolutionary change of the kind championed by the Left.

Not all the conclusions that follow from an empirical survey of political terrorism are as iconoclastic as these. It was evident, even in the 1960s, that campaigns of political terrorism were becoming more common in the more prosperous European and Latin American democracies. They also were more persistent in these countries, but less deadly than in the poorer, nondemocratic countries of the Third World. The powerful authoritarian countries, the Communist ones in particular, have remained largely free of terrorist activities. In the conclusion to this chapter some inferences are drawn about the structural characteristics of countries that seem most conducive to political terrorism. The first task, though, is to review some evidence and interpretations of trends and patterns in political terrorism on a global scale, relying mainly on the 1961-1970 data mentioned above.

This study has two limitations. It is restricted to terrorist actions and campaigns carried out by internal groups; thus it does not include the international terrorist acts by various Palestinian groups that began in 1967. The second is that its empirical generalizations cannot be proved to apply to terrorism in the 1970s. They should be taken as hypotheses, ones that have a solid basis in "contemporary history," against which to evaluate more impressionistic evidence about the immediate present.

Definitions and Data

Intrinsically, terrorism is a state of mind. Political terrorism, presumably, is the state of mind of political actors who are paralyzed by the threat of unpredictable attack. No one has ever attempted to document systematically the existence of such a state of mind in beseiged officials or activists, few of whom would admit to it in any case. So by default the concept has come to be employed to characterize the kinds of actions that are assumed to induce "terrorism." The circularity of this definition is obvious. Those who feel threatened by political violence dramatize the imputed intentions of their assailants by labeling them political terrorists. Governments are among those accused of using such tactics as a means of controlling their subjects. Neither Idi Amin of Uganda nor the new rulers of Cambodia, both of whom rule by terror, would be flattered by the label. The tactics are more widely used by groups opposing governments, but they are much more likely to call themselves "revolutionaries" than "terrorists," and only some of them justify their choice of tactics by reference to an explicit theory of terrorism.[1]

This chapter surveys the use of "terrorist" tactics by private groups for political purposes. The interpretative problems are sidestepped by using an empirical definition of this kind of "political terrorism" that makes no a priori assumptions about what effects the users hope to accomplish by their actions or about how their would-be victims react. The definition has three objective elements. The first is that destructive violence is used, by stealth rather than in open combat. Explosives and incendiary devices are the archetypical weapons of political terrorism, but there are others, including sniping, kidnapping, hijacking, biological agents, and atomic devices, the latter two thus far feared rather than used.

The second element in the definition is that some, at least, of the principal targets are political ones. Political targets include public buildings, political figures and groups, and the military and police. Terroristic acts often are aimed at private targets as well, sometimes for dramatic effects, sometimes because of their political associations, sometimes simply because rebels have many axes to grind.

The third definitional element is that these actions be carried out by groups operating clandestinely and sporadically. This restriction is needed to distinguish the practitioners of terrorism from armed bands of rebels and revolutionaries who operate more or less continuously from areas that they control at least in part. In practice the distinction is not always easy to apply because rebels sometimes use both kinds of tactics. Generally, though, we have excluded from the data all instances of "terrorist" activity that, as in South Vietnam for example, were an intrinsic part of an ongoing movement of armed revolution.

All three elements must be present for an act or set of actions to be considered "political terrorism" in the context of this study.[2] The groups responsible for such actions are called "terrorists" here, but without assuming that they would describe their actions or aims in the language of terrorism.

Data on the world-wide incidence of political terrorism, as defined here, were collected by me and my assistants for the decade of the 1960s as part of a larger study in which information was systematically gathered on all instances of civil strife reported in major news sources. The procedures and sources have been described elsewhere.[3] Because "event counts" are in bad repute in studies of conflict behavior,[4] it should be emphasized that this study was not concerned with events per se, but with identifying the who, what, when, where, why, and how of manifest political conflict. For terrorism, for example, our efforts were aimed at isolating "campaigns" or waves of actions that could be ascribed to particular groups. For each such campaign, as for all instances of open conflict, information was recorded on the identity and motives of the participants; their numbers and organization; the targets and duration of action; the government's retaliatory response, if any; the number and identity of casualties; and the presence and nature of external support—all insofar as the information could be found in news and supplementary sources.

This study includes an analysis of the data on political terrorism identified in the larger study, beginning with an enumeration of the events and continuing with an analysis of their other properties. The reader must understand that these data are not a complete or wholly representative portrait of political terrorism in the decade of the 1960s because of the selective nature of journalistic reporting and the fact that not all countries were surveyed. These two limitations need explanation before the data are examined.

First, the information in journalistic sources gives most emphasis to the larger and more dramatic campaigns of terrorism. It is reasonable to assume that virtually all campaigns that lasted for more than 6 months, or that involved repeated attacks on national political targets, are represented in these data. Isolated instances of bombing and assassination, especially those in out-of-the-way places, are only "sampled" by the press. Readers are asked to assume, as we do, that these data provide a sketch—not a precisely accurate portrayal—of the more serious episodes of political terrorism in the 1960s. They should be reminded too that for the purpose of a global mapping of terrorism, or any common kind of conflict, there are no open alternatives to relying on journalistic accounts. Systematic information of this sort simply is not regularly compiled and made available to scholars by the governments of the world, by the United Nations, or by any private group.[5] Broad surveys are not an alternative to in-depth studies of particular terrorist campaigns and countries, but they are an essential complement to them.

The second limitation on the data is that they refer only to eighty-seven political entities in a world that now has nearly twice that many autonomous states. The smallest and least developed countries of Africa and Asia are excluded and so is China, not because they are unimportant but because news about them is so sparse, or so controlled, that it is unreliable even for our general purposes. The eighty-seven countries nonetheless have some 90 percent of the world's population aside from China. Virtually all of Europe and both Americas are included, and so the findings for those regions have some claim to generality. The eighty-seven countries are listed in Appendix I; note that Hong Kong, Northern Ireland, and Puerto Rico are among them.

For the comparisons that follow, the eighty-seven countries are divided into more homogeneous sets, or clusters, so that the effects of level of economic development, type of political system, and geocultural region on characteristics of terrorism can be seen. The countries were divided into three "developmental" clusters on the basis of their per capita gross national product in the 1960s. The three "political" clusters refer to conditions in 1965 and distinguish among the multiparty democracies, autocracies (principally the Communist states, but also countries like Spain and Taiwan with tightly controlled conservative dictatorships), and countries with "mixed" political systems. The last category might better be labeled "uninstitutionalized," because it consists of Third World countries with untried or chronically unstable political systems. The three regional sets are largely self-explanatory. The European cluster includes Eastern and Western European countries, Israel, and the English-speaking countries of North America, Australasia, and Southern Africa. The two exceptions are Spain and Portugal, which for historical and cultural reasons are included in the Latin cluster, along with Puerto Rico and the independent countries of Latin America and the Caribbean. All other countries are in the Afro-Asian cluster. The clusters to which each country is assigned are shown in Appendix I.

Patterns of Terrorism, 1961-1970

The kinds of acts called terrorism are neither new nor rare. Medieval and French Revolutionary examples have been cited by Paul Wilkinson. The Righteous Assassins, a medieval Muslim group, systematically used murder for political purposes. The Jacobins developed a secular ideology of terrorism and used it to justify their policies against suspected counterrevolutionaries.[6] Walter has documented the use of systematic terrorism as a recurring technique of political control in some African kingdoms before the European conquest.[7] Bombings have been common in a number of European societies and in North America ever since high explosives became widely available, which is to say since the last part of the nineteenth century. Bombings are so common, in fact, that many pass almost entirely without notice except by their targets and the police. For example, the London police reported that 139 bombings and attempts occurred in that city in 1974.[8] Many such actions have private not public motives. In Quebec, where political terrorists were active in the 1960s, police reported that 43 bombings occurred between 1972 and 1975, of which 40 were attributed to warfare between underworld factions and only 3 to political activity.[9] More detailed evidence comes from a survey by the Internal Revenue Service of the United States, covering 15 months in 1969 and 1970. A total of 4330 bombings and incendiary attacks were identified, with the police being able to identify the group responsible in about 1560 cases. Of this number, 56 percent were associ-

ated with student protest (not all of it political, by any means); 33 percent were
attributed to racial extremists, black and white; 8 percent to criminal activities;
2 percent to labor disputes; and 1 percent to attacks on religious institutions.[10]

Our data for the 1960s for eighty-seven countries are restricted to political
terrorism, and we made no attempt to count specific terrorist acts. Instead we
have tried to identify "campaigns," that is, series of terrorist acts carried out by
the same group. The results are summarized in Table 1. There is evidence for
136 campaigns of multiple attacks that covered a wide area or extended for a
substantial period, or both. We also have evidence on 199 more limited episodes
of bombings and assassinations.[11] About 150 of these appeared to be single, un-
connected events: one bombing or one successful or attempted assassination.
Some such events were reported from sixty-three of the eighty-seven countries;
numbers of each type are listed by country in the Appendix. Not too much reliance ought to be placed on these numbers because many such isolated acts go
unreported and others may be part of campaigns whose common source could
not be established from the evidence available.

A more adequate index of the extent of political terrorism is the number
of deaths that resulted from terrorist acts. It is clear from the data in Table 2

Table 1 Incidence of Political Terrorism in 87 Countries, 1961-1970

Group and number of countries	Isolated episodes[a]	Terrorist campaigns[b]
All 87	199	136
Countries grouped by region		
European (30)	74	51
Latin (22)	70	56
Afro-Asian (35)	55	29
Countries grouped by type of regime		
Democratic (35)	105	72
Autocratic (19)	21	21
Mixed (33)	73	43
Countries grouped by level of development		
High (29)	68	56
Medium (29)	82	50
Low (29)	49	30

[a]Single instances and short-lived waves of political bombings and assassinations.
[b]Campaigns involving multiple actions extending over a wide area or a long period, or both.

Table 2 Deaths Reported from Political Terrorism in 87 Countries, 1961-1970[a]

Group and number of countries	Isolated episodes	Terrorist campaigns
All 87	167	4455[b]
Countries grouped by region		
European (30)	26	245
Latin (22)	48	2580
Afro-Asian (35)	92	1630[b]
Countries grouped by type of regime		
Democratic (35)	46	1140
Autocratic (19)	13	615[b]
Mixed (33)	108	2700
Countries grouped by level of development		
High (29)	26	667
Medium (29)	64	908[b]
Low (29)	77	2880

[a]In the events tabulated in Table 1. Many of these figures are rough estimates, and for approximately 5 percent of all instances no estimates of any kind can be made.
[b]Excluding an estimated 6000 deaths caused by the OAS terrorists during the last year of the Algerian war of independence.

that the terrorist campaigns are relatively much more intensive and deadly in their consequences than the more limited episodes. But how serious was terrorism as a threat to life and limb? In the entire decade about 4600 people—including terrorists as well as their victims—were reported to have lost their lives. If the latter stages of the Algerian war are added, the number exceeds 10,000. If Algeria and the four other most deadly campaigns are excluded (in the Camerouns, Guatemala, Cuba, and Venezuela), the death toll was well under 2000. These figures can be compared with our estimate that 3 million people lost their lives in all civil strife in the 1960s,[12] or with the fact that nearly 1000 murders occur in the city of Chicago each year.

More of the political impact of terrorism is due to the threat it poses, which looms far larger to officials and mass media audiences, than to the objective harm done by terrorists. One way of assessing the degree of threat is to consider the duration of terrorist campaigns. In this jaded world, a single day's wave of bombings is not likely to cause more than a passing ripple of anxiety; sustained campaigns like those of the Tupamaros in Uruguay or the Provisional

Table 3 The Estimated Duration of Terrorist Episodes and Campaigns, 1961-1970[a]

Approximate duration	Percentage of episodes and campaigns			
	All (in 87 countries)	European (30)	Latin (22)	Afro-Asian (35)
Total number of cases[b]	*335*	*125*	*126*	*84*
1 day or less	67%	60%	68%	75%
2-6 days	8	5	12	7
1-10 weeks	10	14	10	4
3-8 months	8	14	5	6
9-18 months	4	5	3	5
More than 1½ years	3	3	2	4

[a]From coded information on the episodes and campaigns tabulated in Table 1. The duration of each is the time elapsed from the first action that can be attributed to a group to the last, as of the end of 1970. Some guesswork was involved in ascertaining, first, whether a set of actions was attributable to one group or several, and second, when a group ceased terrorist tactics.
[b]Data on duration were ascertained for all 335 episodes and campaigns. It is likely that some of the episodes of brief duration were parts of longer-term campaigns by unidentified groups.

IRA in Northern Ireland are much more likely to create the panic and paralysis sought by advocates of revolutionary terrorism. Information on the duration of terrorist episodes and campaigns is shown in Table 3, from which it is evident that three-fourths of them are come and gone in less than a week. The data are subject to some error, of course, but where the larger campaigns are concerned they are more reliable than either the counts of deaths or numbers of events. Such campaigns usually have dramatic beginnings that are well recorded in the press and can be dated from then to the last recorded bang. Table 3 shows only percentages; in numbers, there were twenty-eight campaigns of 3 to 8 months duration, fourteen that lasted about a year, and ten that were considerably longer— though the evidence for sustained activity throughout the period is doubtful for many of them.

    The most interesting things to be learned from the data in Tables 1 through 3 concern the distribution of terrorist activity among different groups of countries. Unlike most other forms of political violence, terrorist campaigns and episodes in the 1960s were more common in European and Latin countries than in Afro-Asian ones; in democratic states rather than in autocratic or new Third-World political systems; and in the most prosperous rather than the poorer countries. This comparison is deceptive, though, because *all* forms of civil strife are more deadly in poor, Third World nations. A more accurate comparison, showing the proportion of recorded deaths from political conflict in the 1960s in each of the three regional groups of countries that were due to terrorism, is as follows:

European countries	17%
Latin countries	12%
Afro-Asian countries	0.5%

Terrorism was responsible for a much larger proportion of much smaller numbers of deaths from conflict in the older countries than the new.

In relative if not absolute terms, terrorism was already in the 1960s a more serious problem in the more developed, European and Latin democracies than in other parts of the world. The duration of terrorist campaigns in these countries also appears to have been longer: Table 3 shows that the longer campaigns were heavily concentrated in these countries. Of the eighty-four campaigns that lasted more than a week, forty-four—more than half—were European and twenty-five of the remainder were Latin. When the democracies alone are examined (not shown in Table 3) they have no less than fifty-two of the eighty-four more durable campaigns, compared with eighteen in the autocracies and fourteen in the new Third World states.

A decade is too short a time span to warrant much attention to "trends," but it is evident from Figures 1 and 2 that substantial changes did occur in the incidence of terrorism during the period under review. The number of reported

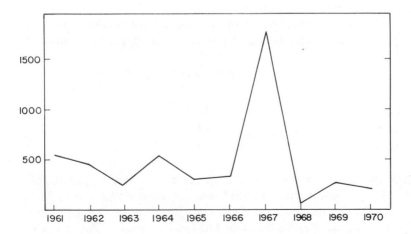

Figure 1   Deaths reported from political terrorism in eighty-seven countries, by year.

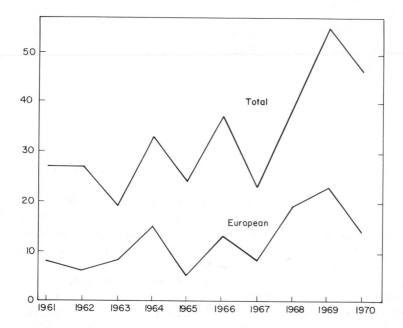

Figure 2 Number of episodes and campaigns of political terrorism in eighty-seven countries, by year of inception, all and European.

deaths per year declined, except for 1967; all deaths in a campaign are attributed in this analysis to the year of its inception, and a particularly deadly campaign began in Guatemala that year. The number of new episodes and campaigns was increasing while deaths decreased, as shown in Figure 2. The increase was most pronounced in the European and Latin countries, as these 5-year totals show:

	Events begun 1961–1965	Events begun 1966–1970
European countries	40	85
Latin countries	44	82
Afro-Asian countries	34	50

These are the main points evident in this survey of patterns of terrorism during the 1960s. Political terrorism was a relatively common tactic in all kinds of nations throughout the decade. It is not a new phenomenon, though its incidence evidently increased during the second half of the decade. The great majority of terrorist campaigns were short-lived, and, with a few notable exceptions, they have not been particularly deadly. Probably most striking is the fact that political terrorism was relatively less common in poorer, authoritarian, and Third World states than in the prosperous democracies of Europe and Latin America. In this respect it is very different indeed from other kinds of political violence. Lest you jump to the conclusion that political terrorism was being widely used as an instrument of class revolutionary struggle in capitalist society, it should be pointed out that its advocacy for that purpose dates from the late 1960s. Moreover we have not yet examined any information on the kinds of groups that used these tactics or their motives. Those are the tasks of the next two sections.

Characteristics of Terrorist Movements, 1961-1970

The actions of political terrorists are more readily observed than the nature of the groups responsible for them. Nonetheless, the sources used for the survey provide considerable information on the kinds of organizations believed to be responsible, including estimates of their size and social composition. This information is summarized in Tables 4, 5, and 6.

Most terrorist actions in the 1960s were carried out by clandestine political groups, as might be expected: This evidently was the case for two-thirds of all actions in which the responsible group was identified, slightly more in the European countries and slightly less in the others (see Table 4). There was virtually no difference between terrorist groups in the Latin and Afro-Asian countries in this regard, so they are not separately shown. More interesting is the frequency with which legal political parties and other above-board political movements have been involved in terrorism. In these cases—nearly one-fourth of the total—the use of terrorist tactics is not necessarily advocated by the organization's leaders. Quite the contrary, as a rule. But the legitimate organization provides the context and cover for violent action for some segment of its members. In the European states, interestingly enough, communal groups are frequently implicated in terrorist activities—a category that includes racial terrorism in ethnically diverse states like the United States and the terrorist campaigns of regional separatists, for example, in Canada, the United Kingdom, Belgium, France, Italy, and Switzerland. Note how rarely communal groups were responsible for political terrorism in the Third World; separatist sentiments in Africa and Asia were more likely to inspire civil wars than terrorist campaigns.

It is easier to identify the organizations responsible for terrorist campaigns than it is to assess the class composition of their membership. In one-third of the cases some estimate could be made, sometimes on the basis of general information (Peronist terrorist groups, for example, are predominantly working class), sometimes from specific information available to the press or police. This information, summarized in Table 5, overrepresents the larger and more publicity-conscious groups. About one-half of these groups draw their membership from

Table 4 Group Context for Terrorist Actions, 1961-1970[a]

	Percentage of episodes and campaigns		
Type of group	All (in 87 countries)	European (30)	Other (57)
Total number of cases[b]	*245*	*108*	*137*
Clandestine political groups	66%	69%	64%
Conventional political groups	23	13	31
Communal groups[c]	9	17	3
Other groups[d]	2	2	2

[a]Derived from coded information on the nature of groups said to be responsible for the events tabulated in Table 1. The data have been adjusted in two ways. First, 16 large-scale terrorist campaigns are excluded from these comparisons; second, campaigns that lasted longer than 1 year are counted separately for each year that they were in progress. The maximum number of cases, after these adjustments, is 336.
[b]This information could not be ascertained for 91 of 336 terrorist episodes and campaigns. Groups responsible for the larger and more persistent campaigns are overrepresented here.
[c]Groups based on a particular regional, linguistic, ethnic, or religious segment of a national population.
[d]Including economic associations and military groups carrying out extralegal terrorist actions.

Table 5 Principal Socioeconomic Classes Represented in Groups Responsible for Terrorist Actions, 1961-1970[a]

	Percentage of episodes and campaigns in which represented		
Classes	All (in 87 countries)	European (30)	Other (57)
Total number of cases[b]	*112*	*51*	*61*
Lower class only	30%	25%	33%
Middle class only	15	18	13
Lower and middle classes	40	39	41
Regime class only[c]	7	4	10
Regime class and others[c]	8	14	3

[a]See Table 4, note a.
[b]This information could not be ascertained for 224 of the 336 episodes and campaigns. Groups responsible for the larger and more persistent campaigns are overrepresented here.
[c]Regime classes include members of the political elite and disaffected military and police personnel.

Table 6 Estimated Membership of Groups Using Terrorist Tactics, 1961-1970[a]

Estimated membership	Percentage of episodes and campaigns			
	All (in 87 countries)	European (30)	Latin (22)	Afro-Asian (35)
Total number of cases	*335*	*125*	*126*	*84*
Less than 50	86%	81%	91%	86%
50–500	8	10	7	5
More than 500	6	9	2	9

[a]From coded information on the episodes and campaigns tabulated in Table 1. For single episodes, membership in the groups responsible usually can only be guessed at, and most of the "less than 50" estimates are of this sort. Membership in groups carrying out the larger campaigns is more often estimated in the sources, though a good deal of guesswork is involved here too.

a single class, more often from the working class than any other. Many of the "middle-class" groups are composed mainly of students, who also are the "middle-class" element in a number of the lower- and middle-class alliances. There are no marked differences among the regional groups of countries. An instructive comparison can be made between the class composition of these groups and those of larger revolutionary groups. Whereas only one-half the terrorist groups involve cross-class membership, virtually all large-scale revolutionary groups on which we have comparable information draw substantially from two or more classes, very often including disaffected members of the military and the civilian political elite.[13] On this limited evidence, political terrorism appears to be a tactic of political activists who lack the broad base of support needed for large-scale revolutionary activity.

There is rarely any precise basis for estimating the number of members in terrorist groups. Even the concept of membership is ambiguous, because many groups rely on noncombatant supporters and intermittently active sympathizers. Such information as is available about groups responsible for limited campaigns suggests that the hard-core activists are very few indeed, say between five and twenty-five. The "Angry Brigade," which was responsible for a dramatic series of bombings in London from 1968 to 1971, was put out of action by the arrest of eight members and the conviction of four of them. Massive car bombings in London in March 1973, inspired by events in Northern Ireland, were laid to a group of 10, all arrested and convicted.[14] In each instance there may have been more activists than were caught and many supporters for whom there were no grounds for arrest, but the point stands that when terrorist groups *are* broken by the police they usually prove to have few members. Such information seldom is known in the case of small groups. Estimates for larger terrorist groups are more readily available from the police, from political experts, and quite often from the groups themselves. These kinds of estimates are obviously unreliable, but on the grounds that some estimate is better than none, Table 6 summarizes the coded information. For the small groups it usually involved forced judgments (that is, guesses) that the groups were quite small. The estimates for larger groups are mainly from the journalistic sources. If anything, the estimates probably over-state the size of terrorist groups. Only twenty-one groups are supposed to have had more than 500 members, and eleven of them were in the European countries. Muslim terrorists operating in France in 1961-1962 are one example; student revolutionaries and racial terrorists in the United States are others, and the Pro-visional IRA is yet another.

The Objectives of Political Terrorism, 1961-1970

There is not much ambiguity about the kinds of people and places that are the immediate objects of terrorist attacks. In the larger campaigns a variety of targets are often chosen: public buildings and private businesses, public figures and the police, political rivals and people chosen at random. Coded information on ter-rorists' targets in 1961-1970 is shown in Table 7, about which a note of clarifica-tion may be needed. The three general categories shown—property, public per-sons, and private persons—are not mutually exclusive; a group that hit targets of each type is counted under each heading. Within each general heading, though, the categories *are* mutually exclusive.

Places are more often chosen as targets than are public persons, although when a government building is bombed the act can be assumed to convey a mes-sage to someone. The preference for property targets was particularly pronounced in the European countries; in Afro-Asian countries terrorists were less solicitous about human life, as was evident from the data on deaths. In Latin countries, places and people were about equally likely to be chosen as targets. Whereas near-ly all terrorist episodes and campaigns included some public targets, whether people or places, a quite substantial proportion of terrorist action was also aimed at private persons (and property, which is not shown separately). Private targets were particularly in favor among European terrorists, about one-third of whom attacked private groups—mostly political or communal ones.

The people who are the most likely targets of terrorist action are politicians and officials, with the military and police coming in second. These two groups were attacked in roughly 40 percent of terrorist episodes and campaigns; victims chosen apparently at random made up only 8 percent of the cases. (The category "various public persons, groups" refers in most instances to campaigns in which both officials and security personnel were attacked.) Random terrorism has

Table 7   Principal Targets of Terrorist Action, 1961-1970[a]

Type of targets	Percentage of episodes and campaigns			
	All (in 87 countries)	European (30)	Latin (22)	Afro-Asian (35)
Total number of cases[b]	*319*	*117*	*125*	*77*
Property targets	*67%*	*86%*	*65%*	*43%*
Domestic only	45	76	31	19
Foreign only	16	9	19	21
Foreign and domestic	6	1	14	3
Public persons and groups	*53*	*36*	*57*	*71*
Domestic political figures only	20	11	18	38
Military or police only	11	13	14	4
Various public persons, groups	13	9	13	22
Foreign political figures, groups	10	4	15	9
Private persons and groups	*24*	*35*	*17*	*18*
Private political groups only	6	10	4	3
Random victims only	8	4	10	12
Other and various	10	20	2	4

[a]From coded information on the targets of terrorist attack; see Table 4, note a. Italicized percentages add to more than 100, because terrorists often take action against several different kinds of targets.
[b]This information could not be ascertained for 17 of 336 terrorist episodes.

gained a great deal of notoriety; it is evident from these data that in the 1960s it was uncommon, and in European countries very rare indeed. It was somewhat more characteristic of terrorist action in Third World countries, but nowhere was it the prevailing tactic.

Because people are among the targets of perhaps two-thirds of all terrorist episodes and campaigns, it is worth asking what proportion of cases do in fact cause death or injury, and to whom. The coded information compiled in Table 8 shows that in over one-third of all episodes and campaigns, and nearly one-half of the European ones, no one was reported to have been either killed or injured. When casualties did occur, they were principally among "noncombatants," which

Table 8 The Identity of Casualties in Episodes and Campaigns of Political
Terrorism, 1961-1970[a]

Casualties	Percentage of episodes and campaigns			
	All (in 87 countries)	European (30)	Latin (22)	Afro-Asian (35)
Total number of cases[b]	*298*	*109*	*118*	*72*
No casualties reported	*37%*	47%	42%	24%
Noncombatants	54	45	52	69
Military or police	14	13	12	18
Terrorists	14	11	15	17

[a]From coded information on the identity of persons killed or injured in episodes and campaigns of terrorism; see Table 4, note a. Percentages add to more than 100 because in many
instances casualties were suffered by several of the groups listed.
[b]This information could not be ascertained for 38 of 336 terrorist episodes and campaigns.

is to say the political and private, national and foreign persons categorized in
Table 7. Security forces and the terrorists suffered casualties in only a small
fraction of cases—14 percent in each instance. As has been seen from other indicators, terrorism in European countries was likely to be less risky for all concerned than elsewhere. One object lesson to be drawn from these data is that
political terrorism has been a relatively low-risk tactic for those who use it. Rioting and guerrilla warfare—two alternative forms of violent political action—can
be shown to cause disproportionately large numbers of casualties among rioters
and guerrillas by comparison with either the security forces or, usually, noncombatants.[15]

Though the targets of terrorists are unambiguous, their purposes are not
always so clear. For larger groups, the "propaganda of the deed" is usually accompanied by outspoken claims and demands. Smaller groups may issue manifestos and give interviews as well, but some are content to let their actions speak
for themselves. In about four-fifths of all instances, objectives were attributed to
terrorists in the sources or could be inferred from the nature of the action. The
coded data are summarized in Table 9. Political objectives of some kind are present almost by definition; the exceptions, all European ones, are terrorist actions
aimed at political targets with social or economic purposes in mind. The most
striking feature of the data is the rarity of revolutionary motives for terrorist
action. Only 8 percent of all episodes and campaigns had as an explicit, primary
objective the seizure of power or the advancement of a particular revolutionary
ideology. To this should be added many of the 14 percent of cases categorized
as having "several of the above (political) motives," and some of those said to
have diffuse political purposes." Even by this generous interpretation of the

Table 9 The Reported Purposes of Episodes and Campaigns of Political Terrorism, 1961-1970[a]

	Percentage of episodes and campaigns			
Purposes	All (in 87 (countries)	European (30)	Latin (22)	Afro-Asian (35)
Total number of cases[b]	*270*	*106*	*95*	*69*
Political purposes	*97%*	*93%*	*100%*	*100%*
Seize power	5	5	1	12
Oppose specific political policies and actions	17	24	16	10
Oppose specific public figures	13	7	18	17
Oppose private political groups or figures	6	9	3	3
Oppose foreign governments' policies, personnel	13	7	16	17
Several of the above	14	15	9	17
Diffuse political purposes[c]	30	27	37	23
Economic purposes[d]	*11*	*13*	*7*	*13*
Social purposes	*27*	*46*	*12*	*20*
Promote an ideology	3	2	3	3
Protect interests of a social group[e]	13	26	2	7
Other and diffuse social purposes	12	18	6	10

[a]From coded information on the objectives attributed to the groups responsible for terrorist episodes and campaigns; see Table 4, note a. The objectives are those claimed by the groups themselves, if reported, or if not, those attributed to them in the sources.
[b]This information could not be ascertained for 60 of the 336 episodes and campaigns.
[c]Instances in which political motives of indeterminant kinds could be inferred from the pattern of action.
[d]Specific economic purposes, not shown separately, include seizure of goods, changes in the distribution of wealth, and retaliation against business and labor organizations.
[e]Actions in support or defense of a regional, ethnic, religious, or linguistic community, including those seeking autonomy.

data, though, no more than about one-fourth of all terrorist episodes and campaigns had revolutionary intent, compared with 30 percent that were explicitly focused on particular public figures and policies, and another 19 percent whose purpose was to do harm to private political groups or foreigners.

On a global basis, then, we can conclude that political terrorism in the 1960s was at least twice as likely to have limited objectives of the kinds expressed in conventional politics and political demonstrations as they were to have revolutionary objectives. None of the regional groups of nations deviate markedly from this pattern, except that the seizure of power is distinctly more common an objective among Afro-Asian terrorists than among those elsewhere. The European terrorist groups conformed to the general pattern, with one notable exception. Social motives were considerably more common there than elsewhere; this is another manifestation of the prevalence of separatist and communal bases and objectives of a number of European and North American terrorists in the 1960s.

International Aspects of Political Terrorism

It is widely believed, on the basis of some well-publicized instances, that there are networks of support and communication among terrorist groups and that many receive material support from foreign governments. The data for 1961-1970 show that only 19 of 335 terrorist groups were reliably reported to have gotten material support, training, or safe bases from which to operate outside the country in which they were active. Of these 19, there were 5 each in the European and Latin countries and 9 in Afro-Asian countries. Twice as many more may have received such support, on the strength of government allegations or indirect evidence given in the sources. Neither of these figures takes account of financial assistance or ideological encouragement, which might add significantly to the percentages shown in Table 10.

Terrorist groups in the 1960s were much more likely to direct their attacks at foreign targets than they were to receive foreign support. Information on this point was incorporated in Tables 7 and 9 and is summarized in Table 10. Altogether, just over one-fourth of all terrorist episodes and campaigns had some antiforeign elements, in purpose or target or both. But only about one-half of these —13 percent of the total—were primarily or exclusively antiforeign.

Guillen and Marighella advocated that terrorism be directed against the representatives of foreign imperialism, and that injunction evidently was especially influential in Latin countries. One-third of Latin terrorist groups included foreign (mainly North American) property among their targets; 15 percent targeted foreign officials and businesspeople. All told, 40 percent of terrorist events in the Latin countries had a significant antiforeign element. Moreover there was a substantial increase in the number that did so, from eighteen in the first half of the decade to thirty-two in the second half. The comparable figures for the Afro-Asian countries are lower, though they too increase sharply in the second half of the decade. European terrorists were least likely of all to attack foreign targets, despite an apparent increase in attacks on targets associated with the United States in the late 1960s.

Table 10 Transnational Elements in Political Terrorism, 1961-1970

	Percentage of episodes and campaigns			
	All (87 countries)	European (30)	Latin (22)	Afro-Asian (35)
Total number of cases	*335*	*125*	*126*	*84*
External support for terrorists[a]				
Specific foreign support	6%	4%	4%	11%
Suspected foreign support	12	9	3	29
Foreign objects of terrorist attack[b]	27	13	40	27
Total cases with external support or objects[c]	40	24	44	58

[a]"Specific foreign support" refers to episodes and campaigns in which the terrorist group was reliably reported to have been provided an asylum, operating base, supplies, training, or military advisors by one or more foreign countries. "Suspected foreign support" refers to instances in which some kind of foreign support or encouragement was alleged or implied to have been provided in the sources, but without specific evidence being cited. Many of the latter are very dubious.
[b]Cases in which any antiforeign purposes or foreign targets were identified; from the data summarized in Tables 7 and 9.
[c]Less than the sum of the figures above because cases with both external support and foreign targets are counted once only.

On the objective evidence, then, there was a very significant transnational element in political terrorism, even in the 1960s, and since then it appears to have increased rather than decreased. But it could not be argued that most or many terrorists have been the Trojan horses of foreign subversion, except possibly in the ideological sense. The more common manifestations of their "international-ism" were xenophobic attacks on foreign political presence and economic pene-tration.

Some Conclusions on the Conditions and Consequences of Political Terrorism

Few countries have been free of episodes of political terrorism. On the evidence reviewed here, the tactics so labeled have been a persistent feature of political life in a significant number of countries, and an occasional one in most others. We have also seen that in a number of respects the evidence of the 1960s contra-dicts some common views about the nature of political terrorism. Most campaigns were very brief, involved very few activists, and caused more noise than injury. In European countries the principal targets were property, and casualties were uncommon.

The revolutionary dimensions of political terrorism also prove to have been a good deal less significant than common belief would have it. In fact, political terrorists are readily distinguishable from revolutionary and secessionist movements in a number of respects. They are much smaller in number than were the armies and cadres of, say, the Algerian or Angolan nationalists or the National Liberation Front in South Vietnam or the secessionists of the Southern Sudan or Northern Iraq or even Fidel Castro's guerrilla bands in 1958. Not only did they lack the manpower, most of them also lacked the broadly based class alliances and support that are characteristic of most revolutionary movements. Most striking of all, less than one-fourth of them had explicit revolutionary objectives.

Even if it is argued that many terrorist movements have had covert revolutionary aims, they have been singularly unsuccessful in achieving them. Only a handful of the 335 episodes and campaigns reviewed here appear to have had any lasting effects on national political systems at any time between 1961 and 1977. Terrorism by Algerian Muslims in France during the Algerian War may have contributed to the war weariness that led to a negotiated settlement. On the other side of the Mediterranean, terrorism by the OAS in Algeria certainly did not keep Algeria French, but made it all the more imperative for the *colons* to leave after independence. Terrorism in Northern Rhodesia, now Zambia, shortly before independence was a factional fight between nationalist parties jockeying for power and did not measurably affect the timetable for independence. In Latin America, the activities of Peronist terrorists helped pave the way for the return of Peron in 1972, the consequences of which were so antirevolutionary that they stimulated still more terrorism. In Uruguay the Tupamaros pushed what had been a relatively open, democratic government into dictatorial repression in 1973, a condition whose theoretically revolutionary consequences in the long run will have to be weighed against the present certainty of the elimination of both the revolutionaries and political freedom. In Brazil a decade of urban guerrilla activity has not shaken the military government's grip on power, nor has it had any visible effect on Brazil's economic boom.

Only in European countries can one find instances in this period of favorable political changes that might be attributed to terrorist activity. In the Alto Adige region of northern Italy, the German-speaking population gained a greater measure of autonomy in the late 1960s after a period of terrorist activity. A terrorist campaign in Quebec in the 1960s coincided with a federal policy of devolution that markedly increased the autonomy of all the provinces. But in both these cases there was intensive political activity and pressure of a more conventional sort in the same direction, and to attribute to the terrorists the principal role in the outcome is romantic. In Northern Ireland, though, it is evident that the IRA can claim some of the credit for the British government's decision to suspend the Stormont Parliament and assume direct rule. Whether that will prove to have been a gain in the long run is another matter, but at least it was a change in a political situation that had been frozen for 50 years.

The upshot of this quick sketch is that in perhaps a half dozen instances in the last 15 years, in the 87 countries being considered, terrorism has been associated with structural changes that might conceivably be said to advance the cause advocated by the terrorists. Some of these changes have been reformist, some reactionary, none revolutionary. On the basis of the record to date, the revolutionary potential of political terrorism is vastly overrated. Where it has had any impact at all, other powerful political forces were pushing in the same direction.

Despite the lack of revolutionary success, the political use of terrorism flourishes, particularly in the more prosperous democracies. Terrorist campaigns are not so common, nor as enduring, in the new nations, and they are quite uncommon in authoritarian nations, both Left and Right. The evidence is not consistent with the view that political terrorism is a specific response to repressive government. In some cases, like South Africa and Spain, it *is* a response to repression, but where it thrives is in the kinds of political systems that have a track record of accommodating diverse political views and demands. No doubt that is one explanation for the commonality and persistence of political terrorism in Western and Latin democracies: Terrorists *can* act with more impunity in quasi-open societies than in police states.

The next question is why some people chose terrorist tactics rather than the more conventional methods of political participation and protest. The militants' most likely answer is that conventional tactics don't work. What the militants are less likely to acknowledge is that they did not, or thought they could not, muster enough popular support to play effective electoral or pressure-group politics. Political terrorism in democratic societies, and in some others as well, is principally the tactic of groups that represent the interests and demands of small minorities. Revolutionaries in Western countries have adopted terroristic tactics *because* they are revolutionaries in societies where the great majority of the population finds the status quo tolerable. In the poorer and weaker nations of the Third World, discontent is sufficiently widespread that revolutionaries have much more promising material with which to work than high explosives.

The use of terrorism for nonrevolutionary purposes in democratic societies is equally understandable in these terms. It is a dramatic way of calling attention to demands and interests of *any* sort that cannot get a hearing by conventional methods. The existence of mass media operating without government controls and an attentive public virtually guarantee that a dramatic act of terrorism will bring attention to the group's demands. Terrorism is a cheap and easy way of doing so, and one that carries relatively little risk. Whether it will gain the terrorists more than attention is another matter; for groups that are otherwise impotent, calling attention to their cause probably is a gain.

Anonymous acts of terrorism cannot so readily be explained in these terms, and they are relatively numerous—the fact that nearly a third of our cases of terrorism were coded as having "diffuse political purposes" is an index of their frequency. There are three kinds of explanations, each of which applies to at least some such acts. Some are manifestations of factional political squabbles—especially true in Italy and Argentina, for example—in which, from the point of view of the target groups, the medium is a message that needs no further translation. Others are tokens of some militants' millenarian faith that violent propaganda undermines the legitimacy of corrupt rulers. And some, probably including many nonpolitical acts of terrorism, reflect a "bombing for the hell of it" mentality that finds sufficient satisfaction in the act itself.

This interpretation can be brought to a tentative conclusion by saying that political terrorism is almost always a tactic of the weak. In authoritarian political systems it is a dangerous tactic for the users and is easily suppressed. In more open and prosperous societies it has flourished, partly of course by imitation, but mainly because conditions are favorable to it. First, there are increasing numbers of small groups in complex societies who are resentful at getting short shrift in the political and administrative process. This is not the place to ask whether their *resentement* has subjective or objective roots; its existence is evident enough. Second, the means for terrorist action are ready at hand for those alienated enough to choose them; guns and explosives are readily obtainable, and targets are accessible. The attention of the media usually is assured. Far from least important, security measures are sufficiently uncertain that the terrorists are very likely to get away with it.[16]

There is not much more to be said about terrorists who have "nonnegotiable demands" that are beyond the capacity of political agents to satisfy. They will be treated as security problems, neither more nor less. But something more can be said about political terrorists who have specific, negotiable demands. Once they have the public's attention they can use it, as the Palestinians have done at the international level. In some countries political terrorism may evolve into a specific bargaining tactic, a mechanism of regular influence for groups that have no other effective leverage on the centers of power. There is a precedent of sorts in the development of the strike as a technique of labor protest. In the industrializing societies of the eighteenth and early nineteenth centuries, labor organizations and strikes were regarded with something like the fear and hatred that political terrorism inspires in contemporary societies. They too were treated as a security problem until they reached such proportions that accommodation to labor demands became an economic imperative. You may recoil from the implication that terrorists' demands might have the same status of workers' rights to organize, bargain collectively, and strike. The point is that standards of what is a legitimate grievance—and what is a legitimate way to express it—change. It is not likely but conceivable that some kinds of political terrorism will eventually become a functional equivalent, in the political arena, of strike activity in the economic sphere: a recognized, perhaps even ritualized means by which groups exert political influence when the now conventional methods of democratic political participation prove inadequate.

Acknowledgments

The data used in this study were collected under the supervision of the author and two principal research assistants, Charles Ruttenberg and Jean Hardisty. The research was supported by the Advanced Research Projects Agency (ARPA) of the Department of Defense (1965-1967) and subsequently by the National Science Foundation. Robin Gillies carried out the statistical analyses at Northwestern University. The paper was written while the author was on research leave at the Institute of Criminology, University of Cambridge, with fellowship support from the German Marshall Fund of the United States. A version of this paper, which was prepared for the Southwestern Social Science Association annual convention, Dallas, March 1977, was presented to the Conference on International Terrorism, Department of State, in March 1976.

Appendix Countries Included in the Study of Political Terrorism, 1961–1970

European Countries

	ECO	POL	TE	TC
Italy	1	1	18	9
U.S.A.	1	1	5	14
France	1	1	8	9
S. Rhodesia	2	2	4	4
S. Africa	1	2	3	4
Greece	2	1	6	1
Britain	1	1	6	0
Ireland	1	1	5	1
Canada	1	1	1	4
N. Ireland	1	1	3	1
Israel	2	1	2	1
Belgium	1	1	3	0
Germany (West)	1	1	2	0
Australia	1	1	1	0
Austria	1	1	0	1
Germany (East)	1	2	0	1
Netherlands	1	1	1	0
Switzerland	1	1	1	0
Yugoslavia	2	2	1	0
Bulgaria	2	2	0	0

Latin Countries

	ECO	POL	TE	TC
Argentina	2	3	22	9
Brazil	2	1	7	10
Dom. Rep.	3	3	3	8
Ecuador	3	3	7	1
Colombia	2	1	3	4
Bolivia	3	3	5	1
Peru	2	3	4	1
Puerto Rico	1	1	1	4
Spain	1	2	2	3
Venezuela	1	1	1	4
Chile	2	1	4	0
Guatemala	3	3	1	3
Panama	3	3	3	0
Portugal	2	2	2	1
Cuba	2	2	0	2
El Salvador	3	3	1	1
Mexico	2	1	1	1
Nicaragua	3	3	0	2
Uruguay	2	1	1	1
Costa Rica	2	1	0	0

Afro-Asian Countries

	ECO	POL	TE	TC
Philippines	2	1	8	4
Ghana	3	3	6	0
Turkey	2	1	6	0
Algeria	2	2	3	2
Jordan	3	2	2	3
Lebanon	2	3	1	4
Congo (Zaire)	3	3	3	1
India	3	1	3	1
Syria	3	3	4	0
Cambodia	3	3	1	2
Camerouns	3	3	1	2
Japan	1	1	3	0
Kenya	3	3	2	1
Nigeria	3	3	0	3
Indonesia	3	3	2	0
Iran	2	2	2	0
S. Korea	2	3	1	1
Pakistan	3	3	2	0
Singapore	2	1	1	1
Hong Kong	2	2	0	1

ECO	POL	Country	TE	TC
1	2	Czechoslovakia	0	0
1	1	Denmark	0	0
1	1	Finland	0	0
1	2	Hungary	0	0
1	1	New Zealand	0	0
1	1	Norway	0	0
1	2	Poland	0	0
1	2	Rumania	0	0
1	1	Sweden	0	0
1	2	USSR	0	0
2	1	Jamaica	0	0
3	3	Paraguay	0	0
2	3	Iraq	1	0
3	3	Sudan	0	1
3	3	Tanzania	0	1
3	3	Thailand	1	0
3	3	Uganda	1	0
2	2	Taiwan	1	0
3	3	Burma	0	0
3	3	Ceylon	0	0
3	3	Malagasy	0	0
3	1	Malaysia	0	0
2	3	Morocco	0	0
2	3	Tunisia	0	0
2	2	UAR	0	0
3	3	S. Vietnam	0	0
3	3	Zambia	0	0

ECO: 1 = developed, 2 = developing, 3 = least developed.
POL: 1 = democracy, 2 = autocracy, 3 = mixed.
TE: Number of terrorist episodes.
TC: Number of terrorist campaigns.

Notes

1. Two influential contemporary advocates of political terrorism as a distinc-
    tive revolutionary tactic are Abraham Guillen, a Spaniard living in exile in
    Uruguay, and the Brazilian Carlos Marighella. Guillen's 1966 book *Strategy
    of the Urban Guerrilla*—in Donald C. Hodges, trans. and ed., *Philosophy of
    the Urban Guerrilla: The Revolutionary Writings of Abraham Guillen* (New
    York: Morrow, 1973)—was the progenitor of Marighella's more widely
    known "Minimanual of the Urban Guerrilla," *Tricontinental Bimonthly*
    (Havana: January-February 1970): 16-56, reprinted in *Revolutionaries on
    Revolution,* ed. Philip B. Springer and Marcello Truzzi (Pacific Palisades,
    Calif.: Goodyear, 1973), pp. 147-183.
    The former work is concerned mainly with strategy; the latter is a detailed
    prescription of tactics. A critical survey of the antecedents and nature of
    contemporary urban terrorism is Anthony Burton, *Urban Terrorism:
    Theory, Practice, and Response* (New York: Free Press, 1975).

2. For a more general discussion of the concept of political terrorism see Paul
    Wilkinson, *Political Terrorism* (New York: John Wiley, Halsted Press, 1975).

3. The *New York Times* was the principal source, supplemented by informa-
    tion from regional news sources and, in some instances, the scholarly liter-
    ature. For a description of the coding guidelines, sample code sheet, and
    data set see T. R. Gurr, *Comparative Studies of Political Conflict and
    Change: Cross-National Data Sets* (Ann Arbor: Inter-University Consor-
    tium for Political and Social Research, 1978), Part I. The full data set is
    available from the Consortium. A summary analysis of the 1961-1970
    data for eighty-seven countries is T. R. Gurr, "Political Protest and Violence
    in the 1960s: The United States in World Perspective," in *Violence in Am-
    erica: Historical and Comparative Perspectives,* ed. Hugh Davis Graham
    and T. R. Gurr, revised college edition (Beverly Hills: Sage, 1979). For a
    more complete analysis see T. R. Gurr with Jean Hardisty, *World Patterns
    of Political Conflict* (Beverly Hills: Sage, Forthcoming), Part I.

4. For a technical criticism see Charles G. Doran, R. E. Pendley, and G. E.
    Antunes, "A Test of Cross-National Event Reliability," *International Studies
    Quarterly* 17 (June 1973): 175-203. A conceptual critique is included in
    T. R. Gurr, "The Neo-Alexandrians: A Review Essay on Data Handbooks
    in Political Inquiry," *American Political Science Review* 68 (March 1974):
    243-252.

5. The events classified as bombings and assassinations in the strife data set
    are treated in this study as "episodes," though some instances refer to
    series of such acts. The events classified as small-scale terrorism and large-
    scale terrorism are treated here as "campaigns." The definitional distinc-
    tion used to demarcate bombings and assassinations from terrorist cam-
    paigns in the coding instructions was that the latter involved the use of a
    variety of methods of attack.

6. Wilkinson, *Political Terrorism.*

7. E. V. Walter, *Terror and Resistance: A Study of Political Violence* (New York and London: Oxford University Press, 1969).

8. *Report of the Commissioner of Police of the Metropolis for the Year 1974* (London: HMSO, 1975), pp. 20-21.

9. Chicago *Sun-Times,* September 7, 1975.

10. The survey was conducted by the Alcohol, Tobacco, and Firearms Division of the IRS and covered the period from January 1, 1969, through April 15, 1970. A follow-up study by the Conference Board for 1972 is described in the *New York Times,* October 8, 1973, pp. 53ff.

11. The most comprehensive and systematic collection of data on internal conflict, consisting of counts of "events" and conflict deaths for the years 1948 to 1967, is in Charles L. Taylor and Michael C. Hudson, *World Handbook of Political and Social Indicators,* 2nd ed. (New Haven, Conn.: Yale University Press, 1972). An updated edition is forthcoming but their data do not separately distinguish instances of terrorism. A narrative survey of terrorist activity as reported in the world press from 1968 through 1974 is Lester A. Sobel, ed., *Political Terrorism* (New York: Facts on File, 1975).

12. From the 1961-1970 civil strife data set described in note 3.

13. Ibid.

14. Sobel, *Political Terrorism,* p. 217; *Report of the Commissioner of Police of the Metropolis for the Year 1973* (London: HMSO, 1974), pp. 14, 38.

15. From the 1961-1970 civil strife data set described in note 3.

16. Ambassador Douglas Heck, director of the U.S. Department of State's Office for Combatting Terrorism, recently observed, on the basis of international evidence, that terrorists have an 80% chance of escaping without punishment and a 50% chance of obtaining their demands (speech at the National Student Conference, The Citadel, Charleston, S.C., March 4, 1977). A detailed analysis of the successes of terrorists taking hostages is Brian Jenkins, Janera Johnson, and David Ronfeldt, *Numbered Lives: Some Statistical Observations from 77 International Hostage Incidents* (Santa Monica: RAND Corporation, P-5905, July 1977).

2

The Urban Context of Political Terrorism

P. N. Grabosky*

Department of Political Science
University of Vermont
Burlington, Vermont

Introduction

There can be little doubt that most of the terrorist activity that has taken place during the past decade has occurred in urban areas. The Tupamaros, the Palestine Liberation Organization, the Irish Republican Army, the Weather Underground, and numerous other groups have achieved their reputaions by virtue of actions undertaken in areas of large, concentrated populations.

Although the cities of the world in the decade of the 1970s might appear to be the setting for terrorist activity of unprecedented frequency and magnitude, urban terrorism is far from a uniquely modern phenomenon. Assassination exists as a time-honored form of political behavior and one with a long urban heritage (Burton, 1975, pp. 1-2). The very term *terroriste* first appeared nearly two centuries ago in reference to the suppression of counterrevolution in the cities and countryside of France. The last quarter of the nineteenth century saw the emergence of significant terrorist activity in Russia, France, Italy, Spain, and elsewhere (Joll, 1964, pp. 117-148; Maitron, 1951; Gross, 1969; Hyams, 1974, pp. 31-93; Johnpoll, 1976). Johan Most, a German immigrant in the United States,

Present Affiliation: Office of Crime Statistics, South Australia.

51

published articles on techniques of bombing and incendiarism in the late nine-teenth century; his *Revolutionäre Kriegswissenschaft* was a forerunner of Mari-ghella's "Minimanual of the Urban Guerrilla."

Nor has coercive intimidation in the urban setting been the monopoly of revolutionaries, insurgents, or angry individuals acting alone. Repressive terror was practiced by the secret police of the Russian czars centuries before the for-mation of the NKVD (Deacon, 1972; Hingley, 1970). The grim practices of recent rulers in Brazil, Chile, Uruguay, and Spain constitute a small reminder of the barbarities of Nazi and Fascist terror during the 1920s and 1930s. Ur-ban terrorism, then, can hardly be viewed as a uniquely modern form of dis-sident political behavior.

Any discussion of urban terrorism must confront a set of fundamental ques-tions. What, if any, is the relationship between the urban setting and the terrorist act? Why is contemporary terrorist activity predominantly urban? Is there any-thing specifically *urban* about the terrorism that occurs in cities? Does terrorism "just happen" to occur in urban areas, or is there something in the structure of cities that produces or facilitates this form of political behavior? These questions are of special importance given the tendency of most commentators on urban terrorism to ignore them, or, at best, to deal with them superficially and implicitly.

What is it, then, that characterizes cities? What structural factors distinguish cities from other social systems? The first hallmarks of the urban system are popu-lation size and density. Cities are inhabited by relatively large numbers of citizens living in relatively close proximity. Cities also tend to be heterogeneous, much more so than rural areas within the same society. Although racially or ethnically pluralistic societies may be characterized by regional concentrations of the various component groups, it is the urban places within these societies where these various social groups are likely to be found in closer proximity. Social heterogeneity is also likely to be a recognizable feature of an urban social structure; social dis-tances between rich and poor neighborhoods tend to be greater than spatial dis-tances. A corollary of these conditions is a characteristic familiar to most ob-servers of urban society: anonymity. In the city, there are more strangers about; any one individual is less conspicuous, particularly so in large, dense, and socially differentiated populations. Although it may not be accurate to speak of the uni-versal atomization of urban life, one can argue that in some cities, and to an in-creasing extent, people make a point of not knowing their neighbors' business.

Yet, at the same time, ironically, one of the more significant characteristics of urban societies is the interdependence of their members. Unlike more primi-tive social systems wherein individuals or families may be self-sufficient, urban living is marked by a differentiation of productive responsibilities. Complex eco-nomic, transportation, and communications systems, themselves interdependent, demand a certain level of cooperation uncalled for in simpler social settings. One other phenomenon merits mention here, for as one of the most significant trends in modern human civilization, its influence on social life and on terroristic activity is indisputable. The phenomenon is that of urbanization. Moreover, the pace at which this process has accelerated during the past decade alone is truly staggering. The growth rate of many Third World cities, attributable to urban drift as well as to natural population increase, can reach from 3 to 8 percent each year; cities have doubled in size within a decade. It is estimated that by 1985, the population of the Mexico City metropolitan area will reach 17 million; Sao Paolo, 16 million; Calcutta, 12 million; and Buenos Aires, 11 million. By 1990, over 70 percent of the Brazilian and Mexican populations will inhabit metropolitan areas, and over 85 percent of the population of Argentina will be urbanized (Wilsher, 1975).

Thus, one explanation for the prevalence of terroristic activity in urban areas is the increasing salience of urbanization per se. And yet, it would be grossly simplistic to suggest that the link between cities and terrorism merely reflects the truism that there is a greater abundance of everything in cities. The pages that follow draw from examples widely dispersed over time and space but do not pretend to present a systematic survey of urban terrorist activity. Rather, they are intended specifically to show how the structure of cities conditions various aspects of terrorist organization and practice, both repressive and insurrectionary.

The Recruitment, Organization, and Logistical Support of Urban Terrorists

The urban location bears upon the recruitment of prospective terrorists in a predictable manner, for it is the city that nurtures dissidence in general. Much has been said of the close juxtaposition of great wealth and abject poverty that may be seen in urban areas, and of the socially dislocative effects of urban migration (Moss, 1971, pp. 5-8). Those who find themselves toward the bottom of the socioeconomic ladder might be regarded as prospective participants in riots or unplanned collective disorders; however, they tend *not* to engage in terrorist activity. Indeed, most contemporary terrorists, whether in Japan, Uruguay, the United States, or Germany, appear to have been drawn from the ranks of the middle classes.

It is the cities where universities provide for large concentrations of young members of the middle class. It is the city where these individuals tend to be exposed to fundamental principles of social justice and at the same time are confronted with the realities that so blatantly contradict those principles. And, of no little significance, it is the city where these individuals tend to be exposed to varieties of revolutionary theory (Hobsbawm, 1973, p. 221). Thus it is the young middle class, particularly the middle-class student population, from which most contemporary urban terrorists have been recruited.

Women, too, have become increasingly visible participants in urban terrorist operations. Among the specific individuals whose names have been prominent in recent years are Ulrike Meinhof, Fusako Shigenobu of the Japanese Red Army,

Bernadine Dohrn and Kathy Boudin of the Weather Underground, and Leila Khalid, the Palestinian nationalist who participated in two separate aircraft hijackings in 1969 and 1970. This noticeable female presence may be attributed to a number of urban-related phenomena. Urban operations often demand less in the way of brute physical strength and endurance than do operations in mountainous or rural terrain. Cities, moreover, tend to serve as the loci for the emergence of feminist activism; it seems logical that the participatory inclinations of women (whether they involve conventional or unconventional forms of participation) would be greater in urban areas. One need only look to the *Narodnaya Volya* and to the suffragettes for illustrative historical examples (Woodcock, 1962, chap. 13; Ramelson, 1967).

In addition, the secrecy and cover essential to urban operations can be enhanced by the participation of females, who continue to arouse less suspicion than do males. Women, for example, played an essential role in the unobtrusive transport of weapons during the "Battle of Algiers" and were strongly represented among the Tupamaros.

One aspect of terroristic activity that is perhaps most significantly conditioned by the urban context is that of organization. The conventional image of the rural guerrilla *foco,* living and raiding as a group and usually not integrated with surrounding villages, is generally inapplicable in the urban context. To a much greater extent than in rural areas, very significant violence in a city can be wrought by an individual acting alone or by two or three persons acting in concert. The phenomenon of the solo practitioner of terrorist activity, aloof even from informal membership in a dissident group, is not historically uncommon.

The uniquely urban organization of larger insurgent groups is most apparent, however, in their cellular structure. Traditionally, the organization is structured hierarchically, with the membership divided into small groups of from three to five persons, each comprising a cell (de Rocquigny, 1959, p. 96). In the ideal organization, there exists no lateral communication between cells, nor vertical communication upward in the hierarchy. Thus, members of different cells remain unknown to each other, and the identity of a superordinate is known only to one member of a subordinate unit. Compartmentalized organizational structure was a characteristic of the Tupamaro group in Uruguay (U.S. Senate, 1974-1975, pt. 5, pp. 295-297), but, like many other characteristics of contemporary urban terrorism, is by no means without precedent. The *Charbonnerie* in nineteenth-century France was divided into *ventes,* each member knowing only those of his *vente* (Hyams, 1974, p. 57).

Another example of a typical clandestine organization operating in an urban environment was the ALN during the Algerian revolution (Heggoy, 1972, pp. 237-238). Here one finds not only a cellular structure, but one characterized by functional differentiation. The operating force of the ALN was made up of several cells, each of which performed a specialized task; among these were units assigned to arson, assassination, sabotage, bomb fabrication, and bomb detonation.

Urban activists of the National Liberation Front in South Vietnam during the early 1960s were also organized on a cellular basis, although at an apparently lesser degree of specialization (Mallin, 1966, pp. 87-90). The primary end served by the cellular structure of urban terrorist groups is, of course, that of security. Moss (1972, p. 222) contends that compartmentalization for the urban guerrilla is the functional equivalent of the secret camp in the jungle, but compartmentalization can provide even greater protection. In theory, should any given member of a group be captured, his or her limited knowledge of the group's membership and operations would be of minor intelligence value.

Among the best discussions of the organization of urban insurgent groups is that of Kohl and Litt (1974). They suggest that a hierarchically arranged cellular structure can easily mobilize its component units for action but is vulnerable to "decapitation." A decentralized organization, on the other hand, although durable, is burdened with problems of coordination. Kohl and Litt see the optimal compromise in the form of strategic centralization and tactical autonomy. Such a system leaves action units free to operate on their own initiative within guidelines established by a central command (Kohl and Litt, 1974, pp. 21-22).

The urban setting, moreover, permits combatants to live separately and fight together and to disperse and reassemble at prearranged times and places with little difficulty. This was one of the main themes articulated by urban guerrilla theorist Abraham Guillen (Hodges, 1973, p. 240). Such arrangements significantly enhance the security of the insurgent group, because they minimize the possibility of discovery by accident or of attack by surprise. The near ubiquity of telephonic communications in most Western cities greatly facilitates what might be termed "periodic mobilization"; even the threat of wiretapping can be circumvented through the use of public telephones.

The organization of insurgent activities in the urban environment lacks one other characteristic more common in the rural context: the folk-hero leader. Urban insurgent groups lack the equivalent of a Mao, Fidel, or Che largely because survival in cities is often enhanced by a posture of anonymity (Segre and Miller, 1973, p. 21). Those urban terrorists who do reach public attention often do so posthumously or when in custody; those who seek personal publicity run a greater risk of identification and apprehension.

The materials necessary for the conduct of terrorist activity are conveniently few—weapons and explosives constitute the bare requisites. These and whatever additional logistical support might be required by terrorists are readily available in the average urban economy. Arms, medical supplies, food, lodging, and the means to obtain them are without question more readily available in the city than in the countryside. All may generally be obtained on the open market. Existing public or private transportation facilities, moreover, provide means of conveyance that are both dependable and unobtrusive (Neuberg, 1970, pp. 226-228). Intelligence information is often close at hand. For those insurgent groups in need of more specialized skills and services, such as mechanics and printers, these too are easily obtained (Russell, Miller, and Hildner, 1974, p. 39; Barrett, 1973, p. 19).

Materials for disguise or camouflage may also be acquired with little difficulty in cities. Argentine Montoneros obtained numerous police uniforms, either from assassinated or embarrassed officers or from raids on police stations. Tupamaro activists have also appropriated police uniforms to enhance the element of surprise in subsequent operations. In addition, members of the Uruguayan group seized a large quantity of wigs from a Montevideo beauty parlor (Kohl and Litt, 1974, pp. 214, 288, 350-351). Perhaps even more important than the availability of these materials is their proximity to the ultimate site of terrorists' actions. The two factors together combine to obviate the necessity of maintaining vulnerable supply channels and storage facilities.

The funds necessary to sustain activists and their operations may be readily obtained, whether by legal or extralegal means. Terrorists need not resort to the bank robbery or the kidnapping for ransom in order to support themselves; loans or casual labor are easily arranged. Other means of support include the use of fraudulent or stolen credit cards or forged checks (U.S. Senate, 1974-1975, pt. 1, p. 6). Subsistence in jungle or mountainous environments is not nearly so simple.

One of the more elaborate urban logistical systems, too elaborate in the opinion of some commentators, was that of Uruguay's Tupamaros. The group's facilities included prisons situated beneath the basements of certain Montevideo houses where hostages such as American agronomist Claude Fly were detained for prolonged periods. The basements of certain Montevideo commercial establishments served as hospitals that were fully equipped with supplies and surgical facilities seized from three complete Uruguayan army field hospitals (U.S. Senate, 1974-1975, pt. 5, pp. 297-307). These clandestine medical centers were staffed by volunteer personnel who worked normally in city hospitals. The rather heavy logistical infrastructure of the Tupamaros was criticized by Guillen, however, as inhibiting the group's mobility (Hodges, 1973, pp. 266-268).

Terrorists have also capitalized upon the modernization of international transportation systems. The easy transit of terrorists across national boundaries, indeed across continents, permits them to draw upon the assistance of sympathizers around the world. It has, for example, been alleged that the Japanese United Red Army members who carried out the shootings at the Tel Aviv airport in 1972 were trained in North Korea, equipped with funds in Germany and with arms in Italy, and received further training in Syria and Lebanon before their mission in Israel (U.S. Senate, 1974-1975, pt. 5, pp. 183-184; Segre and Adler, 1973, p. 22).

The gathering of intelligence by terrorist groups through direct infiltration of their targets or adversaries has a long history. Perhaps the most intriguing tale of terrorist intelligence gathering is that of Iveno Azev, the Russian terrorist leader who served in the highest levels of the czar's secret police (Hingley, 1970; Deacon, 1972, chap. 9). But other revolutionary groups were also dramatically successful in gaining direct access to their adversaries. During the 1920s members of the Irish Republican Army were serving in Scotland Yard, the Dublin Metropolitan Police, the British Army, the Royal Irish Constabulary, and various public service organizations (Hyams, 1974, p. 100). Lohmey Heruth Israel, an Israeli independence movement, was represented in the British Army in Cairo, where members of the movement were instrumental in the assassination of Lord Moyne, the British Minister Resident (Hyams, 1974, pp. 160-162). More recently, members of the Tupamaros were serving in any number of Uruguayan government agencies.

Although there is nothing inherently urban about infiltration, the transfer of crucial information may be accomplished more expeditiously and less obtrusively in cities. Impending operations of police and military units and plans and movements of prospective kidnap or assassination victims can be communicated quickly, thus providing a significant offensive or defensive advantage. Nevertheless, the most regular practitioners of infiltration have tended to be, and remain, government agents. This and other countermeasures are discussed shortly.

Strategic Considerations of Insurgent and Repressive Terrorists

The ultimate objectives of insurgent terrorists may vary widely, depending on the general context of their activities. Whether the goals in question are limited to the nihilistic destruction of persons and property or extend to complementing a broad-based revolutionary movement, their ends may be well served by operating in urban areas.

For the nihilistic terrorist, with no other aims than the destruction of persons, property, or symbols of authority, an urban setting is perhaps most desirable. Here is where targets are most varied and abundant; here is where the impact of a destructive act is most widespread. Most terrorist activity in cities, however, is undertaken with broader ends in view. Insurgents seek to accomplish revolution; authorities seek to repress dissent.

Perhaps the most significant strategic consideration is the need to publicize the terrorist group's existence, its aims, and its strength. Indeed, the task is not merely one of publicizing these properties but also of magnifying them. The attention-seeking goal of the terrorist is well served in the urban environment not only because of the plethora of potential targets that exist there but also because of the greater visibility of cities and what takes place within them. Just as "propaganda by the deed" was generated in Russian cities of the late nineteenth century by members of *Narodnaya Volya* and other insurgent groups, so too are contemporary urban terrorists better able to propagandize.

The advent of the electronic media has greatly facilitated the attention-getting goal of contemporary urban terrorists, particularly in those societies that enjoy a free press. Public attention is more readily attracted by actions undertaken in urban areas. It is here where the immediate audience is greatest and where representatives of print and electronic media are readily available and quite eager to report one's behavior (U.S. Senate, 1974-1975, pt. 4, p. 240).

A reporter-photographer team from *Der Spiegel,* for example, once accompanied part of the Baader-Meinhof Group on a raid in Hamburg. The IRA has held secret press conferences for British journalists, and the Provisional wing has granted exclusive interviews with its leaders. At one point, an American documentary team was able to film an IRA bombing mission (U.S. Senate, 1974-1975, pt. 5, pp. 273-275).

It should be noted that operations in rural areas do not preclude media coverage; North American coverage of the Cuban revolutionary Twenty-sixth of July Movement in the Sierra Maestra was rather extensive. Nevertheless, urban operations are more visible, and their practitioners potentially more accessible, than are their rural counterparts.

A closely related consideration of many urban terrorists is that of receiving favorable publicity, media coverage that will elicit sympathy for the group within the general public. Others still will resort to extreme acts for the purpose of attracting attention per se to advertise their interests and to gain recognition.

One further consequence of the extensive media coverage accorded the activity of contemporary urban terrorists is the enhancement of their fear-generating capabilities. As one commentator contends, "the continuous, voluminous, comprehensive coverage of terrorism in countries consistently threatened by it has contributed to the impact and fear-generating capacity of very small groups of people" (U.S. Senate, 1974-1975, pt. 5, p. 274). Such coverage is of significant assistance to groups such as the wing of IRA who are engaged in a war of attrition against the British government on British soil. They are little concerned with their public image among Britons and seek not to gain their sympathy but rather to exhaust their patience.

Among the more newsworthy activities of urban insurgent groups, serving to demonstrate daring and strength as well as to project a favorable image, are "Robin Hood" type actions. The power and intrinsic appeal of the Robin Hood myth has been exploited by numerous terrorist groups during the past decade, with considerable success. The spatial proximity of affluent and poor residential areas in the typical city permit such sudden, dramatic gestures as the hijacking of a bakery truck by Tupamaros in 1963 and the distribution of its contents among residents of a poor neighborhood (U.S. House, 1974a, pt. 2, p. 3283). A similar action, involving the donation of hijacked milk to the poor people of Tucuman, Argentina, was accomplished by the Argentine People's Revolutionary Army (ERP) in 1972 (Sobel, 1975, p. 87).

Such "hunger commando" methods, although not terroristic per se, are sufficiently bold that they portend future actions of a more drastic and violent nature. Yet, at the same time, they tend minimally to alienate members of the general public (Kohl and Litt, 1974, p. 24). Acts that might best be termed "altruistic extortion," kidnappings followed by the demand that ransom be paid to underprivileged groups, were a characteristic practice of the Argentine ERP from 1971 to 1973 (Kohl and Litt, 1974, pp. 344-364). In 1973, the mere *threat* of future attacks on employees of the Ford Motor Company's Argentine affiliate induced the company to donate $1 million worth of food, medical supplies, and educational items to the poor. The classic North American example of this practice was the food distribution program established in the aftermath of the Patricia Hearst kidnapping in 1974 (Sobel, 1975, pp. 85, 87, 94, 96, 197-198; Baumann, 1973, p. 84; Jenkins, 1975b, p. 44).

When urban terrorism occurs in conjunction with a rural insurgency, it may serve a number of ends. The greater visibility of urban operations generally tends to project an image of strength and to attract local or global attention. For example, while the Cuban revolution was generally regarded as a primarily rural enterprise, the Twenty-sixth of July Movement was able to demonstrate its strength in Havana most impressively. At one point, the sabotage of a power facility caused a 2-day blackout of downtown Havana, and a coordinated set of smaller bombings resulted in a series of forty explosions within a 15-minute period (U.S. House, 1974a, pt. 2, p. 3180). In addition, even a small urban terrorist complement to a primarily rural insurgency can force substantial investment of enemy manpower in urban security activity. This can serve to tie down government troops in urban areas, thus providing rural comrades with greater freedom to operate. The Algerian example is perhaps the best illustration (O'Ballance, 1967, p. 54; Moss, 1972, pp. 142-143; Silverman and Jackson, 1970, p.62). Finally, the urban adjunct to a larger rural operation can provide symbolic satisfaction and serve a general morale-boosting function by accomplishing very dramatic and visible deeds (Thornton, 1964, p. 80). The bombing of the U.S. embassy in Saigon by NLF terrorists in 1965 could only have reinforced the enthusiasm of their colleagues throughout South Vietnam (Silverman and Jackson, 1970, p. 66).

One of the more fundamental considerations of terrorist activity, and one that takes on even greater significance in the urban context, concerns the question of selectivity. For nihilistic terrorists—those who operate without political or moral constraints—the question of selectivity is less significant; it is merely a function of the individual's personal whim. For those terrorists (be they insurgent or governmental) who wish to influence political behavior and public policy, however, an urban setting constitutes a complex operating theater.

Most urban terrorist operations call for some degree of discriminate targeting. Given the aforementioned density and interdependence of urban social systems, however, this is by no means easily accomplished. Operations involving sabotage or assassination run the risk of harming innocent bystanders. Such accidental consequences are regularly seized upon by an adversary to discredit the insurgents in question or, in addition, to justify the implementation of draconian countermeasures. Indeed, governments have not infrequently resorted to the use of *agents provocateurs* to induce insurgent groups to undertake counterproductive actions (Deacon, 1972, pp. 119-129). Occasionally, government agents themselves have engaged in terroristic activity that was subsequently blamed on an insurgent group. Again, the urban environment provides a much more favorable setting for such covert actions than do sparsely populated wide open spaces.

However, for some insurgents, such as the IRA activists in British cities during the mid-1970s, selectivity was a less than paramount concern. Although bombings in the Underground and in the Tower of London may generally be regarded as indiscriminate, violence appeared to be directed at affluent Londoners, not generated aimlessly. The IRA in this case was engaged in a war of attrition against what they viewed as a colonial government. Moreover, they were operating in foreign territory, at some distance from their base of support. As such, the insurgents sought more to influence people than to win friends.

At other times, terrorism can be employed indirectly to mobilize a hitherto quiescent populace and to build an insurgent movement. In a heterogeneous society where separatism or national liberation is at issue, this might involve the attempt at polarizing racial or ethnic groups. In a bicultural urban setting, communal groups exist in close spatial if not social proximity. Indiscriminate violence directed at members of the dominant group is employed in order to provoke similarly indiscriminate retaliation. As the two groups become increasingly polarized, members of the underdog group are more readily recruited to the revolutionary cause. This general strategy was employed with some success in Algiers by the ALN (O'Ballance, 1957, pp. 53-54) but with a notable lack of success by the FLQ in Montreal (Moss, 1972, pp. 122-123).

A strategic principle that has been central to numerous insurgent campaigns in relatively homogeneous societies involves the attempt to weaken public support for the existing regime. Ultimately, this is designed to render its eventual downfall all the more readily attainable. Such a strategy may be based on one or both of the following themes. On one hand, an insurgent group may, through its persistent attacks on persons, property, or essential services, demonstrate the incapacity of the regime to maintain order (U.S. House, 1974a, pt. 4, p. 4207). The Tupamaro kidnappings, which will be discussed shortly, were a chronic source of embarrassment to Uruguayan authorities as were their successful raids on Uruguayan military installations and their dramatic prison escapes. As if these operations were not sufficiently vexing, the Tupamaros in addition appropriated official documents that explicitly indicated corruption within the Uruguayan government (Kohl and Litt, 1974, p. 24). Such a strategy is, of course, enhanced by the greater visibility and proximity of targets in urban areas.

A second theme, actually a logical extension of the first, involves a continuing harrassment of the regime to the point at which the authorities mount a repressive counterattack (Burton, 1975, p. 81; Marighella, 1973, pp. 180-181). It is assumed that the repression will ultimately reach a sufficient intensity to produce significant disaffection within the public at large.

The Tupamaro operations indeed provoked repression, but in a rather painful way. The inept civil regime that was the target of Tupamaro actions gave way to a military-backed coup. The resulting repression appears not only to have defeated the Tupamaros but to have discouraged much in the way of overt dissent on the part of the remaining Uruguayan citizenry.

When governments themselves seek to induce a state of extreme fear within a population or subpopulation, their purpose is to consolidate power by discouraging dissent and by fostering an atmosphere of quiescent submissiveness.

> Terrorism affects the social structure as well as the individual; it upsets the framework of precepts and images which members of society depend on and trust. Since one no longer knows what sort of behavior to expect from other members of society, the system is disoriented. The formerly coherent community dissolves into a mass of anomic individuals, each concerned only with personal survival. [Hutchinson, 1972, p. 388; see also Dallin and Breslauer, 1970, pp. 44-45; Thornton, 1964, p. 83].

To this end, atomization and social disorientation, intended *effects* of repressive terror, are common properties of urban societies to begin with.

An atmosphere of terror may be created by various means, some subtle and others less so. Arrests, detentions, and trials, on either a widespread or limited basis, may be grandly publicized. In the initial aftermath of the Russian Revolution, the Cheka promulgated occasional lists of its victims (Hingley, 1970, p. 126). During the 1930s in Russia, the elaborate "show trials" and lengthy public confessions were most prominent and visible in urban areas (Conquest, 1968).

In recent years, repressive regimes have been more secretive about their operations; sudden and permanent disappearances are not uncommon. Regimes that conduct terror without fanfare are able to exploit natural urban social phenomena. Urban societies are much less cohesive than rural communities. Anxiety and uncertainty are significantly more characteristic of urban life, and the potential for mutual suspicion and mistrust is that much greater (Jenkins, 1975a, p. 6).

Secrecy has perhaps as great a terror-inspiring quality as does official promulgation, and the size and density of urban populations allows for greater diffusion, and perhaps inflation, of rumor. Thus the scope of control produced by a successful campaign of repressive terror will be greater in cities. Repressive terror conducted in a secretive manner carries with it one further advantage that is of considerable significance in a world where international consternation is frequently expressed and occasional pressures brought to bear. Although the effects of terror continue to be felt domestically, secrecy permits official protestations of innocence. Chilean and Brazilian governments would not admit to the use of torture during the mid-1970s, but potential dissidents in those countries were well aware of the price paid by their colleagues in captivity.

Urban-Oriented Tactics

Although hit-and-run or "mosquito" tactics are common to guerrillas or terrorists in general, the requisite elements of surprise and speed are directly affected by the uniqueness of an urban terrain. At first glance, it might appear that the disadvantages inherent in the urban setting are dominant. Hobsbawm (1973, pp. 223-224) reminds us that the broad boulevards that characterize many European cities were designed as much for the defense against urban insurrections as for their aesthetic value. Marighella (1973, pp. 160-161) cautions urban guerrilla fighters to be ever conscious of the impediments to mobility, particularly those that would foil a withdrawal or escape; to "avoid entering alleyways that have no exit, or running into traffic jams, or becoming paralyzed by the Transit Department's traffic signals" (p. 100).

Urban terrain, however, holds significant advantages for the insurgent. Given the density of urban populations, the use of the helicopter for counterinsurgency operations is much less advantageous than in rural areas. Barricades and other methods of blocking thoroughfares are among the recommended means of frustrating pursuit (Marighella, 1973, p. 161). It has also been suggested that urban guerrilla activity demands less physical exertion than do rural and mountain operations. Furthermore, in an urban environment there exist more opportunities for actions that do not involve direct contact with an adversary (U.S. House, 1974a, Pt. 4, p. 3179).

The mobility of the urban insurgent is enhanced by the availability of high-speed rapid transit systems in many major cities (Hobsbawm, 1973, p. 230). There exists, moreover, a third dimension to the urban terrain, one which lends itself more readily to insurgent than to counterinsurgent operations. The Tupamaros of Uruguay were literally an underground movement, as was indicated above. In addition, they made use of the Montevidean sewer system for concealment and travel. Certain hatch covers were "booby trapped" to intimidate searchers and to provide an alarm in case the system were penetrated.

The nature of cities provides still further opportunities for the inhibition of pursuit. In societies where street demonstrations are tolerated, a small, hostile assembly in one part of a city can distract official attention from the real target of terrorist activity (Barclay, 1972, p. 86; Callahan, 1969, p. 53). In medium-sized cities, police switchboards may be temporarily blocked by a certain number of simultaneous calls (U.S. House, 1974a, pt. 4, p. 4228). Normal automobile traffic, and consequently official pursuit, can be significantly impeded by scattering tacks along major thoroughfares.

One of the more dramatic tactics of contemporary terrorists is that of kidnapping. The capture and detention of a prominent person has served numerous ends, including publicity, the release of colleagues being held as political prisoners, and the receipt of substantial funds in ransom payments.

The publicity value of kidnapping was adroitly exploited in Brazil by the National Revolutionary Movement of October (MR-8) and in Uruguay by the Tupamaros. MR-8 succeeded in kidnapping the U.S. ambassador to Brazil, C. Burke Elbrick, in September 1969, itself an event that attracted worldwide attention. One of the conditions for Elbrick's safe release was the promulgation throughout Brazil of the organization's revolutionary manifesto (Sobel, 1975, p. 114). The kidnapping and subsequent execution of Italian politician Aldo Moro in 1978 is further illustrative.

The Tupamaros, on the other hand, relied on the prolonged detention of their kidnap victims, thus enjoying sustained media attention and inducing a state of chronic embarrassment on the part of the Uruguayan government. American agronomist Claude Fly was detained in a "people's prison" in underground Montevideo for 7 months following his abduction in August 1970, and Geoffrey Jackson, the British ambassador was imprisoned for 8 months in 1971. The record Tupamaro detention was that of Ulysses Reverbel, who spent no less than 13½ months in custody (Burton, 1975, p. 98).

The alleged kidnapping of Patricia Hearst in 1974 provides a North American example of the publicity value of kidnapping. Her alleged conversion to the cause of her captors, accompanied by the selective release of numerous tape-recorded statements, provided a series of major media events over a period of several weeks. Thus, although kidnappings may be logistically cumbersome, they can provide a good deal more media "mileage" than a single robbery, bombing, or assassination. Moreover, the eventual release of a hostage can serve to minimize an adverse public reaction.

Kidnapping to secure the release of political prisoners has also been a common practice, one that met with particular success in Brazil during the period 1970-1971. Four diplomatic officials, including the ambassadors of the German Federal Republic and Switzerland, and a Japanese consul general were exchanged for 130 prisoners during that summer. Similar exchanges were accomplished in Guatemala, Haiti, the Dominican Republic, Mexico, and elsewhere (Baumann, 1973, pp. 69-93).

The tactic of kidnapping for ransom has been exploited most successfully by members of the ERP in Argentina. Kidnappings in Argentina yielded an estimated $400 million in 1973 alone; the record sum for a single kidnapping ($14.2 million) was paid by the Exxon Corporation in April 1974 to obtain the release of Victor Samuelson (U.S. House, 1974b, p. 170).

The most desirable setting for kidnappings has been the busy urban thoroughfare. There the prospective kidnappers are able to set up an ambush while attracting minimal attention; following such an attack, and the immobilization of the victim's vehicle, a capture and speedy getaway may be easily and unobtrusively accomplished. Other than the potential victim's randomizing his movements, only an armed escort or intensive patrols could serve as adequate preventive measures (Burns International Investigation Bureau, 1973).

Occasionally, in the course of a kidnapping, escape may be precluded. At other times, kidnappers deliberately seek to hold a hostage in public, or at least in a location known to the authorities. The siege that inevitably follows is usually among the most dramatic of terrorist events. In such situations, kidnappers demands may include calls for ransom or for the release of political prisoners; they tend usually to be accompanied by demand for safe passage to a friendly jurisdiction as well. Sieges of this nature tend to take place in and around diplomatic missions and occurred with considerable frequency during the early 1970s.

Illustrative examples include the raid on an OPEC ministers' conference in Vienna in late 1975 that was undertaken by some of the more extreme sympathizers toward Palestine liberation. Earlier in that year, a group of Baader-Meinhof activists invaded the West German embassy in Stockholm in a fruitless attempt to secure the release of their colleagues in custody at home. In some cases such incidents serve merely a symbolic function and represent an explicit attack on the offices or nationals of a target nation.

Depending upon the relative willingness of opposing sides to capitulate, sieges of the nature described here may endure for a number of days. In September 1974 the French ambassador to Holland and ten other hostages were held at the embassy in The Hague for 5 days by three members of the Japanese Red Army. They were released when the Dutch government acceded to the demands of the insurgents for a cash ransom, the release of a Red Army member then in custody, and safe passage out of the country.

A longer siege took place in the Republic of Ireland in 1975 when a Dutch businessman was held by two IRA terrorists for a period of 2 weeks. The insurgents ultimately surrendered, and the hostage was released unharmed.

Perhaps the most dramatic form of kidnapping, and one hardly unique to terrorists, is that which occurs in the context of an airline hijacking. Aside from those who are motivated by personal financial considerations—persons such as the celebrated "D. B. Cooper"—or those with severe personality disorders, the vast majority of skyjackers seek either to obtain the release of certain political prisoners or to express protest against a particular regime. In addition, insurgents almost always demand safe passage to a friendly jurisdiction.

Aircraft hijackings also occur with considerable frequency; between 1968 and 1975, an aircraft was seized on the average of once every 3 weeks (U.S. Senate, 1974-1975, pt. 4, pp. 222-227). Even after the advent of rigorous security procedures, hijackers have been able to exploit the crowded and hurried settings of urban airports to their considerable advantage.

One of the most time-honored of terrorist tactics is that of bombing. In the early seventeenth century, not long after the advent of explosives technology, Guy Fawkes sought in vain to blow up Parliament. Prior to the development of timing and remote detonation devices, most bombs were delivered by hand. This placed the assailant almost equally at risk as the intended victim and placed considerable importance on concealment of the weapon, often destined for delivery along busy city streets. A bomb intended for Czar Alexander III in 1887 was disguised as a copy of Gunberg's *Dictionary of Medical Terminology* (Hingley, 1970, p. 78).

The advent of reliable timing devices permitted bombs disguised as nondescript packages to be left in or around public places. The coming of the motor car allowed prospective bombers a more rapid means of delivery and retreat, as well as a further means of concealment; time bombs were easily left in parked cars (Joesten, 1962, p. 200). Such "car bombs" have wrought significant devastation recently in Jerusalem and Dublin (Sobel, 1975, pp. 17, 242). Similarly, explosives concealed in bicycle frames were used by activists of the National Liberation Front in South Vietnam in the early 1960s (Harrigan, 1966, p. 28). The attachment of explosive devices to an automobile ignition or exhaust system permits a more selective bombing; such a form of assassination, however, requires identification of, and access to, a specific vehicle.

The development of sophisticated detonation technology has also permitted the use of the mails for the delivery of explosive devices. Indeed, a fatal explosive charge can be concealed in an envelope, thus appearing no more threatening than a bulky letter. Package bombs and letter bombs were delivered with some frequency during the late 1960s and early 1970s; although most were intercepted and failed to reach their intended targets, a few were fatal. Although the letter bomb might generally be regarded as a "poor man's weapon," its use was by no means limited to insurgents. Mozambican nationalist Eduardo Mondlane was killed in 1969 while opening a package bomb allegedly posted by Portuguese agents, and numerous officials of the Palestine Liberation Organization were the recipients of letter bombs in late 1972 (Sobel, 1975, pp. 55-56).

Another mode of explosives delivery, dependent upon remote detonation, was employed in the assassination of Spanish Premier Carrero Blanco in December 1973. A device hidden beneath the street was detonated as the premier's car drove over a predetermined spot; the resulting explosion lifted the car five stories in the air. The use of such devices is of course inhibited by the difficulties inherent in the tasks of positioning and detonating them without being discovered. Similarly, the volume of traffic in most urban places precludes the use of "urban land mines."

With the advent of bombing as a tactic of terror, the spurious bomb threat became common. Such a tactic can be disruptive, if not destructive. In 1970, U.S. government buildings were evacuated on 226 occasions; the loss of employees' time was estimated at $3.8 million (Karber, 1971, p. 529). Moreover, the risk of apprehension is minimal, and the disruptive effect tends to vary directly with the complexity of the urban setting.

The credibility of bomb threats can be enhanced through the use of "dummy" bombs, inert packages left in appropriate public places where their "defusing" would cause maximal disruption of urban life. Such tactics were liberally employed by Maoist activists in Hong Kong during the late 1960s; at one point, they even "mined" Hong Kong harbor with prominently marked devices (Burton, 1975, p. 74).

The use of gunfire as a terrorist tactic is hardly in need of descriptive elaboration. Firing into a crowd, or firing at a particular target are commonplace occurrences. One significant recent development, of particular note in the context of large population concentrations, is the use of heavy weaponry in terrorist actions. Early in 1973, a terrorist team was apprehended at the airport in Rome while in possession of a Soviet-made portable SA-7 heat-seeking missile. An anti-tank weapon was fired at the United Nations Building in Manhattan during the 1960s, but the projectile landed in the East River. In January 1975, a Yugoslav aircraft was struck by an explosive projectile intended for an Israeli plane at Orly Airport in Paris.

Authorities too have begun to make use of heavy weaponry in urban operations. Although tanks and armored vehicles have long been used in city streets, a helicopter gunship was employed against a lone sniper in New Orleans in the early 1970s. The continued proliferation and diffusion of such devices would seem to portend their continued use in both insurgent and counterinsurgent operations.

Targets

Whatever the ends of terrorist groups, and whatever tactics they might employ in furtherance of these goals, there is no question that the city provides the best

array of potential targets (Hobsbawm, 1973, pp. 230-231). If the goal is to inflict harm upon, or generate fear within, the public at large, the city is where the
greatest concentration of the public may be found. If the intention is that of attacking government buildings, offices, or officials, from presidents to police officers, the city is where they are situated in greatest abundance. Representatives—
both official and private—of foreign nations are often visible in national capitals
or other large urban places (U.S. Senate, 1974-1975, Pt. 4, pp. 220-222). Corporate headquarters, banks, and other offices of symbolic or strategic value are similarly situated.

Of equal if not greater significance is the urban locus and great salience of
those systems that support contemporary modern society. Communications,
transportation, power, water, and waste disposal services so essential to modern
urban life are extremely vulnerable to disruption. Indeed, the complexity and
integration of these systems further enhances their vulnerability, and the vulnerability of those urban dwellers whose existence depends on them (Moss, 1971,
p. 10; Hillard, 1966; Barrett, 1973, p. 20).

Although the spatial proximity of so many different and interdependent
targets may be characterized as the nihilist's dream, such conditions do pose
problems for the terrorist groups whose ultimate goals depend on support from
the public at large. In such a situation, the choice of targets for terrorist actions
must be very selective. Jenkins suggests that terrorists generally have not attacked
water and power systems for fear of causing prolonged inconvenience and suffering among many people (1972, p. 9). Attempts on the part of the Tupamaros to
disrupt the Uruguayan tourist industry during the summer of 1971 succeeded in
the short run, reducing Uruguayan tourism by 40 percent. The subsequent increase in unemployment, however, served to alienate Uruguayan workers, a potentially important constituency (d'Oliviera, 1973, p. 32; Moss, 1972, p. 213;
Jenkins, 1974, p. 6).

Similar problems confront terrorists who engage in bombing. Even when
great care is taken to isolate a target or to set its detonation for a period when
injury to bystanders might be minimal, the destruction of a building may have
undesirable consequences. The bombing of a Canadian Army recruiting center
in Montreal in 1963 was timed for midnight, with the obvious intention of avoiding both civilian and military casualties. The death of an elderly passerby, however, served to detract substantially from the public image of the FLQ (Morf,
1970, pp. 6-9).

Over the past century there has been a discernible change in the nature of
the targets selected by terrorists. Kings, czars, presidents, and other public officials were the targets of most actions during the late nineteenth and early twentieth centuries, but increasing security precautions have made these targets
less accessible. Rather, one sees the attention of terrorists directed at lesser

public officials—from police officers to diplomatic personnel. Aside from being more numerous, these individuals are less well protected than their more distinguished counterparts (Hyams, 1964, p. 166). For similar reasons, buildings and other physical objects such as monuments and statues have also drawn the attention of modern terrorists.

As prominent officials become less accessible to potential terrorists, essential urban services become more accessible. Street traffic is easily disrupted, and mass transit systems are perhaps even more vulnerable. Sugar poured into the gas tanks of a number of vehicles will soon immobilize them; sand thrown into the grease box of a freight car will ruin the bearings. Such actions per se hardly serve to induce a state of intense fear within an urban population; rather, they might engender some short-term anxiety while complementing other disruptive actions (U.S. House, 1974a, pt. 2, p. 3182; Callanan, 1969, p. 53).

Apart from the context of conventional war, terrorist actions have yet to be directed at large population concentrations. To be sure, scores or even hundreds of persons may be killed in a given attack, and millions of people have experienced the fear of seemingly random violence; but threatening entire urban populations with extermination is unprecedented. Growing attention has been accorded this particular potential threat, however, given the increasing vulnerability of urban populations and the increasing destructive potential of portable weapons.

Concern has arisen of late over the proliferation of nuclear power facilities and their vulnerability to sabotage or to the theft of nuclear materials. A guerrilla group in Argentina allegedly seized temporary control of a nuclear power station in Argentina in 1973 (U.S. House, 1974a, pt. 2, p. 3182). Although unshielded plutonium is dangerous in itself, existing technology makes possible the construction of a homemade nuclear weapon; the destructive power of such a device would be enormous. There exists also the potential for the development of biochemical weaponry that would constitute a similar threat to large population concentrations. The idea of poisoning a city's water supply has already been entertained, if not undertaken (U.S. House, 1974a, pt. 2, p. 3166). Whatever the specific vehicle, the coercive threat inherent in a situation of nuclear of biochemical blackmail is enormous (Woods, 1975; Horrock, 1975; Jenkins, 1975b, p. 23).

Repressive Terror and Terror Countermeasures

Although it would be convenient to distinguish between alternative countermeasures available to liberal democracies and those employed only in more repressive political systems, such a distinction is not entirely appropriate. It was the Canadian government, after all, that imposed martial law in Quebec in 1971. The British and French employed torture somewhat freely in coping with wars of national liberation during the present century; and the U.S. government has condoned, if not actively supported, death squads in certain Latin American nations during the past 2 decades (Jenkins, 1974, p. 5; Hyams, 1974, p. 101; Kee, 1974).

The problem of defending against insurgent terrorist activity has plagued authorities throughout the world, and for good reason. As Jenkins suggests, it is "virtually impossible to prevent a handful of guerrillas from carrying out individual acts of destruction" (1972, p. 8). Moreover, the costs of minimizing the occurrence of terrorist activity, whether through amelioration or through repression, are often excessive. Four general avenues of countermeasure may be suggested, although not all are of specific urban relevance.

The first, of course, is to ameliorate those conditions giving rise to terrorist activity in the first place (Jenkins, 1972, p. 11). A redistribution of wealth or political power is more easily advocated than accomplished, however. Privileged classes and governments have always evinced a tenacious unwillingness to share their advantages with the less fortunate. Although terrorist activity has upon occasion ultimately accomplished meaningful social and political change, it has more often provoked repressive countermeasures. The question is an important one, but of no direct relation to urban issues.

The inhibition of urban terrorist activity through the limitation of opportunity is an alternative that authorities would tend to find similarly unattractive. The potential targets of urban terrorists are of such a nature that they do not lend themselves to concealment or removal. Governments do not close down airports simply because they are vulnerable. Indeed, the reduction of opportunity attending the recall of North American business executives from Argentina constituted in itself an embarrassment and strategic setback for Argentine authorities. Denying prospective terrorists the tools with which to practice their trade is similarly cumbersome. As was related earlier, great damage can be wrought with minimal equipment; sabotage was originally accomplished with nothing more than conventional footwear. It may be possible to control the distribution of high explosives within an urban society, but not the distribution of gasoline.

Some authorities resist social change with the utmost tenacity, whereas communal divisions in many societies may preclude peaceful resolution. The ability of governments to implement a forceful campaign of retaliation may also be inhibited in areas of high population density (Craig, 1971, pp. 124-125).

Manipulation of the mass media is a countermeasure common to most regimes, although the extent of manipulation tends to vary with the degree to which freedom of expression is valued in the society. Authorities in more liberal polities will quite naturally accentuate any discussions or materials that might embarrass an insurgent group or otherwise detract from its public image. In general, authorities seek to project an image of competence and restraint on the part of their own forces. Government countermeasures may also include specific attention to public relations, for the visibility of their actions in the urban context is as great as those of the adversaries. British Army officers assigned to Northern Ireland receive instruction in how to face a TV camera and in the technique of managing media interviews (Cooper, 1973).

In societies where less value is attached to freedom of expression, terrorist activity tends to be met with censorship. The publicity value of much terrorist activity has been noted earlier; it is not surprising, therefore, that authorities might wish to conceal terrorist operations when possible. The government of Uruguay, for example, forbade news coverage of guerrilla activity and actually prohibited the use of the word "Tupamaro" at one point.

A still more extreme alternative involves increasing security precautions of various kinds. This tends to involve increased restrictions on freedom of movement and curtailment of personal privacy. As in the case of the previous category of alternatives, such measures tend to impose significant burdens on members of the public at large.

Liberal democracies have adopted measures of this type with increasing frequency. In most Western cities, public buildings are closely guarded and the airport search has become a way of life for the vast majority of air travelers. Moreover, public concern with conventional criminal activity is sufficiently great that television surveillance of commercial establishments is hardly noticed.

There is but a fine line, however, between these and more intrusive countermeasures. In many cities, curfews are customary, and the carrying of official identification passes mandatory. In Algiers, for example, the cordoning off of the Casbah and the rigid control of egress served as a model for future repressive governments (Kee, 1973).

Reliance upon mass arrests and the indefinite detention of suspects, common techniques of repressive governance during the 1930s, have been frequent in recent decades. In September 1969, following the kidnapping of the U.S. ambassador, the Brazilian police arrested 1800 suspects (Kohl and Litt, 1974, p. 67). Such operations are more readily accomplished in an urban environment but tend to be more obtrusive and provocative than when undertaken in rural areas. Moreover, should they prove to be unsuccessful in locating the suspects in question, such campaigns can be acutely embarrassing to the governments that undertake them (Burton, 1975, pp. 228-229).

There is little question, however, that the customary response to terrorism in most societies has been the use of repressive terror. Reliance on policies of mass arrest, torture, summary execution, and other means of intense coercion enjoy a long tradition (Woodcock, 1962, pp. 345-350). One of the more dramatic tactics of government terror is that of direct assassination of suspected insurgents. The "death squad," a team of assassins usually sponsored covertly by governmental authorities, is most common in Latin America (Kohl and Litt, 1974, pp. 19-20; Jenkins, 1974, p. 6; Sobel, 1975, pp. 123, 133-143; de Onis, 1976). Israeli agents have also employed assassination squads to eliminate adversaries in the Palestine Liberation Organization (Jenkins, 1975b, p. 42; U.S. House, 1974b, p. 52).

The death squad is hardly a modern institution; the "Black Hundreds," an ultra-right-wing anti-Semitic society in early twentieth century Russia undertook the assassination of political liberals, and the British army relied on summary execution to suppress nationalist movements in both Ireland and the Middle East (Hyams, 1974, pp. 101, 104, 139).

In order to enhance public tolerance of such draconian countermeasures, governments may preface them with exceedingly intricate deceptive actions. The place of provocation in a strategy of repressive terror has been noted earlier. It does not tax the imagination severely to speculate upon the possibility of government agents themselves directing terrorist acts against innocent victims and then accusing an insurgent group of responsibility for the deed in question. One noteworthy impediment to the implementation of terror as a countermeasure in the urban context is the density of the population. To a significantly greater extent than do their rural counterparts, urban insurgents swim in a veritable ocean of the people. Cities, even small areas of cities, are not subject to saturation bombing with napalm, phosphorus, or high explosives (U.S. House, 1974a, pt. 4, p. 4241). Thus, the use of fatal force by authorities in urban areas has been limited to carefully prepared ambushes or to other precisely defined settings. Two of the more vivid examples include the killing of Black Panther leaders in Chicago in December 1969 and the massive attack on the SLA in their Los Angeles hideout in May 1974.

There seems little doubt that terrorism will remain a widely practiced form of political behavior and that it will become a phenomenon increasingly common to urban areas. The cities of the world will continue to grow in size, complexity, and hence in vulnerability. The grievances, be they personal or collective, that provide the impetus for terrorist acts are not likely to abate. Nor will there be any dearth of potential recruits for urban terrorist organizations. Large numbers of young people with at least a modicum of education will continue to abound in most urban areas, and all will have been raised in a world where violence has been a common form of political behavior.

Cities will continue to provide ample means of concealment and supply for insurgent terrorists, in addition to offering a rich array of targets, both human and material. Bombing, kidnapping, and assassination appear destined to remain common practices, and means of delivery will become more powerful and technologically refined. The inevitable proliferation of small yet extremely destructive weaponry will greatly enhance the strategic and tactical capability of insurgents (Jenkins, 1975*b*, pp. 18-20; U.S. Senate, 1975, pt. 7, p. 524).

This in turn will stimulate considerable investment by authorities in countermeasures technology. There now exists, for example, a thermal lance that enables a raiding party to slice through a steel door in 6 seconds (U.S. Senate, 1974-1975, pt. 4, p. 205). Other examples of the hardware currently under development for use in urban areas have been discussed by Burton (1975, pp. 231-233). Under these circumstances, it is not difficult to envision a future marked by increasing limitations on the individual freedoms of urban dwellers. Already, citizens in liberal democracies have learned to tolerate searches of personal possessions at airports and other public buildings; brief impositions of martial law have been accepted with only minor discomfort (Moore, 1970, p. 182). In the United States infiltration and provocation of dissident groups is generally acknowledged (U.S. Senate, 1974-1975, pt. 2). In polities where there has been less of a tradition of individual liberty, such impositions are commonplace. Indeed, it is in these societies that the most effective practitioners of terrorism will continue to be governments themselves. Mass arrests, summary executions, and torture will remain grimly familiar means of social control.

Thus fire, plague, and other natural disasters, phenomena that so detracted from the existence of our urban forebears, no longer threaten the quality of life in cities. Future decades, rather, will see urban residents facing more insidious threats—those of their own creation.

Acknowledgments

The author wishes to thank Sue Brannigan, the late Lyman J. Gould, and the editor for their comments on an earlier version of this essay.

References

Barclay, C. N. 1972. "Countermeasures Against the Urban Guerrilla." *Military Review* 52, no. 1 (January): 83-90.

Barrett, Raymond J. 1973. "Urbanization in Developing Countries." *Military Review* 53, no. 3 (March): 17-22.

Baumann, Carol Edler. 1973. *The Diplomatic Kidnappings*. The Hague: Martinus Nijhoff.

Begin, Menachem. 1951. *The Revolt—Story of the Irgun*. New York: Henry Schuman.

Burns International Investigation Bureau. 1973. *Executive Protection Handbook.* Burns International Security Services.

Burton, Anthony. 1975. *Urban Terrorism: Theory, Practice and Response.* New York: Free Press.

Callanan, Edward F. 1969. "Terror in Venezuela." *Military Review* 49, no. 2 (February): 49-56.

Conquest, Robert. 1968. *The Great Terror.* New York: Macmillan.

Cooper, G. L. C. 1973. "Some Aspects of Conflict in Ulster." *Military Review* 53, no. 9 (September): 86-95.

Craig, Alexander. 1971. "Urban Guerrilla in Latin America." *Survey* 17, no. 3 (Summer): 112-128.

Dallin, Alexander, and Breslauer, George W. 1970. *Political Terror in Communist Systems.* Stanford: Stanford University Press.

Deacon, Richard. 1972. *A History of the Russian Secret Service.* London: Frederick Muller.

de Rocquigny, Colonel. 1959. "Urban Terrorism." *Military Review* 38 (February): 93-99.

d'Oliviera, Sergio L. 1973. "Uruguay and the Tupamaro Myth." *Military Review* 53, no. 4 (April): 25-36.

de Onis, Juan. 1976. "Argentine Funds Aided Terrorists." *New York Times,* February 6, p. 7.

Gann, Lewis H. 1971. *Guerrillas in History.* Stanford: Hoover Institution Press.

Gellner, John. 1974. *Bayonets in the Streets.* Don Mills: Collier-Macmillan Canada Ltd.

Gilio, Maria Esther. 1972. *The Tupamaro Guerrillas.* New York: Saturday Review Press.

Gross, Feliks. 1969. "Political Violence and Terror in 19th and 20th Century Russia and Eastern Europe." In *Assassination and Political Violence,* ed. James F. Kirkham et al., Report to the National Commission on the Causes and Prevention of Violence, vol. 8. Washington, D.C.: Government Printing Office.

Harrigan, Athony. 1966. "Combat in Cities." *Military Review* 46, no. 5 (May): 26-30.

Heggoy, Alf Andrew. 1972. *Insurgency and Counterinsurgency in Algeria.* Bloomington: Indiana University Press.

Hillard, J. L. 1966. "Countersubversion in Urban Areas." *Military Review* 46, no. 6 (June): 12-19.

Hinckle, Warren, ed. 1971. "Guerrilla War in the U.S.A." *Scanlan's* 1, no. 8 (January).

Hingley, Ronald. 1970. *The Russian Secret Police.* New York: Simon & Schuster.

Hobsbawm, E. J. 1973. *Revolutionaries.* New York: Pantheon Books.

Hodges, Donald C., ed. and tr. 1973. *Philosophy of the Urban Guerrilla: The Revolutionary Writings of Abraham Guillen.* New York: William Morrow.

Horrock, Nicholas M. 1975. "Mock Poisoning of Subway Is Described to Senators." *New York Times,* September 19.

Hutchinson, Martha Crenshaw. 1972. "The Concept of Revolutionary Terrorism." *Journal of Conflict Resolution* 16, no. 3 (September): 383-396.

Hyams, Edward. 1974. *Terrorists and Terrorism.* New York: St. Martin's Press.

Jenkins, Brian M. 1972. "An Urban Strategy for Guerrillas and Governments." Santa Monica: RAND Corporation.

Jenkins, Brian M. 1974. "Soldiers versus Gunmen: The Challenge of Urban Guerrilla Warfare." Santa Monica: RAND Corporation.

Jenkins, Brian M. 1975*a*. "High Technology Terrorism and Surrogate War: The Impact of New Technology on Low Level Violence." Santa Monica: RAND Corporation.

Jenkins, Brian M. 1975*b*. *International Terrorism: A New Mode of Conflict.* California Seminar on Arms Control and Foreign Policy, Research Paper no. 48. Los Angeles: Crescent Publications.

Joesten, Joachim. 1962. *The Red Hand.* London: Abelard-Schuman.

Johnpoll, Bernard K. 1976. "Perspectives on Political Terrorism in the United States." In *International Terrorism: National, Regional, and Global Perspectives,* ed. Yonah Alexander, pp. 30-45. New York: Praeger.

Joll, James. 1964. *The Anarchists.* Boston: Little, Brown.

Karber, Philip A. 1971. "Urban Terrorism: Baseline Data and Conceptual Framework." *Social Science Quarterly* 52, no. 3 (December): 521-533.

Kee, Robert J. 1974. "Algiers, 1957: An Approach to Urban Counterinsurgency." *Military Review* 54, no. 4 (April): 73-84.

Kohl, James, and Litt, John. 1974. *Guerrilla Warfare in Latin America.* Cambridge, Mass.: M.I.T. Press.

Maitron, Jean. 1951. *Histoire du Mouvement Anarchiste en France (1880-1914).* Paris: Societe Universitaire D'editions et de Librairie.

Mallin, Jay. 1966. *Terror in Vietnam.* Princeton, N.J.: Van Nostrand.

Mallin, Jay. 1971. *Terror and Urban Guerrillas.* Coral Gables, Fla.: University of Miami Press.

Marighella, Carlos. 1973. "Minimanual of the Urban Guerrilla." In *Revolutionaries on Revolution,* ed. Phillip B. Springer and Marcello Truzzi. Pacific Palisades, Calif.: Goodyear.

Moore, Barrington, Jr. 1954. *Terror and Progress, USSR.* Cambridge, Mass.: Harvard University Press.

Moore, Barrington, Jr. 1970. *Reflections on the Causes of Human Misery and upon Certain Proposals to Eliminate Them.* Boston: Beacon Press.

Morf, Gustave. 1970. *Terror in Quebec.* Toronto: Clarke, Irwin.

Moss, Robert. 1971. *Urban Guerrilla Warfare.* London: The International Institute for Strategic Studies, Adelphi Papers no. 79.

Moss, Robert. 1972. *The War for the Cities.* New York: Coward, McCann, Geoghegan.

Neuberg, A. (pseud). 1970. *Armed Insurrection.* New York: St. Martin's Press.

O'Ballance, Edgar. 1967. *The Algerian Insurrection.* Hamden: Archon Books.

Oppenheimer, Martin. 1969. *The Urban Guerrilla.* Chicago: Quadrangle Books.

Prosser, George. 1971. "Terror in the United States: 'An Introduction to Elementary Tactics' and 'Some Questions on Tactics.'" In *Terror and Urban Guerrillas,* ed. Jay Mallin, pp. 51–66. Coral Gables, Fla.: University of Miami Press.

Ramelson, Marian. 1967. *The Petticoat Rebellion: A Century of Struggle For Women's Rights.* London: Lawrence and Wishart.

Russell, Charles A., Miller, James A., and Hildner, Robert E. 1974. "The Urban Guerrilla in Latin America: A Select Bibliography." *Latin American Research Review* 9 (Spring): 37.

Salvemini, Gaetano. 1967. *The Fascist Dictatorship in Italy.* New York: Howard Fertig.

Segre, D. V., and Adler, J. H. 1973. "The Ecology of Terrorism." *Encounter* 40 (February): 17–24.

Silverman, Jerry R., and Jackson, Peter M. 1970. "Terror in Insurgency Warfare." *Military Review* 50, no. 10 (October): 61–67.

Sobel, Lester A., ed. 1975. *Political Terrorism.* New York: Facts on File.

Thornton, Thomas Perry. 1964. "Terror as a Weapon of Political Agitation." In *Internal War,* ed. Harry Eckstein. New York: Free Press.

U.S. House of Representatives. 1974*a*. Committee on Internal Security. *Terrorism.* Hearings, Parts 1–4. Washington, D.C.: Government Printing Office.

U.S. House of Representatives. 1974*b*. Committee on Foreign Affairs, Subcommittee on the Near East and South East Asia. *International Terrorism.* Hearings. Washington, D.C.: Government Printing Office.

U.S. House of Representatives. 1975. Committee on Foreign Affairs, Subcommittee on International Organizations and Movements. *Torture and Oppression in Brazil.* Hearings. Washington, D.C.: Government Printing Office.

U.S. Senate. 1974–1975. Committee on the Judiciary, Subcommittee to Investigate the Administration of the Internal Security Act and Other Internal

Security Laws. *Terroristic Activity.* Hearings, Parts 1-7. Washington, D.C.: Government Printing Office.

U.S. Senate. 1975. Committee on the Judiciary, Subcommittee to Investigate the Administration of the Internal Security Act and Other Internal Security Laws. *State Department Bombing by Weatherman Underground.* Hearings. Washington, D.C.: Government Printing Office.

Wilkinson, Paul. 1974. *Political Terrorism.* New York: Halsted Press.

Wilsher, Peter. 1975. "Everyone, Everywhere, Is Moving to the Cities." *New York Times,* June 22, IV, p. 3.

Woodcock, George. 1962. *Anarchism.* Harmondsworth, England: Penguin Books.

Woods, G. D. 1975. "The Possible Criminal Use of Atomic or Biochemical Materials." *Australian and New Zealand Journal of Criminology* 8, no. 2 (June): 113-123.

3

Political Disintegration and Latent Terror

Peter R. Knauss

Department of Political Science
University of Illinois at Chicago Circle
Chicago, Illinois

D. A. Strickland*

Department of Political Science
Northwestern University
Evanston, Illinois

Tragedy, then, is a representation of an action that is heroic and complete and of a certain magnitude. . . . it represents men in action . . . and through pity and terror it effects relief to these and similar emotions. (Aristotle, *Poetics*, 6)

Theoretical Framework

The streets are completely empty. No one dares venture out. Except for occasional distant explosions, an uncanny silence prevails. Everywhere there is the odor of garbage, sewage, rotting corpses. There is no electricity. No water can be got from the taps. The last of the food is running out. Contradictory rumors are heard everywhere; and all that is certain is that the fighting has reached some sort of stalemate.

This is the terror within terrorism, the root fear that official and unofficial violence will someday, somehow, lead to the complete breakdown of society and that the brutish state of nature, which Hobbes told us lurks just beneath the surface of the political order, will reclaim us. Granted, this is an extreme case in the panoply of human behavior. But given the sieges of Stalingrad and Leningrad during the last war, or conditions in Beirut in 1975-1976, it is clearly an empirical case and not an ideal construct of social science.

The aim of this chapter is to explore the connection between terrorism and the fear of anarchy. On the one side, many scholars have claimed that terrorism

The authors are listed alphabetically and are equally responsible for what follows.
Present Affiliation: Department of Political Science, University of New Mexico, Albuquerque, New Mexico.

is effective just insofar as it paralyzes and disorganizes its intended victims and evokes this very fear of chaos. On the other side, terrorism has been considered, by the same conventional scholars, in isolation from political repression and the "normal" fear of the state.

Hence the question arises: What is the exact distinction between terrorism and politics? Our working hypothesis is that there is no such distinction, and that ordinary politics is suffused with latent and residual terror.

In search of evidence for the existence of a disjunction between normal politics and terror, we shall be looking at examples of chaotic interregna, open cities, and deadly stalemates. Here the question is, How well grounded in reality is the fear of social and political collapse? We shall also refer to certain theories of social contract and anarchism in order to see how the conventional view of terrorism relates to systematic political theory. And finally, we shall examine some relevant cases, most extensively the Algerian situation, in which both authors shared as Fulbright professors at Oran and Algiers, respectively, in 1975-1976.

That there is, from any angle, a paradox about the locus of terror is illustrated by some statements by a leading authority on outlawry (Hobsbawm, 1969). He was able to speak of bandits as filling a void in public order (when they are not creating one), of being engaged in mere jurisdictional struggles with the police, and of becoming legitimate leaders. (Pancho Villa, for example, was eventually made a general in the Mexican Army.)

Far (said Hobsbawm) from fleeing these *banditos* in panic, the peasant typically treats them with politeness and respect. "What else could he be expected to do?" And the fear of marauding outlaws comes to resemble in its empirical manifestations (as distinct from official rhetoric) the everyday fear of the state, or what we shall call latent terror.

Social Disorganization

It is a part of the folklore of terrorism that it intends to, or does, or both intends to and does, paralyze society (Moore, 1954, p. 176; Eckstein, 1964; Thornton, 1964, pp. 77-79; Walter, 1969, pp. 14, 26-27; Hutchinson, 1972, p. 388). To employ the frequent and familiar metaphor, it unravels the social fabric. A French functionary lamented during the onset of the Algerian liberation struggle, for example, that the growing polarization would bring with it a "total collapse of economic life and social structure" (Soustelle, 1956, pp. 123-124). This fear of social breakdown is rarely if ever expressed as a specific fear of *governmental* or *regime* decay, although implicit in its appeal is the belief that government is some sort of barrier between terrorists and the social chaos that they allegedly wish to bring about. More deeply hidden is apt to be an assumption that government itself could not possibly be a source of terror (except, of course, foreign governments that are perceived to be the enemies of our own regime and that are almost by definition themselves regimes of terror). Hegel, himself no friend of terrorism, had commented in relation to the destructiveness of liberation movements that "The victorious faction only is called the government. . . ."

Because the literature commonly insinuates that the *outcome* of terrorism is or would be the collapse of social relations, it is worth asking, in advance of any examination of the political aspects of this phenomenon, what it would be like to live through pure terror and whether social structures, like some physical structures, are such as to be capable of collapsing in on themselves.

It is instructive that the sociologists have shied away from this specter of a total collapse of social life. The *International Encyclopedia of the Social Sciences* (1968) offers no analysis of social disorganization. Leading textbooks tend to contain indices with entries such as: "Social dysfunction (*see* function)." They tend also to psychologize the concept by referring the reader to "anxiety" and "anomie" or to ideologize it by referring to "pathology," "crime," or "deviance" (see Bloch, 1956). This is quite odd, inasmuch as (1) from any macrosociological standpoint "crime" and "anxiety" are compatible with a reasonably stable social organization, and social breakdown must therefore entail something more than variable rates of divorce and alienation, and (2) the same discipline has often enough demonstrated the potential of conflict and extreme environments for *heightening* social cohesion (Coser, 1956; Shils and Janowitz, 1948).

One may even accept the difficult hypothesis that society has a sacred center (Shils, 1975) and profane periphery, without knowing what genuine social *dis*organization would look like. The reason is that the "center," like the "structure" in which it is embedded, is well-nigh impossible to specify. Insofar as it is imagined to be static, it is part of a status quo ideology (Lefebvre, 1971) and bears no resemblance at all to real-life societies (though it is to the old social statics that the metaphor of a structure, undermined and crumbling because of subversion, seems to refer).

But more to the point: Insofar as social collapse is conceived of as a *quality* of change, it is necessary to specify how it differs from other sorts of social change. Here we begin to approach the political dimension, because the aim of terrorist activity is often supposed to be (and is, very explicitly, with the anarchists) the paralysis and destruction of the *state, in the name of* social order. But the immediate difficulty is that when sociologists used to write about social change from "Darwinist" and progressive standpoints (Ross, 1901; Cooley, 1918, 1922), they supposed some degree of "organic degeneration" to be a desirable process, or, as with the later Freudo-Marxists, they thought repression in the service of the existing social structure to be, on balance, a bad thing. This leaves us with the embarrassing *political* question of naming, from among the flux of social decay and regeneration, those changes that are *dis*organizing to the over-all structure.

The impossibility of this task resides in the fact that basic social structure is subjective and interpersonal—that is, it is learned from other people, especially in the early stages of socialization, is stored in individual minds as memories, and is cumulative. Only the more reified modes of thought (that is, the dominant ones in social sciences today) envision social structure, institutions, or the cash economy as if they were "objects" separate from humankind, existing objectively and separate from or despite us and capable of collapsing "under" us or "onto" us. This bizarre albeit accepted point of view is easily refuted by reference to the fact that the money economy does not deteriorate during bank holidays, nor does the occupational "structure" have to be reinvented each time people go home for a night's rest.

Basic socialization, procreation, kinship roles, self-definitions, and language —above all, language—are not readily vulnerable to sudden death or even hijack-ing; nor do whole populations go into paralysis or some analogue of epilepsy. If "social structure" is meant to exclude just these factors, or to consist mainly in relationships qualitatively different from them, then it is very difficult indeed to imagine what the term refers to.

The much vaunted breakdown of civility, or even the deterioration of essen-tial services, is likewise a poor criterion of social disorganization, because it is well known that the decay of manners does not in and of itself destroy society (Turn-bull, 1972) and may even increase cohesion within certain subcultures; and, as previously mentioned, language and self-concept are likely to survive even without electricity, so long as there is a minimum of oxygen arriving to the brain.

It is not, therefore, surprising that we lack a goodly body of theory about social *dis*organization. The specter of total breakdown is something that seems never to happen, except retrospectively, ideologically, and in the minds of schol-ars who would ignore the newer forms of social behavior that replaced the "col-lapsed" ones.

Yet there is a very real sort of breakdown and paralysis, which is conven-tionally assigned to the "personal level" by reified thought. And that is psychosis, maiming, and the death of the organism. It is interesting that the psychoses not only "unnerve" the victim in much the same way that social scientists would like to pretend terrorism does, but that frequently the sufferer goes through a period of *Weltuntergangsphantasie* (a delusion that nature has fallen apart)—in which "everything" is collapsing, or being rejected, and in which political symbols often figure significantly. Without pausing to argue a position on the social determi-nants of nervous breakdowns, we may agree with some of the authorities that terrorism is basically a subjective phenomenon (Wilkinson, 1974).

That terrorism is essentially subjective means that its effect is to excite uncertainty and fear in the mind, thereby eliciting predicted and desired behavior. In its intention and effect, therefore, it is to be distinguished from the overt co-ercion of the victim or his physical destruction. In other words, it has as its aim a political act—compliance—rather than the subversion of social structure proper-ly understood. This is apparent from firsthand accounts of life in the Nazi con-centration camps (Kogon, 1950; Bettelheim, 1960; Rappaport, 1968); and inso-far as it is not apparent in such an extreme example, it shows only that social organization is sacrificed eventually and very slowly to political compliance, or rather that a quasi-novel social life appears as an adaptation thereto.

For all these reasons, we now abandon the quest for a meaningful distinc-tion between social disorganization and social cohesion as hallmarks of terrorism and turn instead to the political factor.

Political Breakdown

In the classical tradition there is, to be sure, no clear line between *the* political and *the* social. As Aristotle said, politics comes first, in the sense that it legis-lates for all other aspects of society. But at the same time it is desirable to make an interior distinction, as did the older political theory, between the *polis* as hu-man community and the *regime* as a particular class within it—namely, as the ("professional") political class. In this narrower sense of "politics" as the struggle for managerial control as between factions and classes, terror finds its *métier*. Here the striving to monopolize power, and the longing to disorganize those who do, have their playgrounds. Societies in the larger sense may change slowly; but regimes exit from the arena in a matter of months, even hours.

Whereas "politics" in the classical sense was the *ordering* of a human com-munity, its choice of *values*, in the modern sense it is the struggle for control over others, almost mindless of the uses of control (Strickland, 1974). Owing to Machiavelli and to Hobbes, the Western view was transformed from one centered on the ethically grounded state to one based on power politics and the merest ambition. "Reason of state" becomes, then, a (question-begging) justification, and considerations of political justice are consigned to the periphery in the in-terests of pure "order," that is, of unadorned domination. Attention has there-fore shifted to *sanction* and to the *probability* of sanction (Weber, 1922; Kelsen, 1945), for a theory that cannot demonstrate its human merit positively has got to do so negatively: Without a monopoly of violence in the state and without a high probability that each delict will be answered by a sanction, "chaos" would ensue, and the social order would collapse.

It is perfectly obvious that terrorism, according to this bankrupt view, is any resistance to the prince (on Hobbes's theory, for instance, any sort of dis-sent means to plunge the community back into internecine warfare); or, reversing signs, that terrorism is the political class's striving for a perfect monopoly of violence. On either account, some further distinctions are appropriate if only because no one now uses "terror" to mean *all* behaviors of the "specialized personnel" who constitute the regime, just as no one uses the term to mean *any* resistance thereto. Open warfare between states, for example, or civil war, is not perceived as terrorism, although propagandists may call specific acts, such as the use of V-2 rockets or saturation bombing, "terror tactics."

Apparently, then, *scale* is one of the indicia of terrorism. But rape and low-level unemployment are not regarded as acts of terrorism. Hence, *which* of the small-scale acts of violence will qualify? Again the answer seems to be that they must be political or, rather, designed to weaken, damage, and disorganize the political class. So when Wilkinson (1974) refers in the opening pages of his book to the "ruthless" and "indiscriminate" nature of political terrorism, we take him to mean something more than the vagaries of the market or of modern urban life. He must have meant ruthless and unpredictable behavior aimed either (1) at the political class or (2) at the general public with a view to disaffecting them from the political class.

In fact the terror within terrorism resides precisely in this gestalt switch: The ruling class publicly defines "senseless violence" as something to do with mayhem, chaos, and an assault on Everyman; the terrorists define their own behavior either (1) as a direct attack on the regime or else (2) as a demonstration to the apathetic public that the rulers cannot protect them after all and ought themselves to be repudiated; and the compliant masses are confounded and frightened by this contradiction.

A further distinction needs to be made between scale and mobilization. As noted, a large-scale, highly mobilized movement may use "terror tactics" without being seen as a gang of terrorists, just as a small-scale, poorly mobilized group, committing the same acts, would be so labeled. It is almost inconceivable that totally unorganized behavior would be so called; indeed it is usually labeled the work of a "lone assassin" or of a small-time criminal. Run-of-the-mill gangland killings are, likewise, conceptualized as "crime" because they are (generally) not attacks on the political class proper, nor are they "random" wastage of the public with an eye to blackmailing the political class.

Highly mobilized violence, irrespective of how random or indiscriminate its effect, is apt to be classified as civil war, insurrection, war, coup d'etat, or chaotic interregnum. In such cases the public fancy themselves to be safer (than with the terrorists) because the conflict is neatly defined and certain rituals control, or used to control, the killing.

Conflicts in which a small part of the community is engaged on less than a career basis (that is, low-scale, low-mobilization violence) are also outside the ambit of terrorism. The classic blood feud, for example, can be labeled a crime (or in some times and places, merely "private" business) just because it is so well circumscribed. The same goes for such episodic violence as cattle rustling, the barroom shootout, duels, or the altogether common murder-suicide of thwarted lovers. So long as the ruling class can maintain the *appearance* of law and order, crime and private redress (which are from a positivist point of view identical) are seen as prepolitical or extrapolitical.

Now we must watch our step, lest, in distinguishing so many things from terrorism there is nothing left but an epithet. If from the official position all terrorism is criminal, and from the terrorists' position it is always a (low-level) form of war, there is no such behavior. To preserve the phenomenon we must reemphasize political breakdown. It is necessary, first of all, for the political class to disguise the fact of its imperfect and perhaps decaying control by assigning the evidence thereof to nature (Jakubowski, 1976), individual madness or "weakness," crime, or (failing all else, and given undeniable evidence of its own falterings) to terrorism. It is necessary, secondly, with each round of violence, for the regime and its competitors alike to make strategic decisions on whether to attribute it to deranged persons acting alone or to a larger conspiracy. In the latter case there is the obvious risk of romanticizing the opposition by casting them in the role of potent, well-organized challengers, or, contrariwise, of dramatizing the lone avenger by *not* positing a network of accomplices.

Thirdly, there is the problem of the apolitical public, who are compliant so long as they believe that the act of terror has been aimed unjustly at themselves (see the case of the London bombings to be discussed shortly) and dangerously anxious when they believe that it shows the government's inability to protect them any longer. Hence the importance to political science of the concept "sanction" and the urgency to the established forces of denying that acts of private vengeance or of political rivals constitute sanctions. Hence, too, the one-sidedness of the literature, which with few exceptions (Walter, 1969; Nardin, 1971), ignores the demoralizing role of the state and attributes uncertainty, fear, insecurity, and social breakdown to terrorism (Moore, 1954, p. 176; Hutchinson, 1972, p. 388).

Political Integration

What holds the political system together then? To conceive of an answer to this simple question we need an anterior understanding of what a political system is (for example, whether it is something more than a regime) and a notion of how it integrates and disintegrates (for example, whether violence harms it or purges it). But the literature does not yield any settled doctrine; for we are still not in agreement over the core meaning of "political."

Nor is the literature on political integration (which ought, by rights, to pro-

vide the obverse definition of political breakdown) very helpful. Definitions of
political integration are a bit mystifying and tell us less than the aforementioned
definitions of social integration. One survey (Hayward, 1971, p. 315) finds "integration" to mean (1) loyalties that are shifting to larger political units, (2) the
ability to ensure peaceful change over time, (3) the establishment and maintenance of a sense of community, (4) the self-maintenance of a system, or (5) collective capacity to make decisions.

If the imagination were to try and extrapolate a notion of political breakdown based on such properties, we should discover immediately that (1) it all
comes down to a tautology (disintegration = failure of integration), or (2) that it
leads back to the ambiguities already exposed in the notion of social disorganization, such that the specifically *political* content of political integration is denied
(political = social), or (3) that political disintegration is equated to political
change, so long as the change is in the direction of smaller units of government
(decentralization). In other words, even if we were willing to stipulate that political integration should have the peculiar meaning of "larger units" of operation
or self-identification, it would not follow that reversion to smaller units would
be a satisfactory definition of political disorganization.

Nor, for that matter, are the definitions that rely on the strength of shared
values merely reversible, because (1) there is no known case where shared values
are completely absent, even among strangers or enemies, and (2) there are plausible theories, including conflict theory and some versions of social contract
theory, that hold that social cohesion and specifically political life are dependent
not on an agreement over (substantive) values but on a congruence of behavior
induced by fear, self-interest, ambition, factionalism, and the like.

The poverty of the formal definitions of famous authors and their disposi-
tion (for example, Weiner, 1971) to speak of "integration" when they mean
power and coercion only gives additional point to our inquiry into what, empirically and phenomenologically, political disintegration could mean.

From an older perspective, political integration is a very undesirable thing.
Those, such as the anarchists, who hold the state in disdain and begin their theo-
rizing on the basis of an intuitive horror of the Leviathan cannot help being interested in finding out what would bring about political collapse. The familiar
justifications that go with this point of view would warrant all sorts of revolutionary activity, not least of all acts of "terrorism."

In the classic formulation, random acts of terror are justified as "propaganda of the deed." Bombings, sabotage, and assassinations are thought to be
legitimate means to show the vulnerability of the regime, to force it to make its
repressive character more explicit, and to command publicity for the terrorists'
ideals. With the exception of the nihilists, these ideals usually pertain to radical
decentralization, communal self-management, and the withering away of statism.

They are not, it almost goes without saying, incompatible with passive resistance, "religious" detachment, and other tactics whose effect is to trivialize the larger political system.

For our purposes in what follows, it will be useful to distinguish two kinds of terror, *latent* and *residual,* that owe some of their inspiration to the anarchist tradition. By latent terror we mean the *ability to arouse* public opinion, such that terrorist attacks have their intended consequences. Without some such concept it would be difficult to explain why people ever react to terror in the first place or to explain the delayed effects of anxiety in disaster situations (Wolfenstein, 1957) or the apparently anesthetizing effect of cumulative terrorism. Underlying the idea of latent terror is a recognition that human existence is fraught with risks to which the normal reaction is fear or anxiety and that a diffused anxiety about the police and other agents of the regime is not the least of these universal apprehensions.

By residual terror we mean more specifically the fears people have of a *recurrence* of something that actually happened to them. In a country like Algeria, for instance, where a large proportion of the present population lost parents and friends in the liberation war, or were themselves injured or saw and heard firsthand things that no human being can forget, the normal predisposition to anxiety is compounded by this residuum. It seems reasonable to hypothesize, in addition, a sort of constant feedback, such that the residual terror of the modern world affects and infects the whole social environment, working on the latent terror even of those too young to have experienced violence directly or to have a clear memory of the actual employment of atomic bombs in 1945.

Political Justice

Injustices are almost always (hypocritically, we should note) supposed to be the property of one's own party, perpetrated upon it by outsiders. The political class is especially prone to portray itself as the font of rectification and to deny its part in injuring anyone (for example, the doctrine of sovereign immunity).

Under the adversary system familiar to Anglo-Saxon law, there is a presumption that one party is at fault and the other virtually without fault; at the very least, it is assumed that the allocation of guilt between the two parties should be made by judges and juries themselves innocent of wrongdoing. Given this naïve pretense, it is easy enough to assign the *cause* of political breakdown to individual aberration or to alien forces—until that is, the public is sufficiently fed up to engage in another gestalt switch and, in good Manichaean fashion, believes that the sheriff of Nottingham is the source of injustice and Robin Hood of justice.

This kind of thinking is encouraged by a version of social contract theory, still dominant in the Western world, that claims in effect that the ruling class rules by reason of some anterior agreement (not up for reconsideration, thank you) and that resistance to the authorities constitutes a breach of contract that, if positively sanctioned or left unpunished, would precipitate civil society back into the state of nature. According to Hobbes, man's basic nature is so vicious that the sovereign is warranted in all necessary ways to terrorize his subjects, so long as they comply and society is somehow kept together. Locke and later theorists took a more benign view of the human condition; but, to make a long story short, they generated a dialectic in which violence is manifest in the struggle between the individual and the state. This is a false problem.

We would appeal, instead, to the older vision of political community, to a vision that pitted justice against stupidity and tyranny. In the classical formulations of Xenophon's *Hiero* and Plato's Socrates, injustice and self-defeat were the root of terror. The tyrant is by definition the one who does not know how to do justice, or the necessity of doing it, and is therefore fated, like Machiavelli's Prince, to idle away his days fretting about attempts on his life and on schemes to punish those who exhibit the slightest insubordination. On this view, political and social disorganization are not the problem, they are rather the norm. The problem is how to arrive for the first time at human relations that are *not* rife with endemic terror, counterterror, and fear of the state.

Case Studies

An essay such as this, replete with qualitative distinctions and aiming to assign a new meaning to "terrorism," cannot establish its claim with empirical data alone. The following cases are, therefore, in a measure impressionistic and anecdotal. But within those strictures we have been, to quote Aristotle, as precise as the phenomena themselves permit.

Particularly in the Algerian case, it should be appreciated that the methodological problem is one of "best evidence," inasmuch as no one method is appropriate and no set of data (above all official statistics) is conclusive. We must stress, therefore, the importance of unobtrusive measures, multimethod inventions, intuition, and logical acuity in dealing with the crucial, subjective side of terrorism: For the stark choice is (1) whether to approximate and to thread our way through the steppes and deserts of ambiguity or (2) to cling to a methodological purity that would preclude saying anything at all about matters of some urgency.

The argument of the previous section is that some degree of terror is endemic to political life in virtually all societies, and the latency or remission of anxiety here and there should not be confused with a clean distinction between terror and its opposite(s). If we were to follow the existentialists, the point would be that life itself is The Stranger's attempt to wrest a measure of meaning and dignity from the ennui, cruelty, and hazard of existence. Following instead the question of limits, the point is how to decipher (and implicitly, how to avoid) situations in which low-grade anxiety runs to panic and social or political breakdown.

First on the continuum of political terror are the conventional forms, apparently random acts of violence that do not greatly disrupt social life. They are customarily reported by the media as the last-resort, desperate, senseless acts of a tiny minority (albeit at least one such case, the assassination at Sarajevo, resulted in a world war) and are represented here by some brief remarks about the bombings in London in the 1970s by the Provisional wing of the Irish Republican Army. Secondly, there are the more systematic and infectious forms of violence, represented here by some comments on the urban riots in the United States in the 1960s. Thirdly, there are the more or less continuous conflicts referred to officially as partisan movements, referred to by the partisans as national liberation movements, and by third parties as civil wars; they shall be represented here by a brief comment on Lebanon in 1975-1976 and by more extended remarks on Cyprus and Algeria.[1]

Peasants, wrote Hobsbawm (1972), would have invented Robin Hood even though he never existed. Otherwise their dream of justice and their hopes would die, and they would become the moral paraplegics, the living dead that, the experts tell us, terrorism produces and maybe aims to produce. Such at any rate is our assumption in looking into certain examples of the delicate balance of terror along quantitative lines.

London

In many respects the bombings of London offer an exceptional case. The famous "consensus" of British society, its present racial mix and its chronic problems with Welsh, Scots, and Irish nationalists notwithstanding, gives the impression of an almost unshakable devotion to the traditional social order. Though this impression collapses at once when one looks at the struggle over income redistribution and the fight over the "social contract" between labor unions and the government, it is nonetheless amazing how little the English are reduced to fearful paralysis by such conflicts. It is commonplace, for example, for older Londoners to remember the period of the Blitz as the most exhilirating time of their lives, a time of social solidarity when almost everyone had a heightened sense of importance, and people of all classes spoke to, and cared for, strangers as never before or since.

Needless to say, the more recent London bombings were also unusual in that the presumed perpetrators, Irish nationalists, were members of an ethnic group assimilated into the English world for several centuries past. The contributions of the Irish to English politics and letters are well known; and Irish workers have settled in England or migrated for seasonal jobs so long that it is impracticable to single out "the Irish" as an identifiable enemy. Perhaps for this very reason, the common public reaction to the bombing of automobiles, shops, banks, and the Underground was cast in the form of a mythic "they," meaning a mere handful of fanatics, almost entirely divorced from what has gone on in Northern Ireland lately or from the long history of Irish-English conflict. "They" (it was frequently said around town) "take it out on us" (the ordinary person) "when their quarrel is with the government." Of course this reaction ignores the rationale, whatever its validity, of the Provos that the public should elect a government pledged to a change of policy in Ulster.

What was most striking to those of us present in London during the Irish bombings, however, was the extraordinary sang froid of ordinary citizens. This is not to deny a universal edginess in the Tube (the Underground) and on the streets; but it does attest to an ability to adjust to everyday terror and, to some degree, to strengthen one's faith in, and reliance on, the state. That is, contrary to the familiar diagnosis that terrorism immobilizes and confuses the general public, in this case it seemed if anything to have the opposite effect.

U.S. Urban Riots

Beginning with the "Free Speech Movement" on the Berkeley campus in 1964, a series of disorders erupted across America. These included the bloody confrontations in Watts, Newark, and Detroit, the violence that followed the second Kennedy assassination and the murder of Martin Luther King, Jr., in 1968, the conjunction of the killings at Kent State and Jackson State with the invasion of Cambodia, and, finally, mass marches on Washington, D.C. That these incidents were not simply the handiwork of black radicals and "effete Eastern intellectual snobs" is shown by the fact that they occurred also in Nebraska and Maryland cities, not to mention the subsequent disclosures of the role of the FBI and the CIA in fomenting them.

In this case, a genuine panic and end-of-the-world mentality was created in those of us who experienced the violence at firsthand. Wholly unprecedented[2] events took place before the eyes of the vast television audience—student sitters-in dragged down the steps of Sproul Hall at Berkeley, their heads bouncing off the marble steps as the police brusquely dragged them by the heels; Black Panthers massacred in a predawn raid on a private, thoroughly bullet-riddled, home; the Chicago police running amok during the 1968 Democratic Convention in Chicago; teargas used against peaceful demonstrators; blacks randomly menacing

whites in Detroit after the killing of Martin Luther King; whites arming themselves and fearing to enter the same central city; curfews imposed; armed troops
with rifles and machine guns at the ready patrolling the streets for the first time
in living memory.

For all that, as uncomfortably close as it came to pandemonium and protracted civil strife, there was little evidence that such real terror brought about
social breakdown, or even major economic dislocation for the country as a whole.
It is true that Lyndon Johnson was forced from office by some of these developments, but racial discrimination and the war in Vietnam did not abruptly come
to a halt; and equally or more true, the election of Richard Nixon and the reactions that followed would, if anything, argue for a strengthening or at least con-
solidation of the traditional order. If a moral is to be drawn from this particular
case, it may be that serious challenges to the state, where they do not succeed,
elicit a real terror, as they did in the French Revolution. And here as there, the
terror is at bottom ideological: It is no exaggeration to assert that the ruling
class views the serious advocacy of alternative *ideas,* outside the framework of
the major parties, as tantamount to a coup d'etat, justifying its own terror tactics
and generating, as in Watergate and its aftermath, the inevitable exposure of its
own secret ideology.

Lebanon

Although the civil war in Lebanon and the Syrian intervention are, with hind-
sight, more easily classified as the kind of violence that goes beyond ordinary
terrorism, its beginnings are closer to the previous case of flash-fire riots and sec-
toral resistance than to civil war. The progression from communal violence (complicated by the Palestinian camps and the Israeli raids on them) to what was apparently a civil war merely underscores our earlier insistence on the quantitative
nature of these distinctions.

What is arresting is that Beirut survived so many months of the sort of violence and uncertainty that "in principle" is supposed to bring both social and
political life to a standstill. Journalists indeed reported in great detail the classic
open-city phenomena: As in Rome in 1944 and in cities that have undergone
police strikes or other lapses of civil authority, there were the horrors of uncol-
lected corpses, moldering garbage, communications blackouts, food and water
shortages, and the killing of innocents. But the same journalists were reporting
in addition their amazement that the system continued to work at all: The water
supply continued to function; food came by sea, through the black market, and
even through enemy lines; despite the departure of many local doctors, international volunteers managed under great difficulty to provide a modicum of care
to the sick and wounded; heavily guarded politicians met amidst gunfire to nego-

tiate a settlement; the telephone and radio worked well enough to get dispatches out and messages about within the city.

Without minimizing the misery and chaos in Beirut and the rest of Lebanon during most of 1976, it is clear that spreading disorder and the uttermost skill of the terrorists did not at first destroy (as distinct from intensifying the divisions within) the existing social system.

Saddest of all, perhaps was the habituation of children to constant bombardment and risk of death. Naturally, they paid the price in nightmares, insomnia, and serious character deformation. Many youngsters were reported to be carrying real guns and using them. Very young children were said to demand toy guns or to make their own out of wood, feeling marginally calm only if they too could have a gun. Women waiting in line for bread were known to curse armed men who crowded in line in front of them. And the hospitals were full of children and women, just as the streets were littered with their bodies, who had caught stray bullets or had defied the brigands once too often.

Thus, after months of terror, the essential services and routines of life finally gave out, not because terrorism can directly paralyze society, but because war can. Consider the following dispatch to the *New York Times* of June 30, 1976, that is, after more than a year of fighting in and around Beirut:

> Until recently, Beirut's 1.5 million residents have managed to live almost normal existences despite intermittent warfare, but that has ended and people are face-to-face with daily misery.
>
> Electricity is gone. Water taps are dry in most houses. The telephone is dead except in spurts of a few hours. Communications with the outside world are cut.
>
> Without power, bakeries are closed and there is no bread. A five-gallon can full of gasoline sells for $20. There is no air-conditioning to ease the Middle East heat, now taking hold for the summer.

Thus far we have been giving examples of terror and counterterror in *cities*. To be sure, there are fewer people to terrify in the countryside, and most guerrilla movements seem to aim eventually at the capture of the capital city, just as most regimes aim to present the capital as the very model of law and order as it exists within the country. That much is consistent with our hypothesis that terrorism is a cryptic coup d'etat—cryptic only to the vast public, who forget that the terrorists are trying to bring down a regime, and who never knew that so-called legitimate governments must sustain their power by a continuing coup known in the literature as public administration, policework, and national security.

Be that as it may, the ambiguities between banditry and terrorism (where, as with Che Guevara's campaign in the Bolivian mountains, it begins in the countryside) and between urban crime and terrorism (where, as in the U.S. riots, the troubles begin in and around major cities) and between professional and amateur terror (where, for example, Tupamaros were locked in protracted conflict with the secret police, or where white-collar ciminals are competing with revolutionaries in stealing from the public)—these ambiguities converge in the next examples, which are of systemic terrorism.

In the cases of Cyprus and Algeria, it becomes patently absurd to try to fix the beginnings and specific locus of the terror. The naive model of a "senseless" attack followed immediately by valiant efforts by peace officers to restore order must here be exposed for what it is. As in revolutionary France, in these cases violence and mayhem are reverberating *throughout* the political system. The distinction between city and country, banditry and crime, war and civil war falls into its proper perspective.

These examples show, we believe, that the conventional way of analyzing terrorism was all along a vain artifact of intellectual caution and "professional" taxologizing. More plausible, we suggest, is the view that terrorism is a political epithet rather than an authentic social phenomenon. It is only by collapsing these unreal categories that one can see the underlying process, the political process in its vicious splendor. (Hobbes, for all his faults, did not shirk from calling the Sovereign a monster.)

Cyprus[3]

The tragic events coup d'ctat, invasion, and subsequent atrocities—in Cyprus the summer of 1974 provide another illustration of the four-way distinction between (1) normal tensions, (2) crisis, (3) political degeneration, and (4) social disorganization. (In what follows, we refer almost entirely to the plight of the Greek Cypriotes, 80 percent of the population, without wishing to minimize the related sufferings of the Turkish Cypriots, about whom we have little or no data.)

The beautiful island-republic of Cyprus, strategically located at the eastern apex of the Mediterranean just 40 miles off the Turkish coast, had been inured to political misfortune. Whatever the "ethnicity" of the indigenous people, ancient Greeks migrated there around 1400 B.C., and the Greek language and later Orthodox Christianity have been the cultural bases of the majority ever since. In search of timber, copper, and safe harbor, however, virtually every imperial power in the area came to this deceptively peaceful and languorous birthplace of Aphrodite. In modern times, the Ottoman Turks governed the island for about 500 years, and the British for about 80.

Resistance to, and assimilation of, these waves of "armed tourists" had left the Greek Cypriotes with a political culture in which a premium is placed upon charm, ingenuity, suppleness, and sometimes submissiveness. Such have been the basic weapons in their arsenal of survival.[4] The lack of natural fortifications except in the peripheral mountains and the location of the capital city in the arid central plain partly explain the delicacy of traditional politics: When Richard the Lion-Hearted paid the coast an unscheduled visit during one of the Crusades, the king of Cyprus is reported to have withdrawn ahead of him; similar reactions no doubt accompanied the earlier and later visits by Phoenicians, Assyrians, Persians, Egyptians, Romans, Arabs, Venetians, and so on, with the Cypriotes withdrawing back across the central plain and ultimately, if the situation required, to the Troodos and coastal mountains.

More than a millennium of Byzantine politics (the ethnarch, lately Archbishop Makarios, was an autonomous prince of the Church already under the Eastern Roman Empire) produced a certain finesse, perhaps comparable to that found in Central European countries that have undergone long histories of ethnic-political conflict. At any rate, after the Ottoman conquest the Cypriotes had to adapt themselves to a minority ruling class that was religiously as well as ethnically foreign, which a few of them did by converting to Islam and intermarrying.[5] It is by no means easy today for a visitor to distinguish Turkish from Greek Cypriotes physiologically.

To the complexity of Cypriote political life was added in 1878 the British hegemony and a whole new world defined by the British empire: another language to be learned; another elite to be accommodated and entertained en route to the nether regions of the empire (Cyprus was also a favorite stopover and retirement village for colonial officers from Africa and Asia); a new metropolis (London, in competition with Athens, Istanbul, Alexandria, and Paris) toward which the ambitious young could look; and above all, a myriad of opportunities for emigration—to Britain itself, America, Australia, South Africa, indeed anywhere a British passport was welcome. As with other relatively poor countries, the modest population of the island was eventually outnumbered by the overseas Cypriotes.

As regards our central problem, the conditions of social and political disintegration, this is a significant complication. In addition to the Anglo-Saxon domination and growing demands for union (*Enosis*) with Greece, the cultural motherland, there was the fact of diaspora,[6] and with it new elements in the Cypriote mentality—nostalgia for the village, obligations to send regular remittances home, and no doubt the torn loyalties that dog the steps of every emigrant.

It would be an exaggeration to call the multiple strains just mentioned, or for that matter the modus operandi of the British administrators, a framework of terror. But as the British empire really began to disintegrate, after World War II, a manifest terror came into being: British officials and their Cypriote collaborators were "liquidated" by guerrillas. A typical method was for the latter to follow a British soldier as he ambled through the crowded "murder mile," Ledra

Street, in the cool of a Nicosia evening. The assassin, perhaps posing as a photographer, would shoot the victim at close range, hand the smoking pistol to a young female accomplice who would deposit it in her handbag and disappear into the crowd as the perpetrator commenced taking pictures of the fresh corpse. Naturally the British retaliated with their own sorts of terror; and before long a full-fledged national liberation struggle was in progress, led on the moral front by the archbishop and on the military front, from the mountains principally, by an austere Cyprus-born Greek soldier, the late George Grivas.

Skipping over the causes of the abrupt British withdrawal, and the ill-starred constitution they left, and the anxiety and disaffection they had tended to stimulate between the two ethnic communities, we arrive at the summer of 1974. It is worth noting here that the events of that summer took place in an unusual environment, as one of the authors can attest from three visits to the island between 1970 and 1973—an environment of languor and world-wariness combined somehow with chronic tensions and pandemic suspicion: Tourism had been at its peak, though one still had to produce a passport to enter the barricaded Turkish quarters or to pass through the UN-patrolled Turkish lines in the mountains. One revelled in swimming and fishing in the "wine-dark sea," even as bodies of young Cypriotes caught in the vendetta were turning up in the nearby orchards.

The blue-helmeted UN soldiers—Irishmen, Finns, Danes, Austrians, and Canadians—relaxed in local *boites* drinking Keo and Carlsberg beer, chatting up the girls. At night, along the Green Line separating the Greek and Turkish forces in Nicosia, one often encountered a handful of Greek Cypriote bons-vivants in the street outside a little tavern, singing the old songs with a ringing, operatic, not altogether sober, bravado; and the occasional Turkish soldier might be seen running the risk of joining them for a glass of Peristiany's brandy, on the pretext of returning the car keys someone had dropped right by the Green Line. The *New York Times* reported similar fraternization—singing back and forth, backgammon games, and the exchange of food and cigarettes—between Greek and Turkish Cypriote soldiers in a stalemate in the Turkish thrust towards Larnaca.

The invasion and subsequent chaos of 1974 ought to be viewed as an escalation and objectification of the antecedent events rather than as the introduction of terror and violence *de novo*. A longing to resolve the old stalemate (following the arrival of Turkish troops back in the 1960s and the withdrawal of most of the Turkish Cypriotes into enclaves) had led to protracted intercommunal talks, which achieved essentially nothing. All the while there were assassinations, attempts on Makarios's life, efforts by the other bishops to oust him, and violent demands for *Enosis* from the Grivas-directed (EOKA-Beta) guerrilla movement, to which the Makarios government responded with the usual counterterror.

Into this living contradiction there arrived, suddenly that summer, all the more woe: the Athens- and perhaps CIA-inspired coup that placed temporarily in power an obscure right-wing journalist, Nikos Sampson, and the simultaneous attempt to murder the Archbishop Makarios; the Turkish invasions and the flight of about one-third of the population; atrocities; capture by the Turks of the richest 40 percent of the island; the collapse of the regimes in Nicosia and Athens. With this as background, we turn to the quality of the terror evoked by the invasions and to the problem of political integration in one of the most dramatic examples of political collapse in modern history.

Under the circumstances, this offers an ideal test of the hypothesis that there is a distinction to be made between social breakdown and political disintegration; for the Turkish Cypriote organization had been, temporarily at least, preempted by Ankara, and the regular government of Makarios was, at best, in exile and a receivership and, at worst, gone forever. Preexisting conflicts between the Grivas guerrilla army, the national guard under the direction of (mainland) Greek officers, a specially created "Auxiliary Security Force" sympathetic to Makarios, the police, and so forth, were as nothing compared to the ambiguity of Nicosia under bomber and mortar attack, the airport closed, the UN troops shot up in crossfire, the roads choked with refugees, communications down, civil authority in abeyance. Hospitals were repeatedly bombed. People huddled in their neighbors' basements. Hearing reports of the brutality of the Turkish soldiers, those who could afford to do so filled their automobiles or wagons with what could be salvaged and made for the mountains or the two British military bases.

As the conflict continued, the economy faltered and collapsed. People fled the country in droves if they had somewhere to go, someone to go to, and the money to get there. Fruit and crops rotted in the countryside, even as food was being imported to feed the soldiers and the refugees. Herds of goats, sheep, and cattle died for lack of care or were slaughtered. Behind one another's lines, Greeks and Turks were subjected to atrocities, denied proper medical care and food, or "merely" suffered the ennui, debilitation, and demoralization that go with unrelieved distress. People are said to have lived in a dream, a nightmare from which they believed they would soon awake and return "home," even though they knew "home" to be a looted, defiled, feces-littered ruin from which even the doors and windows may have been stolen. All the while the vagaries of international politics, to which the Cypriotes are well attuned in the best of times, offered not the slightest ray of hope. Days later the American ambassador was shot dead in Nicosia.

Here is and continues to be as heartrending an example of social-political disintegration as anyone would care to imagine. Yet even in this unhappy case, the degeneration began in the political sphere and infected everyday social life. There is no way to construct a theory that would attribute the political crises to anterior social decay—not, that is, without acknowledging that the rapid social change that was already disrupting traditional life was itself the product of earlier political decision or, more likely, failures of policy.

The politically induced chaos and ennui understandably affected the routine of daily life, preventing essential activities from taking place or from reaching completion. But—"miraculously," as some conservative social scientists would want to add—the social system did not collapse. Life went on, "even" (wrote visiting journalists in the autumn of 1974) in the tent cities. Marriages were performed in the refugee camps with intense devotion, and the ethnic identification of the survivors was heightened. Cypriote nationalism took on new meanings.[7] The ethnarch returned to an emotional welcome. Overseas Cypriotes were forced to reexamine their identities. Athenian political life was profoundly affected, and therewith the role of Greece in the North Atlantic Treaty Organization. One may speculate that a new irredentist ideology, perhaps superseding the older quarrels over the meanings(s) of *Enosis,* is in the making. At all events, the foundation has probably been laid for grievances that will control the futures of two or three generations yet unborn, assuring to the "victors" the doubtful prize of never again resting safely in their newfound beds.[8]

The Cyprus invasions represent, among other things, a translation of long-festering *latent* terror into *objective* terror and back again.[9] What emerges most of all is the fact that the *fear* of social breakdown is not autonomous, is not warranted insofar as it is a fear that interpersonal relations will break down of their own accord or that they *cannot be put back together.* On the contrary, people seem to have survived the most gruesome dislocations, wounds (physical and psychic), and disappointments, sustaining hope against hope, despite the one.underlying fear that they might be physically liquidated before the chance to begin life anew is granted them. Social practice seems to change very, very slowly indeed. But what *does* seem worthy of realistic despair is the degree of political miscalculation, blundering, and immaturity that interrupts and thwarts these social impulses.

The malaise induced by political terror can only (because, as Hegel observed, it is pure negativity) delay life. It cannot positively shape it. It can hinder people's efforts to return "home"—but it can do this only by killing the people and ransacking their houses. It cannot by any manner or means extinguish their resolution to live a decent and continuous life. And that is part of the reason why social disorganization, or death in the sense of a final resignation and a feeling of irrevocable defeat, is impossible. It is impossible, that is, so long as there are some few human beings still really alive, still unafraid of their memories, still capable of thought.

Algeria

There is in our country no place whatever for improvisation, since serenity reigns with all our citizens. [Houari Boumediene, Speech of June 19, 1965]

While the last dramatic scenes of the "Battle of Algiers" were being filmed on June 18, 1965, armored cars and tanks of the National Popular Army were closing off the capital city. Very early the next morning, the President of the Republic, Ahmed Ben Bella, was roused from sleep, betrayed by members of the Palace Guard, and summarily arrested and imprisoned along with other members of the Council of Ministers.

The new government of Colonel Houari Boumediene thus installed itself in power, declaring the coup d'etat an act of national "recovery" (*redressement*). This military government has ruled the Popular and Democratic Republic of Algeria for more than a decade. Until 1976 the "revolutionary power" (Boumediene's euphemism for rule by decree) has steadfastly eroded experiments in democratic socialism initiated in 1962 by Ben Bella and his government. Under the mantle of "collective leadership" the Boumediene group has turned Algeria into a military dictatorship by dissolving the National Assembly, diluting the autonomous FLN party organization, the major trade unions, and other mass organizations, and filling these as well as government posts with individuals loyal to a small group of politicians and military men known as the clan of Oujda.[10] All national elections were abolished and until the spring of 1976, the constitution was a dead letter.[11]

The official rationale for this turn of events is found in Boumediene's tenth anniversary speech commemorating his coup d'etat: The anarchy and demagoguery of the Ben Bella period had been replaced by the order, discipline, and efficiency of the new regime. The premise of power was articulated in the speech he delivered to the party leadership on November 1, 1965:

> If there is one truth that History has consecrated, it is that a country can undertake nothing lasting without a state apparatus which is efficient and stable. The reign of political illusionism had been installed in the wheels of the State, as well as incoherence and confusion. Today, it is necessary for us to build and consolidate a State which, since June 19th, has already its own revolutionary morality, a State based upon a real social commitment in respect of our national values; it is necessary for us to build a State capable of assuring order and discipline.[12]

Beneath the rhetoric of the new chief of state lay some old military realities of power. Under the banners of order, discipline, and efficiency a new Algerian state was in fact built. When divested of their halo images, these slogans meant the depoliticization of the party and the nation, the immiseration of the majority of the people, and, to compound the injury, the creation of a modern Third World oligarchy that terrorizes its own citizens.

The French, it will be recalled, had ruled Algeria with heavy hand for more than a century before the liberation war of 1954-1962. French harshness toward, and degradation of, the native population was compounded by the facts that (1) military governors ruled the country for much of the nineteenth century, often using it as a testing ground of the army's prestige and as a vehicle of their own careers; (2) the *colons,* a goodly proportion of whom were not themselves French, were constantly at odds with the military regime, pressing for even more exploitative policies toward the natives; and (3) most of the Muslims refused to convert to Christianity or to assimilate fully to French culture, thus increasing the already lively disdain for them on the part of the metropolitan French as well as the *colons.* These polarizations, accompanied by the expropriation of the best lands and retributive taxes, only worsened when, during and after World War I, the native labor force became deeply entangled in the French economy, the army, and the factories and plantations of the *colons.* The generations of resentment explain in part the savagery of the war and the harshness of the postrevolutionary regimes.

Ben Bella's goals reversed

It is beyond the scope of this chapter to evaluate the success or failure of the first 3 years of Algerian independence from July 5, 1962, until the overthrow of Ahmed Ben Bella. This period was characterized by intermittent civil war, conflict between the "external" army and the army of the interior, postwar reconstruction, a revival and subsequent brutal repression of Kabylie separatism, and virtually unbridled personal intrigue and machinations. Such cleavages and conflicts are well described by other writers,[13] but, the faults of the Ben Bella regime notwithstanding, it is ridiculous in the extreme to characterize the latter as the cause for "incoherence and confusion" in the state, as President Boumediene did.

An objective view of the Ben Bella period must take into account, we submit, at least three political and socially disintegrating factors that any postwar regime would have to cope with whatever its political orientation. Firstly, the loss of upwards of 1.5 million Algerians during the "monstrous" (that is, in terms of the human price paid for national liberation) 8-year war from November 1, 1954, to the cease fire of May 19, 1962. This population depletion represented the effective loss of one-ninth of the total population of the nation through death, mutilation, and other war-related tragedies. The war was fought with an incredible cruelty on both sides, and all of our former veteran respondents stressed this in their comments: The use of torture was notoriously widespread among the French paratroop and police units; within the FLN units, men were shot for violating the smallest military order or suffered immediate and painful disfiguration (having their noses cut off) even for smoking cigarettes.[14]

Secondly, it has been conservatively estimated that approximately one-third of the economic infrastructure of the country was partially or completely destroyed during the war in the countryside and the vicious battles waged in the cities between the OAS and FLN units. Finally, the flight of over 1 million Europeans (as well as Jews and Algerian collaborators) immediately before and during the "summer of shame"[15] in July 1962 meant the loss of the overwhelming majority of the professionals, skilled workers, and civil servants who had run hospitals, the schools, the factories, the water works, the electrical power generators, the transport industry, and the intensively cultivated farms of the nation. Their rapid departure left this war-racked, decimated country of 9 million in a state of chaos.

It is a credit to Ben Bella and his ministers that government, civil order, and a semblance of national development were maintained under these conditions. The Ben Bella government with its one-party state and its tendency toward the end of its rule to short-circuit decisions away from the national legislature was hardly a model of a constitutional democracy. Nevertheless, Ben Bella's government, we believe, was a genuinely populist civilian regime committed to expanding popular participation in governmental decision making by encouraging FLN accountability and peasant and worker direct participation in the management of the farms and factories that were abandoned by the Europeans.

Our sources who participated in that regime underscore the centrality of three objectives that, if allowed to reach fruition, might well have created some important preconditions for a new Third World form of democratic socialism: the creation of farmers' and workers' *autogestion* (self-management) councils on approximately one-third of the arable lands of the nation; the establishment of a "mixed economy" based upon nationalization of those basic means of production held in foreign hands combined with a continuation of private Algerian ownership of smaller secondary industries, farms, shops, and trades; and the emphasis on a Pan-Arabist, but essentially pro-African, foreign policy grounded on nonalignment.

Ben Bella's foreign policy objectives reflected his idealism in domestic matters. His goal and that of his immediate entourage of internationalist advisers was an Arab nation of 100 million inhabitants. It was his belief that no "new" Arab or African nation could ever hope to break out of the cycle of dependency on the former metropolitan government (or from the potential new form of dependency that "cooperation" with the United States or the Soviet Union implied) without creating a huge human and material resource base out of the former colonized nations of the southern Mediterranean littoral.

For Ben Bella that meant a united Arab republic from "Cairo to the Atlantic" that would unify the three Maghreb states (Morocco, Algeria, and Tunisia) with Libya and Egypt to the east. Such a nation, it was believed, would create a "scientific basis" for "real" African development. According to one of the policy advisers in his government, this objective aimed at building a supranational government over these territories, which he believed would provide the material base for an "African treasury" from which development projects for the rest of liberated Africa could be financed with long-term loans with low interest rates, outside of the intrigues and interference of the Cold War.

This visionary goal has been criticized as being too "internationalist" or simply unrealistic given the centrifugal nationalist tendencies of the postindependence regimes cited. We mention it here to underscore the fundamental difference in orientation and goals between the Ben Bella and the Boumediene governments. Colonel Boumediene remarked on this allegedly dangerous cosmopolitan tendency of the regime overthrown by his June 19 "movement": While referring to Algeria before 1965 as a "country sapped, plunged into an atmosphere of trouble and instability," he also saw Algeria then as "a refuge of numerous adventurers who attempted to use it as a terrain for their experiments in order to realise here that which they were not able to undertake either in their own countries or in other Third World countries." Instead, Boumediene sounded a typically nationalistic note by claiming that "all these reasons . . . incited us to take our responsibilities on June 19, 1965, as the Council of the Revolution: to put an end to a formal legality, and to safeguard the revolutionary legitimacy, the fatherland, and the Revolution."

Against whom was the new military group defending the fatherland, one is tempted to ask. Boumediene was, no doubt, referring to the *pieds rouges* (non-Algerian leftists) in the Ben Bella government (of whom there were in fact only two or three who figured prominently); and perhaps to various representatives of African liberation groups whom Ben Bella openly and generously aided, who had set up headquarters in Algiers.

The subtle intrigues within the Ben Bella government, however, cut short bold experimentation in the domestic and foreign affairs. The members of the Oujda clan, machinations earlier within the party, and continued French pressure combined to undermine the strength of the regime and ultimately spelled its overthrow. Ben Bella himself is still serving a jail sentence of indefinite length and many of his former ministers were detained for 3 years plus long years of house arrest. By 1968, certainly, almost all of the Ben Bella supporters had been removed from the FLN, the trade union movement, as well as the women's and youth organizations, and most importantly from the civil service at all levels of public administration. As one person active during this period confided to us, "While we dreamt noble dreams (*autogestion*, the mixed economy, an Arab nation of 100 millions), they (the Boumediene group) placed a banana peel in our path."

Psychological action: Mystification and depoliticization

Through effective use of the mass media, especially the two countrywide newspapers and television, the Boumediene regime has since 1965 created an Orwellian world of unreality for the Algerian people. "Self-management" has come to mean in practice the end of an autonomous trade union movement and the bureaucratization by loyal followers of Boumediene of the genuinely popular-based workers' and farmers' councils. The "agrarian revolution" (much publicized since 1972 to forcibly collectivize small peasant landholdings into "socialist cooperatives"), when demystified and carefully examined, is merely a euphemism for taking land from the small peasantry (leaving many large landholdings intact). Similarly, "socialism" or its most frequently employed mass media equivalent in the mid-1970s, "the transition to socialism," means in fact a very naked and oppressive form of state capitalism.[16]

In the arena of foreign policy the Orwellian truthspeak is perhaps even more obvious. The frequently used expression by the Boumediene press of "Maghreb of peoples" (instead of a "Maghreb of states") means in fact a conversion from a polity based on respect for the mutual sovereignty of Maghreb states to one based on aiming at the overthrow of contiguous Arab governments, principally that of King Hassan II of Morocco. For those men and women who fought in the war of national liberation, this deliberate falsification of realities must have profoundly disorienting effects.

For example, one of our respondents, a police officer in one of the large northern cities commented openly to one of us about these flagrant contradictions:

> It's like a large feast has been prepared for you (independence), with all your favorite foods and wines all laid out for you in grand style, and just as you are sitting down to enjoy it, someone has taken it all for himself. We wonder why so many have fought so bravely. For what? To substitute one foreign dictatorship for one of our own?

Fidel Castro was even more direct in his criticism. In his final press conference in early spring 1976 in Algiers he is said to have remarked as he contemplated boarding his plane for Cuba: "We now have a new form of socialism in Algeria: socialism for the poor and a new class of millionaires."

One wonders with unbelief how such a situation could come about. At the risk of some simplification we cite at least three processes we observed at work in Algeria during 1975-1976 and that we hypothesize have been a reality since 1965 when Colonel Boumediene and his group seized power: (1) the depoliticization of the FLN and the subsequent depoliticizing effects of this on the nation as a whole; (2) the continuing immiseration of the overwhelming majority of the people; and (3) the creation of a system of state-organized "terror" through the elaboration of the informant-spy system.

Depoliticizing the National Liberation Front (FLN)

The disintegration of the FLN actually began under Ben Bella, owing to a major struggle for power between him and the former Party General Secretary Mohamed Khider.[17] However, from what we can piece together from our respondents, it was never Ben Bella's intention to allow the party to atrophy. His crucial decision to postpone the national constituent assembly until 1964 was taken only very reluctantly in order to isolate Khider who had been using the party's external treasury (for example, in Tunis and elsewhere) as a means of building up his own base of power within the nation by turning the FLN into his own patronage organization. The dismemberment of the mass membership of FLN and its subsequent transformation into a "party of bureaucratized militants"[18] by the Boumediene regime is, again, like *autogestion,* the subject of several articles and one that is too complex to more than summarize here.

The salient explanatory factor behind this process, we believe, is the submerged four-way power struggle within the Oujda clan and among the clan, Boumediene, and the former FLN General Secretary, Kaid Ahmed, now in exile in Morocco. This power struggle, it is reliably reported, has continued since at least 1959 and has involved, in addition to Boumediene and Ahmed, the former (now the late) Minister of Interior under both Ben Bella and Boumediene, Ahmed Medeghri, and, it is presumed, the present Minister of State for Foreign Affairs, Abdelaziz Bouteflika, who also served in this post under Ben Bella after he moved from the Ministry of Youth and Sports. All four were participants in the June 19, 1965, movement for national "recovery." All four paid lip service to the goals of this movement while plotting individually or in tandem to seize state power.

The first to be removed effectively from the political scene was former FLN head under Boumediene from 1965-1972, Kaid Ahmed. His position was always materially the weakest of the four because, lacking a ministerial portfolio, and having no independent source of income, Ahmed was not in a position to derive funds from the state budget. Early on, probably at least as early as 1962, our sources tell us, each of the ministers mentioned above (including Colonel Boumediene who, under Ben Bella was Minister for Defense, and for a time, the Vicepresident of the Republic) had agreed among themselves to divide the Algerian political terrain between themselves. To Ahmed Medeghri, the Interior Minister, was given the administrative apparatus of the republic. From the Ministry of the Interior on down to the regional (*wilaya* or *prefecture*) and municipal (*communal*) levels of government, Medeghri was given a virtual free hand to install men loyal only to himself. He successfully exploited his large budget and generous appointment powers to install *walis* (*prefects* or regional governors) who themselves had authority of tremendous actual and potential power (for example, the right to be the final arbitrator on building contracts in the region and the final decision maker on who should or should not be granted a passport, a birth certificate, a change-of-residence card, and even a taxi or hunting license).

Medeghri, who can in terms of his political orientation be compared with Napoleon, established in his 12 years as Interior Minister a powerful machine of spies, informers, and political patronage of unbelievable corruption that united the fifteen (and by 1974, the thirty) *wilayate* of the country under his careful personal control. One of his most significant powers was the privileged information his network gathered, particularly population figures.

One of our informants mentioned that Medeghri skillfully used census statistics and other similarly rare data in Council of the Revolution meetings as a lever to exact concessions from Boumediene himself. Because the latter had no reliable, independent source of statistics of his own, he was often forced to capitulate to the former's demands. Medeghri, like Kaid Ahmed, was effectively eliminated from the submerged power struggle by 1974. Exeunt two rivals for state power, leaving the field to only the President and his former Oudja comrade, Bouteflika, to continue the struggle.

It is important to note here, in discussing the role of Bouteflika, that our data are the "softest," perhaps the most speculative of this discussion. This is partially due to the fact that since the demise of Medeghri, the Minister of Foreign Affairs has played a low-keyed, "low-profile" role in the affairs of the Algerian state. Bouteflika is, however, perhaps the Algerian political leader best known to foreign observers, owing to his official position as spokesperson abroad for the Algerian government. He was also President of the UN General Assembly in the mid-1970s, and more recently Algeria's representative at the frequent meetings of the OPEC nations.

A skilled diplomat, and a frequent interviewee in various English and French newspapers, Bouteflika has perhaps been the most intelligent actor in the Hobbesian drama in Algeria for well over a decade. Bouteflika was, as of this writing virtually a minister without portfolio. He had simply but dramatically fallen out of favor with the chief of state, it was believed, after his alleged "cooperation" with Medeghri in the latter's machinations against Boumediene during the "hot summer" of 1974. He has had his "political wings clipped," according to one of our sources, and has since 1975 been relegated to a primarily ceremonial role. Bouteflika is seen on Algerian television receiving foreign diplomats and state guests, but almost always in the presence of President Boumediene. The latter, having recently arrogated to himself all authority for foreign policy decision making as well as the defense portfolio, is perhaps overly concerned about Bouteflika's important ties with Western diplomats and businesspeople, particularly French and Americans. Bouteflika (as some of our informants allege) has highly developed political ambitions of his own and would make a formidable opponent to any incumbent.

It is safe to conclude this section by saying that by 1970 all democratic accountability in Algeria had been effectively eliminated by this four-way power
struggle. Kaid Ahmed was driven into exile and political opposition by 1972. He
was replaced by a rather colorless, but loyal follower of the President who knows
how to obey the new guidelines of personal power. The party, like the unions
and other "mass" organizations became, even as early as 1968, a party of bureaucratized "militants." It was forbidden to hold party congresses, to publish party
newspapers, to engage in *any* kind of public or even private criticism of the government, its policies, or its leader. The FLN, the once dynamic revolutionary
organization of militants that had attracted the respect and admiration of much
of the world in its struggle against French colonialism, was converted into a
bureaucratic sycophantic shell. Real power had shifted by the late 1960s to the
Ministry of Interior, the Ministry of Foreign Affairs, and to the President of the
Republic.

Socialism for the poor: The continuing
immiseration of the people

Some general facts of economic life in Algeria will serve as illustrations of
the failure of the present Boumediene regime to respond to the basic needs of
the majority of Algerians. Depending upon the method of calculation and the
definition of "unemployment," estimates from reasonably objective sources (that
is, foreign ones because government statistics either do not exist or are false) suggest that unemployment is between 30 to 50 percent of the active work-age population. This figure, which includes women, applies mostly to the northern cities
where over 45 percent of the population is packed, living in dense squalor, ever
hopeful of finding a job or of getting the requisite papers to leave the country to
find a job in Europe.

The employment problem has been a constant one since the 1930s and
even earlier when many Algerians were forced to emigrate, temporarily or permanently, to France in order to survive or to realize higher material aspirations
for themselves and their families. It is fair to say that the Boumediene regime
has done nothing important to alleviate, improve, or change structurally the situation of the large number of workless Algerians.

Although Boumediene argues that the realization of his goal of 1000 "socialist villages" in the countryside with the ostensible objective of keeping the Algerian peasants on the land and thereby stopping or slowing down the huge rural ex-
odus seems a cogent case, the fact that only about thirty of these villages are actually completed and occupied suggests that he has been either blissfully optimis-
tic or highly deceptive. Furthermore, the Boumediene commitment to "heavy"
industry based on exploitation of hydrocarbons, natural gas, and other natural
resources hardly helps to ease the unemployment pressure. Such a priority may
in fact exacerbate the problem.

The emphasis in the first Three-Year Development Plan and in the subsequent two Four-Year Development Plans since 1966 has been on developing the steel, electronics, and chemical industries by purchasing Western or Russian technology and equipment with capital generated by oil and natural gas. The theory behind this strategy seems to make considerable sense, at least on paper: The oil and natural gas industries are viewed officially as "industrializing industries," or catalytic agents to rapid industrialization because of the huge injections of capital that OPEC prices yield to the Algerian government and hence to its state-owned national enterprises.

The problem as far as unemployment is concerned is that, by choosing this development strategy, Algeria has opted for a high level of technological sophistication, which cannot be remotely met now by recruiting insufficiently trained Algerians. Therefore, the Boumediene regime has liberally opened up its refinery, electronics, and drilling and sounding areas of enterprise to *foreign companies,* which require their own trained personnel and equipment as part of the contractual agreement.

Usually there is provision for the training of Algerians in these contracts, but the number trained in these enterprises is a drop in the bucket compared with the massive unemployment problem the nation faces. Although the government has since 1973 initiated a crash program to train Algerians as well as students from several other African nations in the complex technology of the diverse aspects of petroleum discovery, drilling, and refinery operations, such a program will take several decades to realize and to produce adequate and competent technical personnel.

Boumediene defends this race to catch up to the industrialized nations of the world in perfectly logical terms: delayed gratification; sacrifice of consumer needs and demands until the goals of the national development plans are met. The problem with this rationale is at least two-fold: (1) What is to happen to the masses of Algerians who have pressing basic needs in the interim? And (2) how long will this period of sacrifice continue? On these two issues the "socialist" government of Algeria remains silent or resorts to more pious exhortations to forgo present pleasures for future benefits.

Human failures: High food prices, inadequate housing,
deteriorating transportation, and the poverty of health care

Each of these issues can only be touched upon here briefly. Suffice it to say that if one is unlucky enough to be part of the 30-50 percent of the Algerian population who are unemployed, there is essentially no government welfare system to fall back upon. One is left to one's own resources. This means, in fact, that the unemployed Algerian must live off family resources, wage long and arduous battles with the government bureaucrats to obtain necessary papers to emigrate, or engage in petty theft[19] or beg for their daily bread.[20] The suicide rate in Algeria, particularly among young women, is reported to be the second highest in the entire Third World.

But the lot of the employed Algerian was little better in the late 1970s in terms of meeting the basic human needs of himself and his family. Take, for example, the case of a functionary whom one of the writers interviewed in 1976. This individual (whom we shall call Ahmed) worked in an industrial suburb of one of the large cities of the northern part of the country.

Ahmed worked in a little office tucked away in the city's town hall, the *daira*. He had finished high school a few years before, was married and had a baby. His monthly salary was about $190 a month.

He itemized his monthly expenses for us one day and estimated that he paid $32.50 for housing; $21.25 for taxes and social security; $7.50 for clothing; $20.00 for gas, electricity, and water; $6.00 for transportation; $9.00 for milk for the baby; thus leaving $93.75 for food for the family for the month. "It is not much to eat on with the cost of food so high here," he lamented.

A little research into the price of food in this area during 1975-1976 yielded the following information: The government controlled prices on such staples of the Algerian diet as couscous flour, lentils, rice, and pasta; but prices for all other food items such as fruits, vegetables, and meat fluctuated erratically and were almost always very high. There was a government vegetable store near where Ahmed worked, and this store had posted government regulated prices. It was a small shop and crowded almost every hour of the day it was open, so that one had of necessity to shop around at the privately owned stores. Prices in the latter depended considerably on who you were, that is, whether you had "clout" (*piston*) or not, or how much the proprietor believed he or she could get out of you.

Some specific prices may reveal the difficulty even a salaried employee of the municipality like Ahmed had to try to feed his family on a decent diet. Tomato paste fluctuated between 50¢ a can and $2.50 a can on the black market when the item had virtually vanished from area stores for 4 months. The price of meat was uniform, and uniformly high: chicken oscillated between $3.50 and $5.00 for a kilogram (approximately 2.2 pounds); beef, of all cuts and variety, was $7.50 a kilogram (or over $3.50 a pound); veal and lamb were pegged at $6.00 a kilogram.

With food prices that high, it takes little imagination to conjure up the average meal served up by Ahmed's wife: the diet of the poor, universally; heavy on starch, light on protein, and deficient in important vitamins. The government-controlled fruit and vegetable company, OFLA,[21] had an established policy of exporting to Europe the best locally grown fruits and vegetables. The strategy here, like that followed in the case of oil and natural gas, was to generate foreign currency to allow the country to purchase sophisticated technology, machines, physical plants, and training facilities for the industrial sector.

The prospect for Ahmed with more than 5 years on the job, with a wife and baby, and with no real likelihood of a promotion was not particularly bright. It is not surprising, given the stark facts of this humble functionary's existence, that Ahmed was not the most pleasant and outgoing civil servant one has ever met. In fact, he was a disgruntled, frustrated, even an envious person, who chose to vent his hostilities on ingenuous foreigners as well as on his Algerian clients.

Ahmed, like millions of other urban Algerians, was also deprived of decent transportation, housing, and medical care.

Public transportation is an ordeal to use. The buses are old and dilapidated (very few having been purchased or repaired in the dozen or more years since the French departed), and bus drivers invariably fail to meet their schedules, making workers and civil servants suffer long waits in crowded and smelly terminals.

Housing and medical care needs were similarly massively neglected by the Algerian government. One writer, Andre Fontaine, revealed that from 1962 to 1970, "not a square meter of low cost housing" was built for the Algerian people by their government (Mallarde, 1975, p. 153). The housing construction that has taken place since 1970, we learned, has been almost exclusively to provide living quarters for the managers of the nationalized companies, the police, and military officers. Ahmed was forced to commute 10 kilometers (about 6 miles) each day to his place of work, a trip that consumed at least 2 hours a day. The heat (or depending upon the climate, the lack of heat), the crush of passengers, and the inevitable bad tempers of the ticket collectors did little to enhance Ahmed's feeling of well-being, nor for that matter that of the thousands of others who are forced daily to rely on Algerian public transportation.

Health care since 1974 has been officially free in Algeria. But even President Boumediene admits that "free medicine" is more a political promise rather than a delivered service.[22] The major deficiencies in the Algerian health system are threefold: (1) the complete failure of hospital administration to enforce accountability of drugs, equipment, and personnel in the day-to-day running of hospitals; (2) the consequent absence, often for long periods, of basic drugs in hospital pharmacies and dispensaries; and (3) the resulting reliance upon *private* clinics and pharmacies because the public sector cannot remotely meet the needs of its vast clientele.

The hypothesis we posit here is that protracted economic deprivation reinforces political quiescence and cynicism on the part of the oppressed population. We believe that, through the continuing miserable lot of the overwhelming majority of Algerians in the context of the gradual but planned depoliticization of the only political party, the regime has since 1965 created the necessary conditions for (1) crushing potential political insurgency and (2) acquiescence in a new form of military dictatorship, one that governs in the name of the people but that in fact ignores their elementary human needs.

Bureaucratic arbitrariness and surveillance

The June 19 movement places heavy emphasis on maintaining tight political and social controls to keep a cowed citizenry in line.

Our sources indicate that in the summer of 1976 there were well over 1000 members of the Military Security section, which had principal responsibility to report on the activities of cabinet ministers, union leaders, students, professors, army officers, the police, and peasant leaders. The Military Security reports directly, it is alleged, to the Council of the Revolution, which, since 1970 when he assumed personal power, means in effect Colonel Boumediene alone. This crucial intelligence branch expands dramatically during periods of national emergency, as for example, during the Moroccan-Saharan crisis of 1975-1976.

Clearly the most efficient branch in the government, this organization has an agent, we are told, on every military construction crew in the country, and probably in every municipal bureau in the over 500 communes in Algeria. It is even known to direct a women's section that is specifically charged with spying on the activities of prostitutes and their clients.

There are three other intelligence-gathering bureaus in the government: the *mouchards* (informers) of the Ministry of the Interior; those of the Gendarmerie; and the special agents of the President who are placed, we were told, in every military unit to report directly to his *chef de cabinet* (his executive officer or assistant). In addition to reporting on the movements, the business transactions, the love affairs, and the conversations of the citizenry, these "eyes and ears of the Prince" report on each other.

At peak periods of government paranoia, as in early 1976, many youths between the ages of 16 and 21 were recruited off the streets of the big cities. They are paid by agents of the *Sureté Militaire* to return to the cafes, street corners, and windows of hotels to observe and note down "unusual" behavior on the streets and in the bars. With unemployment rates as high as they are in Algeria, particularly in this age group, it is no surprise that the Military Security finds ready and even eager recruits. Brecht phrased it aptly in the *Three Penny Opera: "Erst kommt das Fressen, dann kommt die Moral"* ("First comes the grub, then come the morals or ideology").

We have personal participant-observer data on the role of student informers and the oppressively inhibiting effects these agents have on classroom participation, the quality of human interactions outside the lecture hall, and the virtual conspiracy of silence and fear that pervades major Algerian universities. One of us was reminded of this early in the first semester in 1975 when a student paused after one of our lectures and said: "I think you should be very careful what you say in class. You know there is at least one government agent placed in every classroom. . . . By the way, it's not me."

The effect of his friendly warning, though meant to be helpful, was very chilling. We learned after months of teaching in two of the major universities that students are equally inhibited. It is difficult to convey the sense of dread and fear that the knowledge of such surveillance has on one's behavior.

Perhaps the obverse side of induced dread or self-censorship is contrived enthusiasm as, for example, in the *Volontariat* program in Algerian universities. Ostensibly a student (and worker) volunteer humanitarian organization created to stimulate student and worker direct involvement in knowledge of the problems of Algerian peasants, many of the members of *Volontariat* whom we taught and interacted with seemed almost like cardboard copies out of Eric Hoffer's *The True Believer.* One of our students, herself a recent participant on the *Volontariat* during the winter break, commented on her role. "It's true," she said. "We went to the steppes to learn the problems of the small peasants (peasants with small landholdings—no more than 50 hectares [about 125 acres] at the outer limit) and to experience their difficulties. But we actually spent most of our time explaining to them, who were woefully ignorant of the facts, how the POLISARIO was the sole legitimate representative of the Saharan people. We learned from the peasants, but *we* were really the educators."

Occasionally the political pacification process of tight surveillance combined with youthful *agitprop* fails. Then the strong arm of the state is exposed as happened at the University of Algiers in the summer of 1975. At a series of meetings, so far as we can reconstruct from a variety of conversations, a conflict emerged within the central committee of the *Volontariat* there, presumably over linguistic issues. Members of the *Frères Musulmans,* a conservative traditional Islamic group, clashed with members of the orthodox Marxist PAGS (*Parti d'Avant-Guarde Socialiste*) during which conflict the former proclaimed the superiority of Arabic over French as the lingua franca of the *Volontariat* program. It was rumored that from three to five students were killed in that dispute, and that scores of others were reported injured. No mention, of course, was made in the government-muzzled press. Some indication of the gravity of the incident was registered a few months later, however, when President Boumediene was moved to remark publicly that he would "never let Reaction come in through the cover of Arabization." This cover-up of student violence in Algiers isolated Boumediene even further from Muslim believers and practitioners. Already hostile to the perceived "atheism" of the Boumediene regime and its increasing reliance upon the Soviet Union for military experts and for material, devout Muslims were in summer 1976 in massive, but still mute, opposition to the military regime.

There are other more recent examples of government repression against actual or potential dissidents. The University of Algiers incident was, however, the most bloody recent case of the military mailed fist in action. Another, more recent incident (which unfortunately cannot be corroborated) was the widely believed story at the beginning of June 1976 that fifteen students had mysteriously vanished after they had dared to criticize the Boumediene regime during the "open and democratic" debates on the draft of the National Charter in a city near Algiers.

Latent and residual terror in Algeria

The three processes we have discussed, the depoliticization of the FLN, the relentless impoverishment of the majority of the people, and the terror-inspiring techniques of the spy and informer system have created the structure for authoritarian rule.

It is, we repeat, difficult to convey the degree of private withdrawal, the generalized feeling of suspicion, fear, and anxiety that we witnessed daily during our months of work and research in Algeria. The bitterness, the arbitrariness, the sheer loss of civility in interactions between Algerians, but also between Algerians and foreigners and between foreigners and foreigners (it is contagious), has to be experienced personally to be believed. The marvel is that under such conditions Algerians behaved so sanely and decently, as if to underscore the revolutionary belief that humankind will not easily accept defeat.

Nevertheless, the isolated, confused and atomized existence of much of Algeria's urban population no doubt manifests itself in the usual pathologies. Unfortunately, no reliable statistics are available on the incidence of alcoholism, assault, rape, and theft. As one of our respondents said, "The statistics died with Medeghri." It is widely rumored, however, that as many as 2 million Algerians are virtual prisoners in their own country without *the right* to acquire the necessary papers (birth certificates, change of residence forms, visas to leave, and so forth) to emigrate. The large number is not the result, we believe, of bureaucratic backlog or inertia, but it is part of a planned strategy of social control and the surveillance of actual or potential political dissidents.

It is estimated, moreover, that *another* 2 million Algerians (out of an estimated total population of almost 18 million in 1976) have been "dossiered." This means that elaborate files are kept by government agents of their "cradle to grave" statistics, their friends and acquaintances, their movements, and their political views.

As for the remaining 14 million Algerians, their lot is exceedingly hard. They must either identify with the oppressor by remaining silent, in order to advance themselves in administrative, educational, technical, or professional hierarchies wherein economic security is fragile but reasonably guaranteed,[23] or leave the country if they can. One of our respondents phrased the Algerian dilemma in somewhat existential terms: "You see what we have become now that we live under a dictatorship? We are a people who have suffered a great defeat. A person is no longer himself. He has lost his identity; he is a mere shadow of himself. He is an animal, and he reacts like an animal. Wary, cunning, and acquisitive."

Another respondent stressed the central role of the mass media in the effectiveness of "psychological action" by the state to confuse the masses about the reality in which they live. "When," she submitted, "the President calls Algeria a revolutionary country without giving any definition for revolution, when he says that it is becoming a socialist society without giving any definition for socialism, and when he repeats that cant day in and day out with the help of the press and television media—he crushes the citizenry with his myths while enriching the new class at the expense of the poor." This psychological warfare further erodes the human base for democracy and for a genuinely popular form of socialism by taking the meaning out of such phrases, compounding the existing cynicism and hopelessness of the people.

Perhaps some perspective can be derived from Isaac Deutscher's comments on the Soviet Union in the late 1940s:

> Within thirty years the Soviet people had repeatedly lost through war, civil strife, purges and famines, their most active, intelligent, and self-less elements, those that might have stiven to safeguard the heritage of the revolution against autocratic despotism. Now one-half of the working class consisted of middle-aged and old men who had experienced and suffered too much to have any militancy left in them; the other half was made up of adolescents who had experienced and understood too little to have a political mind of their own. The silence of a generation lost in the war lay like a pall upon the consciousness of the whole class. The peasantry was even more depressed and passive. Intimidated, absorbed in the labour of recreating the most elementary material conditions of their existence, the mass of people abdicated all political aspiration and withdrew into their private lives. [1949, p. 564]

Conclusions

Observations gained from firsthand experiences in London, the United States in the 1960s, Lebanon and Cyprus, and more recently Algeria were presented as evidence of the essentially subjective nature of terrorism. It was hypothesized, from the first four cases, that the "social inertia" of those societies allowed the majority of the population to reconstruct and continue ordinary daily routines even in the face of random bombings, widespread arson and police terror, and even fullfledged warfare, as in the cases of Cyprus and Lebanon. We were impressed with the tenacity of these social "perpetuating" phenomena in the face of vicious and usually protracted violence by aggrieved minorities to achieve a substantive policy change of their government or a regime change.

In the Algerian case, however, another form of terror was observed—the implicit, and occasionally overt manipulation of state sanctions by the postrevolutionary military regime to maintain political control over its citizens by "terrorizing" them politically, economically, and psychologically.

We recognize both the usefulness and the pitfalls of simple, firsthand observations. Such observations are valuable because the data generated are fresh, are gathered by the researcher himself or herself, often with important visual cues that designate the individual actors for subsequent follow-up, and because they allow the researcher to reduce alternative hypotheses because of useful judgments he or she can make regarding the most plausible interpretations of the behavior of the actor(s) in a given situation owing to the researcher's direct and intimate knowledge of the milieu (Webb et al., 1966, p. 138).

On the other hand, data generated by simple, firsthand observations are subject to some obvious sources of bias. Webb and co-workers outlined one of these by pointing to the "danger that the data-gathering instrument, the human observer, will be variable over the course of his observations. He may become less conscientious as boredom sets in, or he may become more attentive as he learns the task and becomes involved with it" (1966, pp. 138-139). It must be confessed that boredom was, for a time, an important factor (at least in the Algerian case).

George Devereux's caveat concerning an additional danger when gathering material with the simple, firsthand observational method, is also relevant here: "The alien and the unexplored fascinates the human mind and tempts it to fill the gaps in its knowledge with projections—i.e. with the products of its own fantasy which are all too readily accepted even by others as facts . . ." (1967, p. 196). He argued further that "one of the main functional determinants of objectivity may well be not so much the realism and conscience of the observer, *as his awareness that his statements can be checked. . . .*".

No claim is made herein to a monopoly on realism nor to superior moral qualities. We have in these five case studies of political disintegration and latent and residual terror followed three basic methodological rules, mindful always that colleagues and compatriots, students and friends in the societies scrutinized, will make the final judgment on the quality of the data and hypotheses, as well as on the validity of the conclusions. The following rules have been scrupulously obeyed:

1. To write down or record immediately after an interview or conversation each instance of the informant-respondent's description of his or her situation as faithfully as memory and knowledge of the local language could render.

2. To write down impressions and interpretations as frequently as possible (in diary form or episodical personal notes) concerning these experiences.

3. And, so far as possible, to cross check (1) and (2) with extant works, with other scholars on the spot and overseas, and with trustworthy local and foreign observers who have lived in the country for long periods.

It is hoped that, with these controls for bias, the basic wisdom of a French proverb cited by Devereux (1967, p. 197) does not apply to this essay—"He who comes from a distant country can lie with impunity."

Notes

1. In the latter case we shall be examining the residual and latent terror that is a device of a contemporary politico-military elite to maintain its control over the population.

2. Lest we forget, there was another period in American history (the last months of Herbert Hoover's administration) when official incompetence brought the country to grief: Children were literally starving and freezing to death. Crops were rotting in the fields and on the trees. Cattle and sheep were slaughtered and thrown into canyons for the worms and vultures to eat, because government would not sustain the market mechanism. Iowa farmers blocked roads and "senselessly" attacked passing motorists, smashing their cars to pieces, "merely" because the market price was lower than the cost of growing the produce. In some cities, groups of unemployed workers walked out of stores with groceries they refused to pay for; unemployed gas and electricity workers reconnected services for those who could not pay their bills; others dismantled whole buildings or joined forces to replace the belongings of evicted tenants. On a single day in April 1932, one-fourth of the entire state of Mississippi was sold at auction for tax arrears. Mrs. Hoover, the president's wife, meanwhile advised all Americans to be more "friendly and neighborly" with those who had "just happened to have bad luck." Consult Leuchtenburg (1963), pp. 22-28; Bernstein (1960), pp. 322-332; and Piven and Cloward (1971), pp. 61-66.

3. We are extremely indebted to our colleagues Kyriacos Markides and Christos Ioannides for comments on an earlier draft of this section.

4. Markides adds (personal communication, 1976): "When the Greek revolution broke out in 1821 the Greeks of Cyprus turned all their guns over to the Turkish governor to show that they had nothing to do with the revolution. The 1955 rebellion (against the British) was a radical departure from long established cultural patterns of submissiveness."

5. Greeks and Turks lived in relative harmony under the Ottoman *millet* system; and until 1956 there was only one minor incident of intercommunal violence under the British administration. Consult Vryonis (1971), pp. 444-497; Hill (1952), pp. 518-519; and Markides (1977).

6. Ioannides (1976) believes that the diaspora did not play too important a political role, except that the "Anglophiles," who had studied in England, formed a special clique in Cypriote politics and administration. One of the present authors has a distinctly different impression, gleaned, it must be admitted, from contacts with Cypriotes in America and the United Kingdom more than from any expertise in decision making processes in Nicosia.

7. There is now the fear, according to Ioannides (1976) that the mainland Greeks will accept any solution to the Cyprus question that will permit them to continue quietly on the course toward a consumer society within the European Economic Community, consigning *Enosis* to historical oblivion.

8. Along with the despair at being evidently abandoned to impoverishment and along with a more remote but very real fear of genocide or mass migration from the island, the Greek Cypriotes must deal with the grim fact that the victors and their recently imported colonists have not been able to manage the orchards, hotels, and other economic resources in the northern sector, such that even they, the "winners," are worse off.

9. The "latent terror," Professor Markides (1976) reminds us, was located specifically among the Cypriote enemies of the Athenian junta, and became *overt* for those Cypriotes and for their compatriots (themselves a bit oblivious to the growing storm) with the coup against Makarios.

10. Named for the eastern Moroccan city which served as the headquarters of the "exterior" Algerian Army during the war of national liberation. In 1960, Boumediene was named chief of the general staff of this army, the ALN (*Armée de la Liberation Nationale*). Men who composed the membership of this "clan" in addition to Boumediene were Abdelaziz Bouteflika, Cherif Belkacem, Kaid Ahmed, and Ahmed Medeghri. See David and Marina Ottaway (1970, pp. 296-298) for brief biographies of these leaders.

11. In mid-May the Boumediene government widely publicized and distributed copies of the "draft project" of the National Charter (or constitution) of the country. This project was considered an attempt by the regime to legitimize itself by appearing to establish constitutional norms for the system. It was discussed for over two weeks in meetings in factories, farms, and at the universities. The final version of the National Charter was ratified in a national referendum by a vote of 98 percent on June 27, 1976. *El Moudjahid,* June 29, 1976, p. 1.

12. *La Republique,* June 22 and 23, 1975, p. 2.

13. See, for example, Quandt (1976), the Ottoways (1970), and Humbaraci (1966). Humbaraci's main point is that Algerians, because of some alleged "national character" trait, have historically been unable to unite warring ethnic and class groups. This premise is very dubious because of the obvious interethnic solidarity that was sustained under the most vigorous conditions during the 8 years of struggle against French colonialism.

14. Every revolutionary or guerrilla movement must maintain strict discipline over its forces. Some of our respondents, however, remarked that they were personally sickened at times by the human consequences of such military discipline. Many writers have commented on the vicious cycle of polarization-terrorism-discipline-dehumanization and of the difficulty of reversing the process once initiated. We believe that the French government bears major responsibility for the original (that is, historical polarization of the Algerian people by its coerced colonialization of the nation from 1830 on. We are unable to attribute responsibility to either side for beginning the more recent terror of the 1950s during the war for national liberation, but we stress its importance as a formative part of the traumatic memories of the people who lived through this horrible period. See Fanon (1963, appendices) for brief case studies of mental illness resulting from the terror, on both sides.

15. Humbaraci's phrase for the incipient civil war from the beginning of July to at least the end of September 1962 when forces of Wilaya IV were threatening to take Algiers and when conflicts between the external army and the internal army were at their most intense level.

16. For a somewhat satisfactory discussion of this phenomenon see Farsoun (1975). For a longer treatment of the same subject see Viratelle (1974).

17. The best discussion of this is found in Mallarde (1975). See also Quandt (1969), pp. 148-174.

18. The phrase used by our sources is a party of "*encadrement.*"

19. Theft may be "the poetry of the marketplace," but from the standpoint of the victim it can be terrifying. According to our informants, the Algerians themselves, at least in the cities, live in fear of thieves and pickpockets (for example, on the crowded buses). Some stores have guards at the doors whose main job seems to be the preventing of gangs of children from entering or from leaving with stolen goods. Every Algerian we asked about the topic reported having suffered some form of theft within the previous 2 or 3 years. A common explanation was that this is the work of the poor and the unemployed, or of youngsters who, lacking proper adult supervision, had never learned better.
It was routine for members of the foreign community to have been robbed or burglarized. Unguarded property was carried away or dismantled in short order; automobiles and their contents would begin to disappear piecemeal, beginning at the docks, where the men who drove cars from the ships would help themselves to almost anything left in the car. Both authors were victims of theft; and one of us was strong-armed by three young toughs whilst getting on a bus and "liberated" very professionally of the contents of his pockets.

20. There remains for young men the possibility of joining the National Popular Army, but unlike in the armed forces in some Western countries, this is hardly a move in the direction of upward social mobility. The daily pay

of the Algerian *djound* (foot soldier) was 2 DA (or about 50¢) in the spring of 1976 with little opportunity for advancement in rank.

21. *Organization des Fruits et Légumes Algériens.*

22. *La Republique,* June 22 and 23, 1975, p. 3.

23. This option is available only to those who are lucky enough to have been able to attend secondary schools. For the approximately 40 percent of the age group between 11 and 19, their lot as adults is one of fighting for sheer survival because they lack the high school diploma that is the passport for upward mobility in Algeria, as in so many other African and Arab countries.

References

Bernstein, I. 1960. *The Lean Years.* Boston: Houghton Mifflin.

Bettelheim, B. 1960. *The Informed Heart.* Glencoe, Ill.: Free Press.

Bloch, H. 1956. *Disorganization, Personal and Social.* New York: Knopf.

Clegg, I. 1971. *Workers' Self-Management in Algeria.* New York: Monthly Review.

Cooley, C. H. 1918. *Social Process.* New York: Scribners.

Cooley, C. H. 1922. *Human Nature and Social Order.* New York: Scribners.

Coser, L. 1956. *The Function of Social Conflict.* London: Routledge & Kegan Paul.

Deutscher, I. 1949. *Stalin.* London: Oxford University.

Devereux, G. 1967. *From Anxiety to Method in the Behavioral Sciences.* The Hague: Mouton.

Eckstein, H. 1964. "Introduction." In *Internal War,* ed. H. Eckstein. New York: Free Press.

Fanon, F. 1963. *The Wretched of the Earth.* New York: Grove.

Farsoun, K. 1975. *State Capitalism in Algeria.* New York: Middle East Research Project.

Hayward, F. 1971. "Continuities and Discontinuities between Studies of National and International Political Integration." In *Regional Integration: Theory and Research,* ed. L. N. Lindberg and S. A. Scheingold. Cambridge, Mass.: Harvard University Press.

Hill, G. 1952. *A History of Cyprus.* Cambridge: Cambridge University Press.

Hobsbawm, E. J. 1969. *Bandits.* New York: Delacorte.

Hobsbawm, E. J. 1972. *Primitive Rebels.* Manchester, England: Manchester University.

Humbaraci, A. 1966. *Algeria: A Revolution that Failed.* New York: Praeger.

Hutchinson, M. 1972. "The Concept of Revolutionary Terror." *Journal of Conflict Resolution* 16: 383.

Ioannides, C. 1976. Personal communication, July.

Jakubowski, F. 1976. *Ideology and Superstructure.* London: Allison & Busby.

Kelsen, H. 1945. *General Theory of Law and State.* Cambridge, Mass.: Harvard University Press.

Kogon, E. 1950. *The Theory and Practice of Hell.* New York: Farrar, Straus.

Lefebvre, H. 1971. *L'idéologie structuraliste.* Paris: Anthropos-Points.

Leuchtenburg, W. 1963. *Franklin D. Roosevelt and the New Deal.* New York: Harper & Row.

Mallarde, E. 1975. *L'Algérie depuis 1962.* Paris: La Table.

Markides, K. 1976. Personal communication, July.

Markides, K. 1977. *The Rise and Fall of the Cyprus Republic.* New Haven, Conn.: Yale.

Mincès, J. n.d. *Self-Administration in Algeria.* Montreal: Our Generation.

Moore, Barrington, Jr. 1954. *Terror and Progress, USSR.* Cambridge, Mass.: Harvard University Press.

Nardin, T. 1971. *Violence and the State.* Beverly Hills, Calif.: Sage.

Ottaway, D., and Ottaway, M. 1970. *Algeria: The Politics of a Socialist Revolution.* Berkeley: University of California Press.

Piven, F., and Cloward, R. 1971. *Regulating the Poor.* New York: Pantheon.

Quandt, W. 1969. *Revolution and Political Leadership: Algeria, 1954-1968.* Cambridge, Mass.: M.I.T. Press.

Rappaport, E. 1968. "Beyond Traumatic Neurosis." *International Journal of Psychoanalysis* 49: 719.

Ross, E. A. 1901. *Social Control.* New York: Macmillan.

Shils, E. 1975. *Center and Periphery.* Chicago: University of Chicago Press.

Shils, E., and Janowitz, M. 1948. "Cohesion and Disintegration in the Wehrmacht," *Public Opinion Quarterly* 12: 280.

Soustelle, J. 1956. *Aimée et souffrante Algérie.* Paris: Plon.

Strickland, D. 1974. "Control per se." Unpublished manuscript.

Thornton, T. 1964. "Terror as a Weapon of Political Agitation." In *Internal War,* ed. H. Eckstein, New York: Free Press.

Turnbull, C. 1972. *The Mountain People.* New York: Simon & Schuster.

Viratelle, G. 1974. *L'Algérie algérienne.* Paris: Éditions économie et humanisme.

Vryonis, S. 1971. *The Decline of Medieval Hellenism in Asia Minor and the Process of Islamization from the 11th to the 15th Century.* Berkeley: University of California Press.

Walter, E. V. 1969. *Terror and Resistance.* New York: Oxford University Press.

Webb, E., Campbell, D., Schwartz, R., and Sechrest, L. 1966. *Unobtrusive Measures.* Chicago: Rand McNally.

Weber, M. 1922. *Wirtschaft und Gesellschaft.* Tübingen: Mohr.

Weiner, M. 1971. "Political Integration and Political Development." In *Political Modernization,* ed. C. Welch, Jr. Belmont, Calif.: Wadsworth.

Wilkinson, P. 1974. *Political Terrorism.* London: MacMillan.

Wolfenstein, M. 1957. *Disaster.* Glencoe, Ill.: Free Press.

Zartman, I. 1975. "Algeria: A Post-revolutionary Elite." In *Political Elites in the Middle East,* ed. F. Tachau, p. 265. New York: Halsted Press.

4

Societal Structure and Revolutionary Terrorism: A Preliminary Investigation

Harry R. Targ
Department of Political Science
Purdue University
West Lafayette, Indiana

Introduction

The specter of political violence and terrorism has increasingly occupied the public mind and social science inquiry in recent years. Perpetrators of political violence and terrorism are often seen in one of two ways by sectors of the world's citizenry. Members of the middle class in developed societies perceive terrorists as pathological individuals driven by evil demons. Third World peoples, with the exception of most political and economic elites, see violent nongovernmental political actors as fighters for national and, indeed, human liberation.

A more systematic empirical and normative assessment of violent political actors, particularly terrorists, requires an analysis of the societal structures in which they operate. This chapter will develop some themes from views of preindustrial, industrial, and postindustrial societies hypothesizing the sociostructural context in which revolutionary acts of political terrorism are most likely to occur. Viewing antigovernmental terrorist acts by revolutionary groups or individuals as a manifestation of the lack of a large vibrant revolutionary movement, this chapter hypothesizes that terrorist acts are more likely to occur in preindustrial and postindustrial societies rather than in industrial ones. Industrial societies have the potential for building mass-based revolutionary or reformist movements for change, whereas the former, for reasons to be discussed shortly, lack the class and occupational prerequisites for building such a movement. Consequently in pre- and postindustrial societies terrorism becomes a more common form of dissident political expression.

Conceptualizations of Political Terrorism: A Critical Analysis

This chapter will make two assumptions about revolutionary terrorism. The first is that revolutionary terrorism is merely one form of behavior by individuals or groups in support of fundamental change in a given society. It is the threat and use of violence against individuals selected by the terrorists for their symbolic value to galvanize a population through fear or respect. Revolutionary terrorism is not synonymous with revolutionary social movements and is made intelligible only through a thorough analysis of the society in which it occurs and in the context of the size, power, and activities of social movements for revolutionary change extant in the given society. Consequently revolutionary terrorism is a product of historical conditions and forces for change. The hypothesis examined in this chapter suggests that terrorism is a form of political action in historical settings not conducive to mass action for systematic transformation.

The second assumption is that, for reasons analyzed in the following sections, revolutionary terrorism is social, not individual, pathological behavior in that it occurs in social structures and historical settings where the forces for social change are at their weakest. Therefore, although terrorism is one behavior pattern in a whole panoply of revolutionary actions, its importance within a society is inversely related to the revolutionary potential of the people. It represents an act of weakness rather than burgeoning strength. Its occurrence is most likely in those historical settings and social structures where revolutionary potential is less prevalent.

These assumptions contradict prevalent conceptualizations in the literature of political terrorism. For example, Gross (1969) develops two models that seek to explain "systematic" political terror: (1) terror against foreign rule or autocratic political regimes; (2) terror against democratic institutions. In reference to the first model, Gross finds three "antecedent" conditions that relate to acts of political terrorism:

1. The perception of sociopolitical conditions of oppression
2. The existence of a political party with an ideology and the tactics of direct action
3. The presence of activist personality types who are willing to make a political choice and respond with direct action and violence to conditions of oppression (Gross, 1969, p. 466)

In discussing these antecedent conditions, Gross says that the perception of oppression, an ideologically based group, and certain personality types are vital for terrorism to occur. Although this model is derived from the history of Russia and Eastern Europe, little account is taken of comparative sociostructural conditions under which frequent instances of terrorism occur. Rather, the three variables cited, perception, ideology, and personality, suggest what one might call a "psychologized" theory of terrorism, an orientation, even if less pejorative, prevalent among the American public.

Similar antecedents are suggested to explain terror against democratic institutions:

1. Sociopolitical determinant—weakening of shared democratic values and/or crisis of democratic institutions

2. Existence of a party or a temporary conspiracy with the ideology and tactics of direct violence

3. Preassassination process of defamation and actions of the party directed against democratic institutions

4. Presence of certain personality types, with propensities toward overt aggression once the foregoing antecedents are present (Gross, 1969, pp. 468-469)

Here again, one finds psychological, perceptual, attitudinal, or personality variables prevalent in the analysis.

Although Gross tries to understand the necessary conditions for political terrorism and does so primarily in psychological terms, Hutchinson (1972) conceptualizes political terrorism in tactical and strategic terms. She defines the components of revolutionary terrorism as including action for specific political purposes, actions consciously doing physical or emotional harm to persons, actions that evidence "extranormality" (that is, shocking, unpredictable acts), and the threat or use of violence against selected symbolic targets to create a mass psychological effect. Revolutionary terrorism is part of a revolutionary strategy to seize political power. With limited resources or support it achieves psychological and political disruptiveness in the society experiencing the birth pangs of revolution.

For Hutchinson, terrorism is conceptualized in strategic terms devoid of the undertones of abnormal psychology present in the Gross formulation. In fact, psychological variables are seen more as outcomes of the process of terror. The tactic is designed to destroy the mass psychic stability that undergirds support for ongoing political regimes. Although the conceptualization of revolutionary terror without resort to psychologically pathological terms may add more to theoretical understanding, the Hutchinson portrait of terrorism lacks the richness of treatment of conditions antecedent to terrorism. To Hutchinson antecedent conditions are conceptualized in terms of the tactical conception of terrorism. The choice of terrorist tactics is based on what is abhorrent to societal norms. Terror is seen as an economical activity when revolutionary organization is weak and regime repression strong. These antecedent conditions flow from the strategic value of terrorism rather than terrorism from antecedent conditions.

The essays by Gross and Hutchinson are representative of conceptualizations of revolutionary terrorism. They limit the capacity for theoretical understanding of revolutionary terrorism as political behavior and do not lend themselves to assessing the value of such behaviors for bringing about fundamental social change. This is so for several reasons.

First, such discussions of revolutionary terrorism do not account for the broad sociostructural features of societies in which terrorism or other revolutionary activities occur. Such sociostructural features include the nature of the class system and the relationships classes have to the means of production, the level of industrialization, the social relations of production, and the level of organization and consciousness among workers in given societies. It will be argued below that revolutionary terrorism is more probable in societies with particular structural configurations. Essentially, the frequency of revolutionary terrorist acts will occur more often in those societies without broad-based movements for radical change.

Second, as suggested above, theories of revolutionary terrorism and popular views of terrorism are mistakenly psychological in nature or are given to overly rationalized strategic conceptions. To psychologize about terrorism is to ignore the objective reasons for terrorist acts. To rationalize about terrorism is to ignore the sociostructural parameters that impinge upon revolutionary action.

Third, much of the writing on terrorism and political violence of which Gross and Hutchinson are illustrative is ahistorical. There is little sensitivity to the processes of historical change and the historical conditions that facilitate or mitigate against revolutionary activity of one sort or another. As with most social science research, the underlying historical forces are ignored so that the models constructed are based upon logical constructs or sense data. Terrorism, revolutionary movements, and governmental reactions all must be understood in broadly historical and sociostructural terms.

A Structural Model of Political Terrorism

Given the criticisms of the terrorist literature articulated above, this chapter posits a model that suggests the sociostructural contexts in which acts of terrorism are more likely to occur. To do so we elaborate on themes from the Marxist schema of social change as outlined in the *Communist Manifesto* and the writings of Lenin and draw from the works of selected writers on what has been called "postindustrial society." After briefly developing the model, we shall discuss the literature

Table 1 A Structural Framework of Political Terrorism

Structural prerequisites		Behavioral prerequisites		
Societal structures	Revolutionary organization	Tactics	Psychological determinants	Incidences of terrorism
1. Occupational 2. Ruling class control of means of production 3. Character and level of exploitation 4. Ideological structure of society	1. Level of class consciousness 2. Size of existing social movements (and parties) 3. Level of party organization	1. Rational process of selecting efficacious strategies	1. Propensity for extreme acts because of cognitive and emotional structure of individual	1. Terrorist acts or social movement

from which it is taken and shall examine selected data on terrorism to evaluate its utility for explaining and understanding terrorist acts.

Table 1 illustrates the kinds of factors that in combination provide a meaningful basis for understanding and predicting terrorist acts. The most fundamental forces conditioning political action are referred to as *societal structures.* Critical to these structures are what might be called the *occupational* structures of given societies, that is, the extent to which the organization of work roles is socialized, as in industrial capitalism, and/or individuated, as in peasant agriculture or postindustrial service employment. Further, an examination of the character of *ruling class control of the means of production* is in order. Societal settings in which feudal lords represent the dispersal of power and control as opposed to a relatively homogeneous and integrated bourgeoisie may determine the potential of a large-scale revolutionary movement. A ruling class, as in postindustrial society, that is less visible because of owner/manager/expertise connections may limit the emergence of a class with clear coherent revolutionary goals. The character of *exploitation* is integral to the sociostructural setting in which various forms of political action might occur. Preindustrial forms of tithing or labor payments to feudal landlords and postindustrial myths of affluence in a structure that does not produce industrial goods may yield behavioral results that are different from those produced in a society in which an industrial working class provides unpaid labor to capitalists in the Marxist sense. Lastly, variations in the prevailing *ideological patterns* of societies may relate to revolutionary or terrorist potentials. That is to suggest that supernatural and hedonistic/scientist cosmologies may yield behavioral outcomes different from those yielded by ideologies based on conflict and competition.

The second set of factors affecting the frequency of terrorism are referred to as *revolutionary organization* variables. If revolutionary movements or class-based electoral movements represent an aggregate response that limits terrorism, *the level of class consciousness, the size of revolutionary movements,* and/or the level of *radical party organization* in given societies become important. These, it is posited, are largely determined by the structural properties of the societies in which they occur and represent critical intervening links between structure and the nature of behavioral outcomes.

Tactical variables involve rational calculations of costs and benefits from electoral activities, demonstrations, underground propagandizing, or revolutionary civil war as compared with terrorism. They logically follow from the structural and revolutionary antecedents. Similarly, *psychological* variables, that is the conscious and/or emotive commitment to certain kinds of action by certain kinds of persons, presuppose the antecedent factors indicated above. Lastly, we here posit an inverse relationship between visible, sizable revolutionary action for social change that can occur only in certain kinds of societies and *incidences of political terrorism.*

The analysis below will examine the meaning of social structure and revolutionary factors and particular emphasis will be placed on establishing possible linkages between them and the frequency of terrorist acts.

Societal Structure, Revolutionary Organization, and Political Terrorism

Karl Marx claimed that all history is the history of class struggle whether that struggle is between Roman lord and slave, medieval lord and serf, or modern bourgeoisie and proletariat. The industrial capitalist age was a by-product of the struggle between feudal lords, guildmasters, and emerging traders, merchants, and manufacturers. The latter three destroyed the fabric of feudal society, freed peasants from the land, and made them into "free" wage laborers. Using Marx's concepts, the means of production, technology, and property relations were revolutionized, causing the relations of production to be radically transformed. Gradually isolated feudal manors were replaced by free trade, wage labor, manufacturing and modern industry, and increasing local, national, and global networks of communications, trade, and capital concentration.

Of course, Marx is explicit about the proletariat as revolutionary class. In the *Communist Manifesto* he speaks of the gradual but insistent movement of the proletariat to its historic revolutionary character. Workers at an early stage of industrial capitalism struggle against factory owners individually, organize in single factories or by trade, and strike out spontaneously against the instruments of production. This early stage of worker struggle is one in which "laborers still form an incoherent mass scattered over the whole country, and broken up by their mutual competition" (Marx, 1972, p. 342). If the workers organize, this is usually a consequence of action by the bourgeoisie and for the purpose of the bourgeoisie. With the further development of industrial capitalism "the proletariat not only increases in number; it becomes concentrated in greater masses, its strength grows, and it feels that strength more" (Marx, 1972, p. 342). Increasing exploitation of workers coupled with the expanding socialization of production spur the coming together of the working class as a revolutionary class. What results from the development of the proletariat is the development of a "self-conscious, independent movement of the immense majority, in the interest of the immense majority" (Marx, 1972, p. 344). This evolution is nothing short of a "veiled civil war" that will lead to "open revolution" and the overthrow of capitalism.

Of vital importance to the relationship between revolutionary action and terrorism and social structure is Marx's vivid statement that

> wage-labor rests exclusively on competition between laborers. The advance of industry, whose involuntary promoter is the bourgeoisie, replaces the isolation of the laborers, due to competition, by their revolutionary combination, due to association. The development of modern industry, therefore, cuts from under its feet the very foundation on which the bourgeoisie produces and appropriates products. What the bourgeoisie, therefore produces above all, are its own gravediggers. [1972, p. 345]

Marx's characterization of revolutionary potential during the precapitalist and early industrial stage of capitalism therefore is one in which laborers are still an "incoherent mass scattered over the whole country." It is claimed here that terrorism in the form of violent action in protest against exploitation is more likely to occur in precapitalist or early capitalist phases of societal development rather than during a phase of mature capitalism. A mass movement based upon the consciousness and organization of workers has not occurred. Revolutionary acts, as Hutchinson suggests, must be economical, must take symbolic form, and must attempt to catalyze the scattered masses and terrify the beneficiaries of the ongoing order.

Lenin, in a more programmatic way, recognized the necessity of building a mass movement led by a highly disciplined party. He too was aware of the requisite conditions within the social structure of bourgeois society that would serve as a stimulus for revolutionary action and consequently was opposed to those "Left-Wing Communists" who based their revolutionary theory on the "spontaneity of the masses." In counseling against both "economism" and "terrorism" Lenin says:

> The Economists and the terrorists merely bow to different poles of spontaneity; the Economists bow to the spontaneity of "the labor movement pure and simple," while the terrorists bow to the spontaneity of the passionate indignation of intellectuals, who lack the ability or opportunity to connect the revolutionary struggle and the working class movement into an integral whole. [Lenin, 1975, p. 47]

Lenin argues later in "What is to be Done?" that the calls for terrorist acts in 1901 evade the "pressing duty now resting upon Russian revolutionaries, namely, the organization of comprehensive political agitation" (Lenin, 1975, pp. 48-49). Both the economists and the terrorists underestimate the revolutionary activity of the masses. The terrorists engage in "excitants" or false stimuli to encourage the masses instead of building for political "agitation" and organization "of political exposures." For Lenin no other activity can substitute for the task of building mass organization and a revolutionary party.

Lenin indicates in "Left-Wing Communism, An Infantile Disorder" what criteria determine the efficacy of a revolutionary party:

> First, by the class-consciousness of the proletarian vanguard and by its devotion to the revolution, by its perseverance, self-sacrifice, and heroism. Second, by its ability to link itself with, to keep in close touch with, and to a certain extent, if you like, to merge with the broadest masses of the working people—primarily with the proletariat, *but also with the non-proletarian* laboring masses. Third, by the correctness of the political leadership exercised by this vanguard, by the correctness of its political strategy and tactics, provided that the broadest masses have been convinced *by their own experience* that they are correct. Without these conditions, discipline in a revolutionary party that is really capable of being the party of the advanced class, whose mission it is to overthrow the bourgeoisie and transform the whole of society, cannot be achieved. [1975, p. 285, emphasis in original]

The conditions needed for the construction of a revolutionary party and movement emerge only out of long and hard-fought struggle. Without the achievement of these conditions, Lenin says, the activity of revolutionaries is ultimately reduced to "phrase-mongering" and "clowning." A truly revolutionary party "is facilitated by correct revolutionary theory, which, in its turn, is not a dogma, but assumes final shape only in close connection with the practical activity of a truly mass and truly revolutionary movement" (Lenin, 1975, p. 255).

Correct revolutionary theory necessitates the building of a vanguard party that is in touch with, and is part of, the revolutionary potential of the masses. Precipitous acts of terror, as frequently occurred in nineteenth-century Russia, are socially pathological in that they do not serve as a substitute for political organization and agitation. The antecedent condition for successful revolution is a revolutionary party and a revolutionary class that has through its own experience of exploitation reached a consciousness of its historic mission. Antecedent to this organization and consciousness is the sociostructural setting of mature industrial capitalism. By implication, terrorism as a prevalent mode of revolutionary behavior is characteristic of preindustrial or early industrial phases of capitalism, comes from representatives of "an incoherent mass" or the "passionate indignation of intellectuals," and in strategic terms is "an infantile disorder." Therefore, from the Marxist-Leninist perspective it may be hypothesized that revolutionary terrorism is more likely to occur in preindustrial and early industrial societies where the conditions for class consciousness and highly organized workers are weaker than in mature industrial capitalist societies where worker consciousness and organization (even if manifested in Social Democratic or Communist parties) are strong.

The issue of the relationship between social structure, revolutionary organization, and revolutionary terrorism may not end here. Recent writers on the industrial state have introduced the concept of postindustrialism to suggest a qualitative transformation of some states beyond industrial capitalism. Particular attention has been given to social changes within the United States, several Western European nations, and Japan as analysts examine apparent changes in their economies, polities, cultures, and knowledge bases.

Daniel Bell (1973) has been most instrumental in raising the issue of postindustrialism. He suggests that the "concept of the post-industrial society deals primarily with changes in the *social structure,* the way in which the economy is being transformed and the occupational system reworked, and with the new relations between theory and empiricism, particularly science and technology (Bell, 1973, p. 13). More specifically, he suggests that there are five dimensions to postindustrialism.

1. Economic sector: the change from a goods-producing to a service economy
2. Occupational distribution: the preeminence of the professional and technical class
3. Axial principle: the centrality of theoretical knowledge as the source of innovation and of policy formulation for the society
4. Future orientation: the control of technology and technological assessment

5. Decision making: the creation of a new "intellectual technology"
   (Bell, 1973, p. 14)

Bell claims that each of these tendencies in postindustrial society is inter-related. For example, the fundamental principle of postindustrialism (the axial principle) is the use of theoretical knowledge for innovation, control, and policy. Theoretical knowledge leads to an orientation toward planning and predictions about the consequences of policy choices. The knowledge/planning/policy nexus suggests the new impact, if not the power, of the expert. The new modes of decision making, the new powerful actors, the new epistemological foundations for political choice converge with or stimulate the change from a goods-producing or industrial economy to a service economy. The number of industrial workers dramatically decreases and the number of knowledge workers increases. Finally, whereas the industrial revolution created the large corporation and trade union, the postindustrial revolution has created and/or supported the growth of the university and research institute.

Bell suggests that comparatively *preindustrial* society has the following characteristics: primary extraction in the economy; farming, mining, and fishing in the occupational sector; a "game against nature" in "design"; common-sense experience as method; orientation to the past as time perspective; and traditionalism as the root ("axial") principle on which such a society is built. *Industrial* society, in contrast, has the following characteristics: secondary goods production and manufacturing in the economy; semiskilled workers and engineers in the occupational sector; energy as the central technology; empiricism and experimentation as the methodology; short-term adaptation as the time perspective; and economic growth and investment as the axial principle. According to Bell, *postindustrial* society has the following characteristics: trade, finance, insurance, health, education, research, and other tertiary activities in the economy; professional and technical experts in the occupational sector; information as the basic technology; "games between persons" as the design; abstract theory, modeling, simulation, decision theory, and so forth, as the methodology; futurology and future orientation as the time perspective; and theoretical knowledge as the axial principle.

Contrary to Bell's assumption that postindustrial societies have transcended their traditional capitalist characteristics, Lasch (1972) contends that the features of postindustrialism described by Bell are unique to the latest stage in the development of capitalism. Such societies are still capitalist because "the industrial system produces commodities rather than objects for use and that the important decisions concerning production remain in private hands rather than being socially determined" (Lasch, 1972, p. 36).

The defining features of postindustrial society are many. First, poverty is no longer pervasive but is found among isolated sectors of the society. The working class is generally affluent, and the poor are found primarily among ethnic and racial groups, migrant and seasonal workers, and chronically unemployed. Second, the class system evidences marked changes. The demand for white-collar workers exceeds the demand for industrial workers. A new lumpen proletariat of occasional menial labor essentially replaces the working class as the most dispossessed. A "new working class" of clerks, salespeople, technicians, state employees, and teachers comes into being. Although similar to the traditional working class in terms of the lack of access to property and control over decisions, this middle class of workers does not identify with the working class.

Finally, a ruling class consisting of owners and managers of the economy dominates. It is "an amalgam of the *haute bourgeoisie* and the new managerial elite, that controls the great corporations, most of the land, and the higher reaches of government (especially the military). In both its functions and ideology, the ruling class is predominantly managerial" (Lasch, 1972, p. 38). This ruling class of owners and managers is committed to a "corporate liberal" ideology, one that accepts a managed economy, the welfare state, trade unions, and imperialism in world affairs, all justified by "free enterprise." The ideology of corporate liberalism, Lasch says, is disseminated throughout the society and is broadly accepted by the populace.

Further, the postindustrial society creates life-styles and consumption patterns that make the central city irrelevant. Cities and urban life styles decay as life increasingly becomes suburban. The automobile becomes the instrument of vast superfluous production as well as destruction of the environment. The demands of the automobile are illustrative of the principle that "the continuing growth of the system now depends on the creation and satisfaction of false needs, and even then the system finds itself unable to run at full capacity" (Lasch, 1972, p. 41). Lasch refers to market research, public relations, defense, and other governmental programs (such as highway construction) as "subsidized waste." "In the partnership between the government and the great corporations, the former performs all the functions indispensable to the survival of the latter, while the latter retain the profits" (Lasch, 1972, pp. 41-42).

Lastly, formal education becomes more critical in a postindustrial society for two reasons. First, the economy and public bureaucracies need trained personnel on an expanded scale. Second, "mass education is a precondition for mass propaganda on the part of both the state, which seeks to maintain a constant air of crisis, and the corporations, which need to create sophisticated consumers. In other words, mass education is a political even more than it is a strictly economic necessity" (Lasch, 1972, p. 43).

In the long run Lasch's postindustrial society is characterized by contradictions that will presage political instability. However, for the immediate future political stability is fostered by increasing government-corporate integration, the rise of expertise, technical knowledge as an essential *intervening mechanism* (as opposed to the view of theorists like Bell who assume that knowledge is power) in system management, and the manipulative capacities of the ruling class over middle and working classes alike. The manipulative feature of postindustrial life is characterized by

> the tendency of political grievances to present themselves as personal griev-
> ances, the tendency for repressive authority to assume the guise of benevo-
> lence, the substitution of psychology for politics, and the pervasiveness of
> the managerial mode of thought. . . . [These] help prevent conflicts from
> coming to the surface and contribute to the illusion that ideology has ex-
> hausted itself. [Lasch, 1972, p. 46]

Other writers on postindustrialism emphasize science, rationalism, and bureaucracy as antecedent conditions that lead to mass manipulation. For example, Erich Kahler in *The Tower and the Abyss* (1957) has argued that humankind has begun to be fundamentally transformed in the twentieth century. The primary characteristic of man in the modern period is his "indivisibility, implying coherent unity, wholeness." Speaking of man as an individual is to imply "that to divide him is to destroy him as a human. As long as he remains human, he must maintain his indivisibility" (Kahler, 1951, p. 4). Contrary to this pervasive definition of man we see today the "disintegration of the individual in all fields of contemporary experience."

The fundamental external change that has facilitated the transformation of man, the indivisibility of him as a social entity, is the movement from social organizations called communities to others called collectives. Communities are groups like the family or tribes that "genealogically" and historically precede individuals who become part of them. They represent the "archaic social entities" out of which individuals grow. They transmit patterns of behavior, life-styles, values, and attitudes. "Communities form traditions; they are the soil, the constantly, silently shifting ground in which the individual is rooted" (Kahler, 1957, p. 7). They act on the individual from within and provide both a moral basis from which to act as a whole person and the sociopsychological environment in which to act as individuals. Communities do not stifle individuality, they provide the only social environment in which it can occur.

The collective, on the other hand, is a "supraindividual" or "postindividual" assemblage of persons for some purpose beyond the individual. "Collectives are established by common ends, communities derive from common origins" (Kahler, 1957, p. 9). Corporations, labor unions, political parties, and nation-states are collectives organized for common purposes above and beyond the individuals that participate in them. About the nation-state Kahler says: "Through the vast scope of its tasks it has become overwhelmingly bureaucratic, a monstrous, rationalized and systematized organization of individuals" (Kahler, 1957, p. 10). Collectives act on individuals from without by intruding on the individual psyche and splitting the personality via mass stereotypes, imposed attitudes and values that have "sunk from consciousness into the unconscious" (Kahler, 1957, p. 10-11).

The collectivization of man began initially when premodern rulers first absorbed applied science and technology and spread rationalism as a creed for their own personal aggrandizement. The combined impetus of science, technology, industrialization, and mass democracy in the modern era have converged in such a way that the human form is being destroyed. "The roots of collectivism are to be found in rationalism and technology and not in any specific social or economic doctrine" (Kahler, 1957, p. 17).

Kahler discusses crucial components of the process of collectivism: Rationalism as a credo evolved into *rationalization* implying the *classification* and *quantification* of organic and inorganic phenomena so that people and things become categories for manipulation. *Scientification* reduces all human and material phenomena (even sexuality) to measurable laws. The passions of people are broken down into party identification and theories of voting behavior and hence their indivisibility is destroyed. Individual intuitions and values are replaced by obeisance to scientific authority. "Science is the supreme, impersonal, collective authority . . ." (Kahler, 1957, p. 21). The splitting of man is reinforced in the economic sector by *specialization* or the replacement of human behavior with functional behavior, in the consumer sector by *standardization* or conformist thinking and behavior, and in the political sector by *anonymity*. In reference to the latter Kahler says: "In big corporations and in modern governments decisions are no longer made by one man alone; they are the result of joint deliberation of a group of people assisted by experts. It is almost impossible to locate the distinct origin of a decision which has become anonymous" (1957, p. 34).

The results of all of this on man are varied. Modern man lacks a definite style of life, is forever subject to manipulation, lacks a sense of personal responsibility, is ready to define right from wrong on the basis of what is good for the state, and has a new "levity" toward injustice.

Theodore Roszak (1969) elaborates on these themes in the light of radical social changes in the 1960s. To him, the characteristic feature of modern society is that it is a technocracy, an organization based upon the confluence of science, bureaucracy, and centralized power. All remaining social problems in a modern society are a function of the lack of appropriate application of technical expertise and/or the result of faulty communication. He quotes Robert McNamara, the prototype technocrat, as celebrating increasingly centralized administration and the application of reason, that is, Kahler's rationalization and scientification, to the making of public policy. The potency of the technocracy is measured more by its power to manipulate than by its power to coerce. Herbert Marcuse's notion of "repressive desublimation" is cited as illustration of the scope and intensity of technocratic infiltration into the public psyche. Roszak applies this notion to suggest that citizens are controlled more and more by the technocracy's partial "liberation" of sexuality from Victorian restraints. Modern man seeks the fulfillment of consumption desires in sex and material benefits as portrayed in *Playboy* magazine. The goal for women is material accumulation and status derived from behaving as objects. The means to contemporary promiscuity come from "right" conduct within the world of business. Men and women are socialized to act appropriately so as to be rewarded with "liberation." This reward structure involves a greater degree of repression and control than of liberation.

Those who protest against the technocracy are subtly manipulated by the system as well. Protest is analogous to the situation where persons are pushing against a door and someone on the other side of the door is applying counterpressure. Suddenly the latter opens the door and those seeking to get in come tumbling to the ground. The outsiders now are under the control of those originally seeking to keep the door closed.

The formulations of postindustrialism by Bell, Lasch, Kahler, Roszak, and others suggest a fundamental transformation of selected societies, a transformation that dramatically affects the possibilities for revolutionary action for social change. First, the change from goods production to service in the occupational sector may represent a movement from the socialization of industrial production to the individuation of service production. With this change, Lasch suggests, workers increasingly perceive themselves as middle class and act on the basis of bourgeois notions of individualism, mutual competition, and commitment to the ongoing order.

Second, the cultural by-products of this new occupational and class structure is a life-style commitment to what Bell sees as an antinomian impulse. Self-gratification replaces social change as a modus operandi of new middle-class thinking and behavior. This creates an ideology of pleasure maximization, compulsive consumption, and hedonism.

Third, as Kahler and Roszak posit, postindustrial man accepts the legitimacy of scientism as the new religion. With this new scientism comes an acceptance of the technocrat's atomized view of the self and social wholes. Man defines himself in terms of externally posited categories. Rather that a holistic class consciousness, men and women increasingly define themselves in terms of their specific work functions, their party identification, their hobbies, and so on, but not as whole persons integrally related to other whole persons. Lastly, postindustrialism is built upon the view (largely a myth) that such societies have moved from economies of scarcity to economies of abundance. It is this myth

Table 2 Linkages Between Societal Structures, Revolutionary Organization, and Political Terrorism

	Type of society		
	Preindustrial	Industrial	Postindustrial
Societal Structure			
Occupation	Agriculture (primary)	Industrial production (secondary)	Service (tertiary)
Ruling class	Feudal lords	Capitalists	Capitalists/technocrats
Exploitation	Extraction of farm produce, natural resources	Surplus value	Surplus value/manipulation
Ideology	Religious, naturalistic	Work ethic, competition	Hedonism, antinomianism
Revolutionary organization			
Class consciousness	Low (peasants prize land, property)	High (socialization of work)	Low (self-gratification replaces social understanding)
Size of social movements	Small	Potentially large	Small
Level of party organization	Small	Large	Small
Political terrorism			
Frequency	High	Low	High
As means of dissident political expression	Central means	Peripheral means	Central means

that masks the pervasiveness of poverty and exploitation domestically and internationally and lends support to the appropriateness of the antinomian impulse. In this social milieu, as Lasch suggests, public problems (that is, structural exploitation) become redefined as personal ones (self-defined psychological disorder).

The social context of postindustrialism inhibits class consciousness, reduces people's perceptions of shared exploitative experiences, and impairs the formulation of radical or revolutionary movements for social change. It is proposed here that terrorist acts become permanent features of the social landscape. Structural attributes of postindustrialism coupled with individuated and antinomian ideological patterns reduce the possibilities for social action. Hence aberrant social action is manifested in terrorism.

Table 2 provides a summary statement of the selected literature summarized above and indicates the central hypothesis of this chapter. Preindustrial societies (and early capitalist societies) are characterized by primary occupations in agriculture or extraction of natural resources, are dominated domestically by feudal lords, and are exploited directly by them through appropriation of primary produce. (This formulation does not deny the interconnections between the rural peasantry and the global political economy but merely suggests the local character of exploitative processes.) Lastly, the prevalent ideology of preindustrialism is religious and/or naturalistic. Industrial societies are characterized by factory production, control by large capitalists, exploitation of labor time, and an ideological structure that emphasizes work and competition. Postindustrial societies introduce service occupations, technocratic components to the ruling class, psychological manipulation and privatization of life as mechanisms of control and exploitation, and hedonism as the ideological pattern.

These structural features of the three societies inhibit revolutionary organization in preindustrial and postindustrial societies and enhance revolutionary potential in industrial societies. Consequently, the expectation is that terrorism as a prevalent mode of political expression of dissent will be found in preindustrial and postindustrial societies. Terrorism is only a secondary mode of expression in industrial societies because mass-based movements for social change are more likely to grow.

Incidences of Political Terrorism

For purposes of examining the central theme of this chapter, we shall survey studies on political violence and terrorism and examine data on terrorism, particularly assassinations. Because of the difficulty of gathering accurate data cross-culturally the following information serves as a preliminary test of the themes described and not a final confirmation. This is particularly true because of the lack of data available concerning most of the variables included in the model.

For purposes of preliminary investigation, we may begin by examining the analysis of the linkages between multiple variables and political violence reported in Kirkham, Levy, and Crotty (1969). Particular attention is given by these authors to two data sets on political assassination gathered by research groups headed by Carl Leiden and Ivo Feierabend.[1]

Kirkham and his co-workers construct an index of the level of development to examine the hypothesis that violence and terrorism are causally linked to national economic development. Eight indicators of development were used: GNP per capita, literacy level, radios and newspapers per 1000 population, rate of urbanization, caloric intake per person per day, number of persons per physician, and the percentage of the population with telephones. Three sets of nations were discerned from the index: traditional, transitional, and modern. It was found that roughly half the traditional societies were unstable (much violence), two-thirds of the transitional societies were unstable, and one-third of the modern societies were unstable (Argentina, Belgium, East Germany, France, United States, and USSR). In reference to political assassinations particularly, only five of twenty-four modern nations had a high frequency of assassinations (more than two in 20 years). These nations were Argentina (nine), Czechoslovakia (five), France (fourteen), Israel (three), and the United States (sixteen). Sixteen of twenty-three traditional nations had high levels of assassinations and twenty-three of thirty-seven transitional societies had a high frequency of assassinations.

Kirkham and his co-workers conclude that "there is a definite relationship between level of development and incidence of political violence, including assassination. Developed countries tend to experience lower levels of political unrest and assassination than do less developed countries" (Kirkham, Levy, and Crotty, 1969, pp. 137-139). The United States and France are seen as "notable exceptions."

The authors further examine assassination data based on a five-nation typology found in the *World Handbook of Political and Social Indicators.* "Traditional primitive" societies have a low assassination rate, "traditional" societies a high rate, "transitional" societies have a lower rate than the traditional but nations with a high assassination rate in this category dwarf those with a lower assassination rate by two to one. Half of the "industrial revolutionary" societies have high numbers of assassinations. Finally, "high mass consumption" societies have a low frequency of assassinations. Of the fourteen nations in this category only two, the United States and France, had more than two assassinations during a 20-year period.

Findings such as these and theoretical discussions of levels of political sta-

bility across regimes point to an inverse relationship between economic development and domestic violence *or* a curvilinear relationship (as the five-nation typology suggests), with modernizing societies going through a period of adjustment
to modernization engendering instability and violence temporarily, then declining. Hibbs aptly summarizes the latter view:

> Many observers have commented on the stabilizing impact of "post-indus-
> trial" affluence. The most common argument is that the high level of eco-
> nomic development achieved by some nations, largely in Western Europe
> and North America, has produced societies without the severe conflicts and
> instabilities generated by the initial process of modernization and indus-
> trialization. Typical of such conventional sociological thinking are the ob-
> servations of Lipset, Dahrendorf, and others about the "new" Europe,
> where the growth of affluence is seen to produce social systems in which
> class conflict is minimized as all classes are integrated into society and
> polity. So large a proportion of the population is now feeling the advan-
> tageous effects of economic development that the age-old obsession with
> the distribution of profits is weakened and the "modern" concern with de-
> velopment is reinforced. The former alienated working class, in the view of
> these theorists, is now at peace with the industrial system, and ideology has
> lost its former relevance as the absence of a suppressed class leaves little hope
> for radicalism. Rational calculation has come to replace ideology and dog-
> ma, permanent negotiation and occasional conciliation have supplanted
> active confrontation and class warfare, and compulsory arbitration rather
> than the general strike becomes the norm. [1973, pp. 21-22]

Theoretical issues are raised by this kind of perspective and the interpretation of the assassination data by Kirkham and his co-workers. For example, of
eighty-four nations' assassination events for a 20-year period, the United States
ranked fifth in assassinations and France eighth. Of the other nations with the
most assassinations (the top ten), five were "transitional" societies—Cuba (twenty-
eight), Korea (twenty), Tunisia (sixteen), Egypt (fourteen), Venezuela (twelve)—
and three were "traditional" societies—Iran (nineteen), Morocco (seventeen), and
Philippines (fifteen).

   In reference to the general hypothesis of this chapter, the propensity to
view the United States and France as aberrations in terms of amount of violence,
terrorism, and/or political assassinations may be ill-conceived. If the propensity
for working-class organization for political change is impaired (whether that organization takes the form of electorally based parties or revolutionary movements to achieve societal transformation) by what theorists like Bell and Lasch
call postindustrialism, then one would explain the high incidences of political
assassination either as a manifestation of aberrational and individualized action
to stimulate the creation of revolutionary consciousness *or* anomic reactions in

the face of the lack of an industrially based movement for social change. Similarly high assassination rates in "transitional" and "traditional" societies may result not from the birth pangs of modernization but from the lack of a revolutionary class in these countries capable of creating and/or carrying out revolution. In other words, a better interpretation of the data above might suggest that political assassinations are aberrant acts more likely to occur in societies where the means of production have not been or are no longer socialized. This condition exists in "traditional," "transitional," and "postindustrial" societies.

Further, Kirkham and his co-workers do not utilize sociostructural or occupational indicators as part of the index of development. Because one of the critical indicators of preindustrial or postindustrial societies is the prevalent occupational structure, assassination data below are examined in terms of percentages of the work force in agriculture, mining and manufacturing, and professional and technical labor.[2] Given the themes summarized earlier it is hypothesized that instances of revolutionary terrorism, in this case assassinations, are more likely to occur in societies that have a plurality of their work force in agriculture as opposed to those societies that have a plurality of their work force in industrial production. Secondly, it is hypothesized that those societies that have a plurality of workers in service occupations are more likely to have instances of revolutionary terrorism than those predominantly characterized by industrial production. (According to Bell, only the United States has a majority of its work force in service occupations.) By examining available data on the percentage of a society's work force in professional and technical labor, elements of the service criteria, we can see whether the magnitudes of workers in these categories affect terrorist activity. The occupational data (see Table 3) among nations experiencing assassination events from January 1965 to October 1968 indicate the following:

1. Of twenty-eight nations (with available data on occupation) experiencing assassination events, seventeen have more than 50 percent of the work force in agriculture.

2. Of the twenty-eight nations, twenty-one have a plurality of the work force in agriculture.

3. Of the twenty-eight nations only six have a plurality of the work force in mining and manufacturing.

4. Of the six nations with a plurality of workers in mining and manufacturing only two, the United States and France, experienced more than one assassination in the 3-year period.

5. Only the United States, of twenty nations (with available data), has as much as 20 percent of its work force in professional and technical occupations.

Table 3 Assassination Attempts, Labor Force in Agriculture, Mining and Manufacturing, Technical and Professional by Nation (January 1965 to October 1968)[a]

Nation	Assassination attempts	Percent of work force in:		
		Agriculture	Mining and manufacturing	Technical and professional occupations
1. Aden	12	—	—	—
2. United States	10	8	29.7	23.1
3. Yemen	6	—	—	—
4. Guatemala	5	73	10.1	3.2
5. Nigeria	5	59	—	—
6. France	4	25	30.4	11.5
7. Congo	3	72	8.7	—
8. Senegal	3	—	—	—
9. South Vietnam	3	—	—	—
10. Brazil	2	57	10.9	7.3
11. Cuba	2	47	16.8	7.7
12. Iran	2	58	10.2	1.9
13. Philippines	2	67	8.4	4.9
14. Spain	2	36	25.9	4.1
15. Algeria	1	68	6.2	—
16. Australia	1	13	29.7	14.6
17. Burundi	1	—	—	—
18. Bolivia	1	53	19.9	—
19. Egypt	1	58	9.8	3.6
20. England	1	5	39.8	11.5
21. Gaza	1	—	—	—
22. Greece	1	48	14.5	4.4
23. Haiti	1	87	4	—
24. Honduras	1	76	6.7	1.8
25. Hong Kong	1	5	32.6	10.9
26. India	1	68	10.7	3.5
27. Israel	1	13	27.4	9.4
28. Lebanon	1	50	—	—
29. Niger	1	97	—	—
30. Panama	1	57	7.4	4.9
31. USSR	1	34	—	—
32. South Africa	1	35	26.9	4.0
33. Thailand	1	78	4.4	1.9
34. Togo	1	—	—	—
35. Venezuela	1	38	13.4	4.9

[a]Taylor and Hudson (1975) present data on percentages of the labor force in agriculture, mining and manufacturing, and technical and professional work roles per nation. Data on some nations is from an earlier year. Because this examination is preliminary the author simply tabulated assassination events from 1965 until October 1968, utilizing the data from the Leiden group. Future work could fruitfully draw upon measures of occupational structure and assassination events over a larger time span.

6. According to Bell, only the United States has more than 50 percent of
    its work force in service occupations.

The assassination data from 1965 to 1968 therefore support the hypothesis
mentioned earlier. The preponderance of assassination events occurred in nations
that are primarily agricultural. The United States and France stand out among the
six nations with more mining and manufacturing workers as to frequency of assassination events. Citing Bell again, the majority of workers in the United States are
in service occupations (61.1 percent) and 42.8 percent of French workers are in
service occupations. As Table 3 indicates, the United States has the highest percentage of technical and professional workers among the thirty-five nations listed
and France is ranked third in percentage of such workers.

A recent Facts on File publication entitled *Political Terrorism* (1975) provides a chronology of terrorist acts, including kidnappings, bombings, slayings,
assassinations, and other terrorist acts, by nation from 1968 through 1974. Most
of the nations for which there were reportable terrorist events were preindustrial
societies. For example, Guatemala experienced three kidnappings, two bombings,
and twenty-six assassinations in a period from early 1968 to mid-1973. Uruguay
had eleven kidnappings, one bombing, and ten assassinations between 1969 and
1972. All of these terrorist events had a political focus.

In reference to the United States and France as "aberrations," the former
experienced at least twenty-five bombings and twelve politically motivated slayings between 1968 and 1974, whereas the latter had thirteen bombings and two
slayings (Sobel, 1975). Great Britain, Canada, and the Soviet Union experienced
some bombings but less than did the United States and France. Italy had approximately 22 bombings and political killings during the late 1960s and early 1970s.
(It should be noted that Bell lists Great Britain as having 49.7 percent of its work
force in service occupations and Italy 45.1 percent.)

In sum, cross-cultural studies of political violence find greater incidence of
political instability in preindustrial societies than in industrial societies. The
United States and France are seen as exceptions to the rule. Given the theoretical
discussion throughout this chapter, there seems to be good reason for reinterpret-
ing the findings of such studies. Such a reinterpretation would suggest that level
of modernity alone is not the contextual factor that conditions the propensity for
political violence and terrorism. Rather, as has been argued here, sociostructural
features of societies called preindustrial, industrial, and postindustrial condition
certain kinds of political responses. Traditional and transitional societies have
violence and terrorism, not because of a lack of modernity, but because the social
setting does not afford political actors the opportunity to organize mass-based
political movements for social change. Similarly, the United States and France
should not be seen as unusual in terms of the frequency of political violence. The
sociostructural setting of postindustrialism also inhibits the building of mass-
based movements for social change.

This interpretation of findings on political violence is tentatively confirmed by an examination of selected data on political assassinations and other terrorist acts. Both the assassination data sets of Leiden and Feierabend and chronologies of terrorist acts seem to fit the interpretation given here.

Conclusion

The thesis of this chapter is that violence, terrorism, and indeed political action are conditioned by societal structures. One motivation for exploring the issue of terrorism is the propensity of analysts to see terrorist acts in psychological terms and to ignore the structural roots of dispositions to engage in terrorism. Another practical motivation for such inquiry revolves around the issues of revolutionary change. For those seeking to bring about radical changes, strategy questions are of vital import. If postindustrial societies are in fact qualitatively different from industrial societies in terms of structural preconditions for viable social movements, then activists must compensate for these differences in building a movement. High incidences of terrorism may reflect the lack of understanding of the structural changes occurring in such societies.

Therefore this chapter raises questions about political terrorism relating to theory, data, and practice. In reference to theory, the argument stated here offers a challenge to research findings on political violence and terrorism. Using several indicators of development, Kirkham and his co-workers find a curvilinear relationship between level of development and incidences of political violence and an inverse relationship between the level of development and incidences of political assassination. Kirkham and his co-workers further utilized a five-nation typology from the *World Handbook of Political and Social Indicators* to analyze assassination data. Again they find a curvilinear relationship, with "transitional" and "industrial revolutionary" societies experiencing the greatest number of assassination events. Figure 1 illustrates these relationships.

The indicators used by Kirkham and others to delineate types of societies do not utilize occupational and other sociostructural indicators of development elaborated on in this chapter. Consequently, nations with similar occupational structures are separated on the basis of nonstructural indicators. The literature examined here argues that the most fundamental forces affecting the nature of movements for social change are structural and include occupational, ruling-class, exploitative, and ideological variables. With these variables in mind, distinctions were made between preindustrial, industrial, and postindustrial societies. Given the thesis developed in this chapter, high incidence rates of political terrorism were predicted to occur in preindustrial and postindustrial societies and low incidence rates in industrial societies, as illustrated in Figure 2. Consequently, the thesis elaborated here contradicts prior work on violence and terrorism.

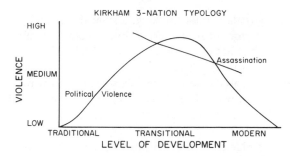

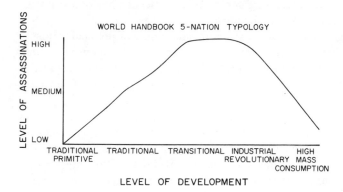

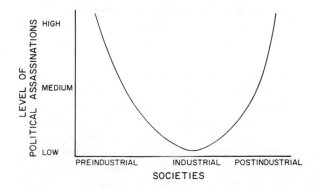

Figure 1 Level of development, political violence, and assassination.

Figure 2 Political terrorism in preindustrial, industrial, and postindustrial societies.

Because the analysis here contradicts prior thinking, further theoretical work is in order. This work should proceed at two levels. First, analysts should examine in greater depth the basic distinctions between preindustrial, industrial, and postindustrial societies. Particularly, the distinction between industrial and postindustrial societies should be explored. Much debate exists in the literature already as to the real meaning of work patterns in developed states. Scholars and activists have taken varying positions on the existence of a new service force as opposed to a factory work force. Conflicts abound over interpretations of available evidence and whether demographic changes constitute qualitative changes in occupational structure. Similarly, there are debates on the assumptions of postindustrialists as to changes in the nature of ruling classes, patterns of exploitation, and ideology. These issues are central to an understanding of social structure in developed states and should be pursued.

Second, linkages between social structure and modes of political action should be pursued. After further clarification of central sociostructural variables, theorists must develop clear positions and gather data on linkages between these variables, political organizations, individual action choices, and acts of violence and terrorism.

As to data and method, further work is in order as well. First, researchers should develop complete data sets on terrorist acts cross-culturally and longitudinally. These data should be related to a multiplicity of indicators relating to preindustrial, industrial, and postindustrial societies. Also data on the intervening variables, that is, revolutionary organizational, tactical, and psychological variables, should be gathered to develop causal connections between societal structures, intervening forces, and terrorist acts. These data should facilitate an analysis of the frequency of terrorist acts as they may relate to occupational structural transformations over time.

Second, the complexity of historical change requires some in-depth case studies of representative societies to tap the richness of detail implied in the theorists examined earlier. Only through the interconnections of aggregate data analysis and historical research can a thorough test of the structural model of political terrorism be performed.

The theme of this chapter involves critical prescriptive questions. If the occupational structure is being radically transformed in postindustrial societies, for example, then new organizing strategies are in order. Individuation of work processes might suggest that organization for social change may be more likely in the neighborhood or community rather than the work place. The postindustrial view of American society might suggest further problems and possibilities for political organization to channel anomic acts of individuals and small groups into mass-based movements for social change. This chapter can only suggest possible modes of explanation of terrorism versus other forms of action. It is the task of those seeking change to refine or reject this explanation and on that basis to develop systematic notions of organization for change.

Notes

1. For a discussion of the research by Leiden and Feierabend and a presentation of their data see Kirkham et al. (1969).
2. Data reported on labor force participation is taken from Taylor and Hudson (1975).

References

Bell, Daniel. 1973. *The Coming of Post-Industrial Society.* New York: Basic Books.

Gross, Feliks. 1969. "Political Violence and Terror in Nineteenth and Twentieth Century Russia and Eastern Europe." In *Assassination and Political Violence,* ed. James F. Kirkham, Sheldon G. Levy, and William J. Crotty, pp. 421–476. Washington, D.C.: Government Printing Office.

Hibbs, Douglas A. Jr. 1973. *Mass Political Violence, A Cross-National Causal Analysis.* New York: John Wiley.

Hutchinson, Martha Crenshaw. 1972. "The Concept of Revolutionary Terrorism," *The Journal of Conflict Resolution,* pp. 383–396.

Kahler, Erich. 1957. *The Tower and the Abyss.* New York: Viking.

Kirkham, James F., Levy, Sheldon G., and Crotty, William J., eds. 1969. *Assassination and Political Violence.* Washington, D.C.: Government Printing Office.

Lasch, Christopher. 1972. "Toward a Theory of Post-Industrial Society." In *Politics in the Post-Welfare State,* ed. M. D. Hancock and G. Sjoberg, pp. 36–51. New York: Columbia University Press.

Lenin, V. I. 1975. *The Lenin Anthology,* ed. Robert C. Tucker. New York: W. W. Norton.

Marx, Karl. 1972. *The Marx-Engels Reader,* ed. Robert C. Tucker, New York: W. W. Norton.

Roszak, Theodore. 1969. *The Making of a Counter Culture.* Garden City, New York: Anchor.

Sobel, Lester S., ed. 1975. *Political Terrorism.* New York: Facts on File.

Taylor, Charles Lewis, and Hudson, Michael C. 1975. *World Handbook of Political and Social Indicators.* New Haven, Conn.: Yale University Press.

part **II**

The Practice of Political Terrorism

5

Transnational Terrorism

Edward Mickolus*

Department of Political Science
Yale University
New Haven, Connecticut

In the last decade the world has seen the rise of a new type of actor on the global stage: the transnational terrorist group. These bands have engaged in numerous types of acts to gain headlines and increase public awareness of their causes, being willing to engage in the assassination of government leaders, sabotage of critical facilities, bombing of embassies and foreign corporations, assaults on military installations, skyjackings, kidnappings of diplomats and business executives, and the takeover of embassies and holding of their staffs for ransoms. How great a problem are we faced with? Are there any trends we can discover? Is the problem worsening? Can any nation consider itself safe from such attacks? Are certain nations being singled out for this type of attack? What groups are engaged in such activity? What is it they want? Why do they resort to these methods? And, finally, what does the future hold in store for the world?

*Present Affiliation: International Issues Division, Office of Regional and Political Analysis, Central Intelligence Agency, Washington, D.C.

Defining Terrorism

Definitions of terrorism vary tremendously, both among governments and among individual researchers. Incidents considered terrorist by South Africa are merely the legitimate acts of freedom strugglers in the eyes of many Third World nations. Indeed, it has become so hard to satisfy all the governments of the world that in the United Nations one does not officially discuss "International Terrorism" but rather Item 92: Measures to Prevent International Terrorism Which Endangers or Takes Innocent Human Lives or Jeopardizes Fundamental Freedoms, and Study of the Underlying Causes of Those Forms of Terrorism and Acts of Violence Which Lie in Misery, Frustration, Grievance and Despair, and Which Cause Some People to Sacrifice Human Lives, Including Their Own, in an Attempt to Effect Radical Changes. Such a view borders on accepting the motivations of the terrorists and is also difficult to operationalize. For purposes of the present discussion, we can consider our research to be concerned with the use, or threat of use, of anxiety-inducing extranormal violence for political purposes by any individual or group, whether acting for, or in opposition to, established governmental authority, when such action is intended to influence the attitudes and behavior of a target group wider than the immediate victims and when, through the nationality or foreign ties of its perpetrators, its location, the nature of its institutional or human victims, or the mechanics of its resolution its ramifications transcend national boundaries. We can further isolate transnational terrorism from other forms of violence by making the following distinctions: International terrorism is such action (as described above) when carried out by individuals or groups controlled by a sovereign state. Examples would include attacks in Europe against Palestinian liberation groups by Israeli intelligence agents, the anti-Basque campaign recently launched in the south of France by the Spanish police, and so on. Transnational terrorism is such action when carried out by basically autonomous nonstate actors, whether or not they enjoy some degree of support from sympathetic states. Examples include the kidnappings of U.S. business executives overseas, the hijacking of international flights, and the machine-gun attacks on international airports by members of the Popular Front for the Liberation of Palestine (PFLP). Domestic terrorism is behavior that has the aforementioned characteristics of extranormal violence but does not involve nationals of more than one state. It is the domestic parallel to transnational terrorism in that it is carried on by basically autonomous nonstate actors but only affects citizens of one state. The bombings in New York City by the Weather Underground, attacks by the Irish Republican Army and Ulster Defense Association upon the civilian population in Northern Ireland, and attempted assassinations of governmental leaders by nationals of that state are examples. State terrorism includes terrorist actions conducted by a national government within the borders of that state and is the domestic parallel

Table 1 Types of Political Terrorism

		Direct involvement of nationals of more than one state?	
		Yes	No
Government controlled or directed?	Yes	International	State
	No	Transnational	Domestic

of international terrorism. Examples include genocide in Nazi Germany, the po-groms in the Ukraine, and incidents of torture in police states. Schematically, we can locate transnational terrorism as being one cell of political terrorism, as shown in Table 1. Other types of nonpolitical terrorism, such as criminal terrorism in which the sole object is personal gain, are beyond the scope of the present inquiry.

Transnational terrorism has often been described as violence for effect. It differs from military concepts of war as a strategy in that it does not attempt to hold a specific piece of territory by dint of military engagement. Rather, it at-tempts to give the impression that the terrorist group is able to strike with im-punity; that the small, numerically weak band of terrorists should be considered a credible threat, and that governmental authorities cannot guarantee security to members of the society under its protection. Hence, although wars, be they civil wars, colonial wars, international wars, irredentist battles for a territory, and so on, may lead to great fear in noncombatant populations, their primary objective is the securing of populations and territory tactically as well as strategically.

Annual Trends

Not all activities of groups that have engaged in acts of terrorism can be classed as terrorist. Although the Montoneros in Argentina may kidnap business execu-tives and conduct armed attacks upon military and police facilities, they also en-gage in more widely accepted political pursuits, such as funding political parties, conducting meetings to discuss politics, and so on. Although such activities are the work of the same organization, we somehow do not normally consider the latter actions to be terrorist in nature when engaged in by others. It is the use or threat of use of extranormal violence that disturbs us. There are basically two general types of such violence: (1) incidents in which the terrorists attempt to injure or kill individuals and/or damage or destroy property, and (2) incidents in which individuals are taken hostage, and destruction of property and injury to the hostages are conditional upon the response of a target group to the demands of the perpetrators. In Table 2, we note seven kinds of destructive incidents and four types of hostage situations.[1] *Kidnapping* is an incident in which a diplomat

Table 2 Transnational Terrorist Incidents, 1968–1975

Incident type	1968	1969	1970	1971	1972	1973	1974	1975	Total
Kidnapping	1	4	28	15	11	30	21	32	142
Barricade and hostage	0	0	2	1	4	8	11	17	43
Skyjacking	33	79	70	37	38	19	7	6	289
Takeover of nonair transportation	0	0	3	0	1	0	1	1	6
Bombing	29	55	42	45	61	90	33	78	433
Letter bomb	2	1	1	1	147	49	1	3	205
Armed attack	2	6	6	9	4	10	7	10	54
Murder or assassination	6	4	10	6	5	11	3	18	63
Arson or Molotov cocktail	0	1	10	8	1	15	1	6	42
Theft or break-in	0	4	6	0	0	1	2	3	16
Sabotage	0	0	0	1	3	0	1	0	5
	73	154	178	123	275	233	88	174	1298

or business executive is taken to an underground hideout and held until a monetary ransom is paid, prisoners are released, the group's manifesto is published, or some other demanded action is carried out. *Barricade and hostage* situations include incidents in which the terrorists seize one or more hostages but make no attempt to leave the original scene of the crime. Negotiations are carried on with the perpetrators themselves effectively being held hostage, unable to leave the scene at their choosing. Such scenarios frequently occur at the end of an incident in which the seizure of hostages was not the terrorists' primary aim, for example, a bank holdup in which the robbers were discovered by the authorities before they were able to escape, with the group seizing any hostages who happened to be handy; an attack on an airport lounge or residence, in which hostages are seized as pawns to be used to secure free passage away from the site of the murders.

Skyjackings* involve the alteration of the direction of an airline flight due to actions by the terrorist. We can distinguish between those situations in which the hijacker is merely seeking a means of transportation to a nation giving him asylum (the old "Take this plane to Cuba" skyjacking), situations in which the hijackers force the pilot to land the plane, release the crew and passengers, and blow up the plane without making any ransom demands (engaged in for the shock value of the action), and incidents in which the skyjackers make specific demands upon governments or corporations, threatening the safety of the passengers and crew.[2] *Takeovers of nonair means of transportation* involve hijackings of transport media including trains, ships, and automotive vehicles.[3]

Bombing* involves the attempt, whether successful or unsuccessful, to explode a device that will cause some amount of damage. Timing mechanisms are usually employed, and the incident is not considered part of a general armed assault. *Letter bombs* are devices that are sent through the mails and are intended to explode when attempts are made to open the envelope. They range in size from a large parcel to a first-class letter. *Armed attacks* involve assaults upon facilities using missiles, hand-held weapons, grenades, thrown bombs, and/or incendiary devices. They range from machine-gun and grenade assaults upon airport lounges to rifle shots taken at an embassy from a fast-moving car.

Murder and assassination* involve the attempt to kill a specific individual for political purposes.[4] *Arson and the use of the Molotov cocktail* involve the attempt to set afire a selected installation. Bombs that are of an incendiary nature are included in this category rather than in the explosive bombing classification. *Theft or break-in* involves the forcible entry of facilities and an illegal attempt to acquire money or documents from the installation. The robbery of individuals by political terrorists is also included here. *Sabotage* entails the attempted damage of facilities by means other than explosives or incendiary devices.

We can see trends in such incidents over the past 8 years. Kidnappings are by far the most popular hostage incident, showing a wavering but rising trend line over time. In 1975 there were more kidnappings than in any other year in recent memory. Moreover, the probability that the kidnappers will successfully seize a hostage in the attempt has grown dramatically since the early 1970s. We have also seen a steady rise in barricade and hostage incidents, with no known failures to take hostages in the 8 years studied. Again, 1975 saw the establishment of an annual record in this category, as well. The situation changes with respect to air hijackings. Improvements in security procedures made in 1973, as well as the unwillingness of countries to grant asylum to hijackers, have made this type of incident a comparative rarity. Nonair transportation takeovers are infrequent annoyances rather than common threats. Overall, if we consider kidnappings, barricade situations, nonair takeovers, and only those skyjackings that involve hostage negotiations, we find an erratic rise in the total number of incidents, with a rise in the probability of successfully seizing hostages.

In the category of destructive acts, bombings have become the most popular type of activity and are a continuing threat to embassies, consulates, and corporation facilities. The IRA and PFLP have also been targeting bombs against more generalized civilian populations. Letter bombs appear to follow no pattern, with the 1972 and 1973 peak years showing a wave of bombings by these two groups, rather than a worldwide phenomenon being conducted by many organizations. It appears that most bombs are sent from the same post office on the same day, but that the targets are worldwide. Because of their general unreliability in successfully harming the chosen target (many letter bombs are intercepted by police or explode in post offices, injuring innocent workers and leading to negative publicity for the terrorists) as well as the technical sophistication required to make them, other terrorist groups do not seem to have picked up the practice of using letter bombs.

Armed attacks and murders appear to be following a cyclical trend, which may be slowly rising, with 1975 setting annual records in both categories. Arson peaked in 1973, a year in which, subtracting intercepted letter bombs, the greatest number of incidents occurred. Thefts and sabotage are comparatively rare. Although the total number of incidents appears to have peaked in 1972 and 1973, we can by no means say that terrorism no longer presents a threat. Methods that have proved too difficult to engage in or relatively ineffective, such as skyjackings and letter bombs, have been replaced by other methods that appear to the terrorists to satisfy their goals. This gloomy conclusion is further supported by Table 3 and Figure 1, which present statistics on all casualties from transnational terrorist operations. Here we find a very disturbing rise in deaths, injuries, and total casualties.[5]

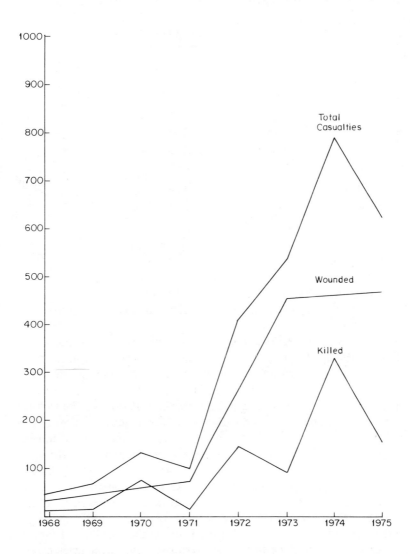

Figure 1 Casualties from transnational terrorist incidents.

Table 3 Annual Casualties from Terrorist Actions
(Includes Terrorists, Police, and Foreign and Domestic
Noncombatants)

Year	Killed	Wounded	Total
1968	11	31	42
1969	12	46	58
1970	73	60	133
1971	18	73	91
1972	142	273	415
1973	90+	455	545+
1974	330	461	791
1975	155	468	623
Total	831	1967	2798

Geographic Trends

What sites have transnational terrorists chosen as the targets of their operations? Tables 4 and 5 give us some idea of the location of the more frequent types of attacks.[6]

Conventional wisdom argues that most terrorism occurs in emerging Third World nations. Although this may be true for cases of domestic terrorism, this does not seem to be correct when analyzing transnational forms of political terrorism. Nearly half of the incidents reported in the past 8 years have occurred in what are considered to be Westernized, highly affluent nations.[7] The United States reports more bombings and skyjackings with international implications than all of Latin America combined. Again discounting the inflationary impact of the letter-bomb figures, transnational terrorism is very infrequent in the developing countries of Asia and Africa. Eastern European nations have been virtually immune to attacks, suffering only sporadic skyjackings by people seeking political asylum in Western nations. Latin America outdistances the Middle East for second place in total number of incidents. Argentina leads the world in kidnappings of foreigners and is second to the United States in the bombings of foreign facilities. Middle Eastern nations do not have terrorist groups with developed undergrounds that would be useful in attacking the types of targets they seek (for example, there are few Israeli diplomatic or military installations available) and so do not engage in certain types of incidents on Middle Eastern soil to the extent that one would otherwise expect. Rather, they have resorted to the barricade-and-hostage scenario. Latin groups, on the other hand, do have the de-

Table 4 Location of Incident, by Region and Incident Type

Location	Barricade and hostage	Skyjacking	Kidnapping	Murder	Armed attack	Bomb	Letter bomb	Arson	Total
Atlantic community	19	131	15	35	23	272	50	27	572
Middle East	12	30	18	13	17	56	6	7	159
Asia	5	18	4	6	2	11	54	2	102
Eastern Europe	–	18	–	–	–	–	–	–	18
Latin America	4	82	77	9	8	92	3	7	282
Africa	1	8	20	3	1	1	3	–	37
Total	41	287	134	66	51	432	116	43	1170

Table 5 Location of Incident, by Country, Region, and Type

Location	Barricade and hostage	Skyjacking	Kidnapping	Murder	Armed attack	Bomb	Letter bomb	Arson	Total
Atlantic community									
Austria	2	1	—	1	—	1	—	1	6
Belgium	—	—	—	1	—	1	1	2	5
Canada	—	2	2	1	—	2	—	—	7
Cyprus	—	—	—	2	2	1	—	—	5
Denmark	—	—	1	1	—	2	—	—	4
France	4	5	3	6	4	18	1	1	42
Gibraltar	—	—	—	—	—	—	1	—	1
Greece	2	4	—	1	2	25	—	—	34
Ireland	—	—	2	—	—	3	1	1	7
Italy	—	5	1	3	—	16	—	6	31
Netherlands	4	1	—	—	—	5	—	1	11
Northern Ireland	—	—	2	1	5	8	—	—	16
Norway	—	—	—	1	—	—	—	—	1
Portugal	—	1	—	—	—	1	1	—	3
Spain	1	2	2	4	—	3	—	2	14
Sweden	2	1	—	1	—	4	—	—	8
Switzerland	—	3	—	—	1	3	6	—	13
West Germany	1	6	1	3	3	16	1	3	34
United Kingdom	3	2	1	3	1	57	31+	—	98
United States	—	98	—	6	5	106	7	10	232

Middle East								
Algeria	1	1	—	—	—	—	—	22
Bahrain	—	1	—	—	—	—	—	11
Dubai	—	2	—	—	—	—	—	12
Egypt	—	5	—	1	1	—	—	17
Iran	—	2	1	3	—	3	—	9
Iraq	—	1	—	—	—	—	—	1
Israel	6	1	1	—	4	8	1	21
Jordan	1	1	3	4	1	6	—	1	17
Kuwait	1	—	—	1	—	—	—	2
Lebanon	1	10	9	3	10	13	4	2	52
Libya	—	1	—	—	—	—	—	11
Morocco	—	—	—	—	—	2	—	2
Saudi Arabia	—	—	—	—	—	1	—	1
Sudan	1	—	—	1	—	—	—	1
Syria	—	1	—	—	—	—	—	1
Tunisia	1	1	—	—	—	—	—	1
Turkey	—	3	4	4	1	23	1	4	36
Yemen	—	2	—	—	—	—	—	2
Latin America								
Argentina	1	8	39	3	4	59	—	1	115
Bahamas	—	1	—	—	—	—	—	1
Bolivia	—	1	4	—	—	—	—	5

Table 5 (continued)

Location	Barricade and hostage	Skyjacking	Kidnapping	Murder	Armed attack	Bomb	Letter bomb	Arson	Total
Latin America (continued)									
Brazil	—	8	7	2	—	1	1	4	23
British Honduras	—	1	—	—	—	—	—	—	1
Chile	—	2	—	—	—	5	1	—	8
Colombia	—	23	5	1	1	1	—	—	31
Costa Rica	—	2	—	—	—	—	—	—	2
Cuba	—	1	—	—	—	—	1	—	2
Dominican Republic	1	2	2	—	—	—	—	—	5
Ecuador	—	6	—	—	—	1	—	—	7
El Salvador	—	—	—	—	—	3	—	—	3
Guatemala	—	—	4	2	—	—	—	—	6
Haiti	1	—	—	—	—	1	—	—	2
Honduras	—	1	—	—	—	1	—	—	2
Jamaica	—	1	—	—	—	—	—	—	1
Mexico	—	11	4	—	—	12	—	—	27
Netherlands Antilles	—	1	—	—	—	—	—	—	1
Nicaragua	1	1	—	—	—	—	—	—	2
Panama	—	1	—	—	—	—	—	1	2
Paraguay	—	—	1	1	—	—	—	—	2
Peru	—	1	—	—	—	3	—	—	4

Puerto Rico	—	3	—	—	—	3	—	—	6
Uruguay	—	1	9	—	2	1	—	—	13
Venezuela	—	6	2	—	1	1	—	1	11
Africa									
Angola	—	2	3	—	—	—	—	—	5
Chad	—	—	1	—	—	—	—	—	1
Ethiopia	—	4	11	2	1	1	—	—	19
Kenya	—	1	—	—	—	—	—	—	1
Somalia	—	—	1	—	—	—	—	—	1
South Africa	1	1	1	—	—	—	—	—	3
Spanish Sahara	—	—	1	—	—	—	—	—	1
Tanzania	—	—	1	1	—	—	1	—	3
Uganda	—	—	1	—	—	—	—	—	1
Zaire	—	—	—	—	—	—	1	—	1
Zambia	—	—	—	—	—	—	1	—	1
Asia									
Afghanistan	—	—	—	1	—	—	—	—	1
Australia	—	2	—	—	—	5	—	—	7
Bangladesh	1	—	—	1	—	1	—	—	3
Burma	—	—	1	—	—	—	—	—	1
Cambodia	—	—	—	—	—	3	—	—	3
India	—	3	—	—	—	—	54	—	57
Japan	—	2	—	1	1	1	—	2	7

Table 5 (continued)

Location	Barricade and hostage	Skyjacking	Kidnapping	Murder	Armed attack	Bomb	Letter bomb	Arson	Total
Asia (continued)									
Malaysia	1	–	–	–	–	–	–	–	1
Nepal	–	1	–	–	–	–	–	–	1
New Zealand	–	–	–	–	–	1	–	–	1
Pakistan	1	–	–	1	1	–	–	–	3
Philippines	1	4	2	2	–	–	–	–	9
South Korea	–	2	–	–	–	–	–	–	2
South Vietnam	–	3	–	–	–	–	–	–	3
Thailand	1	1	1	–	–	–	–	–	3
Eastern Europe									
Czechoslovakia	–	6	–	–	–	–	–	–	6
Finland	–	1	–	–	–	–	–	–	1
Poland	–	4	–	–	–	–	–	–	4
Romania	–	2	–	–	–	–	–	–	2
USSR	–	5	–	–	–	–	–	–	5

Other Actions:

Takeover of nonair means of transportation: Poland, 2; Cuba, Lebanon, Thailand, and the United States, 1.

Theft or break-in of facilities: United States and Uruguay, 3; Lebanon, 2; Argentina, Ireland, Japan, Jordan, Portugal, Sweden, and the United Kingdom, 1.

Sabotage not involving bombs: Jordan, Kuwait, Netherlands, the United Kingdom, and West Germany, 1.

Table 6   Victims of Terrorist Actions, by Region

Region	Total number of incidents	Regional victimization index
North Atlantic	769	42.7
Middle East	197	10.4
Latin America	176	7.3
Eastern Europe	63	9.0
Asia	55	3.1
Africa	31	2.2
Other	31	n.a.

veloped undergrounds and have not needed to resort to the barricade approach. Hence, we see that logistic constraints at times may rule out the imitation of tactics of other groups.

Are certain nations being singled out as victims of attacks? In Tables 6 and 7 we find that although many nations' citizens suffered in one or two incidents, Westernized, industrialized nations are the most popular targets of attacks. Citizens of the United States have been the victim in over 30 percent of all events,[8] with the British also facing a serious security problem. The Regional Victimization Index[9] illustrates the preference of terrorists for North Atlantic targets.

Again we find that transnational terrorism has not yet affected Asia and Africa to the extent that it has other regions. Eastern European Communist nations have been relatively safe when one discounts skyjackings by domestic dissidents. Only the USSR and Yugoslavia have been subjected to other attacks, by the Jewish Defense League and Croatians, respectively. The immunity of these nations may be due to their verbal and material support of many of the contemporary terrorist groups. In the Middle East, it is not surprising to find Israeli citizens most harassed. The more moderate nations in the Arab-Israeli conflict also find themselves singled out for attack, with Palestinian terrorists frequently being ambushed by unknown attackers.[10] Latin Americans frequently attack non-Latins as victims, with those perceived to be rich capitalists being singled out. Overall, nationals of the poorer nations who are victimized are most often their nation's ambassador to another country or a manager or president of a multinational corporation's local subsidiary. Hence, although no one country can feel perfectly safe from terrorist attack, the problem appears to be primarily one for Westernized, capitalist nations.

Table 7 Victims of Terrorist Actions, by Nationality and Region

Nation	Number of incidents	Nation	Number of incidents
North Atlantic		North Korea	1
Austria	7	Pakistan	1
Belgium	2	People's Republic of	
Canada	11	China	1
Cyprus	1	Philippines	6
Denmark	3	Singapore	2
France	24	South Korea	3
Greece	18	South Vietnam	4
Ireland	6	Taiwan	1
Italy	29	Thailand	1
Netherlands	15	Africa	
Portugal	7	Angola	1
Spain	34	Ethiopia	14
Sweden	4	Gabon	1
Switzerland	14	Ivory Coast	1
West Germany	36	Kenya	1
United Kingdom	121	Liberia	1
United States	435	Malawi	1
Vatican	2	Mozambique	1
Asia		Nigeria	1
Australia	5	Rhodesia	1
Bangladesh	1	Senegal	1
Hong Kong	1	South Africa	5
India	9	Tanzania	1
Indonesia	4	Zaire	1
Japan	12	Latin America	
Malaysia	1	Argentina	18
Nepal	1	Bahamas	3
New Zealand	1	Bolivia	2

Table 7 (continued)

Nation	Number of incidents	Nation	Number of incidents
Brazil	14	Jordan	19
British Honduras	1	Kuwait	3
British West Indies	1	Lebanon	22
Chile	11	Libya	2
Colombia	27	Morocco	1
Costa Rica	3	Palestinians	20
Cuba	14	Qatar	1
Dominican Republic	7	Saudi Arabia	10
Ecuador	8	South Yemen	1
Haiti	2	Syria	1
Honduras	2	Turkey	11
Jamaica	1	United Arab Emirates	1
Mexico	22	Yemen	2
Netherlands Antilles	2	Eastern Europe	
Nicaragua	3	Czechoslovakia	8
Panama	4	East Germany	1
Paraguay	3	Finland	1
Peru	3	Poland	9
Puerto Rico	7	Romania	2
Uruguay	5	USSR	30
Venezuela	13	Yugoslavia	12
Middle East		Other	
Algeria	7	CENTO	3
Dubai	1	OAS	2
Egypt	12	Foreigners	26
Iran	7	(that is, source unspecific	
Iraq	5	about nationality of victim)	
Israel	71		

Links of Terrorist Groups

Contacts between terrorist groups and with sympathetic governments appear to be growing. Various groups have been funded, armed, and trained by nations such as the Soviet Union, the People's Republic of China, Cuba, North Korea, and radical Arab nations. It has been reported that Colonel Qaddafi recently gave Carlos (an infamous transnational terrorist) $2 million for his attack of the OPEC ministers' meeting in December 1975.[11] Soviet-made Kalashnikov machine-guns and SA-7 Strela portable missiles have been discovered in the hands of arrested terrorists. It has been argued that governments have found conventional forms of warfare too expensive and may resort to hiring mercenary terrorist groups to disrupt enemy societies,[12] a tactic that is far cheaper and permits the government to deny involvement in the terrorist action.

But what is far more disturbing to many are the growing contacts between terrorist groups. Palestinians have apparently trained Latin Americans, members of the Baader-Meinhof Group of West Germany, members of the Irish Republican Army, and Japanese anarchists. Latin groups that have acquired fantastic ransoms[13] reportedly have been funding less affluent, but possibly more violent, smaller groups. Such groups have held many worldwide meetings, including the recent meeting in Trieste of a score of European separatist groups, the confederation of four major Latin American guerrilla groups, and the frequent meetings of the members of the Palestine Liberation Organization, which at times has served as the forum for ten separate groups that have engaged in terrorist tactics. Such groups have also conducted joint operations, such as the skyjackings and barricade-and-hostage episodes of the Japanese United Red Army and the Popular Front for the Liberation of Palestine, as well as kidnappings engaged in by coalitions of the Revolutionary Movement of the 8th, Action for National Liberation, and Popular Revolutionary Vanguard in Brazil. Terrorist groups have also engaged in operations designed to secure the release from prison of members of their own and other organizations. If such trends continue, and terrorists are able to rely upon each other for funding, training, arms, and technical skills, they may develop a greater autonomy from their current nation-state mentors and not be subject to whatever restraints are now placed upon their activities by these nations. More spectacular, grisly incidents may be the result.

The Economics of Terrorism

In economic terms, how great a problem has transnational terrorism been? In answering this question, we could simply tally the number of individuals killed and wounded due to terrorist attacks (see Table 3) and add the dollar damage due to bombings, armed assaults, arson and sabotage, the amount of ransom paid in hostage situations, dollar losses due to thefts, and dollar losses due to extortion payments. The casualties total far less than deaths due to automobile accidents in 1 year in the United States.

But this considers only the direct costs of terrorism. We should also note the flight of foreign capital from nations experiencing terrorist campaigns, as well as decisions not to invest in those countries in the first place. Added in should be opportunity costs for hostages, and opportunities lost while a given corporation consolidates its losses after an attack. The costs of security measures taken to prevent attacks is also high, and must include the costs of metal detectors, skymarshals, bodyguards, security training for corporation, airline, and embassy staffs, as well as more intangible costs, such as randomly rerouting airline flights, ships, motorcades, and home-to-office travel to evade attacks. Other intangible costs include the personal anxiety faced by victims and possible victims of attacks, as well as whatever anxieties are faced by the terrorists themselves.[14] Finally, we could include the costs of all academic and governmental research on terrorism, as well as the costs of policy staffs assigned to develop national responses to terrorism, such as the Cabinet Committee to Combat Terrorism. When all of the above factors are considered, transnational terrorism is indeed a costly problem.

But is such activity cost-effective? We need to assess the cost-effectiveness of terrorism for the terrorists themselves. What does it cost to launch a terrorist operation in terms of manpower, arms, time, planning, money, security precautions, and so on, and what types of benefits may the guerrillas expect from such actions?[15] The answer to the first part of the question depends upon the type of operation envisioned—a simple arson requires a glass bottle, gasoline, and a wick, whereas some kidnappings by the Tupamaros in Uruguay involved more than fifty persons.

But what is it that terrorists are seeking? Strategically, some groups aspire to control of the apparatus of the state. As far as can be determined, no campaign of terrorism by itself has ever led to the fall of a government, although the independence of Algeria and Israel can be attributed in part to pressure on colonial authorities by the sustained attacks by the FLN and Irgun, respectively. At a somewhat lower level, many seek policy changes, ranging from greater autonomy for a province of the country to increased wages for union members.

At a tactical level, terrorists have sought changes in sentences, elimination of torture, or the outright release of specified political prisoners, including members of their own groups. Monetary ransoms are also frequently mentioned, along with extortion payments.[16] Terrorists have met with varying degrees of success in such endeavors.

But where terrorism has proved to be overwhelmingly effective is in the securing of publicity for the groups' actions and views. Dramatic actions are able to attract sensation-seeking television and newspaper coverage, which tends to give an impression of strength that the group does not possess. Among other objectives, terrorists are attempting to demonstrate that they can attack at will and that the government is unable to meet its obligation of guaranteeing the security of society. They attempt to embarrass the government and corporations viewed as exploiters by releasing damaging information secured in interrogation of hostages or by theft of documents, as well as by clever maneuvering of hostage negotiation situations. For example, the terrorists may demand that the government donate food to poverty-stricken peasants, casting themselves in the role of Robin Hoods while forcing the government into the position of refusing a charitable demand or giving in to a group of criminals. Corporations refusing monetary ransoms are portrayed as caring more about finance than the lives of the hostages. Terrorists also use such media coverage as a forum for expounding their political views, frequently demanding the publication of the group's manifesto as well as granting interviews to press reporters. In these ways, a small group can acquire the publicity of a major political campaign.

The ability of terrorists successfully to attract publicity appears to differ according to the type of action engaged in, as well as the government's response. Events that once outraged the community, such as the bombing of an embassy, are now quite commonplace, with the perpetrators finding their attempts being used as fillers on the obituary and classified ads pages. In some regions even indiscriminate bombings of civilians have become a tacitly accepted part of the hazards of everyday living. Such atrocities eventually reach the level of diminishing returns, having dulled the public's sensitivities with endless repetition. In order once again to capture the headlines, groups must resort to innovative schemes, such as the current rash of embassy takeovers. The public is presented with a dramatic scenario, with the lives of hostages depending on the bargaining skills of two powerful contestants—the terrorists versus the government. But even the barricade scenario appears to be becoming a passing fad, and terrorists may soon be forced to devise a new incident model to gain attention. In the words of Professor Robert A. Friedlander of Lewis University College of Law, "Without publicity, terrorism is the weapon of the impotent."

Short of doing nothing or raffling off the keys to the presidential mansion, governments have shown a variety of responses to terrorist attacks, with varying degrees of success. It is the government's task to demonstrate that official duties to society can be carried out in the face of the terrorist threat and to decrease whatever amount of influence the terrorists have. Five strategies, some being employed in tandem, are frequently seen:

1. The government can work with the press to alter public perceptions of the might of the terrorists. This can range from a complete ban on the reporting

of terrorist actions (exemplified by Argentina in 1976), to banning the use of the name of the terrorist group (as occurred in Uruguay during the height of the Tupamaros' activities), to more subtle methods. These can include "black propaganda" (placing in the press a story falsely attributed to terrorist authorship, which puts the group in a bad light), falsely reporting terrorist actions to the press, and so on. Such types of responses frequently misfire, at times leading to an increase of clandestine support for the revolutionaries, especially among the skeptical media. Other governments have attempted to work with the press by carefully explaining what is going on during an incident, lessening speculation, which frequently is counterproductive. The government can also caution the press against revealing possible government plans during an event, such as reporting the movement of extra troops to a barricaded area in preparation for a surprise attack. Governments have been more successful in attempting to create legitimate negative publicity for terrorists by using such methods, rather than completely blacking out all information.

2. The government can make the perpetration of a particular type of incident so costly to the terrorist that he or she will be deterred. The elaborate preflight search procedures by Israeli security guards appear to have eliminated skyjacking of El Al flights. Full-scale armed attacks by large groups of terrorists are at times the only way in which a head of state can be assassinated. Such manpower resources are luxuries not available to many violence-prone groups. Those unwilling to lose their own lives for the cause will channel their talents into other types of operations.

3. The government can abide by a publicly stated policy of not granting concessions in the face of terrorist threats. This makes the perpetrators at the scene of the incident appear powerless as time drags on, and one frequently finds the terrorists surrendering without injury to their hostages or others. However, there is some legitimate question as to whether this type of governmental response is also successful in deterring future attacks. The U.S. Department of State points with pride to its record of obtaining the release of over twenty hostages since January 1975, without the U.S. government granting any terrorist demands. (Some reports indicate that concessions were granted by corporations or other private groups.) Although this is a laudable measure of success, can we also label it a successful policy of deterrence? Why were hostages taken in the first place if the terrorists were aware that concessions would not be granted? Many governments have taken the same no-concession position on hostage negotiations but have also been faced with new incidents.

4. The government may engage in a nationwide crackdown on the terrorists by enacting emergency measures that severely limit civil liberties. The Canadian government was successful in eliminating the threat from the Quebec Liberation Front by such a strategy. Of great importance is that Prime Minister Tru-

deau reinstituted civil liberties once the crisis had passed. This has not been the case with all governments. Uruguay was able to wipe out the Tupamaros by similar actions but has not revoked the emergency powers, changing that country from a democracy to a state run by the military. Such indiscriminate, society-wide repression is often precisely what the terrorists seek. The government thus temporarily cures a symptom, while adding to the cause of the infestation of terrorism.

5. "Death Squads," vigilante organizations with or without extraofficial support, frequently arise in the face of terrorist threats to security. Such groups have received mixed reviews. On the one hand, they add to the general feeling of dread in the society brought on by an increasing disregard for normal, nonviolent legal measures for dealing with political demands. However, they are viewed by others as doing the job of the police, in rooting out terrorists who have led the country to this situation. Vigilantes are also sometimes credited for ridding neighborhoods of common criminals. At times a variant of such groups, again with or without the blessing and participation of official intelligence and security organizations, go overseas to attack transnational threats to the public order. This tactic can lead to a temporary increase in security, as terrorists burrow ever deeper underground, but does not treat the fundamental causes of the terrorism. Such tactics may also lead to a worsening of interstate relations, as is evidenced by the Tunisian and Egyptian response to Libyan sorties.

These five strategies are all short-term measures that governments have taken to respond to an immediate terrorist threat. Ultimately, governments need to attack the causes of such types of political violence. Unfortunately, without a theory of terrorism's causes, modern social science can furnish few guides to authorities in ending this scourge. We also may discover that political violence cannot be eliminated completely, and governments are fundamentally forced to resort to the above five stopgap measures.

Identity and Motivation of Transnational Terrorists

Despite common conceptions, terrorists differ as to types of tactics chosen, motivations, and their respect for life. Table 9 identifies the groups who engaged in the more prevalent forms of transnational terrorism,[17] which is summarized regionally in Table 8.

Again we note that Latin American groups, along with the Eritrean Liberation Front (ELF), with their extensive undergrounds, are able to engage in standard kidnap situations that require great resources. Middle Eastern groups, lacking this infrastructure, have resorted to actions that leave them more open to police attack but that also receive greater press coverage and involve a larger num-

Table 8 Region of Nationality of Group Claiming Responsibility for Incident, by Incident Type

Region	Kidnapping	Barricade and hostage	Skyjacking	Bombing	Armed attack	Murder
Africa	18	–	7	1	1	2
Asia	4	10	4	–	1	2
North America	3	–	6	33	2	2
Europe	6	7	3	69	5	5
Middle East	7	19	32	51	23	20
Latin America	44	3	11	82	5	6

Table 9 Group Claiming Responsibility for Incident, by Country of Members' Nationality, Region, and Incident Type

Country	Group	Kidnapping	Barricade and hostage	Skyjacking	Bombing	Armed attack	Murder
Africa							
Angola	Popular Movement for the Liberation of Angola (MPLA)	3	—	—	—	—	—
Chad	Toubou rebels	1	—	—	—	—	—
Ethiopia	Eritrean Liberation Front (ELF)	11	—	7	1	1	2
French Somaliland	Liberation Front for the Somali Coast	1	—	—	—	—	—
Spanish Sahara	Saharan nationalists	1	—	—	—	—	—
Zaire	People's Revolutionary Army	1	—	—	—	—	—
Asia							
Bangladesh	Bengali guerrillas	—	1	—	—	—	—
Burma	Shan insurgents	1	—	—	—	—	—
India	Kashmiri nationalists	—	—	1	—	—	—
Japan	United Red Army	—	4	1	—	1	—
Nepal	Nepalese Communist Party	—	—	1	—	—	—
Pakistan	Black December	—	1	—	—	—	1
Philippines	Kabataang Makabayan	—	—	1	—	—	—
	Moro National Liberation Front	—	1	—	—	—	—
	Philippine nationalists	2	—	—	—	—	—
South Molucca	South Moluccans	—	3	—	—	—	1
Thailand	Pattani Liberation Front	1	—	—	—	—	—

North America						
Canada	Canadian-Hungarian Freedom Fighters Federation	—	—	—	—	—	1
	Quebec Liberation Front	2	—	—	—	—	—
Puerto Rico	Armed Commandos of Liberation	—	—	—	1	—	—
	FALN	—	—	—	17	—	—
	Puerto Rican Resistance Movement	—	—	5	1	—	—
United States	Black Panthers	—	—	5	—	—	—
	Black Revolutionary Assault Team	—	—	—	3	—	—
	Jewish Armed Resistance	—	—	—	1	—	—
	Jewish Defense League	1	—	—	7	2	1
	Republic of New Africa	—	—	1	—	—	—
	Revolutionary Action Party	—	—	—	2	—	—
	Revolutionary Affinity Group 6	—	—	—	1	—	—
Europe						
Indeterminate	National Youth Resistance Org.	—	—	—	2	—	—
Cyprus	EOKA-B	—	—	—	—	—	1
France	Action for the Rebirth of Corsica	—	1	—	—	—	—
	Committee of Coordination	—	—	—	2	—	—
Greece	EAN–Greek Antidictatorial Youth	—	—	—	1	—	—
	Greek Militant Resistance	—	—	—	1	—	—
	Greek People	—	—	—	1	—	—
	Popular Revolutionary Resistance Group	—	—	—	1	—	—

Table 9 (continued)

Country	Group	Kidnapping	Barricade and hostage	Skyjacking	Bombing	Armed attack	Murder
Greece	Resistance, Liberation, Independence (AAA)	—	—	—	4	—	—
Italy	Ordine Nero (Black Order)	—	—	—	1	—	—
Portugal	ARA	—	—	—	1	—	—
Spain	ETA–Basque Nation and Homeland	3	—	—	—	—	1
	GARI	1	—	—	—	—	—
	Hammer and Sickle Cooperative	—	—	—	1	—	—
Switzerland	Les Beliers-Jura	—	1	—	—	—	—
United Kingdom	Black Liberation Front	—	1	—	—	—	—
	IRA–Provisional Wing	1	2	2	45	5	1
West Germany	Baader-Meinhof Group	—	—	—	3	—	—
	Holger Meins Commando	—	1	—	—	—	—
	Meinhof-Antich Group	—	—	—	1	—	—
	Second of June Movement	1	—	—	—	—	—
Yugoslavia	Ustasha and other Croatians	—	1	1	5	—	2
Middle East and Northern Africa							
Algeria	Soldiers of the Algerian Opposition	—	—	—	2	—	—
Iran	Iranian Peoples' Strugglers	—	—	—	—	—	2
	Iranian terrorists	—	—	1	1	—	1
Israel	Masada-Action and Defense Movement	—	—	—	1	—	—

Jordan						
Jordanian National Liberation Movement	—	—	—	1	—	—
Lebanon						
Lebanese Revolutionary Guard	—	—	1	—	—	—
Revolutionary Socialist Action Organization	—	—	—	—	1	1
Palestine						
Action Organization for the Liberation of Palestine	—	1	—	—	—	—
Al Saiqa	—	—	—	—	1	—
Arab Liberation Arm	—	—	—	—	1	—
Arab Liberation Front	—	—	—	—	1	—
Arab Nationalist Youth for the Liberation of Palestine	—	—	—	2	—	—
Arab Nationalist Youth Organization for the Liberation of Palestine	—	—	—	1	—	—
Black September	7	3	11	2	3	—
Eagles of National Unity	—	—	—	1	—	—
Eagles of the Palestine Revolution	—	—	—	—	1	—
El Fatah	1	—	4	3	1	1
Moslem International Guerrillas	—	—	—	—	1	—
Nationalist Organization of Arab Youth	—	2	—	—	—	—
Nationalist Youth Group for the Liberation of Palestine	—	—	1	—	—	—
Organization for the Victims of Zionist Occupation	—	—	—	1	—	—

Table 9 (continued)

Country	Group	Kidnapping	Barricade and hostage	Skyjacking	Bombing	Armed attack	Murder
Palestine	Organization of Sons of Occupied Territories	—	—	1	—	—	—
	Organization of Victims of Occupied Territories	—	1	—	—	—	—
	Palestine Liberation Army	1	—	—	—	—	—
	Palestine Liberation Organization (PLO)	—	—	—	1	—	—
	Palestine Popular Struggle Front	—	—	1	2	1	—
	Palestine guerrillas	—	1	3	9	11	7
	Popular Democratic Front for the Liberation of Palestine (PDFLP)	—	1	—	—	—	—
	Popular Front for the Liberation of Palestine (PFLP)	2	4	14	17	4	2
	PFLP-General Command	—	1	—	—	—	—
	Punishment Squad	—	1	—	—	—	—
	Seventh Suicide Squad	—	1	—	—	—	—
	Squad of the Martyr Patrick Arguello	—	—	—	—	1	—
Turkey	Turkish People's Liberation Army (TPLA)	4	—	1	1	—	—
Latin America							
Argentina	Argentine rightists	—	—	—	—	—	1

Comite Argentino de Lucha Anti-Imperialisto	11	—	—	5	—	—
ERP–People's Revolutionary Army	1	—	3	11	2	—
FAL–Argentine Liberation Front	—	—	—	—	—	—
FAP–Peronist Armed Forces	—	—	—	15	—	1
MANO–Argentine National Organization Movement	1	—	—	—	—	—
Montoneros	4	—	—	1	—	—
Peronist guerrillas	—	—	—	1	—	—
Bolivia Bolivian peasants	1	—	—	—	—	—
ELN–National Liberation Army	1	—	—	—	—	—
Brazil ALN–Action for National Liberation	3	—	1	—	—	—
MR-8–Revolutionary Movement of the 8th	1	—	—	—	—	—
VAR-Palmares–Armed Revolutionary Vanguard-Palmares	—	—	1	—	—	—
Chile Chilean refugees	—	1	—	—	—	—
Leftist Revolutionary Movement	—	—	1	—	—	—
Colombia ELN–National Liberation Army	1	—	2	—	—	—
Invisible Ones	1	—	—	—	—	—
United Front for Guerrilla Action	—	—	—	1	—	—
Cuba Anti-Castro Cubans	—	—	—	14	—	—
Cuba Movement 4	—	—	—	1	—	—
Cuban Power 76	—	—	—	1	—	—

Table 9 (continued)

Country	Group	Kidnapping	Barricade and hostage	Skyjacking	Bombing	Armed attack	Murder
Cuba	Cuban Scorpion	—	—	—	1	—	—
	Cuban Youth Group	—	—	—	7	—	—
	El Poder Cubano	—	—	—	20	1	1
	Secret Organization Zero	—	—	—	1	—	1
	Youths of the Star	—	—	—	1	—	—
Dominican Republic	Dominican guerrillas	—	—	—	1	—	—
	United Anti-Reelection Command	1	—	—	—	—	—
Guatemala	FAR–Revolutionary Armed Forces	2	—	—	—	—	1
Haiti	Coalition of National Brigades	—	1	—	—	—	—
Mexico	Armed Communist League	—	—	1	—	—	—
	Mexican guerrillas	1	—	—	—	—	—
	Peoples Revolutionary Armed Forces	1	—	—	—	—	—
	23rd of September Communist League	1	—	—	—	—	—
Nicaragua	FSLN–Sandinist Front of National Liberation	—	1	1	—	—	—
	MoPoCo	1	—	—	—	—	—

Uruguay						
OPR-33—Organization of the Popular Revolution-33	1	—	—	—	—	—
Tupamaros	6	—	—	1	2	—
Venezuela						
People's Revolutionary Army-Zero Point	—	—	1	—	—	—
Red Flag	1	—	—	—	—	—
Other						
Unknown	—	3	2	193	19	24
Individuals or groups who engaged in incident as a one-time event and were not involved in a campaign of terrorism	4	3	230	5	4	6

ber of hostages per incident—that is, barricade and hostage events and skyjackings. They also have a near monopoly on armed assaults and assassinations, tactics that also do not require large support groups.

Very few groups exhibit an extensive repertoire of tactics. Only the ELF, Popular Front for the Liberation of Palestine, Jewish Defense League, Irish Republican Army, Japanese United Red Army, Black September, and Argentina's People's Revolutionary Army have a consistent ability (or preference) to vary their operations.

Most other groups appear to specialize in only one type of incident—for example, the Puerto Rican FALN consistently chooses to bomb selected targets. Many other groups, which may engage in a great deal of domestic terrorism, surface into the transnational level only once or twice—for example, the Argentine Liberation Front, Bolivian National Liberation Army, and Quebec Liberation Front. Finally, many groups mentioned in Table 9 are names given to cover the organization behind the incident. For example, many have reported that Black September was an appendage of El Fatah and would engage in particularly gruesome operations that would shock the world and bring great publicity to the Palestinian conflict but would not bring public outcry against El Fatah itself. Such ploys may have also been used by anti-Castro Cuban groups.

Unfortunately, we have no well-developed theory that suggests why some groups choose to engage in terrorism and others do not. One can point to feelings of relative deprivation and note inequality of distribution of land and income, lack of political participation of the masses, the shock of changing societies, and so on. One may find it relevant to consider societal structure, including rigid social and economic class hierarchies, as well as political institutionalization. One could also note that society's history of other forms of violent behavior and attempt to create a theory based upon a "culture of violence" view. Still others could point to racial, religious, ethnic, or linguistic antagonisms within the society. These macro-level explanations must then be linked to a discussion of the weakness of the groups that are attempting to articulate their grievances. Terrorism appears to be engaged in by small bands, rather than large organizations with extensive popular support, and has been called the weapon of the weak. Finally, these societal and organizational factors must be further linked to a study of the type of personality that would be attracted to this kind of political expression. Other groups have arisen to become vigilante terrorists established to fight "primary" terrorist groups. Examples of such pairings include the Ulster Defense Association versus the Irish Republican Army, the anti-ETA versus Basque nationalists, the Jewish Defense League versus the Palestine Liberation Organization, and the Argentine Anti-Communist Alliance versus numerous Argentine leftist groups.[18] Much work remains to be done in explaining terrorists' motivations and the causes of their behavior. A preliminary typology of transnational groups, based upon apparent motivations, is offered in Table 10.

Table 10 Types of Terrorists

Group type	Examples
Territorialists	Separatists, irredentists, independence movements, exile organizations—for example, ETA, ELF, IRA, Ustasha, PLO
National revolutionaries	ERP, Montoneros, ALN, ELN, official IRA
Global anarchists	Japanese Red Army, Baader-Meinhof Group and its splinters, Carlos's associates
Criminal gangs	Mafia, groups that publicly cloak their actions in political rhetoric, but whose intent is personal gain
Psychotic individuals	Security guard who seized Israeli Embassy in South Africa in 1975, many skyjackers
Hoaxes	Brian Lee's kidnapping in Uganda
Cover names	Black September, Cuban groups
Vigilantes	Argentine Anti-Communist Alliance, extraofficial Latin American "Death Squads"

But given that political terrorism by autonomous actors may be caused by the aforementioned societal, organizational, and personality factors, why do some groups choose to internationalize their struggle and involve citizens of foreign countries? A number of reasons can be offered. Their grievance may well be against a country other than their home country that is perceived by them to have exploitative policies. Thus, they choose American and Western business executives as victims of attacks. The terrorists may also believe that attacking foreigners will lead the victim's government to exert pressure upon the host government to capitulate to the terrorists' demands. We have also noted the lack of an underground of some groups. Being unable to engage in prolonged military confrontations with the army, they resort to spectacular incidents to give a false impression of strength. Publicity is increased if the target is a foreign diplomat rather than a backwater village. This publicity may have a contagion effect upon other terrorist groups, who observe the success of other terrorist operations. Finally, groups such as the Japanese United Red Army preach world revolution and are insensitive to territorial borders.

Responding to the Terrorist Threat

Unfortunately, the international response to transnational attacks has been feeble. The UN General Assembly members have quibbled over who is and is not a terrorist and have not managed to agree on a common definition of, much less a solution to, the problem. They have managed to approve a convention on the protection of diplomats, but only nine nations have ratified this 1973 agreement, and it is not yet in force. Other relevant conventions include the 1963 Tokyo Convention on Offenses and Certain Other Acts Committed on Board Aircraft, the 1970 Hague Convention for the Suppression of the Unlawful Seizure of Aircraft, the 1973 Montreal Convention for the Suppression of Unlawful Acts Against the Safety of Civil Aviation, and the 1971 OAS Convention to Prevent and Punish Acts of Terrorism Taking the Form of Crimes Against Persons and Related Extortion That Are of International Significance. Unfortunately, many states that support terrorist groups have refused to ratify these conventions. Effective sanctions against states who disregard the prosecution or extradition clauses have not been created. And finally, these conventions cover only a small part of what can be viewed as terrorist acts.

Bilateral treaties have also been resorted to, among the most important of which is an agreement between the United States and Cuba on skyjacking that has effectively shut off the flow of hijackers to that island nation. But the right of asylum in Latin American countries is a time-honored tradition in Latin international law. Governmental leaders recognize that they may one day be requesting asylum when and if they are ousted from power in the next revolution. It is not in their personal interest to in any way restrict this practice, and any proposals to place a global, regional, or bilateral ban on the granting of asylum to political offenders (either the terrorists instigating the incident or the prisoners whose release is demanded) will be met with great resistance in these countries.

On the national level, many governments have resorted to draconian measures to root out terrorist groups, torturing prisoners, establishing strict curfews, and creating a quasi-permanent police state. But this may be precisely what the terrorists are attempting to provoke. Such measures must be applied nationwide if the government is reasonably to expect to hit all of the group's cells. Unfortunately, many individuals uninvolved in the hostilities will be adversely affected by such measures and can be expected to resent deeply such incursions on their liberties. It is the terrorists' hope that this animosity will surface and that the government will be faced with a nationwide revolutionary movement with broad popular support.

Suggestions are also made to establish a no-ransom policy, which would deter terrorists from engaging in future incidents. But the acquisition of money or the release of prisoners may merely be bonus effects of the incident, with the real purposes of the terrorists being served by the extensive media coverage that their operations receive.

As has been shown in our discussions, all governments have faced or may have to face this growing problem. No one solution, such as toning down present media coverage, will stop terrorism. But a combined program of greater security measures, worldwide cooperation by governments and those concerned about the problem, better intelligence efforts, a well thought out incident negotiation policy, attempts to meet the justified grievances of those whom the terrorists claim to represent, and a self-restrained media may well bring about a lessening of the problem.

The Future of Transnational Terrorism

Here we can only speculate on what the trends we have seen may portend for the future. Among the possibilities are:

1. Terrorists may shift from one of the types of political terrorism listed in Table 1 to other types. For example, governments may co-opt stateless revolutionary transnational groups and send them to disrupt the societies of their perceived enemies. Domestic terrorists may discover that going transnational gives them greater publicity and more leverage in bargaining with governments. Domestic terrorists may come to power and discover that they must resort to state terrorism to keep revanchist populations in line.

2. Transnational terrorists may choose new victims for their operations. Installations using sophisticated but delicate equipment are particularly vulnerable, and much damage to valuable facilities can be caused by the simple bomb. Among these targets are offshore drilling rigs, the Alaska Pipeline, airport control towers, computerized rapid transit, and nuclear reactor sites.

3. We shall probably observe increased cooperation among transnational and domestic groups, with more joint operations, intergroup training, funding, arming, and so on. This may result in greater autonomy from sympathetic governmental sponsors, with the subsequent lack of restraints this implies.

4. With highly destructive weapons becoming cheaper and more easily carried, we may see the use of more sophisticated weapons by terrorists and more spectacular incidents. With the large number of incidents occurring in any given year, terrorists must resort to increasingly theatrical escapades in order to attract any publicity to their cause. A bombing of an embassy goes virtually unreported, buried on the back pages next to the classified ads. But an attack on a nuclear facility by groups using hand-held launchers of heat-seeking missiles would capture the front pages for days (if not the facility).

5. With the increasing sophistication of terrorist technology, *some* of their operations may in fact become less destructive. For example, clandestine bugging of some embassies is a relatively simple task once entry has been gained. Rather than setting time bombs during an embassy takeover, could a guerrilla technician more profitably spend his time planting listening devices in strategic locations in

order to give the group information about future precautions that will be taken by the embassy to prevent more incidents of that type, about embassy-police liaison regarding the conduct of the nationwide search for the perpetrators, and about other matters?

6. High-speed jet airliners and international telephonic communications will continue to make the planning and execution of transnational events on any continent easier than they would have been even a decade ago.

7. A few words must be devoted to what many view as the greater horror story of the near future: a nuclear bomb in the hands of terrorists. Among other questions to be answered are: Why hasn't anyone stolen nuclear material by now? Why would a group want to steal it? What are the characteristics of a group wishing to kill thousands of people? What are the characteristics of a group who would use the bomb to ransom a city? What types of demands could be made, and agreed to, that could not be made in incidents threatening a lower level of destruction? What kind of effect would such an attack have upon the group's public support? What would be the reaction of the public to such a situation of high stress? Do any of the terrorist groups active today possess the requisite skill to manufacture a bomb? Would it be more cost-effective for the group to resort to other methods, such as chemical or biological warfare, aerosol attacks, sabotage of major life-support systems, plutonium dispersal devices, and so on? Is the theft of nuclear material to make a bomb the only type of terrorist threat to society involving nuclear facilities?

If present trends continue, the future for the world looks bleak indeed. Although less than 3000 casualties due to transnational terrorism is not large compared to other causes, such as conventional warfare, accident, and illness, terrorist actions have lessened societal freedoms and the sense of security, diverted resources to protection against attack, and led to strains in state relations. Concerted and cooperative international action will be needed to stem the tide.

Appendix: Chronology of Terrorist Activity: January 2—March 9, 1976

At the time of the writing of this paper, it is too early to include 1976 data on our graphs and charts. However, to give the reader some idea of the continuation of trends mentioned in the text, this peek into the new year is presented. Incidents with an asterisk (*) are not considered to be acts of transnational terrorism that would be included in the ITERATE data set, but they are still of interest.

January

2nd   Israel—A fire that authorities believe was set by arsonists caused millions of dollars worth of damage to the three-story building housing Haaretz, a leading Israeli newspaper. The fire was the biggest in Tel Aviv's history, officials said.

5th   Philippines—Two Filipino gunmen held a JAL DC-8 and its crew for 10 hours before surrendering to Philippine authorities. The two brothers, who demanded to be flown to Tokyo, initially held 219 passengers as well. The brothers released the passengers after 5 hours, then freed the crew and surrendered after the Japanese government refused to grant them permission to land in Tokyo. There was no violence. Before giving up, the brothers had demanded a pardon, a ban on publishing their photos, and an improvement in "living conditions."

5th   West Germany—A time bomb exploded outside the Yugoslavian consulate in Stuttgart, causing no injuries.

7th   *Ireland—A British Airways Boeing 747, diverted to Shannon airport by a bomb scare, resumed its flight to Miami after 8 hours on the ground. The jumbo jet, Flight 661 from London to Miami with 212 passengers and 18 crew aboard, was 400 miles over the Atlantic when it was ordered to turn back to Shannon.

8th   Jamaica—One man was killed and a second wounded when two gunmen opened fire outside the U.S. consulate in Kingston. In an earlier attack, several hundred demonstrators, many of them throwing stones, protested at the consulate over South Africa's presence at a meeting of the IMF.

9th   Israel—A time bomb exploded in a Jerusalem supermarket crowded with pre-Sabbath Israeli shoppers, injuring eight persons. Police rounded up 130 Arab suspects for questioning and began tighter security.

9th   France—In Paris, fire bombs were thrown at the two headquarters buildings of UNESCO, causing some damage but no casualties. The Jewish Self-Defense Front claimed responsibility for the attacks.

12th   United States—In New York City, three pipe bombs were discovered outside UN headquarters a few hours before the Security Council was scheduled to open a controversial debate on the Middle East with PLO participation. The three bombs, discovered by a city electrician inspecting a subway maintenance entrance near the UN library, were set to explode half an hour before the Council was to have met. The explosives, said a UN security official, could have torn up half of the library building. No group has claimed responsibility.

12th   United States—A bomb was found in front of the Iraqi mission to the United Nations. A Jewish defense organization claimed credit for the midnight incident.

13th Israel—Israel said its troops killed four Palestinian guerrillas in a shootout near the Lebanese border. The four had crossed the border from Lebanon armed with submachine guns and axes for a terrorist mission. Leaflets found on the guerrillas' bodies identified them as members of the Palestinian Rejection Front, a coalition of guerrilla groups opposed to any political settlement of the Middle East situation. Statements released by the PRF in Damascus and Beirut said their commandos had carried out a mission inside Israel. The Beirut statement said the commandos then blew themselves up, along with a number of hostages taken from a nearby farming settlement. Israeli sources mentioned no hostages. The Palestinian statement said the raiders were trying to free thirty prisoners, including Archbishop Hilarion Capucci, who is serving a 12-year sentence in Israel on charges of smuggling weapons to Arab terrorists.

14th United States—In San Francisco, a group linking itself with international revolutionary causes claimed it had planted a powerful bomb that heavily damaged a new financial district skyscraper housing the Iranian consulate. The bomb exploded after a telephoned warning to the UPI. The group said the bombing was carried out "in support of the Iranian people's struggle to rid themselves of the CIA-backed Shah." The group proclaimed solidarity with revolutionary groups in Angola, Greece, Puerto Rico, and Iran, as well as with terrorist organizations. Two persons who had been in an office on the fourteenth floor of the forty-one-story Embarcadero Center were slightly injured by flying glass from the blast, which caused $200,000 in damage.

16th *Switzerland—In St. Moritz, Swiss authorities dispatched security agents to this winter resort following reports that the terrorist "Carlos," who had led the attack on OPEC in December, might arrive at the same time as the Shah of Iran.

16th Portugal—Bombs were hurled at a Soviet freighter in the northern port of Oporto. There were no injuries nor serious damage.

17th United States—In New York City, police said an anonymous call to the United Nations warning of a pipe bomb led to the discovery of a piece of pipe in bushes on the UN grounds. Examination showed the sealed pipe to be empty.

26th USSR—Sources in Tel Aviv said Ben Gurion Airport went on alert for 90 minutes after a Swedish airport received a radio message from a Soviet Jew who hijacked an Aeroflot plane over Moscow. It appears that the hijacker was overpowered and returned to the USSR.

29th Argentina—In Buenos Aires, fifteen terrorists, including two women, burst into the offices of the local subsidiary of the Bendix Corporation and killed two Argentine executives.

31st *Uganda—A plane piloted by a PLO officer crashed into Lake Victoria. It was the third recent crash involving PLO pilot trainers working in Uganda.

February

3rd   *Central African Republic—CAR President Jean Bedel Bokassa escaped an assassination attempt at the airport of the capital, Bangui. Informed sources in Chad said all contacts with the CAR were cut off. Paris reports said two body-guards of the president were killed in the grenade assault.

3rd   Afars and Issas—Four gunmen of the Front for the Liberation of the Somali Coast hijacked a schoolbus carrying the children of French military officials. They were later reinforced by two others, and Somalia also brought up forces near the border, apparently to back the guerrillas. They demanded the immediate and unconditional independence of the French territory without the referendum planned by France, release of all political prisoners and departure of all French troops from Djibouti. On February 4, French military sharpshooters opened fire on the bus and killed the six terrorists threatening to slit the throats of the thirty captive children. According to the French account of the shootout, the French force killed five gunmen in the initial volley. But a sixth, hidden on the floor, managed to squeeze off a burst of fire and killed one child while wounding four, plus the bus driver and a woman social worker. He was gunned down.

4th   Afars and Issas—After the assault, police announced that 7-year-old Frank Rutkovsky was still missing. He apparently was taken across the border into Somalia during the night or morning. The guerrillas demanded that France free political prisoners in Djibouti and halt deportation of civilians as a precondition to the boy's release. France sent three warships to the Red Sea area as tension rose with Somalia over the incidents. On February 7, the child was handed over to the French embassy in Mogadishu.

5th   Italy—Two men on the grounds of the Egyptian embassy in Rome opened fire with submachineguns when challenged by police. The intruders successfully escaped.

6th   France—Four days after Iran announced the execution of two more Marxist terrorists, three explosions destroyed the offices of an Iranian firm in the Mont-parnasse Tower, the tallest building in Paris.

7th   West Germany—In Frankfurt, Yugoslavian Consul Edwin Zdove was gunned down outside his home, possibly the work of Croatians.

9th and 10th   *India—H. L. Batra, secretary to the vice chancellor of Meerut University, opened his mail to find a 2-foot-long cobra raising its hood in attack. The snake was captured and clapped into a jug. Officials called in a snake charmer who said the cobra belonged to a deadly species. In New Delhi, a worker at the central government's Public Service Commission opened a package and found a live, poisonous snake inside.

12th   United Kingdom—IRA leader Frank Stagg died in a British jail on the sixty-first day of a hunger strike. A wave of terrorism and rioting followed. Within hours of Stagg's death, gunmen opened fire on a British army patrol and a police car in Northern Ireland. British police disarmed a 20-pound bomb in a London subway station during rush hour. Bombs exploded in Belfast and Dungannon on a day in which over 100 incidents were reported.

12th   Portugal—Bombs damaged a town hall in northern Portugal where an exhibition of Soviet photographs was under way.

17th   Lebanon—A Palestinian student was arrested and charged with shooting two professors at the American University of Beirut. He may have been acting out of revenge, having been expelled in 1974 for radical activity.

20th   France—Bombs exploded outside Algerian consulates in Paris and Strasbourg, as well as outside the Air Algeria offices in Lyons, smashing windows but causing no injuries. The bomb in Lyons caused the most damage, smashing the windows of nearby apartments and those of a French airline company, UTA. So far no one has claimed responsibility for the blasts.

20th   *Philippines—Heavily armed men, believed to be Moslem rebels, ambushed a bus carrying fifty people as it went up a hill near New Calamba. At least twenty-one persons were killed and several others were wounded.

23rd   Lebanon—The Canadian Embassy was taken over by Mohammed Haymour and six of his relatives. The gunman, a former Canadian resident, claimed he was bilked out of ownership of an island there by his wife and a doctor. He also charged that he had been illegally expelled from Canada on grounds of insanity. He demanded that Canada fly his four children to Lebanon and threatened to kill the hostages. Eight women hostages were allowed to leave during negotiations, and the band finally surrendered after 8 hours, releasing their last fifteen hostages. Police said there were no injuries.

27th   Greece—Homemade bombs exploded in front of two American banks in Athens, causing slight damage.

27th   United States—Several shots were fired from an M-1 rifle at a Soviet diplomatic residence. A woman claiming to represent the Jewish Armed Resistance called UPI and said the organization did the shooting and threatened to kidnap Soviet diplomats unless a Soviet Jewish teenager was allowed to emigrate to Israel.

27th   Venezuela—A Marxist group calling itself the "Group of Revolutionary Commands" claimed credit for the kidnapping of William Niehous, vice-president and manager for Owens—Illinois Glass Manufacturing Company in Caracas. They warned that he would be killed if any actions were taken against leftist groups in Venezuela. No ransom demands have been received.

March

2nd *Japan—Claiming that it was acting against the oppression of the Ainu people, the East Asia Anti-Japanese Armed Front set a time bomb that blasted a crowded government building in Sapporo, killing two office workers and injuring eighty-five others.

4th United Kingdom—A bomb, believed planted by the IRA, devastated a commuter train in London, minutes after hundreds of rush-hour passengers had disembarked at a railway station. Eight people traveling in a second train alongside the empty train suffered shock in the explosion. Two more bombs exploded in central London, with at least one injury reported.

9th United States—In New York City, the Jewish Armed Resistance claimed responsibility for the bombings of Czech and Soviet airline offices.

Notes

1. In the tables and figures, only incidents of transnational terrorism, as defined, are included. Events related to the Vietnam conflict are not included, nor are the numerous cross-border raids between Arabs and Israelis against military targets. Plots to engage in actions classified as terrorist, but which were discovered before the carrying out of the operation, are not included, nor are threats to engage in such actions.
    Data were obtained from chronologies provided by the U.S. Department of State, the Federal Aviation Administration, the RAND Corporation, the U.S. Information Agency, the U.S. Senate and House of Representatives, staff reports for congressional committees, Facts on File, plus reports found in Associated Press dispatches, the *New York Times, Washington Post, Chicago Tribune, Detroit Free Press,* and *The Economist.* Due to omissions in reporting for some incidents, grand totals for the tables presented herein may disagree.

2. Skyjackings must have the attributes of our definition of transnational terrorism in order to qualify for inclusion. Incidents that did not involve a crossing of a border (such as events involving the payment of ransom and parachuting of the hijacker from the plane within the territorial confines of the nation of embarkation), domestic attempts to hijack a plane to another country that involved no injuries in the resolution of the incident, and incidents that involved only one nationality of passengers, crew, hijacker, and destination and embarkation point of the flight are thus not included.

3. Although skyjackings and nonair takeovers can become barricade and hostage situations, these incidents are not treated in the barricade-and-hostage category if they occurred in transit. Hence, the multiple skyjackings of

the PFLP in September 1970 are treated as skyjackings, although negotiations were conducted on the ground.

For a discussion of trends in hostage situations, what the terrorists seek, and the policy debate over the proper response to such demands, see Edward Mickolus, "Negotiating for Hostages: A Policy Dilemma," *Orbis* 4 (Winter 1976): 19.

4. A score of definitions have been offered for assassination. Rather than attempt to distinguish between the political murder of a low-level official and a high-level official (if such an arbitrary cut-off point could be established) or to categorize on the basis of the motivations of the killer and other criteria, a general category of political murder and assassination is used. To qualify for inclusion, such acts must satisfy the conditions of the definition of transnational terrorism.

5. The casualty totals for 1974 are all the more distressing when it is noted that the data currently on file in the ITERATE Project (*International Terrorism: Attributes of Terrorist Events*), which is based upon the sources mentioned in note 1, are incomplete. I have had access to classified and proprietary data on the 8 years studied and am able to report that the present sources are not reporting all incidents. Hence, the rather comforting decline in the number of terrorist events shown in Table 1 for 1974 is misleading and is due to error in the data rather than restraint by the terrorists.

6. The location of an incident is considered to be the place in which the incident began, while its year is that date on which it became known to individuals other than the terrorists that a terrorist incident was taking place. In the case of skyjacking, the location is the nation in which the plane had last touched ground before the hijackers made their presence as hijackers known. In cases in which the embarkation point is not known, the location is considered to be that nation in which the plane landed and the negotiations took place, where appropriate. If both of the above do not apply, the nation of registry is used.

7. The location of an incident need not be a nation-state. Protectorates, colonies, and mandated territories may also experience terrorism, and are considered by the government to be different types of security and administrative environments, not comparable to the metropole. Hence, areas such as Puerto Rico and Gibraltar are included as locations, despite the legal citizenship of their residents.

8. The grand total for Tables 6 and 7 is greater than that for Table 2 due to the multiplicity of nationalities of victims in some incidents.

9. The Regional Victimization Index is computed for each region by dividing the number of incidents in which any citizen of that region was the victim of an attack by the number of nations in the region whose citizens were reported as victims in at least one attack.

10. However, reports frequently allege these attacks to be the work of members of Israeli intelligence.

11. *Washington Post,* February 9, 1976, p. C-5.

12. An interesting discussion of this possibility is included in Brian M. Jenkins *International Terrorism: New Mode of Conflict,* Research Paper no. 48, California Seminar on Arms Control and Foreign Policy (Los Angeles: Crescent Publications, 1975).

13. Ransoms in Latin America have ranged from as low as a tractor demanded and received by Bolivian peasants to $60 million in cash, $1.2 million in food for peasants, and the publication of a manifesto in selected foreign newspapers received by the Montoneros from Bunge y Born in 1975.

14. Such neuroses have been described in the work of Fanon.

15. Henry McFarland of the Economics Department of Northwestern University and I are presently conducting research on the economics of kidnapping, noting the utility to the terrorists of their demands being met, publicity garnered, and so forth, against the costs of the operation, such as the expectation of arrest, conviction, and jailing, the probability of release in subsequent incidents, the monetary costs of the operation, and so on.

16. Despite the popularity of the United States as a provider of hostages, the U.S. government is rarely the target of terrorist demands. Terrorists have tended to single out corporations or make demands that do not mention a particular target (for example, "We want $4 million for his safe return") when holding American hostages.

17. The name of the group claiming responsibility for the incident is as reported, rather than the identity of the group which police or the press speculate as having been involved. Often groups give "cover" names to be able to deny the responsibility of the umbrella organization for particularly hideous crimes or for operations that failed to achieve the objectives of their perpetrators. Actions that occur less frequently than those mentioned in Table 9 are listed here, with the name of the groups responsible for such incidents:

Theft:	4	Jewish Defense League (United States)
	3	Palestinians, Tupamaros (Uruguay)
	2	Irish Republican Army (United Kingdom)
	1	Japanese students, Ethiopian students, ERP (Argentina), unknown
Arson:	27	Unknown
	5	Revolutionary Force 7 (United States)
	2	Palestinians
	1	Black September, Irish Republican Army, Jewish Defense League, Movement of Youth-

		ward Brothers in War of the Palestinian People, Proletarian Revolutionary Action Group (Chile or Italy), Puerto Rican Liberation Front, Bandera Roja (Venezuela), National Liberation Armed Forces (Venezuela), one-timers
Sabotage:	2	Black September, unknown
	1	PFLP
Letter bomb:	80	Palestinians
	59	Black September
	40	Irish Republican Army
	24	Unknown
	3	El Poder Cubano
	1	Yanikian Commandos (Turkey)
Nonair takeover:	5	One-timers
	1	Palestinians

When the nationality of the perpetrators is known, but no organizational name is available, it is so noted—for example, "Palestinians" or "Iranian terrorists."

18. Vigilantes do not appear to conduct transnational operations.

6

Ethnic and Student Terrorism in Western Europe

Raymond R. Corrado
Department of Political Science
Simon Fraser University
Burnaby, British Columbia

Introduction

The recent hijackings in the Middle East and the kidnappings and assassinations in certain regions of Latin America confirm that terrorism is an integral part of the political scene in these areas. However, Western Europe has the longest history of terrorism and therefore is the richest source for exploring its political role. It is particularly in nineteenth- and twentieth-century European history that one can trace most distinctively two basic rationales for contemporary terrorism: (1) nationalism and (2) classic ideologies, for example, anarchism, fascism, and communism. Both ethnic nationalist and ideological terrorism involve the use of violence in the form of assassinations, bombings, torture, and other methods of physical intimidation to achieve either the independence of an ethnic group or groups or a revolutionary restructuring of society. Terrorism in this chapter is viewed as an explicitly political tactic employed by self-appointed individuals who are members of small clandestine groups who want to destabilize a political regime by making the cost in lives prohibitive, intimidating major social groups, and creating economic and political chaos.

Terrorist tactics and goals are similar to those of guerrilla warfare, except that terrorists rarely occupy or exclusively control territory and usually operate in small deliberately dispersed cells rather than as large formal concentrations of soldiers. Also, the terrorism we are concerned with is largely confined to urban areas where terrorists remain inconspicuous. Although the intention of a guerrilla army is normally to achieve a specific military objective by direct application of its own resources, the immediate aim of a terrorist group is to generate fear and confusion at random among noncombatants in the hope of undermining confidence in the police and military forces. Whereas the target for orthodox military operations is the military capacity of an opponent, the target for terrorists is the political legitimacy of a regime or government.

Favorable conditions for ethnic and ideological terrorism exist when there is a highly visible social group that sees itself as oppressed in political and/or economic terms; a monolithic and repressive government or political regime; and few structural vehicles for redress. Another important factor in the existence of terrorism is the need for a concrete symbol of repression—a historical act or acts that involved government violence against an ethnic or working-class group, especially if the structure of government has not changed substantially since the original violent act. In effect, it seems that ideological and ethnic terrorists need historical precedents that allow them to perceive recent history and contemporary government behavior as continuously repressive and as requiring drastic and violent action.

One of the major themes in this chapter is that favorable conditions for terrorism are waning in Western Europe. It is increasingly difficult for terrorists to isolate the oppressed and the oppressor and to convince the former that violence is the solution to their oppression. The inability of terrorists to gain significant popular support reflects the gap between values and perceptions of the terrorist and those of most of the public. Chapter 7 will describe this value and perceptual gap and present an analysis of why it exists.

Historical Overview of the Changing Conditions for Terrorism in Western Europe

Since the French Revolution, terrorism has periodically affected European politics. As a result of Napoleon's attempts to rebuild the internal political structures of various European states, a significant number of university students, the middle class, and the intelligentsia, although bitterly opposed to Napoleon's armies, were inspired to support revolutionary and nationalistic values. The reaction to this by the conservative elites and other segments of the European societies became an important factor in the violence and turmoil that frequently characterized European politics in the nineteenth century, particularly during the struggle for liberal reforms in the German states and the British Isles. Ideol-

ogies such as communism, anarchism, and fascism provided additional rationale
for the terrorism that took place in the nineteenth and twentieth centuries, including the events that shaped World Wars I and II, the Russian revolution, and the
fascist dictatorships. Ethnic terrorism was also linked to the creation of the Irish
Free State and Ulster in the British Isles.

    Following World War II, there were few incidents of terrorism in Europe be-
cause fundamental change had occurred. The war experience was traumatic; in
addition to the physical devastation, there was the emotional shock of the savagery of Nazism. Major structural changes took place that affected every European country, such as the division of Germany and the onset of the Cold War.
In addition, the creation of the European Economic Community (EEC) inter-
locked the economies and, to a lesser degree, the political systems of the key
Western European countries. The North Atlantic Treaty Organization (NATO)
joined the military forces of some of these countries as did the Warsaw Pact for
Eastern European countries. The latter countries were also linked economically
through COMECON and politically as satellites of the USSR. In addition, Britain,
France, Belgium, and the Netherlands all lost their colonial territories. An equally dramatic economic change took place in Western Europe. While West Germany
led the way with a complete material recovery, the economies of most of the
other members of the EEC had also undergone impressive changes. Thus, the
material standard of living had increased to the point that much of the class-
based political conflict of the pre-World War II period had been mitigated so that
most political parties adopted essentially moderate positions on formerly bitterly
contested class-based or ideological issues.[1]

    The conditions necessary for terrorism, an oppressed working class or a de-
prived ethnic group, were now waning.[2] It was difficult to identify oppressed or
exploited masses in any Western European country. The slums of the major European cities were only partially inhabited by indigenous people; the majority were
immigrants who, for the most part, were temporary workers. Depopulation often
occurred among the more disadvantaged ethnic groups from the economically
peripheral areas such as Wales and Scotland in the United Kingdom, Brittany in
France, Galicia in Spain, and Calabria and Sicily in Italy. People were migrating
from these ethnic regions to be absorbed in the expanding work forces of the
more dynamic industrial regions of Western Europe. It appeared that cultural
homogenization was the trend throughout Western Europe. Consequently, eth-
nically-based socioeconomic and political interests were giving way to more func-
tionally based interests. With rapidly expanding service economies, most Western
European students were pragmatic toward the job market. They were named
the "skeptical generation," wary of extremism because of the lessons of World
War II and the continuing Soviet threat.

Terrorism in Western Europe: Revolt of the Traditionalists

In spite of these major structural changes, the use of terrorist tactics increased in the late 1960s. Why did ethnic terrorist groups spring up in Wales, Scotland, Corsica, and the Jura where there was little tradition of terrorism and why did it return to Northern Ireland, the Basque region of Spain, and Brittany? Why did ideological terrorists surface in Spain, Brittany, Italy, and Germany? It is beyond the scope of this chapter to provide answers based on a detailed account of all Western European terrorist movements. Instead, I shall propose the general thesis that these terrorists are reacting, each in their own way, against modernization and are unlikely to engage in other than sporadic terrorism as long as Western European countries retain pluralist political systems and develop advanced industrial economies. I shall illustrate my thesis through an examination of the evolution of the Irish Republican Army in the British Isles, basically ethnic terrorists, and the Red Army (the Baader-Meinhof Group) in West Germany, who illustrate ideological terrorism.

Although fundamental differences exist between ethnic and ideological terrorists, there are also basic similarities that account for the simultaneous reappearance of both types in the 1960s. In his opposition to modernization, the ideological terrorist reacts negatively to the advanced industrial society values of competitiveness, materialism, and decommunalization. The ethnic terrorist also reacts negatively to values such as decommunalization, but positively to materialism, equality of opportunity, and nationalism. In both cases, in their objection to "modern" values, these terrorists are participating in the revolt of the traditionalists in the advanced industrial society. In both the Baader-Meinhof Group and the IRA Provisionals, members are willing to sacrifice their lives and those of others while resisting most of the dominant political, social, and economic values of the societies in which they live, despite the fact that many of the conditions that sparked the growth of ethnic and ideological terrorism have been drastically mitigated. Instead they cling to values identified with nationalist and ideological movements of the nineteenth century. Further, although both groups acknowledge the necessity of gaining mass, popular support, they base their appeal on a single dimension, although the politics of pluralist advanced industrial societies are characterized by multidimensional values.[3]

Ideological Versus Ethnic Terrorism

Major differences between the IRA and the Baader-Meinhof Group account for the persistence of ethnic terrorism compared with the more fleeting existence of ideological terrorism. The goals of the IRA have always been precise: the severing of all ties to Britain and the creation of a sovereign Irish republic for the thirty-two counties of Ireland. Force has always been considered the major means to achieve these goals. Irish ethnicity has been the basis for both recruitment into the IRA and the support of the general population.[4] The goals of the Baader-Meinhof Group are identified in more general terms, such as the development of a proletarian army to facilitate the initial stages of a revolution. Such an army could be created only by demonstrating the repressive character of the West German police and military. The means are quite clear: the use of force "to liquidate the chiefs and hangmen servants of the military services and the police." A source of recruitment for the Red Army was the student movement and, in particular, the SDS. The appropriate level of consciousness was difficult to achieve initially in the absence of a radical situation in the universities. The basis for popular support in West German society would be the "oppressed people," particularly the workers. Thus, the IRA has clearly defined goals, means, and bases of popular support, whereas only the means of the Baader-Meinhof Group are explicitly defined. To ask individuals who identify themselves with one ethnic group to kill individuals of other ethnic groups in order to obtain sovereignty is more concrete and immediate than to ask individuals to kill police and military officials who stand in the way of some abstract notion of an authority-free society run by Worker's Councils.

The Evolution of the Irish Republican Army (IRA)

The birth of the Irish Republican Army (IRA) can be traced back to Irish armed resistance to the Norman invasion in 1169, which was followed by Henry II's lordship of Ireland. The Tudor monarchy, including the Catholic Queen Mary, sought to enhance their control of the Irish by various plantation schemes in which land was confiscated and granted to English subjects. It was in large part a commercial as well as a military enterprise. James I, a Scot, contributed to the alteration of Ireland by instigating "a full-scale movement of population of all classes from landlords to hoodcarriers" from the Scottish border areas to Ireland. Whereas most of the earlier settlers were Anglican and strong supporters of the monarchy, many Scots were Presbyterians and distrustful of the monarchy.[5] These Scots were concentrated in the nine counties of northeastern Ireland known as Ulster.

    A rebellion broke out in southern Ireland in the mid-seventeenth century that supposedly resulted in the massacre of English men, women, and children. Whether or not this massacre in fact took place, Oliver Cromwell and his New Model Army retaliated by systematically laying to waste many major Irish towns and by killing most of the inhabitants. Following Cromwell's successful Irish campaign, more land was confiscated and on this occasion Cromwell himself, as well as his key military subordinates, became major landowners in Ireland. There was little doubt that Cromwell viewed the Irish as savages, which, along with the brutality of the military campaign and the extensive confiscation of Irish land, played a significant part in the perceptions by many Irishmen that the English were evil usurpers.[6] The seventeenth century ended with another major humiliation when Protestant William of Orange defeated Catholic James II at the Battle of Boyne. William's conquest ended any immediate hope that the Catholics would regain their lands in Ireland. Instead, a series of laws were passed that deprived Catholics of legal, social, political, and economic power and proscribed the practice of their religion. It was these events of the sixteenth and seventeenth centuries that solidified the hostility between many Irish Catholics and the Irish Protestants and English.[7]

Socioeconomic Division of Ireland: North and South

By the mid-eighteenth century Ireland had undergone a major restructuring. The majority of the Irish population consisted of Catholic tenant farmers living on small plots of land. In the six northeastern counties, the majority of the population were Presbyterian tenant farmers along with a small group of freeholders. The large landowners throughout Ireland were Anglican. Both Catholics and Presbyterians were officially discriminated against politically; the Dublin-based and *de jure* autonomous government of Ireland was totally dominated by the Anglican aristocracy.[8] The land-tenure system was also crucial in Ireland because Catholics were subject to a "whim-tenure" system involving short-term leases with little tenure, price security, or incentive for land improvement. In comparison, the Presbyterians were subject to the "Ulster custom" which involved long-term tenure and facilitated land improvement.[9] Attempts by landlords in Ulster to lease their lands to Catholics under the economically more favorable whim-tenure resulted in the formation of the secretive Anglican Orange Lodges.[10] Its members employed terrorist tactics to discourage interference with landlord tenancy rights. Presbyterians, in turn, resorted to terrorist tactics to prevent Catholics from underbidding them for tenancy rights. Sectarian animosity was thus reintensified in Ulster, while the often absentee landlord system in southern Ireland was less provocative.

    The beginning of a mixed economy occurred in the eighteenth century with Belfast and Dublin as the main industrial-commercial growth centers. The evolution of the urban middle class in Ireland followed the general European pattern. They were strongly influenced by the Enlightenment, and the Irish Presbyterians, in particular, were affected by the American Revolution. The imperial economic policies of England toward Ireland were facilitated by the aristocratic-mercantilist integration of the British Isles. England was the major market for Irish agricultural products, but it also was a main competitor for the nascent Irish linen industry. Many of the Irish middle class maintained that England imposed unfair economic regulations that favored English industry at the expense of Irish industry. The Dublin Parliament was seen as a dupe of the English aristocracy.

The Tone Rebellion, the Act of Union, and
Favorable Conditions for Terrorism

In Belfast, an Irish Presbyterian, Wolfe Tone, created a nonsectarian organization called the United Irishmen to force the complete independence of Ireland from England. It seemed that only violent action would create a nonsectarian Republic of Ireland. In 1798 Tone led a rebellion, with the assistance of the French, but it was quickly quashed. He then committed suicide to dramatize his Republican goals. The English reacted with the 1801 Act of Union of Ireland and England, which abolished the Irish Parliament. Westminster was now the main legislative and executive body for Ireland. Ireland was allotted 100 members of Parliament and a Lord-Lieutenant to act as the Crown's appointed representative to Ireland. As an integral part of Britain, Ireland would receive economic benefits. Protestants would be assured of a permanent majority and Catholics would be more likely to see reforms under a Westminster government. Britain, in turn, would be less concerned about the influence of foreign governments in Ireland. Thus, from the British perspective, the Act of Union was hardly a blatantly imperialistic or totally self-serving policy decision.

Nevertheless this Act of Union provided the basis for the evolution of Republican terrorism. It was seen as the ultimate British assault on Ireland; there was no longer any pretense of autonomy. Robert Emmet led the first small and futile rebellion in 1803. During the nineteenth century, major structural changes then took place that had an enormous influence on the course of terrorism in the British Isles. In the economic sphere, Ulster in the North became the industrial center of Ireland while the rest of Ireland floundered. At the beginning of the nineteenth century, the South had had a mixed economy while the North had been largely agricultural. The introduction of coal in British industries left the southern-based Irish industry at a considerable disadvantage.[11]

In the North, the "Ulster custom" of land tenure facilitated the growth of cottage industries (most importantly, linen manufacturers). Tenure security and less volatile rent increases permitted local capital accumulation and the creation of a domestic market for manufactured products. Also, the use of off-season agricultural labor, unlike the year-round labor system of the South, meant that the northern industry withstood the initial challenge of British industry while the southern industry collapsed. By the end of the nineteenth century two distinct economic regions existed in Ireland:

... The South had a vast subsistence level peasantry which was slowly re-
covering from the years of the Great Famine and a thin upper stratum of
landlords and trading bourgeoisie. Industry was not far developed. In
Ulster, on the other hand, the economically dominant class was the industrial bourgeoisie, and this class was in the process of achieving political
dominance as well against the landlord class. Belfast was a rapidly expanding modern industrial center. . . .

In short, the South was a kind of neo-colonial society while Ulster was
no more nor less than an integral part of the British economy.[12]

The Great Famine had a related and equally profound impact on Irish society. Most dramatically the Irish population, through death and emigration, was
cut in half. The enmity toward England was directly intensified by the exporta-
tion of much of the drastically reduced potato crop to England in the midst of
the famine. One argument was that had these exports not taken place there
would have been enough food to have prevented the death of over a million Irishmen. British economic imperialism, whether legal or not, was seen as a culprit in
the Irish tragedy.[13]

The Great Famine also laid the groundwork for the Republican movement
involving the Young Ireland Movement and the Fenians in the nineteenth century
as well as the contemporary IRA. The vast majority of those emigrating went
either to the urban centers of England or to the United States. The Irish experience in the U.S. Civil War along with a successful integration into the dynamic
U.S. economy meant that both military experience and, more importantly, money
would be available to the Republican movement in Ireland. In addition, for the
next 100 years the Irish in England were able to provide the various Republican
terrorist organizations with the infrastructure to attack England directly.

The Irish Republican Brotherhood (IRB) was founded in 1858. It was a
secret organization committed to violence against Britain in order to create an
Irish republic. It had two main branches, one in Ireland and one in America,
which collectively were popularly identified as Fenians.[14] One of IRB's most
dramatic attacks on Britain occurred when they assassinated Lord Frederick
Cavendish, chief secretary of state for Ireland, in 1882. The resulting outrage of
the British public played an important role in the defeat of Prime Minister William Gladstone's attempt to pass a Home Rule Bill for Ireland.[15]

Pluralist Politics: Competition for the Fenians

The Gladstone Home Rule Movement reflected another major structural change
in Ireland—the growth of a constitutional Irish political party. The extension of
suffrage to the middle and working classes and the elimination of political restrictions against Catholics and Dissenters meant that the Irish electoral bloc

became important in the competition between the Liberal and Conservative parties for dominance in Westminster. The Presbyterians in Ulster, through their Unionist party, proved an important source of support for the Conservative party while the Catholics were even more important to the Liberal party. The Irish party clearly undercut the Fenians, primarily because options were now available for redeeming the grievances brought about by the Act of Union.[16] Home Rule meant that an autonomous Ireland was the immediate and far less costly alternative to an Irish Republic. The Irish Parliamentarian movement also attracted the support of key interest groups such as the Catholic church, certain trade unions, and many business organizations. By the 1890s, Ireland was "killed with kindness: Catholic restrictions removed, inequities of land system resolved, Irish language replaced by English, commercial success, Empire."[17] This is not to say that Britain was now viewed favorably by Irishmen. However, fundamental changes had begun that could have virtually negated most of the conditions favorable to terrorism in the British Isles. Gladstone and many members of the Liberal party simply did not propound the intense proimperialist view that characterized earlier generations and still characterized many Conservative party members (moreover, Gladstone himself was popular among the Catholic Irish). Even the Conservative party played a role by enacting legislation favorable to Ireland. According to the Irish statesman and historian Conor Cruise O'Brien, significant political and cultural ties now existed:

> On the left, ideology and a common language produced the idea of the identity of interest and the solidarity of the English and Irish working class. Among the educated, a knowledge of English literature—and generally an ignorance of Irish and other literature—developed a special spiritual bond, cutting across history and religion. It must be very difficult really and thoroughly to hate a people on whose language and literature one is brought up. Certainly the only educated Irishman I ever knew whose anti-English feeling seemed to me unquestioning and without flaw was a man whose first language was French.[18]

A major roadblock to Home Rule was removed when the archconservative House of Lords was reduced to a debating society. Still, in the midst of these important changes in the relationship between Ireland and Britain, there remained a major obstacle in the way to constitutional resolution of Irish nationalism—Protestant Ulster.

Ulster: The Basis for Terrorism

Because of the industrialization of Belfast, Catholic immigration into the area increased considerably. Between 1800 and 1830, the ratio of Protestants to Catholics decreased from ten to one to three to one.[19] The Catholic proletariat was, therefore, growing substantially and constituted a direct threat to the growing Protestant proletariat. The Protestants protested that the Catholics were willing to work for starvation wages. Adding to the economic strains between Catholics and Protestants in Ulster, was the ascendency of the conservative faction within the Presbyterian church. The liberal influence that had been an important element in the urban Presbyterian bourgeoisie no longer acted as a mitigating influence on long-standing sectarian hate. At the same time, the Orange Order was reactivated, and Presbyterians were allowed to join.[20] The political unification of the Anglicans and Presbyterians was paralleled in the economic sphere with the rapprochement of the Protestant urban and rural factions. Both agricultural and industrial exports from Ulster were dependent on free trade with Great Britain because the South simply did not provide a comparable market. Southern Ireland, while also dependent on exports, required tariff protection until its industries could evolve sufficiently to compete with British industries. Thus, the urban Presbyterian and rural Anglican elites were united by economic self-interest in opposing the southern industrial and agricultural need for protective tariffs, as well as by the removal of discriminatory policies against the Presbyterians. The final impetus for this unification of the two major Protestant sects in Ulster came with the introduction of the first Home Rule Bill in 1886. Integration with Britain had been perceived as a critical advantage to Ulster, and the Home Rule threat to this arrangement cemented the unification of Ulster Protestants. The Orange Order became the organizational basis for this unification, because "its system of local lodges, affiliated to a Grand Lodge in each County, supplied the ready-made framework for an effective organization."[21]

The Unionist movement in Ireland was then concentrated in Ulster, while the nationalist movement was based primarily in the South. The Unionists were united through the Orange Lodges, while the nationalist movement was split into the Parliamentarians of the Irish party, the nonviolent Republicans in the Sinn Fein, and the violent Republicans in the Fenian or Irish Republican Brotherhood. In spite of these divisions in the nationalist movement, there remained the general polarization of Ireland into the Ulster and southern regions. It is in the context of this intense and total polarization that terrorism became a factor in the politics of Ireland.

Easter Rebellion: The Creation of the
IRA and Its First "Victories"

In 1912, it finally appeared that the Liberal-Irish party coalition would pass a Home Rule Bill for Ireland. The Conservative-Unionist coalition provided the parliamentary opposition, and out of the Orange Lodges came the Ulster Volunteer Force (UVF) to provide armed opposition. The UVF was not an idle military threat to Britain and the rest of Ireland because it involved 100,000 volunteers and the support of key members of the British garrison in Ulster and the military in general. There was a possibility of civil war in Britain.[22] Given such a political-military coalition, the response of the nationalists was in kind: In 1913 the Southern Volunteers were formed. Members of the Irish Republican Brotherhood infiltrated the Southern Volunteers, but the Parliamentarian leader, John Redmond, controlled most of the 170,000 members of the Southern Volunteers. However, before a major violent confrontation could take place in Ireland, World War I broke out. It was evident that to many Irishmen, Britain was no longer villain because most of the Southern Volunteers followed Redmond's command to fight with the British forces. A substantial minority of 10,000 soldiers refused to follow Redmond, and they became the nucleus for the Easter Rebellion.

As early as 1848, the IRB theoretician John Mitchell advocated striking Britain when it was preoccupied with a crisis such as war. The Southern Volunteers who had remained in Ireland were to stage an armed uprising in Dublin that would spread throughout Ireland and force the British out. The plan was largely instigated by IRB leaders and opposed (at the last minute) by the leader of the Volunteers, who had been unaware of the proposed insurrection. Only 1200 Volunteers showed up for the rebellion. The opposition within the Volunteers plus the subsequent lack of popular support during the actual uprising reveal the difficulty of employing force in the context of a pluralist society where other options and tactics are available. The events of the Easter Rebellion also reveal how government response to armed insurrection can create overnight support for terrorism where it did not exist previously. The rebellion was put down by the British army within a week, because the uprising was limited to certain occupied buildings in Dublin. The popular support did not materialize until fifteen of the sixteen leaders of the rebellion were executed after secret trials. The executions appeared "hasty, vindictive and cruel,"[23] and additional sympathy was created by the imprisonment of 1800 Volunteers in Wales and by the subsequent hunger strikes of many of the prisoners.

In addition, the British government's decision to pass a conscription bill antagonized the Irish public and created further support for the Republican terrorists. An important non-Republican organization, Sinn Fein, became Republican. It included the only leader of the Easter Rebellion to survive, Eamon de Valera. Although the British banned all Republican groups and jailed their leaders, the Sinn Fein contested most seats in the 1918 general election and won all but four. Its elected members of Parliament refused to take their seats at Westminster and, instead, formed the Dàil Eireann, the National Assembly of Ireland. However, the British government ignored the Sinn Fein and the Dàil. In addition, without the conscription issue of World War I, active support for the Volunteer movement (now known as the Irish Republican Army (IRA) dissolved. Although the polarization of the Irish public and the British government on the nationalist issue provided ideal conditions for terrorism, one key ingredient was missing—the violent act of provocation. As the stalemate was gradually being accepted by the Irish public, a leader of the IRA said: "If this goes on, we'll have to kill someone, and make the bloody enemy organize us."[24]

Britain was most vulnerable to attack through the Royal Irish Constabulary, particularly in the countryside. When sixteen policemen were killed by the IRA, the British responded with their own unofficial terror campaign. Suspected IRA and Republican supporters were shot and full-scale violence spread throughout Ireland. In Ulster, Orangemen set up a Special Ulster Constabulary and proceeded with their own terrorist campaign against the Catholic population. To bolster the Royal Ulster Constabulary, which was having considerable difficulty controlling certain countryside areas from the IRA, the "Black and Tans" were brought in from Britain. Because few native Irishmen were recruited for the Black and Tans and most members were poorly trained, they relied even more than usual on indiscriminate brutality in their war with the IRA. Terrorism quickly became guerrilla warfare, with the British controlling the urban areas and the IRA controlling key areas of the countryside. A stalemate ensued.

The Treaty of 1921: A Legacy of IRA Bitterness

Support for the British military campaign in Ireland diminished rapidly in Britain especially because there appeared to be little support for the massacre that would have been necessary to subdue the IRA.[25] In the 1921 general elections, the Sinn Fein received overwhelming support in the South while the Unionists achieved similar success in Ulster. The British prime minister, Lloyd George, succeeded in passing the Government of Ireland Act, which facilitated the creation of the Irish Free State. As a British dominion, Ireland would become virtually a sovereign state even though its citizens would owe their allegiance to the British king. British troops were to withdraw, and Ireland and England were to relate as equal states. To placate the Unionists, Northern Ireland would be allowed to declare its unwillingness to remain a part of the Irish Free State and would be a part of Britain even though it would have its own regional Parliament—Stormont. Stormont would be officially dependent on the British Parliament at Westminster for the devolution of its executive and legislative power. Also, Northern Ireland would continue to have direct representation at Westminster by retaining its seats in the House of Commons.

Lloyd George met with a delegation from the Dàil in order to obtain a treaty that would allow for the peaceful implementation of the provisions of the

Government of Ireland Act. The "Treaty-men" in the delegation and the Dàil represented the view that the creation of the Irish Free State met the need for self-government while retaining important economic and political ties to Britain. This position was supported by most of the business community and the Roman Catholic hierarchy. The "stepping-stone" position reflected the view that once the Irish Free State came into existence, a republic could peacefully evolve. Underlying this moderate view was the realization that Britain could not be defeated militarily, that the human cost of the continued warfare was simply too high, and that Ulster was at least temporarily a separate problem from the issue of immediate autonomy from Britain. In comparison, the "doctrinaire Republican" view was that nothing short of an Irish republic (composed of every county in Ireland and necessitating total withdrawal of British troops) could be the focus of any peace treaty with Britain.[26]

The key vote, which resulted in a majority of the delegation favoring Lloyd George's proposed treaty, belonged to the IRA leader Michael Collins. He was a legendary hero within the Republican movement because of his ingenuity in eluding capture and the bold but calculated ruthlessness of his terrorist tactics against the British intelligence operations in Ireland. Collins voted for the treaty, primarily because he adhered to the "stepping-stone" view. Collins understood that his position would be deeply resented by many in the IRA and that he was in their eyes a traitor. The fundamental difference between Collins and the doctrinaire Republicans in the IRA appeared to be the unwillingness of the latter individuals to acknowledge that twentieth-century Britain was not nineteenth-century Britain. They clung to the view that Britain was, in fact, being defeated militarily in Ireland and that force was the only effective means to combat British imperialism. It appears, on the other hand, that Collins understood that Britain had the clear military advantage but would use it only when forced against the wall. In effect, the IRA had made their point to a sufficient portion of the British public and political elite that the costs of the traditional imperial ties between England and Ireland were too high, especially in light of the dominion option. The complexity of pluralist politics was understood by Collins; gradual, nonviolent tactics, after a certain point, were more effective in gaining a Republican Ireland than violent tactics. Compromise, not zero-sum ultimatums, was an accepted tactic in the pluralist process. If the "doctrinaire Republican" view had been accepted by Lloyd George, then it was likely that either the Conservative party would have come into power and negated the treaty, or a civil war would have occurred. The fear of civil war and a loss of political power were the reasons for Lloyd George's rejection of the Republican "solution" to the problem of Ireland. Furthermore, if the Irish delegation had not accepted the treaty, then Britain would have stepped up its military campaign against the IRA. To Collins, this was seen as too risky and costly, given the chance to achieve a republic.[27] With regard to the partition of Ireland, Collins felt that Ulster was not economically viable and would have to join the South.[28]

Civil War: The Dénouement of the IRA

The Dàil accepted the treaty sixty-four votes to fifty seven. Along with the Easter Rebellion, this event marked a watershed of unfavorable conditions for the IRA. A majority of the political representatives of the southern Irish public as well as most key interest groups, such as the Roman Catholic church, supported the treaty. Many members of the IRA followed their leader Collins, as did members of other Republican organizations. The split in the Republican movement was further dramatized by Eamon de Valera's denunciation of the treaty and his subsequent leadership of the opposition. The deep and rancorous division over the treaty led inevitably to a civil war. The Irish Free State (IFS) immediately created an official army in cooperation with Britain, and, in 1925, the civil war began. The IRA simply collapsed under the combined impact of the resources of an Irish Free State and Britain. The Catholic church condemned the IRA and removed the right of sacraments from them, so they were never able to gain the popular support required for guerrilla tactics or conventional battle engagements against the IFS army. With the rapidly increasing isolation of the IRA, de Valera ordered the IRA Volunteers "to dump their arms" and stop fighting. It was not unconditional surrender; it was to be a temporary lull, yet it marked the end of the IRA as a major political factor in the, politics of southern Ireland. The Irish government "showed no sudden burst of magnanimity. The army was not demobilized and the swollen intelligence section with policy detectives continued to track down Republicans on the run."[29]

A strong majority of the Irish people backed the IFS. The government party, *Cumann na n Gaeldheal,* handily defeated the Republican party, Sinn Fein, sixty-four to forty-four in the postwar elections. The final blow to the IRA in the South occurred when de Valera left the Sinn Fein and created his own political party the Fianna Fail. He left because he disagreed with a central Republican principle—abstentionism. According to this principle, Republicans refused recognition of the IFS and demonstrated their defiance of Britain by running for elections but not taking their seats in the Dàil.

Thus, another major and legendary Republican leader had abandoned terrorism as a tactic for obtaining an Irish republic. Clearly, de Valera understood that the accessibility of pluralist politics in Ireland and the decline of imperialism as a widespread value in Britain were complementary vehicles for obtaining his Republican goal.[30] After his party came to power in 1932, de Valera introduced a bill to abolish the oath of allegiance to the British crown and to cease payment of land annuities. Britain countered with tariffs on Irish imports that badly hurt the

Irish agricultural interests. At the same time Irish industry now had the protection from British industry that was necessary for its growth. These dramatic moves, in addition to the de Valera-led campaign against the IRA, resulted in key members leaving the IRA to join Fianna Fail and in the arrest of other members. Considerable dissension resulted, and the IRA split into bickering factions. Fundamental disagreements arose concerning the need to develop a revolutionary socialist program versus the need to maintain the traditional nonpolitical role of the IRA. In the midst of the ferment caused by the radical *Saoaire* faction in the IRA, de Valera introduced a constitution that created a new state, Eire (Ireland), in place of the Irish Free State. He also signed the Anglo-Irish agreement with Britain that ended the economic war and allowed Ireland to retain the British treaty ports. Finally, Ireland would be allowed to remain neutral in light of the impending war. Ireland was thus virtually a republic in all but name. Single-handedly de Valera had demonstrated the success of nonviolent tactics.[31]

While de Valera had isolated the IRA in the South, the Royal Ulster Constabulary (RUC) had done the same in the North. Unlike the ambivalent policies of the Fianna Fail toward the IRA, the Unionist-controlled RUC constantly harassed and monitored the IRA. The Protestant majority, which was spread out strategically through most of the counties in Northern Ireland, provided an extensive and reliable intelligence network for the RUC. Since the formal partition of Ireland in 1921, Catholics were, in general, viewed suspiciously as either potential or actual Republicans. The slightest provocation between the two sectarian communities was dangerous because of the Protestant perceptions and their overwhelming military superiority. In addition to the armed RUC, the "Special B Forces" provided an auxiliary police force. The British army also maintained garrisons in Northern Ireland. The RUC acted swiftly when they believed that the IRA was active. In June 1935, for example, the RUC carried out their typical strategy in dealing with the IRA: A sectarian riot occurred on the Orange holiday of July 12, and two men were killed and fifty wounded, so the RUC blocked off Protestant and Catholic areas with barricades and isolated the less populated Catholic enclaves. Then the "orgy of murder, arson, looting, assault, sniping and terror" was allowed to run its course in the Catholic communities.[32] Thus IRA attempts to carry out various terrorist campaigns in the North usually left the indigenous Catholic population exposed to severe retaliation. It was understandable therefore that IRA initiatives did not receive widespread Catholic support.

In the face of the de Valera-imposed isolation of the IRA in the South and the difficulty of maintaining any terrorist momentum in the North, the IRA suffered another major factional split over tactics. Key southern leaders of the IRA felt that an explicitly political nonviolent strategy had to be devised to regain the ever-dwindling support of the Irish public. Northern IRA leaders felt, however, that a bold military strategy in the North was the answer to the IRA doldrums.[33] The factional dispute turned vicious when a military campaign in the North aborted, and the bombing campaign in England resulted in the severe antiterrorist Prevention of Violence Bill of 1939. This bill allowed for a tight control of immigration, the right of deportation, the registration of all Irish in Britain, and the detention of suspects. In light of these dismal failures, IRA traitors became easy scapegoats. Intensive street warfare, kidnapping, and torture tore apart the IRA, and, due to dwindling financial support, the IRA turned to bank robberies. All this turmoil contributed to the growing IRA image of being "little more than the Celtic branch of the Chicago gangsters."[34]

The disarray of the IRA continued after World War II. Disenchanted Republicans abandoned terrorism and formed a political party, *Clan na Poblachta,* that became part of a coalition in the Dàil that ousted de Valera. A Republic of Ireland was declared in 1949. The British government reacted by reiterating that the six northern counties in Ireland were under the control of the Stormont government. Until recently, these events virtually ended the IRA's role as a terrorist organization in the South. With a republic now in existence in the South, all terrorist activity was to be limited to the North. Sinn Fein became the official political wing of the IRA. In spite of these moderate trends, factional disputes continued in the IRA, and electoral support for the Sinn Fein dropped to a barely significant 3 percent.

For southern Ireland the trend toward a republic, which effectively began in 1916, was completed in 1949. There were two Irelands at this point and the overwhelming majority of the southern Irish appeared to accept this fact. This was evident because only the "doctrinaire Republican" organizations, the IRA and Sinn Fein, received insignificant public support in terms of recruitment, money, and votes.[35]

Rapprochement Between the Irish Republic and Britain

By the early 1950s, it was clear the Republic of Ireland had come full circle in terms of its relations with Britain. Irish industry, although hardly as extensive as Britain's, was oriented to the British market, as was Irish agriculture. The fate of the two economies was intertwined as much as it had been during the colonial era. British cultural influence still remained a powerful factor in Ireland. For example, in spite of government attempts to reactivate the Gaelic language, English has remained the chief language of the Irish.

An elaborate communications and transportation network links the two countries, and given the large Irish communities in major British cities, they are well observed and traveled. It is doubtful that the legacy of centuries of British colonialism has disappeared completely, but there is a generation now that has directly experienced only a Republican Ireland. It will be evident later that a very small but significant minority of individuals in the Republic of Ireland still are committed to a "doctrinaire Republican" view. This minority continues to call on what they perceive as the latent sympathies of the public to support Republican or IRA terrorism.

One of the most telling illustrations of the above changes in the South occurred when de Valera (who had returned to office) reopened the Curragh prison in order to carry out the internment of IRA members who were participating in the "border campaign" in the North. In 1956 the IRA had undertaken an extensive terrorist campaign in the North that took most government officials in Ireland and Britain by surprise. The Stormont government responded with the internment of known and suspected IRA members. Using the South as a sanctuary, the IRA had hoped to offset the inevitable loss of men and material in the North with its protected supply in the South. The IRA assumed that de Valera would not agree to internment because of the explicit IRA policy of avoiding violence in the South. If de Valera would not act out of his traditional Republican sympathies then he would, at least, avoid antagonizing the Irish electorate. However, there was little outcry against internment in the South, and the IRA border campaign ended in failure, largely because of the simultaneous internment of IRA suspects in both the North and the South.[36] With the end of the border campaign in 1961, the IRA virtually ceased to be an active terrorist organization until the end of the 1960s.

IRA Factionalism: Tradition Versus Change, IRA Provisionals Versus Officials

During this lull, another major division occurred within the IRA that had profound impact on the course of terrorism in the British Isles—the split between the IRA "regulars" and the IRA "Provisionals." This split was the culmination of a trend that had begun immediately before World War I, when James Connolly, one of the leaders of the Easter Rebellion, advocated a socialist society in the midst of a highly conservative, clergy-influenced Irish society. Socialism was not easily distinguished from communism in the eyes of the Irish Catholic hierarchy; hence both ideologies were strongly opposed.[37] There were other brief attempts to influence the IRA toward socialism, such as the creation of the *Saoaire* movement in the 1930s. These attempts resulted in dissension within the IRA ranks and the more formal hostility of the Catholic church. Nonetheless, it was difficult to ignore the economic hardships that afflicted many Irishmen of the North and the South, in the cities and on the farms. While the worker in the South suffered an extremely low standard of living from the lack of industrial growth, the Catholic worker in the more industrialized North suffered from systematic and blatant discrimination in jobs and housing. Emigration was one solution, but it did not create a favorable environment for the Republican cause. In addition, there was the increasing danger that in the South, the British Labour party or any party that specifically addressed itself to economic problems would win the allegiance of the working class (as was the case in Wales and Scotland). Equally distasteful was the prospect that materialist values would take priority over Republican principles. If this happened, then, from the IRA perspective, an entirely negative chain of events would be set into motion: The main concern for working-class individuals would be obtaining "a good job," buying a house or occupying a low-cost Council house, leisure activities, and maintaining the appropriate trade and tourist relationships with Britain and other countries that facilitated these values. There would be little support for doctrinaire Republican values in Ireland once the working class became similar to the middle class. Stability was essential for the tourism and capital investment that had become so critical to the Irish economy. IRA terrorism created an unfavorable image of Ireland abroad and dangerously aggravated relations with a now largely ignored Northern Ireland.

By the mid-1960s, it became evident that this had in fact taken place in the Republic of Ireland. Economic conditions for working-class and middle-class Catholics, however, were far more complex and confusing in Northern Ireland. The southern economy still had not created the standard of living that existed in the North, but it had improved substantially since the pre-World War II period. Significant economic changes also had occurred in the North. Most importantly, massive welfare legislation introduced by the Labour government in 1945 significantly improved the standard of living of Catholics despite the continuing high levels of unemployment and the systematic discrimination in employment and housing. The British welfare policies had a direct impact on Irish Catholics in the North in spite of the Unionists concerted efforts to interfere with this legislation. The IRA had to cope, therefore, with a Catholic population in the North, which actually benefited economically from the various post-World War II British governments. A prevalent view was that despite Unionist discrimination against them, the Catholics in the North were often in a better situation economically than their working-class Catholic brethren in the South.

These changes in the North and in the South were viewed by certain IRA leaders as the causes of the miserable failure of the "border campaign." The IRA received little support, even in the counties in Northern Ireland that had Catholic majorities and so were easily isolated by the RUC (especially because internment removed many of the experienced IRA regulars and the key leaders). The unexpected lack of popular support in both the North and South was seen by the IRA leader, Cathal Goulding, as a reflection of traditional IRA misunderstanding of the class structure of Northern Ireland and its relationship with British imperialism.[38] The official IRA view now was that the Catholic and working Protestant classes were kept divided by sectarian hate, which was exploited by the British capitalists.[39] A united, socialist, Republic of Ireland would be a critical step in combating this British imperialism. The IRA could gain popular support in the North and the South primarily by exposing this British capitalist exploitation of both Catholic and Protestant sections of the Irish working class. Force would remain a tactic, but other more subtle, political constitutional means would be even more important. Among most of the key IRA leaders, Marxism was essential for understanding and preparing the way for a united Republican Ireland.[40] The inevitable resistance of the traditional and doctrinaire Republicans was immediately evident when they began to ignore policy orders from the Goulding leadership. The latter aggravated the tension by promoting Trinity College students to head the Belfast IRA branch, which was the bastion of the "old-style" Republicans.[41] By 1967, the dissension decimated the ranks of the IRA: In a very candid recollection, Goulding maintained that "we called a meeting of local leadership throughout the country to assess the strength of the movement. We discovered we had no movement."[42] The RUC was also aware of the IRA predicament because, despite its traditional paranoia over the presence of the IRA, it had informed the Stormont government that the IRA was no longer a threat.[43]

Northern Ireland and the Civil Rights Movement:
The Saving Conditions for Terrorism

A turning point in the fate of the IRA occurred when the civil rights movement arose in 1967 in Northern Ireland. The civil rights movement provided further evidence of the basic changes in Northern Ireland, because it was a Catholic middle-class movement.[44] With the U.S. black civil rights movement as a guide, middle-class Catholics organized the Northern Ireland Civil Rights Association (NICRA) and pressed for moderate political and economic reforms. They demanded one-man one-vote with no gerrymanderrying of electoral constituencies (which had been used to ensure Protestant control of government units where Catholic majorities existed), no public housing discrimination, and a repeal of the Special Powers Act (which allowed for the suspension of certain key civil rights), and the disbanding of the "B-Specials", parapolice units.[45] There was no mention of British imperialism and unification with the South. Thus, in addition to the IRA, the nonviolent Republicans of the Nationalist party and the Northern Irish Labour party, Catholics could also turn to the NICRA. With their new "political" orientation, the IRA did not participate in the civil rights movement in a dominant manner. Reform was not opposed by the IRA, even though it might have temporarily weakened sympathies for its own Republican goals, because the lessening of sectarian tension brought about by reforms would contribute to the more immediate goal of the IRA, unification of working-class Protestants and Catholics. The IRA thus had a temporary political vehicle in the NICRA that they could utilize in lieu of the traditional violent tactics.[46]

The civil rights movement had a dramatic impact on the IRA for different reasons, however, because the reaction of the Protestant extremists (the "ultras") to the civil rights movement was violent. The ultras, such as Ian Peasely, saw the civil rights movement as a subterfuge for the IRA and, accordingly, met it with force. Despite the unprecedented attempts by the Unionist leader of the Stormont government, Terrence O'Neill, to meet some of the demands of the civil rights movement with a moderate reform package, the violence escalated.[47]

In the midst of the turmoil, the IRA made a fateful political move that precipitated its formal division. In accordance with the basic Republican principle of abstentionism, IRA policy had always dictated backing only those candidates who refused to take their seats in Stormont or Westminster. This policy was changed when the IRA backed the People's Democracy candidate, Bernadette Devlin, for a seat in the Westminster Parliament, which was traditionally held by a Unionist because of the divisions within the Catholic majority in the constituency. Devlin's victory and her subsequent visibility in the mass media angered both doctrinaire Republicans and the Protestant ultras. The former were angry that the IRA had contributed to Devlin's victory by foregoing abstentionism, whereas the latter were upset at the prospect of the increased political power and unification of the Catholics.[48] In addition, the doctrinaire Republicans maintained that the IRA leadership's new policies had deliberately left Catholics unarmed and at the mercy of the Protestants. To the IRA dissidents, the RUC violent 3-day siege of the Catholic Bogside region of Derry confirmed the necessity for armed resistance. Even the IRA leadership now deliberated about arming the Catholic population, but events moved quickly when the British and Irish governments became directly involved. The rampant violence of August 1969 shocked the Labour government and the British public. British troops were sent into Belfast and Derry to separate the Protestant and Catholic enclaves. The Dublin government established a special cabinet group that was led by hard-line Republicans who favored arming the Catholic population. This policy involved secret financing of the IRA to purchase arms. Distrust between the IRA leadership and the Dublin government (headed by Jack Lynch) resulted in contacts between the latter's representatives and the IRA dissidents. In their anger over the betrayal of traditional Republican principles, and with the apparent promise of financial support, the IRA dissidents formed the Provisional Irish Republican Army (the Provos).[49]

Official Versus Provisional: Tactical Compromise or Violence

Now there were two terrorist organizations, the "official" IRA and the "provisional" IRA, struggling for the allegiance of the Catholic Irish in both North and

South. A significant difference between the two groups is expressed by the euphemism "the officials go to Mass once a year; the Provos once a week": The Provos were in the traditional vein of the Republican movement, which stressed Irish nationalism, Roman Catholicism, conservatism, and terrorism.

Marxism was a "foreign" ideology and anathema to the traditional Irish Catholic. The Provo leadership was more concerned with preserving Irish traditions than with creating a revolutionary and atheistic society. This view of the Republican movement also involved a deep distrust of tactical changes, even in the face of "inglorious failures" such as the border campaign.[50] Despair seemed an important element among many of these individuals: "Mostly they are damaged people—damaged by unemployment, by the long years they spent in confinement, by the sheer hopelessness of their vision of life in Belfast."[51] They clung to the doctrinaire Republican view of the British as the major culprit and chief obstacle to a thirty-two-county Irish republic. In addition, any rapprochement between Catholics and Protestants in Northern Ireland would occur only in the context of a united Ireland, and a united Ireland would occur only if the British army was forced to leave. This view of the Irish Republican movement varied little from Wolfe Tone's view in 1798.

What gave the Provos faith in the utility of terrorism was their assessment that unfavorable conditions for compromise in Northern Ireland were becoming increasingly evident. Even before the bloody clashes of August 1969, Catholics and Protestants had become polarized over the existence of Northern Ireland. In Richard Rose's classic study of Northern Ireland, *Governing Without Consensus,* the survey evidence clearly indicated that while most Protestants accepted the legitimacy of the Stormont government, most Catholics did not.[52] Ireland was the main focus of identity for most Catholics, but the majority of Protestants identified with Britain.[53] National identity, religious affiliation, and support for, or opposition to, Northern Ireland were interdependent, and the complexity of these relationships resulted in a highly divided society. In addition, religion remained a crucial variable in dividing northern Irish society because secularization had not occurred; traditional religious beliefs and regular church attendance, for example, were common among both the Catholic and Protestant communities. Rose's survey revealed a situation that was potentially favorable to terrorism:

> Because Catholics see discord in nationality terms whereas Protestants see it in religious terms, politics in Northern Ireland involved ideologically unrelated politics. Disaffected Catholics claim that the appropriate solution is nationalist—to abolish the Border to create a 32 county Republic of Ireland. Protestants see their regime as a bulwark of religious faith against Catholics within the 6 counties, against the mere Catholic pale, and against the forces of error and darkness everywhere growing stronger in a threatening and increasingly ecumenical world. By their own standards, each side is right, and uncompromisingly so.[54]

To take advantage of the extreme polarization, the Provos had first to deal with the fact that most Catholics were opposed to violence, both in principle and in practice.[55] In particular, it had to be shown that the British army was a violent and repressive tool of the Protestant majority and of British imperialism and that only the Provos could protect the Catholic population from Protestant and British violence. At first, the opposite reaction occurred among Catholics when the British army was brought into Northern Ireland. The British soldiers were welcomed by the Catholic community as protectors against the Protestant mobs and the RUC, which had been invading the Catholic areas since August 1969. At the same time (and at the prodding of the British government), reforms were initiated in housing and with regard to the severe reduction in the police role of the RUC and the disarming of the B-Specials. Still, there were no major political reforms, and the economy visibly suffered as investors were frightened away. Seven percent of the work force was unemployed; the largely Catholic Derry had 12 percent unemployed.[56]

The Provos Become Protectors of Catholics

From the summer of 1970 until the summer of 1972, the British army and government precipitated the very conditions that the Provos desired. Instead of cancelling the provocative Orange Marches in 1970, Stormont and the British government allowed them to take place. Violence erupted during the marches, and the British army resorted to tear gas in a Catholic area of Ballymurphy in Belfast. The effect was traumatic:

> The smoke rolled in clouds down the streets and gulleys of the estate, choking rioters and peaceful citizens in their homes alike. The Army never grasped how "radicalizing" in its effect CS was: but the first Ballymurphy riot . . . was a classic demonstration of the fact. A weapon so general produces inevitably a common reaction among its victims: it creates solidarity where there was none before. One knowledgeable local thought afterwards that those Ballymurphy riots gave the first great boost to the Provisional IRA recruiting campaign.[57]

Also, during these riots an extremely vulnerable Catholic enclave of 10,000 people, known as the Short Strand, was completely isolated in a Protestant enclave of 60,000. Only the Provos were armed and able to come to the defense of the Catholics. Finally, the British army engaged in a massive arms search in a major Catholic ghetto of Lower Falls. All these events were a boost for the Provos in the Catholic community—especially, the image created of the British as imperialist and a tool of the Unionists, and the inherent danger of the IRA official strategy of compromise.

With new support in the Catholic community (particularly in recruitment), the IRA went on the offensive and began to shoot British soldiers.[58] It was extremely difficult to prevent these killings, given the highly visible presence of British soldiers in Catholic areas. The Provos could attack and disappear quickly using "safe houses" where arms could be hidden. By the summer of 1971, in frustration and in response to a highly volatile situation among Protestants who were growing increasingly angry at the impotence of the British army in the face of the IRA terrorist tactics, the British government introduced its most drastic antiterrorist measure—internment. Internment meant that IRA suspects were rounded up throughout Northern Ireland and sent off to prison camps; the reaction in the Catholic community was one of outrage. The mass media covered these events extensively and rumors of torture and indiscriminate brutality against innocents as well as IRA members spread rapidly. A dramatic sign of Provo support in the Catholic community was that, despite the internment, the Provos were actually able to escalate their violence against the British army. The leaders of the Provos appeared in public in Catholic areas to demonstrate the ineffectiveness of internment; they had sufficient support to move publicly and could replace Provo internees with young men from the Catholic ghettos.

The bitterness between the Catholics and the British army reached its peak on "Bloody Sunday" in early 1972. The British army shot and killed thirteen Catholic demonstrators. The Provos responded by gradually shooting thirteen British soldiers in revenge. As long as the British government—partly in response to pressure from the Unionist leadership—resorted to violence, the doctrinaire Republican tactics and goals employed and advocated by the Provos received significant support within the Catholic community. Although the official IRA also used terrorist tactics during this period, their belief in the efficacy of compromise with political groups in order to facilitate a nonsectarian working-class coalition seemed out of place amid the violent polarization of the two religious communities.

Direct Rule, Compromise, and Attempted Political Reform: A Change in British and Provo Strategies

Internment had not worked. Violence had escalated enormously and four times the number of killings took place in the year following internment than had occurred the previous year.[59] The Stormont government, which had pressed so unrelentingly for internment, had miscalculated the Catholic backlash that ensued. Aggressive military tactics of the British army against the IRA in Catholic communities, in the absence of any major political reforms, played directly into the hands of the Provos. When the Stormont prime minister, Brian Faulkner, refused to hand over law-and-order functions to British officials, the British government exercised its prerogative to suspend the Stormont government. Northern

Ireland was now to be ruled directly by Westminster through a secretary of state who would be a member of the cabinet. William Whitelaw was appointed to this post, and he immediately switched the emphasis from military to political tactics in order to end the civil strife. Whitelaw quickly sought to reduce the terrorist battles between the IRA and the British army, and between the IRA and the Protestant paramilitary Ulster Volunteer Force (UVF).

The disentangling began with a truce between the British army and the two wings of the IRA. Whitelaw and other British politicians, such as Harold Wilson, unofficially recognized the Provos by engaging in discussions with Provo leaders concerning the basis for a settlement. The British wanted to return the "government" of Northern Ireland to its inhabitants. The main question was what political structure would this government take. In addition to the withdrawal of the British army and the release of all political prisoners, the Provos demanded that the structure of the government of Northern Ireland be determined by all Irishmen in a thirty-two-county election. The Provos "conciliatory" gesture to the Protestants was a proposal for the adoption of a federal structure in which Ulster was to be a province. Although certain individuals in the Provo leadership may have seriously believed in the feasibility of their proposal, others were surely not so committed.[60] When the inevitable British rejection came, the Provos resumed their bombing campaign.

Since the introduction of internment, Provo terrorism had turned uglier, with the use of highly explosive car bombs in crowded business districts, frequented mainly by Protestants. Even though warnings were issued at the last moment, the slightest mishap would result in disastrous carnage.[61] One of the worst Provo bombings occurred in July 1972 on "Bloody Friday" when eleven civilians died. This incident had followed another Provo truce that brought about face-to-face discussions between the Provo leadership and Whitelaw. News of the truce angered Protestant ultras of the Ulster Defense Association into indiscriminate killings of Catholics. The British response to "Bloody Friday" was the removal of barricades in the "no-go" areas of the Catholic communities of Belfast and Derry. This display of military force was preceded and followed by a series of major political initiatives by the British government concerning a new constitutional government for Northern Ireland. Whitelaw sought out the views of most of the constitutional political parties at the Darlington Conference in the summer of 1972. A British government Green Paper followed, which assured the Protestant majority that Northern Ireland would remain a part of the United Kingdom unless they voted otherwise. To the Catholic minority, the promise of political participation in all aspects of a future government was given. Basic democratic principles would guide the British in facilitating the Northern Irish political parties' attempts to create a constitutional government. A plebiscite, known as the "border poll," was held on the issue of the unification of the two Irelands. Although most Catholics boycotted the plebiscite, 57 percent of the total electorate voted to remain in the United Kingdom.[62] Still, the "Irish dimension" was not ignored, because a Council of Ireland, including representatives of Westminster, Dublin, and Belfast, would meet to discuss any potential changes in the institutional relationships among the three governments. Whitelaw and Westminster intensified the political reform momentum with the Constitutional Act of 1973. This act allowed for a Northern Irish assembly and executive with specific legislative and executive functions. "Power sharing" between Catholics and Protestants would also be institutionalized: The executive had to include representatives other than just majority party members from one of the sectarian communities. In addition, no discriminatory bills would be allowed.[63]

The British political initiatives were cautiously accepted by the two leading parties of the Protestant and Catholic communities, the Brian Faulkner-led Unionists and Gerry Fitt Social Democratic Labour party. The parties representing the extremist positions in the Protestant and Catholic communities rejected the initiatives. Naturally, the Provos opposed the political reforms, seeing them as part of the continuing treachery of the British government. The reforms were seen as superficial and deceptive because they would simply maintain the British-Ulster imperial relationship and inhibit the creation of a united Ireland.[64]

Elections were held in the summer of 1973. The Protestant vote was split between the compromise elements of the Unionist party and the new Loyalist Coalition, which opposed the political reforms. The Catholic vote was divided among three proreform parties. Whitelaw announced a "power-sharing" executive with a Protestant, Brian Faulkner, as chief executive and a Catholic, Gerry Fitt, as chief executive officer.[65] Between mid-1973 and early 1976, various elections were held to ratify informally and formally, the British-inspired, power-sharing formula for a Northern Ireland government. The final result was that the Protestant community rejected the political reforms by supporting both the Loyalist Coalition and a 14-day general strike instigated by the antireform Ulster Workers Association. The power-sharing executive collapsed, the assembly was prorogued, and a subsequent constitutional convention ended in disarray in March 1976.[66] Direct rule from Westminster was introduced for the second time in 4 years.

Provo Reaction to British Reform Tactics

For the Provos, the favorable conditions for terrorism that peaked with internment and "Bloody Sunday" had been seriously eroded during the reform period. Most importantly the Protestant community lost its political hegemony in Northern Ireland when the Stormont government was suspended. Protestant political power had been monolithic, because the Unionist-Orange Lodge connection had constituted a political machine that completely dominated local government and Stormont. The breakup of the Unionist party finally occurred in 1973. There were, in addition, various paramilitary organizations and an Ulster Workers Association, which also represented other factions of the Protestant community. Although many of these political and military organizations formed coalitions against the Catholic community, the British, and the IRA, they remained independent from one another.[67]

The potential now existed, as demonstrated in the power-sharing executive scheme, to form coalitions across sectarian lines. Even though the power-sharing executive had failed, it broke a 50-year tradition of total exclusion of the Catholic community from political power in Northern Ireland. Catholics could at least see the possibility that a vote for a moderate political party, such as the Social Democratic and Labour party, would not be the futile gesture it once was under the Unionist-controlled Stormont government. One of the major roadblocks in developing Catholic allegiance to a Northern Ireland government, the absence of meaningful political participation, was removed, with the possibility of establishing a new constitution and government.

The British government and army still seriously antagonized the Catholic community, especially in sensitive border areas such as Armagh county. However, the attempt to enact concrete political reforms, along with change in British army tactics, complicated the simple view of the British government as a tool of the Protestant supremacists. The British army switched to a low profile in Catholic areas and reduced its numbers from 22,000 soldiers to 14,000. A concerted effort was made, then, to recreate the image (prevalent before 1971) of the British army as "security forces." Finally, the British government undertook a major analysis of the economic plight of Northern Ireland as a first step in the rehabilitation of the rapidly declining economy.

In the face of such dramatic and total policy changes, the Provos undertook a major tactical shift in its relations with the British by initiating a long-term truce with the British army. The two short truces that occurred in 1973 were overshadowed by the truce that began in 1975 and is still in effect. In return, the British army gradually released most of the internees who had not been convicted of any violent crimes but were suspected IRA members. On occasion, Provos and British soldiers still shot at one another, but the decline in the number of British soldiers killed was immediately evident.

The Provos were clearly in a dilemma with their new policy. As doctrinaire Republicans, they were committed to the use of force against the British, yet political realities demanded more. In addition to truces, the Provos adopted an elaborate socioeconomic policy. Some viewed this policy as socialist,[68] but in the light of public statements by key Provo leaders, the program was essentially populist.[69] This change from purely terrorist or military tactics to a "revolutionary" vision of the Republic of Ireland was designed to offset the Provo image of that of a group of simpleminded and violent romanticists who were essentially fascists.

The paradox was that with the truce, the Provo role as the armed protectors of the Catholics in the North was unnecessary. Allegiance to the Provos could now be rechanneled toward the various constitutional political parties, especially the Socialist Democratic and Labour party. This party was led by Gerry Fitt, who had established his credentials within the Catholic community during the violence of the civil rights movement and through various firm political actions against the Unionists during the existence of the Stormont government. Fitt challenged the Provos in their area of strength—the Catholic working-class communities.[70] Another aspect of the Provo dilemma was that although they did develop an elaborate political, economic, and social policy for all of Ireland, they remained terrorists. As such, it was extremely difficult for them to compete with constitutional political organizations that were able to work within the British instigated political reform. Ironically, it was the Provisional truces with the British that facilitated British attempts to create political reform, because the British army could reduce its antagonizing presence in the Catholic community while the British government could concentrate on reform initiatives.

The Provisional leadership was also aware that its strength in the North depended substantially on its image in the South. As long as the Provos were perceived as "protectors" of the Catholics in the North, then the Fianna Fail-led Dublin government retained its ambivalent relationship with the Provos. As has been the case with other *Taeoischs* ("prime ministers") in the South, Jack Lynch resented and distrusted the presence of a terrorist organization, especially one that did not recognize the legitimacy of the popularly based constitutional government of the Republic of Ireland.[71] As long as the Protestants and the British in the North appeared to threaten the Catholics, then it was difficult to ignore the traditional sympathy aroused by the doctrinaire Republicanism of the Provos. Periodic restrictions were placed on the Provos, as was the tradition with previous IRA organizations, but as long as their violence was restricted to the North and as long as an imminent or actual threat to the Catholics existed, the IRA was given a free rein in the South. Moreover, open violent clashes in the North led to both overt and covert financial support from the Dublin government and the business community. Thus the Dublin government had to contend with the danger of legitimizing a nonconstitutional or terrorist organization in its midst at the risk of antagonizing the British and jeopardizing economic lifelines to Britain.

Provisional support peaked in the South when internment and "Bloody Sunday" in the North led to a covert attempt on the part of key cabinet members of the Lynch government to arm the Catholic population in the North. The notorious "arms trials" of 1973 resulted in the acquittal of the participants who had illegally imported arms into Ireland. Despite the denials of Lynch, the clear impression was that his government had committed an illegal act. Lynch dismissed the cabinet members who had instigated the arms deal. One of the dismissed, a major Irish politician, Kevin Bolard, created a new political party that openly supported doctrinaire Republicanism. Once the British switched to a policy of political reforms, however, the "arms trial" took on a different perspective. An unemotional assessment of what might have occurred if the "hardliner" or pro-Provisional view had become the policy of the Irish government was that a devastating war would have broken out that the South would not have been able to win. The economic cost would have been astronomical, given the Republic of Ireland's fragile economic base and near total economic dependency on Britain. At least one important Irish politician who held this view, Connor Cruise O'Brien, became a cabinet member in the coalition government that replaced Lynch's Fianna Fail government.[72] Although the Lynch government had begun the crackdown on the Provos by arresting their leadership, the subsequent Cosgrove government would prove even less tolerant especially after the Provos began their indiscriminate bombing campaign in England and in the Republic of Ireland, as well as accelerating the sectarian violence in the North.

The Provisionals appeared at first to be disoriented by the British-initiated political reforms, but with the stalemate brought about by Protestant opposition to the political reforms, violence remained the main weapon. Only the targets would change. Civilian casualties remained high throughout the extended truce period, because the Provos and Protestant paramilitary groups (for example, the Ulster Defense Association, UDA) carried out a bloody policy of mutual retaliation. A shooting in the Catholic community automatically meant the Provos would randomly shoot a Protestant in revenge. The brutality increased as "kneecapping" and "hooding" were introduced by both sides.[73]

As the violence escalated in Northern Ireland, it spread into England and southern Ireland. At first only military barracks or facilities were bombed by the Provos and possibly other IRA factions, but then indiscriminate bombings in crowded public places followed. Favorite targets were pubs, restaurants, underground stations at rush hour, and historic sites such as the Tower of London.

This change in tactics was based on the assumption that the British and Irish would ignore the Provos as long as the terrorism and violence were restricted to Northern Ireland and British troops were not a primary target. By spreading violence into England and Ireland, the Provos could force the British government to withdraw its army and let the Protestants and Catholics decide their own fate. If the costs of continuing were made too high, the British might choose to wash their hands of Ireland as they had done in Palestine and Cyprus.

The reaction in Britain and the Republic of Ireland was the opposite; stiff antiterrorist acts were passed that facilitated the arrest and detention of terrorist suspects and severely restricted the movement in and out of Britain that had been traditionally so important for the IRA. The Provisionals responded by attempting to assassinate their most vocal British opponents including Conservative members of Parliament Hugh Fraser and Edward Heath. Although most of these attempts failed, there were casualties. The most recent strike at British or Irish political leadership took place in the summer of 1976 when the British ambassador to Ireland was blown up in his car. Although the Provos deny that they were responsible for the assassination of the British ambassador as well as for many other terrorist acts in England, they are usually identified with these acts, and the result is increased antagonism from many of the British and Irish.

Further Factionalization of the IRA and
Terror in the Catholic Communities

At a minimum, the Provos had to retain the general sympathy of the Catholic community in the North in order to remain a viable terrorist organization. Internecine warfare among the various factions of the IRA was a major obstacle to retaining this sympathy, especially after the British army resorted to a low profile in the Catholic communities. Although the "official" IRA and the Provos still engaged in isolated confrontations, the major clash occurred between the IRA "officials" and a new splinter group, the Irish Republic Socialist Party. This group maintained that the "officials" were not sufficiently socialist. The bickering turned into violent confrontations mainly in the Catholic areas. According to Gerry Fitt, "the feud between the rival Republican movements has brought a reign of terror of the type never inflicted by any of the loyalist (Protestant) paramilitaries."[74]

Many innocent bystanders were killed or injured in these IRA factional conflicts and in IRA engagements with the British army and the Protestant paramilitary groups, which alienated many in the Catholic community. For similar reasons, many were alienated from terrorism in Protestant communities. In the summer of 1976, massive rallies were held in Belfast by Catholic and Protestant mothers protesting the accidental killing of three children. Although the Provos have traditionally dismissed these protests as British-inspired,[75] it is difficult to dispute their importance as a barometer of IRA support in the Catholic community since the British have adopted their low profile. It is likely that antiterrorist protests will continue and possibly increase as long as IRA factional disputes and sectarian revenge bombing and killing continue. Terrorist acts against the leaders of the antiterrorist movement will likely alienate the Catholic and Protestant community even further. The recent attempts to assassinate some of the leaders of the women's peace movement and the mistaken shooting of an innocent woman and her daughter reflect the desperation of the current Provo strategy.

Current British Policy Toward Provos and Other Terrorists

As long as "an acceptable level of violence" continues, attrition and exhaustion will be the main problem facing the Provos and the other paramilitary groups. Max Hastings, who has been a sensitive observer of British policies in Northern Ireland believes that "In effect they [British officials] are saying that four or five deaths a week for the next decade are politically less alarming than the several hundred deaths that might well take place in a matter of months if the British government attempted to impose any drastic solution on Ulster.[76]

The policy of an acceptable level of violence, according to British Prime Minister James Callaghan, apparently will grind down the terrorists and the "Irish troubles, as a heath fire will in time burn itself out."[77] This policy is particularly threatening to the Provos who cannot point to a discriminatory and Protestant-dominated political system, because there is no such system with direct rule; there is only an inconspicuous and impartial secretary of state. It is more diffi-cult for the Provos to portray themselves as protectors of the Catholic commu-nity, because the British army now has a low profile there, and this, in turn, has caused antagonism in the Protestant community. Most of the violence that occurs is instigated by the Provos and the other paramilitary groups. So to a large extent, the Provos will be "protecting" the Catholic community from Provo-related vio-lence; the conditions for further terrorism will hardly be favorable once the gen-eral population reaches this conclusion.

Provo Misperceptions of Britain and North and South Ireland

There were two occasions when IRA terrorism contributed to major changes in British policies toward Ireland. The effective IRA guerrilla struggle in 1920 was an important factor in the events leading to the creation of the Irish Free State. The IRA, particularly the Provos, also played a central role in the violent events that led to the suspension of the Stormont government and the constitutional attempts to include the Catholic population in a new government of Northern Ireland. In both these instances, the conditions for terrorism were favorable. It was essential that British policies alienate most of the Catholics so that the IRA could secure "safe-houses," maintain a constant supply of recruits, and obtain financial support from Catholics in Ireland and the United States. The actions of the Black and Tans in 1920 and the British army in 1970 severely antagonized the IRA host communities and consequently created the necessary conditions for support there. Except for these two major exceptions, the trend of British policies toward Ireland since the Home Rule Movement began in the late nine-teenth century has been to avoid antagonizing the Irish, Protestant and Catholic, by withdrawing from direct or highly visible participation in Irish political affairs.

The creation of the Irish Free State and the North Irish province allowed the British to avoid constant involvement in Ireland until the late 1960s. The trend in British-Irish relations then (even with Northern Ireland a part of the United Kingdom), has been for the various British governments to leave Ireland alone as much as possible. This policy weakened a necessary condition for IRA terrorism—the perception by Irish Catholics that the British wanted to maintain imperial control of Ireland. The remaining condition for the imperial view of Britain was Northern Ireland. However, once the British government made it clear that any government in Northern Ireland had to include Catholics, it became evident that Britain was no longer ignoring and antagonizing Irish Catholics in the North by exclusively supporting Irish Protestants. And, there was the strong sentiment in Britain that the question of a united Ireland was ultimately a problem to be settled by the Irish North and South and not the British. If the basic condition for IRA terrorism has been eroded seriously since 1971, then why does the IRA (especially the Provo faction), persist? The answer involves the misperceptions by the IRA of contemporary Ireland, Britain, and the international economic environment.

First, the Provo view of Irish and British politics is essentially the same as that of the nineteenth-century Fenians. They feel that Britain is imperialistic and that therefore its people and leaders are not to be trusted. In their view, Britain is still an eighteenth-century colonial society determined to drain Ireland in a neomercantilist fashion of its economic growth potential.[78] The various Dublin governments and the industrial elites, out of crude self-interest, have cooperated with the foreign (including British) industries that were economically exploiting Irish industry.

Second, there is the Provo view that reform or compromise, which is basic to pluralist politics, is unacceptable because it nullifies the sacrifices made by the IRA.[79] In effect, once IRA soldiers are either killed or captured, only complete victory in the form of an immediate thirty-two-county Republican Ireland is acceptable.

Third, there is the curious anomaly that the British and Dublin governments are not quite constitutional in their dealings with the IRA. "Blatantly undemocratic" attempts to jail the IRA leadership during the reform period beginning in 1973 are decried by the Provos.[80] This reflects a seriously distorted view of counterinsurgency tactics in the face of terrorist-inspired crises.

Fourth, while it is admittedly difficult to establish which one of the factions of the IRA, Protestant paramilitary organizations, or even British counterinsurgency operatives are active in any particular terrorist act, the Provos insist that the Irish and British press associate them duplicitously with indiscriminate bombings. The Provos deny that they unduly jeopardized innocents with their car bombings in public places, and they are angry when the mass media in Ireland and other pluralist societies then depict the Provos as a terrorist organization.

The truth according to Provo leader Sean MacStiofain is that adequate warnings were always given but that they were surreptitiously ignored by British officials or their supporters, and that the mass media in Ireland, Britain and the United States in particular do not report the truth when casualties occur. Part of the self-righteousness of the Provo view of casualties rests on the belief that they are too well organized to make the mistakes that injure innocents on the scale presented in the mass media—and that British instigated "black operations" are behind much of the violence. In effect, British agents and their tools, the Irish government, actually plan for innocents to suffer in order to discredit the IRA.[81]

Fifth, there is an insistence that the British and Irish publics perceive their nations as eighteenth-century colonial entities. In reality, as indicated in Britain and Ireland by the overwhelming majority votes supporting entry into the European Economic Community, both countries have concluded that a decrease in their respective sovereignty or independence is the price of potential economic growth. However, the Provos opposed Ireland's entry into the EEC because it would merely strengthen Britain's control of Ireland. What the Provos perceive as imperialism and colonialism most people in Britain and Ireland perceive as mutually beneficial economic interdependency. Provos fail to realize that nationalism can assume different meanings. Many southern Irish value their standard of living and physical security to such an extent that they are willing to define nationalism as a republic of twenty-six rather than thirty-two counties, in order to avoid sacrificing themselves or any of their children in a bloody and full-scale civil war. Furthermore, the disruption to the Irish economy just as it is beginning to produce a decent standard of living would be catastrophic.

Sixth, the Provos fail to acknowledge that the territorial and emotional bases for nationalism can change. By 1949, it was clear that a republic existed in name and fact throughout most of Ireland. Only the six counties of Northern Ireland remained as a motivating force for the existence of the IRA. But once the Stormont government was abolished, and the British were determined that a pluralist democracy be the foundation of any future government in Northern Ireland, then the Provos again were placed in the position of advocating violence on the basis of their minority definition of Irish nationalism.

Seventh, there is the Provo failure to recognize the depth of the feelings of the majority of the Protestant community and the widespread support their feelings have in Britain. According to the Provos, Northern Ireland came into existence in the seventeenth century because of British imperialism, and the subsequent treaties and acts of Parliament involving the creation of the province of Northern Ireland merely ratified this original imperialist event. That the majority in Northern Ireland were Protestants was not relevant because Northern Ireland was an aritficial creation of British imperialism. Also, Irish Protestants were not indigenous Irish—that is, Irish Catholics, in spite of 3 centuries of Irish ancestry. Thus, the Provos dispensed with the link between the majority view and principles of self-determination within Northern Ireland. But the problem is that Ulster Protestants, the British, and many Irish in the South have not: because most of Northern Ireland (the four eastern counties) has been distinctively Protestant Irish for over 3 centuries, it is difficult to convince these people that they are colonial usurpers.

Provos: The Revolt of the Traditionalists

Why then do the Provos insist on using terrorism in the face of such unfavorable conditions? There is no questioning the sincerity of most individuals who join the Provos, because the physical and emotional costs are enormous. Given that the economic, social, and political structures of Ireland, North and South, and the relationship between Ireland and Britain have changed drastically, it is likely that these changes are a significant element in the formation of the Provo view. Most Provos want an Irish society based on a mid-nineteenth-century Fenian view: an Irish island (a republic) of Gaelic speakers who could thumb their noses at the English because they would be *totally* independent of England politically, socially, and economically.[82] Instead, the Provos live in a twenty-six-county Ireland with English as the dominant language, an English-based judicial system, a British-focused economy, and a British-dependent destiny. The difference between mid-nineteenth-century Ireland and contemporary Ireland is that the majority in the Republic of Ireland have themselves decided to live with the above picture of the Irish republic. There have been definite rewards attached to this vision of Ireland, based in large part on values associated with a pluralist industrial culture, such as political choice and urbanism. There is also acceptance of the economic fact that Ireland has few natural resources, a small population, and little indigenous capital, and that dependency on larger national and international markets is the price most countries are willing to pay in order to achieve the high standard of living associated with advanced industrial society.

According to a prominent historian of the IRA, J. Bower Bell, most of its members have been "steeped in their own history, traditionalists to the core; Irish Republicans have misinterpreted the past, selected inappropriate tactics, and applied a useless strategy."[83]

A History of the German Student Movement and the Birth of the Baader-Meinhof Group

The history of the IRA is long and complex, dating back to the early seventeenth century. An Irish Republican (nationalist) movement was nearly continuous from 1798 to 1976 and provided a consistent rationale for the Fenian and IRA terrorists from the mid-nineteenth century until today. In contrast, the history of the Baader-Meinhof Group (BMG) is far shorter and considerably less complex. The Baader-Meinhof Group came into existence only in 1968. The conditions that facilitated its growth can be traced to those of the original German student movements of the early nineteenth century, although, unlike in the history of the IRA, these conditions were not continuous; there were long periods during which the student movements were nonexistent or politically docile. Specifically, the student ideological terrorists of nineteenth-century Germany have an even more truncated history than the student movements that exhibit many of the characteristics of the BMG. The main thrust of the following history of the German student movements will be to delineate the conditions that both turned these movements to terrorism and away from it. With a few major exceptions, the student ideological terrorists have been isolated and defeated by the various German governments and their police forces, in large part because these terrorists have had little popular support. The German student terrorists had a communal experience and a commitment to traditional or romantic values that were inconsistent with the dominant values of the middle and working classes of their particular society. Because, like the nineteenth-century student terrorists, the BMG is committed to values that are anachronistic or romantic, their terrorism can be seen as the revolt of traditionalists.

The Foundations for Contemporary Ideological Terrorism: The Nineteenth-Century German Student Movements

Student movements in the multitude of German states prior to the nineteenth century were based primarily on immediate self-interests such as housing and financial support. The Napoleonic invasion and occupation of the German states politicized the students: They first fought Napoleon's armies, and then embraced many of the values that the French Revolution and Napoleon had championed. Nationalism (involving the unification of the German states) and democratic reforms (involving popularly elected governments) were the specific goals of the original student movements. Yet, many of the liberal values associated with broad democratic reform were ignored and even opposed by the Universal German Students' Association in 1817. This student association, or Burschenschaft, replaced many of the once dominant and apolitical aristocratic fraternities. Its members supported a religious conception of German nationalism, a united Germany that they would call the Christian German Republic. The Burschenschaft had an authoritarian organizational structure. Terrorism in the form of assassinations was seen as a key tactic necessitated by the conspiratoral organization of those who opposed democratic reforms and German nationalism. According to this student association, a particularly devious group opposed to democratic reform and nationalism was the Jews, whom they accused of conspiring with Napoleon against Germany because they had supposedly avoided service in the Prussian army. Anti-Semitism, conspiracy, and terrorism, therefore, were characteristics of the original German student movement.

An advantageous condition for the Burschenschaft was that it was the only existing national organization (facilitating its communications and movement throughout the German states). Also, the center for this movement was in the more provincial areas such as the University of Jena, which had a tradition of liberalism and student activism.[84]

Conditions were favorable for terrorism in the early nineteenth century because of certain historical events and the structure of German society. Napoleon had redefined the boundaries of certain German states in order to create new entities, such as the Rhineland Confederation. This introduced the restructuring of German states on the basis of a common identity, or *Volk*.[85] Because the victories of Napoleon's armies over the German states, including Prussia and Austria, had been attributed in large part to French nationalism, many among the German students and the middle class reasoned that the German people could resist foreign invasions only if a German nation-state existed.

Liberal reforms, most particularly representational government, had become popular among students at the end of the eighteenth century primarily because of the American and French revolutions and the success of the constitutional monarchy in Britain. Most of the German states still had an absolutist monarchy with feudal laws governing relationships between the aristocrats on the one hand and the burghers and peasants on the other. Property rights especially favored the aristocracy politically and economically. For members of the Burschenschaft, the presence of absolutist monarchical and feudal socioeconomic structures were directly to blame for the military weakness of the various German peoples in comparison with the French.

Many in the middle class and among university students believed that through the "wars of liberation" against France the goals of a united Germany and a liberal democratic government would be attained. The patriotic experience of defeating Napoleon would awaken Germans to the necessity of German nationalism. The Prussian monarch also had promised a constitution based on "a more just social order." However, even though there was a brief period of liberal reform in Prussia during the Napoleonic period, the defeat of Napoleon brought about a reactionary atmosphere.[86] In particular, Prussia aligned itself with two of the most conservative states in Europe, Russia and Austria. The "Holy Alliance" of the major European countries was designed primarily for military cooperation against any liberal or reformist movements in the member countries.

Historically it appeared that the polarization of major segments of German society had occurred; both nationalism and liberalism had motivated many Germans in the war against Napoleon, but most of the controlling political elite in the German states reverted to a pre-Napoleonic view of German society and consequently opposed these values.[87] Thus, the presence of a disillusioned middle class from which the Burschenschaft recruited its student members represented an important, but still only potential, source of a broad-based support for terrorism. (Aristocratic students had turned to the more fashionable student *Corps.*)

The initial tactics of the Burschenschaft included mass rallies, the largest of which was held at Württemberg in 1817, and which ended in the burning of books written by reactionaries.[88] The violent element in the Burschenschaft was epitomized in one of its leaders, Karl Follen. He adopted a distinctive dress style including long hair, beard, black velvet coat, and dagger. Follen believed that the redemption of the German nation could be accomplished by a direct act of will.[89] In the face of mounting government persecution, Follen maintained that there was "nothing immoral or illegal in the pursuit of liberty; one should be prepared to die violently in this pursuit."[90] Other more moderate elements in the student movement concentrated on drafting a German constitution that could serve as a model for the various German states and a united Germany and tried to win the support of certain German princes who were favorably disposed to their goals. Although only a small minority were committed to the "gruesome ritual of the death wish, the terrorism and the heroism of the first student-movement," they were sufficient in number to undertake dramatic assassination attempts.[91] The attempt to kill the president of the state of Wiesbaden failed, but a German ally of the Russian czar was assassinated.

The Metternich-inspired German governments reacted swiftly with antiterrorist laws such as the Karlsbad decrees. The repression was severe; professors perceived as sympathetic to the terrorists were expelled from the university, while other sympathizers were forced into exile. Rigid censorship and the curtailment of freedom of speech accompanied the forced abandonment of the Burschenschaft.[92] Both the German student movement and its terrorists dissipated quickly after 1820, and, with a few exceptions, little was heard from them until 1848.

Why were the Burschenschaft terrorists so easily defeated, even though a potentially supportive middle class existed and the enemy, an oppressive aristocratic elite, was both highly visible and monolithic? There had been a severe economic recession following the wars of liberation because of the influx of English manufactured goods.[93] The policy of free trade of the land-based aristocracy was not supported by the urban middle class. The latter needed tariff protection because much of its wealth was tied to the emerging urban-centered industries not yet competitive with British industries, whereas the former needed free access for its agricultural products in Britain and other nations. Many of the political and economic values of the middle class were thus being slighted by the German governments, and there appeared little hope for any immediate change in these conservative policies, given the strength of the monarchist regimes in Prussia and Austria.

Despite these conditions, the failure of the student terrorists is partly attributable to the fact that the population was still predominantly rural and generally not sympathetic to urban middle-class and working-class values. Also, intense opposition came from the bureaucratic and military elites in the German states, which were still dominated by aristocrats, particularly in Prussia where the Junkers symbolized these relationships. In addition, the European environment was hostile to terrorism, particularly since the formation of the Holy Alliance in 1815. The Russian czar and Metternich were particularly cautious and aggressive toward liberal leaning-states such as Württemberg. As long as they remained on favorable terms with Prussia, Russia and Austria could exert considerable influence in the smaller German states.

Although these structural factors undoubtedly inhibited middle-class support for the student terrorists, an equally critical and unfavorable condition was the romanticist image of these terrorists. The student terrorists appeared too deeply committed to romanticist and idealist values to realize that these values were largely incompatible with the liberalism with which many of the middle class identified. The middle class was primarily concerned with concrete and immediate political and economic reforms, while the student terrorist as a romanticist was

> always preoccupied with distant goals whose realization transcends and defies the limitations of time and space. Romanticism at its best offers the sublime spectacle of a prodigious quest of the religious and metaphysical meaning of life, nature and art. At its worst it plunges its protagonists into a chaotic world of shapeless phantasms and hapless meanings.[94]

Even though the student terrorists and the middle class held certain goals in common, they were separated by radically different visions of the ideal society.

In addition the appearance of many of the terrorists, such as Follen with his beard, long hair, cloak, and dagger, was alien to most middle-class sensibilities. Generational bitterness also characterized many of the student terrorist relationships with the older middle class.[95] Although German romanticism and idealism affected the middle class in general, it seemed to have had a radicalizing impact primarily on students. Thus, the fanaticism of the student terrorists was threatening to both the aristocracy and the moderate elements of the middle class, student and nonstudent alike. The inability of the student movement to take advantage of the middle-class sympathy for their goals was dramatically illustrated in the 1848 rebellion in Austria. The polarization of the conflict between the middle class and the reactionary Hapsburg monarchy resulted in a full-scale rebellion. Students, the middle class, and workers all combined militarily to take control of Vienna. Metternich, the symbol of German antiliberalism and antinationalism, had to flee Austria in the wake of the successful insurrection. But,

as discussed earlier, the radical element of the student movement quickly alienated both the middle-class and working-class participants in the revolutionary
government that controlled Vienna. Once the solid front dissipated, the military
forces of the monarchy quickly regained control.[96]

Austria remained essentially an autocratic society. The rebellious events
in Austria in 1848 were repeated throughout much of Europe. In Berlin, the rebellion was also defeated, but the Prussian monarch then introduced a constitution that partially satisfied the demands for liberal reform.[97] Between 1848 and
1870 the call for more liberal reforms was largely muted as Prussia, led by the
"Iron Chancellor" Bismarck, forged the unification of most of the German states
and peoples through economic and military means. Until the post-World War I
period, the German student movement remained quiet.

German student movements like the Burschenschaft clearly played an important role in pushing for liberalism and nationalism periodically during the
first half of the nineteenth century. The student terrorists, however, had a less
effective impact in promoting these goals. Undoubtedly, it was their terrorism
that brought about the reactionary Karlsbad decrees, which buttressed the autocratic monarchies. Still, the student terrorists had set a violent precedent that
could be linked to the more extensive and more successful 1848 rebellions in
Berlin and Vienna.[98] The limited democratic reforms that resulted in a constitutional monarchy in Prussia indirectly paved the way for a united Germany because the more liberal Rhineland states could at least see liberalizing tendencies
in Prussia, unlike what they saw in Austria.

One of major impacts of this original student movement was on the early
twentieth-century youth movements. The latter movements were characterized
by many of the romantic social values that characterized the former movement.
However, the German middle class moved steadily away from this romantic
vision of German society, as urban, industrial socioeconomic structures and an
extensive political party system developed rapidly. These changes in German
society from the first half of the nineteenth century to the initial three decades
of the twentieth century were so extensive that the student movements in the
latter period played an insignificant role in Germany even though the conditions
for terrorism were near ideal.[99]

Weimar Germany: Student Movement Subservience to
Nonstudent Ideological Terrorists

By the end of World War I, Germany was in a state of chaos. The Second German
Empire had dissolved with the abdication of the kaiser. Extreme polarization of
major social groups existed in the midst of the ensuing political vacuum. In Berlin and other major cities, the dominant group was the radical workers organiza-

tions, whereas in the rural areas of East Prussia, it was the Junker aristocracy, and in the towns in the southwest, the Catholic conservatives. Further, in each area, there were groups ideologically opposed to the dominant one.[100] On top of the deep political polarization, there was continued economic hardship. Also, war-embittered military units and individual soldiers started to return from the battlefronts. Terrorism from both the radical Left and Right and large-scale rebellions, which could be effective as long as the police and military remained disoriented, occurred throughout Germany.[101] However, the terrorist organizations, although they included individual students, were not student movements. Even though civil order was eventually restored by the German army[102] and the Social Democratic party, terrorist groups such as the Vehme continued periodic assassinations of prominent political leaders. Right up to 1932 and the creation of the Third Reich, Germany was rarely stable politically and economically.[103] The polarization of key segments of the German population was evident in the multiplicity of political parties, which represented nearly every significant cleavage.

In terms of using terrorism as a political tactic, this period was a critical illustration of the need to employ constitutional techniques as well in order to obtain political goals. The short history of Adolph Hitler and his National Socialist Workers party reflects this necessity. A combination of the disruptive tactics of terrorism and the intimidation of opponents by a private army alone had not worked for Hitler,[104] yet these tactics combined with constitutional measures involving a political party ultimately proved successful in the pluralist industrial society of Weimar Germany. Political organization was critical because the existence of public support for radical political goals was most convincingly demonstrated through elections. Once Hitler established the legitimacy of his Nazi party, he dramatically increased the likelihood that his radical vision of German society would be partly accepted by, and partly forced on, the German people. In her classic work on totalitarianist violence, Hannah Arendt demonstrated the crucial interplay of terrorism and constitutional tactics that ultimately paved the way for the Third Reich.[105]

Students were absorbed into the more broad-based and better organized nonstudent ideological movements in part because they lacked the ability to forge such political movements themselves. The university experience still was limited to a small percentage of the public, and because students were together for a limited time, organizational membership was unstable. Both Hitler and Lenin viewed with disdain radical terrorist movements such as those led by students. They were seen as idealistic, ineffective, and, worst of all, counterproductive to revolution. From their perspective, the student experience was far too limited to allow these individuals to communicate effectively with the segments of the public that were needed to promote a revolution.

For the first half of the twentieth century, there were virtually no effective student terrorist movements in Europe, although terrorism was an important and effective tactic in the hands of such paramilitary political organizations as the parties in Austria, Germany, and Italy. Throughout the 1940s and 1950s West German students generally were characterized as the "skeptical generation" who were largely apolitical.[106] Clearly World War II, the allied occupation, and the Cold War had a profound and unfavorable impact on student movements in general and even more so on student terrorists.

The Division of German Society and the Demise of Major Conditions for Terrorism

Although some observers of post-World War II Germany might argue about the depth of cultural change that took place, no one disputes the fact that drastic structural changes occurred. These resulted in the virtual disappearance of the conditions essential to terrorism that had existed with the autocratic role of the post-Napoleonic period and led to the "polarized pluralism" of the Weimar Republic. As discussed above, in these earlier periods, a major segment of the German population became alienated and, consequently, susceptible to terrorism. The persistence of these conditions throughout the pre-World War I and Weimar periods was largely a result of the dominant position of Prussia, which played a decisive role because of the size of its largely rural-based, conservative Protestant population, its domination of the bureaucratic and military elites, and its opposition to the goals of the centrist (primarily Catholic) and leftist political parties.[107]

The importance of Prussia was abolished when, between 1945 and 1948, large regions of eastern Prussia were incorporated into Poland while the rest formed the core of a new country, the German Democratic Republic (GDR). While East Germany (GDR) continues to have an influence on the politics of West Germany, Prussia per se is no longer a factor.[108] More directly for student terrorism, the issue of the two German states has not been a viable one for mobilizing the population or organizing terrorist acts because the East German student movements have been directly under the authoritarian control of the government and Communist party.

Allied Occupation and the Rise of a Stable Political Party System

World War II, the elimination of Prussia as a distinctive political force, and the onset of the Cold War were crucial factors in the evolution of the political party system in Germany. East Germany quickly became a de facto one-party system, while West Germany settled into a stable two-and-one-half party system. Four important sources of potential opposition to the West German government were mitigated quickly. First, the creation of the GDR meant that there were approximately equal numbers of Catholics and Protestants in West Germany.[109] Second, the urban-rural cleavage declined in importance because West Germany consisted of the predominantly urban regions of Germany. Third, many of the conservative-nationalist parties were discredited because of their identification and cooperation with the Nazi regime. Fourth, at the other ideological extreme, the Communists were tainted by their identification with the Soviet-imposed dictatorial regime in East Germany.[110]

In addition, the occupation powers turned to the ideologically moderate politicians and community leaders for guidance in reestablishing the party system in West Germany.[111] Extremist parties were not permitted to form initially, which allowed the members of the former Catholic Centrist party to organize a nondenominational Christian Democratic party (CDU) consisting of a coalition of groups from the moderate center to the conservative Right, and a Bavarian regional party, the Christian Socialist Union (CSU). The socialist Social Democratic Party (SPD), which had maintained its organization throughout the Third Reich, also was allowed to resume active party politics. The third group that played a significant role in the establishment of a stable political party system in Western Germany was the Free Democratic Party (FDP). Like the CDU, this party was ideologically moderate to conservative. These three political parties dominated the initial elections and, consequently, played a central role in drafting the Basic Law, the constitution for West Germany.[112] The Basic Law established a federal system with considerable decentralization of political power. Because the state, or Länder, boundaries were restructured, no one Länder could dominate as Prussia had under the previous constitutional arrangements.[113] Another critical provision insisted on by the Allies was the need for a party to obtain at least 5 percent of the vote in order for it to have representation in the lower house, the Bundestag.[114] This seriously limited the growth of the small splinter political parties that had plagued the Weimar party system. There were other provisions (many added subsequently) that were essentially designed to enhance the stability of the executive without making him too autonomous from a parliamentary majority[115] and to discourage further the formation of extremist or splinter parties.

It was difficult originally to assess the stability of the new party system itself apart from the presence of the perennial chancellor from the CDU party, Konrad Adenauer. He was a dominant political figure with apparent widespread personal popularity among the electorate. Still, the coalition majorities that were prevalent throughout much of Adenauer's rule were cohesive enough to pass crucial legislation (especially in the economic area). Beginning in 1953, the SPD opposition gradually modified its socialist goals in order to overcome its image as a predominantly working-class-oriented party. In effect, the SPD after 1959 became a "catchall" party and attempted to appeal to the broadest spectrum of the electorate.[116] This move to the center is reflected in the SPD campaign policy slogan "as much competition as possible—as much planning as necessary. . . ." There were only slight policy differences, such as the extension of the welfare state, that separated the two major political parties. Both the CDU-SPD Grand Coalition in 1963 and the subsequent SPD-FDP coalition victory in 1968 were further indications of a stable party system, the former reflecting the ability of two main political parties to cooperate and the latter—led by SPD leader, and then chancellor, Willy Brandt—reflecting peaceful change in leadership.[117] Both broad-based coalitions and acceptance of parliamentary leadership changes had been lacking in Weimar Germany and in the previous periods.

Even on the once critical partisan issue of religion (particularly the role of the Roman Catholic church) the SPD has attempted to structure its policies so that the Vatican and the German Roman Catholic hierarchy would view them more favorably.[118] Another major development relating to the evolution of a stable political party system is the fact that the West German bureaucratic elite is essentially favorably disposed toward pluralist politics. By comparison, bureaucrats in the previous periods were anti-political party elitists in sympathy with the conservative elites and authoritarian political systems of the post-Napoleonic, second Empire, and Weimar periods.[119]

Along with dramatic changes in the German political structure with the formal division of Germany into two independent states, there have been changes in the social and economic structures now that East and West Germany are considered postindustrial or advanced industrial countries. The social makeup is primarily urban middle and working class with a high standard of living, reflected in the rapid growth of the service-oriented economy. An important question is whether these structural changes have been accompanied by changes in cultural attitudes, particularly in the political sphere. There is survey evidence that there has been a consistent increase in favorable attitudes toward pluralist democracy, including a competitive political party system.[120] It is difficult to assess the depth of these beliefs but their widespread presence is one of the distinguishing characteristics of the Bonn republic when compared with its predecessors. It is likely that these favorable attitudes toward pluralist democracy are linked to the massive economic growth in the West German economy,[121] a point to be discussed later at greater length.

With regard to terrorism, the political changes, structurally and culturally, signify an unfavorable environment for terrorism in West German society because there are virtually no outstanding cleavages that facilitate the polarization of any substantial segment of the population. It is extremely difficult to see any obvious oppressive characteristics in the "organized pluralism" of the West German political system. It is not a question of whether or not oppression exists, but rather whether it is visible and can be identified clearly to the oppressed.

Economic Miracle and Political Stability

The stability of the West German political system relates directly to the "economic miracle" and the changing social structure. The dramatic economic growth of the last 25 years has been referred to as Germany's second economic revolution.[122] The first one occurred during the Second Empire and was largely controlled by the aristocrat-dominated elite, which inhibited a total reorganization of the social and political structure.[123] The fact that many of the old political values remained in the Second Empire, despite an economic revolution, paved the way for the polarization that occurred in the subsequent Weimar Germany.[124] The second economic revolution, with a major assistance from the population shifts initiated by the Nazis during the Third Reich, completed the restructuring of German society.[125] Traditional cleavages based on religion and class remain politically important but in a refined manner: Church attendance and trade union membership have been the best predictors of party support in the Bonn republic. Still, the socioeconomic bases of support for the SPD and CDU do not reflect the polarization of any major segment of the West German population. In a Western European perspective, "the relatively low working-class composition of the SPD makes it one of the least working-class socialist or communist parties in Western Europe."[126] This is in marked contrast to the previous periods when the SPD support was nearly exclusively working class, and the party and its supporters maintained a self-encapsulated existence apart from non-SPD members. Now there are formal and legally sanctioned employee-trade union cooperative organizations as well as other institutions that facilitate political and economic communication that cuts across many of the traditional class-based cleavages. Finally, West Germany has the highest standard of living in the world and one of the most extensive welfare state systems. These characteristics have contributed directly to the integration of the working class into West German society.

Although the once isolated working class has fared well, so also has the middle class, whose major interest is to avoid the inflation of previous periods (especially Weimar). Of the major Western industrial powers, West Germany has suffered the least from inflation. Economic growth, with a few exceptions, has been steady since 1948 and is reflected in the frequent upward revaluation of the West German currency. Because the general economic growth has outpaced the growth of the domestic labor market, foreign workers are prevalent in many of the working class occupations. However, this enormous economic growth has favored the middle and upper classes because the extensive welfare state system has not required a major redistribution of income away from these classes to the working class. Instead, West Germany retains one of the most inequitable distributions of wealth and income of the advanced industrial countries.[127]

The Radicalization of the German Socialist Student Alliance (SDS)

An additional reason for the stability of the political party system was that it had incorporated most of the important social groups within its organizational structures, including university students. Both of the dominant political parties, the SPD and the CDU, had student affiliate organizations. The largest and most powerful of these student or university groups was the SPD's German Socialist Student Alliance (SDS), which spawned the student terrorists and the Baader-Meinhof Group of the late 1960s and 1970s. Prior to the evolution of the SDS into a violent extraparliamentary opposition, it was a typical student party movement of the post-World War II period, representing the more extreme or more ideologically doctrinaire positions on most political issues. Tension between the parent organization and the SDS intensified as SPD policies, particularly on such defense matters as rearmament, became virtually identical to the policies of the ruling Christian Democrats. This policy shift occurred after the SPD's electoral defeat in 1957 and reflected the rationale that "the SPD leadership adopted a determined course to achieve 'respectability' among the broad depoliticized voting masses with their wariness of socialist experiments."[128] By 1961, the SPD had expelled SDS members and substituted a more malleable student organization in its place. The SDS fear that the SPD had abandoned doctrinaire socialism was confirmed when the SPD entered the Grand Coalition and subsequently supported an emergency powers bill that dramatically increased state police powers. From the SDS perspective, the SPD had become an establishment party from which no major changes in West German society could be expected, especially because the Grand Coalition destroyed the SDS view of the SPD as an opposition socialist party.

According to Gunter Barsch, the SDS then passed through four radicalizing phases that led ultimately to its demise and to the development of the concerted terrorism of the Baader-Meinhof Group.[129] It is for this reason that the short period between 1964 and 1970 contains the critical conditions for the brief success and failure of student terrorism in West Germany. During the first phase, the SDS had become agitated over foreign policy issues and the university structure. The "Frankfurt School" of radical Marxist theorists, including Jurgen Habermas, maintained that both the capitalist (for example, West Germany) and the state socialist countries (for example, East Germany) were repressive societies.[130] Those theorists in particular asserted that the nineteenth-century Humboldt university system, which emphasized classical and elitist curriculae, had to be altered so that students would be able to undergo the radicalizing experience that would allow them to contribute to changing West German society in a non-violent manner.[131]   Also, Vietnam had become a major issue, in part because West Germany was seen as an ally of the United States and its domination of the Third World countries. Similarly East Germany was linked to the imperial power of the Soviet Union. These views concerning German society, the university system, and the international environment linked the SDS to identical radical university movements in other industrial countries such as the Netherlands and the United States. The radicalization of the Students For a Democratic Society in the United States clearly had a direct impact on the SDS in Germany. The violent rhetoric of the American SDS and also the street conflict of the Dutch Provos set the stage for the second phase when the SDS, led by Rudi Dutschke, adopted terrorist tactics to prepare Germany for the revolution.[132]   Still, the conditions that facilitated the move to student violence were limited to the general structure of the German university system and in particular to the unique environment of the Free University of Berlin.

Student Population Explosion and an Archaic University System

Between 1950 and 1968 the student population in Germany grew from 116,000 to 260,000.[133]   Although the university physical plant also grew, it was simply outdistanced by the enormous growth in student population. Most of the students came from the middle class, with only 10 percent from the working class. Overcrowding was immediate, and, in addition to inadequate classroom and living facilities, there was a poor teacher-student ratio. Most senior faculty were still oriented toward an elitist or Humboldt conception of the German university and, consequently, were unprepared for the decline in intellectual quality of students that apparently occurred with the student boom.[134]

Even with the expansion of university enrollment, Ralf Dahrendorf maintains that "extraordinary inequalities of opportunity existed" within the German education system. The German professor who reached the status of Ordinarius "had the right to determine what would be studied and by whom it would be conducted, the type of exams . . . ; he was totally sovereign."[135]   The Ordinarii also controlled the expanding number of assistant professors. As members of state universities, professors were civil servants with lifetime appointments.

Once accepted into the university level, students were left in relatively unstructured programs with the exception of the physical and natural sciences. Students were allowed to move, with certain restrictions, throughout the university system. The average time spent in obtaining a degree was ten-to-thirteen semesters or 5-6½ years. The dropout rate differed considerably depending on the discipline: A study of the universities revealed that 82 percent of pharmacy students graduated whereas only 65 percent of social science and 37 percent of art students graduated.[136]

The most vocal opposition to the university system was centered at the universities in Berlin, Marburg, and Frankfurt. The Free University of Berlin (FUB) had been created after World War II and became a symbol of the Allies' "democratic" response to the authoritarian educational system that existed in East Germany. It had attracted many major scholars, partly because it had been well financed by American sources and was highly visible because of the long-standing world media attention focused on West Berlin's vulnerable military position in the midst of Cold War politics.

The SDS and other student groups agitated for democratic reforms of the university system during the early 1960s but met with little success. The West German government was more concerned with coping with the first major recession in the economy since the spectacular economic growth of the previous decades. Part of the government's response included raising tuition fees and streamlining the university curriculum by limiting the number of semesters for graduation. Also, policy moves were undertaken to force the curriculae more into line with the needs of the business community.

Government and Student Violence

The second phase of the radicalization of the student movement is marked by the decision of certain student leaders, particularly SDS leader Rudi Dutschke, to use violence. According to Dutschke, two types of violence were justified: violence to protect oneself from the oppressive police forces of the state and violence against oppressive machines or objects of the state such as the newspapers and journal officers of publisher Axel Springer.[137] A turning point in the confrontation between the SDS and student movement and the West German government occurred when the West Berlin police aggressively broke up a massive student demonstration against a visit of the Shah of Iran. A student demonstrator was shot and killed. The primary blame for the killing was placed on Axel Springer, who the SDS claimed had inflamed the police and the public against the student movement by distorting and vilifying the image of its student members. Students attacked the officers of the Springer publishing empire and attempted to stop the delivery of its newspapers. Under Dutschke the SDS then tried "to draw out the conflicts with the police which . . . would stimulate the appearance of class conflict in society . . . to show how the German society had become dominated by the authoritarian personality of its government officials."[138] The organizational base for the student movement was at the Free University of Berlin where an Action Committee coordinated the tactics of numerous student organizations including the SDS.

At the point when violence was adopted as an important tactic in the student movement, critical splits occurred. A faction led by Habermas maintained that student violence would bring about repression that would hinder the unfolding of radical revolution in West Germany.[139] Dutschke and most of the SDS leaders favored increasing the violence. This basic split marked the isolation of the violent factor in the student movement. Dutschke clearly had turned the SDS away from a university reform focus to concentrate on a social revolution. The East German refugee cynically maintained that the presence of high-ranking ex-Nazis in government reflected the moral bankruptcy of the Bonn republic. The capitalist structure was seen as unjust and irrational. Dutschke subscribed to Herbert Marcuse's view that, as members of a marginal group in society, the students could break through the cultural repressiveness of their society and serve as the catalyst for creating a socialist revolution.[140] According to Dutschke, the task was to build a student revolutionary class that would reach and revolutionize the working class. The revolutionary students and workers would penetrate all the critical socioeconomic institutions and thus pave the way in approximately a decade for a neo-anarchist society.

Dutschke viewed himself as a "constructive Christian critic" whose revolutionary zeal depended on his faith in the power of "revolutionary consciousness":

> Others have argued that we must cooperate with the existing trade unions, the liberals, the comparatively democratic state, because the revolution is not now possible. I believe it is possible to extend the limit of what is called possible. For example, the student movement—which has grown tremendously—is creating a prerevolutionary situation. The objective situation of the students is not too different from what it was ten years ago. But today students feel linked to the Third World, especially Vietnam. In other words the change in their minds is changing the circumstances. Consciousness itself is a factor in creating the situation.[141]

Dutschke appeared quite aware of pluralist institutions in German society but seemed to feel that a neo-anarchist utopia was absolutely preferable and achievable in the near future. This second phase of the radicalization of the student movement and the SDS ended with the attempted assassination of Dutschke. He suffered near fatal gunshot wounds in the head. He then left Germany to convalesce in Britain and Denmark and virtually disappeared from the student movement.

The reaction of the student movement to the Dutschke shooting marked the third phase. Bloody riots broke out in Berlin and other cities, with massive student marches. The Springer empire was a main target of the student violence because the students considered his newspapers and journals to be responsible for spurring the reactionary assassination attempts of student leaders by distorting the image of the student movement. This phase began with fairly unified action from the students because both the violent groups such as the SDS and the non-violent ones went into the streets to protest the Dutschke shooting. However, the student movement quickly degenerated into factional disputes over tactics, with the SDS unsuccessfully attempting to gain control. The use of violence, then, was a major cause for driving the student groups irrevocably apart.

The fourth and final phase witnessed the isolation of the SDS as a revolutionary student organization. The SDS itself was decentralized and quickly became a series of uncoordinated information and discussion groups. These SDS groups were further divided when socialist, communist, and anarchist factions competed for the allegiance of the SDS members.[142] It was from the ranks of the anarchist faction that the Baader-Meinhof Group emerged.

The Evolution of the Baader-Meinhof Group

The student movement did have some success in reforming the university governance. The Free University of Berlin, for example, in 1969, had student representation in certain decision-making areas such as faculty recruitment. Student participation in these areas generally was low, which accounted for the dominant role of the hard-core student radicals; they often pushed for extreme positions on issues and were opposed by a majority faculty vote. Many of the radicals engaged in disruptive tactics by occupying buildings and classrooms and shouting down and assaulting professors who were considered reactionary. The West Berlin government's attempt to "democratize" FUB resulted in considerable chaos because of these disruptions, faculty strikes, and resignations.[143]

Although most of the radical and now disorganized student movement focused on increasing student power within the university system, a small group of radicals was planning to focus on creating a revolution in West German society. Most of them had come directly from SDS ranks. Of the original members of the BMG, Andreas Baader and Gustaf Mahler had been a part of the SDS leadership while Ulrike Meinhof had been Dutschke's personal companion. They clearly were influenced by the radical-violent American students; Baader-Meinhof and Gudrun Ensslin assumed the title of "Wetterleute" or Weathermen. Like the Weathermen, the BMG was committed to using terrorist bombings to prepare the way for the revolution. Terrorism was regarded as necessary for two reasons: (1) to "shock the indifference of people" to the oppressive policies of capitalist countries such as the American involvement in Vietnam,[144] and to demonstrate the vulnerability of the police by showing, in Meinhof's words, "that armed confrontation is feasible—that it is possible to carry out actions where we can win. . . ."[145] Terrorism would facilitate the growth of a proletarian army that would mark the initial stage of a revolutionary "free society." While the BMG relied heavily on Marcuse's concepts, they did not elaborate specific criteria or provide

an operational blueprint for their "free society." They declared that the immediate and long-term objectives of their terrorism were:

1. To liquidate the chiefs and hangman servants of the military forces and
   of the police
2. The expropriation of power and productive means that belongs to the
   government of the monopolistic capitalists, large landowners, and imperialists: with small extractions for the individual needs for the urban
   guerrilla and great ones for the necessary requirements of the revolution
   itself[146]

Under the self-proclaimed leadership of Gustaf Mahler, the original members of the BMG proclaimed themselves members of the Red Army faction.[147]
This appellation identified them as part of an international terrorist organization
with large membership concentrations in certain Middle Eastern countries and
Japan. Financial aid and arms from this international Red Army network apparently did support some of the terrorist activities of the BMG. In turn, intelligence
was shared and even individual BMG members or supporters were employed by
the Red Army in terrorist acts in other countries such as Israel.

Between 1970 and 1971 the BMG engaged in a series of terrorist acts involving numerous bank robberies and bombings at American military installations in
West Germany. These terrorist acts resulted in five killings and fifty-four attempted killings. The West German media gave extensive coverage to the activities of
the BMG, including the embarrassment of the police and prison officials when
BMG leader Baader was captured and then set free by other members of the group
in a spectacular jail break. The response of the government was to establish a special counterterrorist police unit with jurisdiction across Länder (state government)
boundaries. The BMG managed to elude capture until 1972 by using stolen cars
and safe-houses in densely populated suburbs. Even when captured, the BMG
leaders utilized their radical lawyers as a conduit to the remaining members. The
primary basis for support outside the actual terrorist organization appeared to be
a group of radical lawyers and radical students and professors at institutions such
as the university of Heidelberg. Sympathy seemed to be limited to a few popular
public figures such as the author Heinrich Böll and certain elements of the West
Berlin Protestant clergy.

By the summer of 1972 all of the original members of the BMG had been
killed or captured. Eventually Mahler committed suicide through a hunger strike,
and Meinhof recently hanged herself while in jail.

Most police authorities figured that the BMG no longer posed a serious terrorist threat, but they cautiously protected their captured terrorists by building
a $5.2 million jail-court house that resembled a fortified bunker. Still, the govern-

ment and police were taken by surprise when remaining members of the BMG took over the German embassy in Stockholm. When Chancellor Helmut Schmidt refused the terrorist demands that their twenty-six jailed compatriots be released, they blew up the embassy. The sporadic terrorism continued; a West German federal judge was murdered in a terrorist reprisal, and the mayor of Berlin, Konrad Lorenz, was kidnapped. The mayor was released in exchange for the release of five terrorists. With the exception of a small protest rally over the death of Meinhof, little has been heard from the remnants of the Baader-Meinhof Group.

Some Psychological Views of the Baader-Meinhof Terrorists

Generational bitterness is the most common explanation for student terrorism. Both nineteenth-century and contemporary student terrorists were viewed as fighting symbolic battles against their parents, especially their fathers. The older generations were seen by the disappointed student idealists as clinging to outmoded values that had brought their societies to failure. The Napoleonic victories in the German states, the failure to enact liberal political reforms in the nineteenth century and the shame and catastrophe of the Third Reich all were attributed to parental failure. Whether through lack of courage or "wrong" values, parents had bequeathed to the late adolescent-early adult generations seriously flawed societies. Part of the generational-bitterness explanation involved the nature of student life: The university experience was unique because it removed students from the constraints of earning a living and family responsibility while subjecting them to an ambivalent situation of leisure, intense exam competition, and unsure future employment.[148] For many students, the university experience also involved a camaraderie and idealism that was unique to this period in their lives, and many wished to maintain these values and organizational links to the university environment well into their thirties.[149]

Although a growing number of university graduates maintained their university ties through traditional fraternities, a minority joined a variety of university-based extremist and ideological groups such as the Trotskyites and Maoists. Because most of these radicals were from the middle class, one explanation of their behavior was the assertion that guilt over middle-class upbringings and the consequent need to prove oneself a "true rebel" were basic to the motivation of radical students.[150] The university experience was uniquely suited to a radicalizing experience, because it reintroduced childhood fears and anxiety concerning success and parental authority. This occurred because "The university setting is rigid and authoritarian, competition is strong and traditional evaluation of students is irrational."[151] This view of the university experience led to the question "Is it the university that is sick and the students that are healthy?"[152] The student terrorist contended that the university, as well as middle-class society, was sick. Some terrorists saw themselves as deprived of the revolutionary experience of the working class but believed that they could still identify themselves as the equivalent of "fellow travelers" of the working class.

With regard to the Baader-Meinhof Group, there is the additional view that many of its members were characterized by intense feelings of hopelessness, frustration, and suicide.[153] The father of one of the leaders of the BMG, Gudrun Ensslin, maintained that she was tragically part of "a generation of youth that were actually mentally disturbed, evidenced by nervous breakdowns and suicidal tendencies."[154] It was also pointed out that many key figures in the student terrorist movements had been social workers who viewed their roles as hypocritical because "concrete" change could only occur by means of a "war on the capitalist society."[155] A former member of the BMG, Beate Sturm, maintained they were "naive and incurably romantic" concerning the revolution they believed would result from their terrorism.[156] They were convinced that once the revolution was set in motion the appropriate radical Marxist or anarchist society would automatically unfold. For the student terrorist, the evidence of success is clear; they have occupied universities, helped topple political figures, and caused hysteria among the police forces. Yet, according to a leading radical Marxist theorist, Jurgen Habermas, this terrorist view of the revolution is disturbing: "So serious a confusion of symbol and reality satisfy the medical criteria of pathological delusion."[157]

Confusion of Revolutionary Symbols and Reality:
Unfavorable Conditions for Terrorism

What exactly do the BMG find so oppressive about West German society that it justifies terrorism? While disparities in wealth remain, it is difficult to maintain that the working class is the victim of an unrewarding capitalist system. The extensive welfare state, trade unions, the SPD, and one of the strongest economies in the world ensure a decent standard of living for manual workers. Civil liberties are considered the undisputed right of all West Germans. The political system is pluralist in the sense that competing interest groups and political parties vie for the control of government offices. The possible decline in competition because of the cooptation of interest groups into formal political parties and bureaucratic channels does not mean that the goals of the interest group go unfulfilled. In fact, these goals are satisfied to such an extent that they are willing accomplices to party government policies. In the same vein, the decline in the differences among political party policies reflects a consensus in the West German electorate rather than any conspiracy on the part of political party elites to deprive West Germans of opposition parties.

In regard to the West German educational system, there were major deficiencies by egalitarian standards. The university system was oriented toward the middle class, although the SPD governments have begun to change this to ensure more opportunities for the working class. In addition, the problems of overcrowding, uncertain postgraduate employment, and outdated curriculae have also been the focus of government reforms. It is still too early to evaluate the outcome of government policies to upgrade university facilities and to restrict the number of students so that there will be job opportunities for all. A recent assessment of the West German universities did find that most students had readjusted quietly following the government initiatives.[158] In any case, government educational policies appear destined to bring the university system more in line with other social and economic institutions in West Germany.

In the international sphere, West Germany does not fit the mold of a major political power such as the United States or the Soviet Union. Although West Germany is a major economic power, it is difficult to view it in classic imperialist terms involving the exploitative policies characteristic of other Western states. Because the close foreign policy links with the United States are directly related to the military presence of the Soviet Union in East Germany, it is also difficult to view this relationship as a part of a grand design to exploit Third World nations.

It is not that disadvantaged groups do not exist in West German society, or that there are not problems in developing a more egalitarian basis for socioeconomic mobility, or that the international economy does not favor West Germany and the United States to the disadvantage of weaker countries. The point is that these grievances exist, but not in the classic Marxist context of class conflict.[159] Why then does the BMG see the solution to social conflict in terms of terrorism and revolution? Terrorism from their standpoint is necessary to awaken the oppressed working class and to threaten the ruling class, in order to prepare for "the revolution." It is not clear, however, that the working class is asleep. Electoral surveys reveal, for example, that working-class trade unionists identify strongly, with the SPD, implying that these individuals are quite conscious of their socioeconomic position and their political system.[160] Most of the working class, far from being alienated, would prefer that the SPD be concerned about inflation and the welfare state rather than about expropriating the means of production.

Although there were conditions in the past that could be viewed by student radicals as a justification for terrorism—major social groups could be seen as oppressed by the class structure of German society—this is not evident in present-day West Germany to most scholarly observers and to the overwhelming majority of Germans. One of the main themes in the previous historical sections is that there are enormous differences between the social, economic, and political structures of the Bonn republic and those of the Weimar, Second Empire, and preunification Germany. Yet, individuals such as Andreas Baader and Ulrike Meinhof turn to terrorism because they are idealists and romanticists. They see problems such as the authoritarian university structure, the lower standard of living of the working class, the poverty of Third World countries, and the complacency of most West Germans in the face of a highly competitive, work ethic society, and they conclude that a change is needed. The student terrorist does not state specifically how society should be restructured, but he or she is certain that it should be. He or she believes that if one has the appropriate revolutionary consciousness, then the ideal is attainable. The proof of success lies in the fact that the student terrorists succeeded in violently challenging the police forces in West German society and intimidating politicians and university officials in regard to university reforms.

In effect, the student terrorist in West Germany and elsewhere in Western Europe (with some exceptions such as Spain) views contemporary pluralist and advanced industrial society as oppressive in totality (just as student terrorists viewed their early nineteenth-century autocratic rural society as an oppressive one) and believes that only revolutionary changes can transform it into an ideal society. Given the obvious complexity of advanced industrial societies such as West Germany, simplistic and abstract concepts about revolution, oppression, and authority appear to be held by frustrated idealists or romanticists who are not revolutionaries but rather reactionaries. With a few minor exceptions, no concerted effort has been made by the BMG to identify operationally with the oppressed working class and proceed to organize it for the revolution. They have never specified whether a nonhierarchical political system could facilitate the economic and welfare values of the working classes once they were "politically liberated." It was evident that what they were offering the oppressed in return for revolutionary sacrifices was "nothing but a distant symbolic identification, and that is not likely to create organic linkages between people and revolutionaries."[161] The terrorism of the BMG can be characterized as "the revolt of the traditionalists" because they long for an ideal society with a minimum of organization, even though they live in a society that is satisfactory (to most of its inhabitants) in spite of its complexities. Like the nineteenth-century student terrorist leader Karl Follen, the BMG wraps itself in the revolutionary symbols that are alien to the very people they hope to revolutionize.

Terrorism in Western Europe: Concluding Remarks

This discussion of the IRA Provisionals and the Baader-Meinhof Group attempted to illustrate the thesis that terrorism in Western Europe is likely to be sporadic and unsuccessful, because most ethnic and student ideological terrorist groups have been operating under conditions unfavorable to terrorism. First of all, in pluralist-industrial societies it is extremely difficult to isolate both "a monolithic

enemy" oppressor and a highly "visible oppressed social group." Although terrorists have no difficulty in defining these two groups, their problem is in convincing
host groups or potential allies of a similar dichotomy. Without a favorable and
extensive host group, terrorists are eventually deprived of recruits, financing, and
safe-houses. Without this support, and even with the inherent difficulties an urban terrorist group poses for the police, the latter's overwhelming resources in
manpower, intelligence, finances, and weaponry usually result in either the defeat
of the terrorists or a severe curtailment of their activities.

Secondly, terrorists in Western Europe have to cope with the overwhelming
material success of most of the economies of this region and the stability of its
political systems. It is increasingly difficult to find isolated and homogeneous
social groups based on either a class or ethnic group in most of the Western European countries. These two types of social cleavage have not disappeared but have
been mitigated by an absolute increase in the standard of living, the emergence of
the welfare state, extensive civil liberties, and the pluralist political process.

Thirdly, it was evident that the rationales of the IRA Provisionals and the
Baader-Meinhof Group were simplistic and based on a distorted nineteenth century view of their societies. This, combined with their obvious sincerity and self-
sacrifice, gave them a romantic utopian image. It was therefore difficult for them
to convince working-class West Germans or even Irish Catholics in the North that
violence is justified by their goals because these goals have been superseded by
the values of the pluralist-industrial society. In an extensive survey of the strength
of acquisitional or materialist values in contrast to those more closely identified
with the values of the student-ideological terrorists, Ronald Inglehart maintained
that in Western electorates, "terrorists or . . . Weatherman type strategy . . . not
only seems counter-productive in the short run; to the extent that it had any real
impact on the economy, it apparently would tend to be self-defeating in the long
run as well."[162]

Not all terrorists in Western Europe can be characterized as traditionalists.
In Franco Spain, for example, some of the Basque terrorists were operating under
an authoritarian political system in which many Basques clearly felt oppressed.
Under Franco, Basque political autonomy was lost, and Madrid pursued economic
policies that were viewed as anti-Basque. However, if the new regime of King Juan
Carlos establishes a pluralist political system, restores economic growth, and grants
the Basque region political autonomy, then the Basque terrorists who demand
Basque independence should follow the pattern of the IRA Provos. Also, the fortunes of the Patriotic Anti-Fascist Revolutionary Front (FRAP) or ideological
terrorist should follow the fortunes of the Baader-Meinhof Group if the above
changes take place in Spain. Both types of terrorism may be viable in Spain given
the present precariousness of Spain's economy and political system.

Although Italy is more pluralist and industrially advanced than Spain, it too has a considerable number of student-ideological terrorist groups on both the Right and Left. If, according to the analysis developed here, the Italian economic troubles are not resolved and the political system becomes stalemated, then it is likely that the ideological terrorists will become more active and possibly more successful in bringing about political chaos. In France, the student-ideological terrorists participating in the spectacular events of the 1963 rebellion in Paris have engaged in only sporadic terrorist acts since then. More favorable conditions for terrorism could occur if a stalemate develops between the president (executive) and the National Assembly (legislature). A Left-Right confrontation is possible if these two structures fall separately to a coalition of leftist political parties on the one hand and a rightist coalition on the other. Chances of a constitutional stalemate, tension, and subsequent increase in the chances for a terrorist movement would be lessened if the French economy resumed its strong growth pattern. The prospects for ethnic terrorism in regions such as Brittany and Alsace are dependent on government policies, decentralization of the structure of representation to the national parliaments, and economic growth. On the whole, conditions for ethnic terrorism are unfavorable in France, given the pluralist political system and the commitment of most major political groups to a basically centralized political structure.

  In sum, ethnic and student ideological terrorists in Western Europe are unlikely to engage in anything more than sporadic terrorist acts as long as these countries maintain pluralist political systems and advanced industrial economies.

Notes

1. For an analysis of the class transformation brought about in Europe by the structural changes occurring after World War II, see "The Changing Class Structure and Contemporary Politics," *Daedalus* 93 (Winter 1964): 271–303. Seymour Martin Lipset is representative of the school of thought that sees a direct relationship between increasing levels of working-class consumption and system participation and decreasing levels of class-based social cleavages. As he states, "Greater economic productivity is associated with a more equitable distribution of consumption goods and education—factors contributing to a reduction of intra-societal tension. As the wealth of a nation increases, the status gap inherent in poor countries, where the rich perceive the poor as vulgar outcasts, is reduced. As differences in style are reduced, so are the tensions of stratification. . . ." The general result of this process, according to Lipset, is an increasing unwillingness on the part of Western publics to adopt the totalistic ideologies of either the left or right—in short, a more firm commitment to the politics of pluralism. See Lipset's, "The Modernization of Contemporary European Politics," in his *Revolution and Counter-*

Revolution, rev. ed. (New York: Anchor Books, 1968), pp. 267-304. A statistical analysis of this trend in Great Britain may be found in Robert Bacon and Walter Eltis, *Britain's Economic Problem: Too Few Producers* (London: St. Martin, 1976), pp. 117-191. For a more detailed study of postwar Europe see Andrew Shonfield, *Modern Capitalism* (New York: Oxford University Press, 1969). For more recent studies of these trends see John W. Brooks and Jo Ann B. Reynolds, "A Note on Class Voting in Great Britain and the United States," *Comparative Political Studies* 8, 3 (October 1975): 360-376. An interesting note here is their finding that while class divisions have decreased in the United States and Britain, regional and religious cleavages do not seem to have risen in response. In this context Campbell found that, in France at least, the most significant factor in electoral polarization appears to be age. See Bruce A. Campbell, "On the Prospects of Polarization in the French Electorate," *Comparative Politics* 8, 2 (January 1976): 272-290. Also see Daniel Bell, *The End of Ideology* (Glencoe, Ill.: Free Press, 1960). Bell seems to approach the attitude that it is not so much that man has conquered his problems—thereby doing away with the need for a "utopian" vision—but rather that man has created an environment of incomprehensibility to the extent that any grand understanding of existence is universally rejected as unrealistic. Finally, see Martin Heisler, *Politics in Europe* (New York: McKay, 1974), for an analytical and substantive discussion of the changing political structures and processes in Western European countries.

2. Two excellent studies of ethnic group interaction are Fredrik Barth, ed., *Ethnic Groups and Boundaries* (Boston: Little Brown, 1969), and Michael Hechter, *Internal Colonialism: The Celtic Fringe in British National Development, 1536-1966* (Berkeley: University of California Press, 1975). Also see Raymond Corrado, *The Politics of Ethnicity: A Challenge to Post-Industrial Society* (New York: Marcel Dekker, submitted for publication).

3. An examination of the similarities to be found among the "pre" and "post" industrial rebels may be found in Ronald Inglehart, *The Silent Revolution: Political Change Among Western Republics* (forthcoming). While both of these groups may be seen as reacting to the same stimuli (that is, bureaucratization, centralized authority, "rootlessness," and so on), it may be argued that the subjective motivations that lie behind these reactions are fundamentally distinct. This is to say that while the tactical orientations adopted by both the "parochial luddite" and the middle-class dropout may be identical, the former acts from a position of a loss of self, and the latter as an affirmation of self. The Sorelian adoption of violence as a cleansing force may be adopted through either desperation or choice. See Hannah Arendt, "Reflections on Violence," *Journal of International Affairs* 23, no. 1 (1969): 1-22.

4. It must be pointed out, however, that the notion of "Irish ethnicity" is, to a large extent, a manifestation of very concrete "Anglophobia." In speaking of the great famine, Roland Gaucher points out that "The first manifesta-

tions of Irish terrorism appeared against this background of poverty. In 1858, a secret society was founded, the Irish Republican Brotherhood, known also by the Gaelic name of Fenians. The rebels recruited their forces primarily from among the peasantry, which had suffered the greatest hardships. They found a fertile and continuous source of aid from amongst those who had emigrated to America and who hated everything British." "Ireland's Rebellion Against England," in *The Terrorists: From Tsarist Russia to the O.A.S.* (London: Secker and Warburg, 1968), p. 176. Also see Tim Pat Coogan, *The IRA* (New York: Praeger, 1970), pp. 1-37.

5. Dudley Edwards, *The Sins of Our Fathers* (Dublin: Gill and Macmillan, 1970), p. 8. See J. C. Beckett, *A Short History of Ireland* (New York: Harper & Row, 1966), pp. 98-101.

6. See Antonia Fraser, *Cromwell* (New York: Dell Books, 1974), chap. 13, and Beckett, *A Short History of Ireland,* pp. 79-82.

7. Many of the contemporary poems and proclamations of the Republican movement bitterly refer to this period. During the Home Rule turmoil in the late nineteenth and early twentieth centuries, many Conservative supporters of the Union of Britain and Ireland employed a sixteenth-century imagery of Irish Catholics. The songs heard during the annual Orange parades in Northern Ireland contain bloody reminders of the religious and cultural significance of the Protestant and British victory at the Battle of Boyne. See Coogan, *The IRA,* pp. 7-10.

8. See Anders Boserup, "Contradictions and Struggles in Northern Ireland," *The Socialist Register,* 1972, pp. 159-161, and Richard Rose, *Governing Without Consensus* (Boston: Beacon Press, 1972), pp. 79-80.

9. Boserup, "Contradictions and Struggles," pp. 159-160, Rose, *Governing Without Consensus,* p. 80, and Beckett, *A Short History of Ireland,* pp. 108-109.

10. See Coogan, *The IRA,* pp. 5-8. Another view of the formation of the Orange Lodges is that they were founded in 1795 in response to an armed attack on Protestants by Irish Catholics who sought to stir rebellion against the king as a prelude to his war against France. The lodges may also have been a response to an anticipated Catholic revolt following the arming of Irish troops for service in the American campaign. See Rose, *Governing Without Consensus,* pp. 80-81. For an analysis of the Orange movements development into the present time, see Boserup, "Contradictions and Struggles," pp. 162-164. Also see F. S. L. Lyons, *Ireland Since the Famine* (London: Fontana, 1973), pp. 13, 289-293.

11. Boserup, "Contradictions and Struggles," p. 159.

12. Ibid., p. 160. Also see Rose, *Governing Without Consensus,* pp. 81-82.

13. See Bob Purdy, *Ireland Unfree,* Red Pamphlets no. 2, 1972, pp. 10-11, and Gaucher, "Ireland's Rebellion," p. 176. Also, for a more extensive analysis see R. Dudley Edwards and T. Desmond Williams, *The Great Famine* (New York: New York University Press, 1957), chap. 3.

14. Coogan, *The IRA,* p. 13.

15. Ibid., p. 14.

16. See Conor Cruise O'Brien, *States of Ireland* (New York: Random House, 1972), pp. 85-88, and Lyons, *Ireland Since the Famine,* pp. 172-180.

17. J. Bowyer Bell, *The Secret Army: A History of the IRA 1916-1970* (Cambridge, Mass.: MIT, 1974), p. 12.

18. O'Brien, *States of Ireland,* p. 67.

19. See Boserup, "Contradictions and Struggles, p. 162, and Rose, *Governing Without Consensus,* pp. 85-85.

20. Boserup, "Contradictions and Struggles," pp. 161-164, and Rose, *Governing Without Consensus,* pp. 85-88. Also see Liam de Paor, *Divided Ulster* (Baltimore: Penguin Books, 1970), pp. 57-59.

21. Boserup, "Contradictions and Struggles," p. 162.

22. O'Brien, *States of Ireland,* pp. 85-88, and Lyons, *Ireland Since the Famine,* pp. 313-327.

23. Bell, *The Secret Army,* p. 13.

24. Ibid., p. 19.

25. Ibid., pp. 20-27. See also Tom Barry, *Guerrilla Days in Ireland* (Dublin: Anvil Books, 1971). For a more detailed study of this period, see Nicholas Monsergh, *The Irish Question: 1840-1921,* 3rd ed. (Toronto: University of Toronto Press, 1976).

26. See Bell, *The Secret Army,* pp. 29-66, for a detailed analysis of this subject in terms of the general feeling toward incorporation of the North and the cleavages present in the South on the questions of gradualism and republicanism.

27. Ibid., also see Coogan, *The IRA,* pp. 100-104, 225-252.

28. O'Brien, *States of Ireland,* p. 101.

29. Bell, *The Secret Army,* p. 40.

30. O'Brien, *States of Ireland,* pp. 100-106.

31. Bell, *The Secret Army,* p. 139.

32. Ibid., p. 123.

33. Coogan, *The IRA,* pp. 65-93, 116-135, 288-308.

34. Bell, *The Secret Army,* p. 217.

35. Coogan, *The IRA,* chap. 12.

36. O'Brien maintains that there is a deep tradition in the South of ignoring Ulster. Concerning the tense events in Ulster over the 1912 Home Rule Bill he remarked: "Most of the people of Catholic Ireland, outside of Ulster itself, knew little or nothing about the real situation in Ulster. Their political leaders, who did know did not tell them. . . . The conviction of

the Catholic people, that there was no Ulster problem . . . became part of the environment of every nationalist politician. It has remained so, though in modified forms, into our own day." O'Brien, *States of Ireland*, p. 79.

37.   Ibid., p. 78.

38.   See the *London Sunday Times* insight teams, *Northern Ireland: A Report on the Conflict* (New York: Random House, 1972), pp. 15-24. For a very personal interpretation of the influence and results of Marxism within the IRA, see Sean MacStiofain, *Memoirs of a Revolutionary* (Edinburgh, 1975), pp. 99-139.

39.   *Northern Ireland: A Report on the Conflict*, pp. 23-26 and MacStiofain, *Memoirs of a Revolutionary*, pp. 99-110.

40.   *Northern Ireland: A Report on the Conflict*, pp. 23-26 and MacStiofain, *Memoirs of a Revolutionary*, p. 105.

41.   Bell, *The Secret Army*, pp. 363-364, and MacStiofain, *Memoirs of a Revolutionary*, p. 135.

42.   *Northern Ireland: A Report on the Conflict*, p. 26.

43.   Ibid., p. 27.

44.   The emergence of a Catholic middle class was long delayed in comparison to its Protestant counterpart, and the delay was not a historical accident. Catholic economic mobility was systematically hampered in Northern Ireland by the all-powerful and extensive Unionist machine. Socioeconomic relations were controlled by the Orange Lodgers, and, therefore, the employment practices of the privately owned industries were used to prevent any significant hiring of Catholics. A blatant example of the effectiveness of this discrimination involved the well-paying Belfast shipyards where only 700 of 10,000 workers were Catholic. Jobs in the rapidly expanding public sector were controlled mainly by local government authorities who were overwhelmingly tied to the Unionist party machine. Thus, Catholics were also discriminated against in the public sector. With mandatory mass education and government-assisted secondary education, however, a small middle class did emerge. See Rose, *Government Without Consensus*, pp. 278-280 and chap. 4, and Boserup, "Contradictions and Struggles," for a more detailed class perspective.

45.   See Richard Rose, *Northern Ireland: Time of Choice* (Washington, D.C.: AEIPPR, 1976), pp. 52-53. Also see Max Hastings, *Barricades in Belfast* (New York: Taplinger, 1970), p. 62.

46.   *Northern Ireland: A Report on the Conflict*, pp. 47-49.

47.   Ibid., pp. 50-55 and chap. 4.

48.   Ibid., pp. 71-74.

49.   According to one of the founders of the IRA Provos, Sean MacStiofain, the Dublin government had no part in creating the Provos. He maintains that

Dublin's mythical role was designed to buttress Fianna Fail's electoral strength in the South and that it was an attempt by the IRA regulars to discredit the Provos. See MacStiofain, *Memoirs of a Revolutionary,* pp. 138-141.

50. Even though the IRA never achieved a total victory in its conflicts with its enemies, Britain, the Irish Free State, and Northern Ireland, defeats were often thought of as "glorious failures." Audacity and ingenuity character- ized many of the IRA activities against the British army and the RUC, such as undertaking an arms raid on a supposedly impregnable army ammunition dump. Few of these escapades succeeded, but they seemed to create public sympathy for the mouse tweaking the lion's tail.

51. *Northern Ireland: A Report on the Conflict,* p. 195. Maria McGuire, in her book *To Take Arms,* (New York: Macmillan, 1973), appears to adopt this view of the Provo leadership and points to their intransigence as the main reason for her supposed defection. (There is question as to whether she ever truly belonged to the Provisional IRA.) This view of the Provos is completely rejected by the Provo leader, MacStiofain. He sees himself and his followers as stable individuals with a positive view of life in general. See MacStiofain, *Memoirs of a Revolutionary,* p. 135.

52. Rose, *Governing Without Consensus,* chap. 7.

53. Ibid., pp. 207-209.

54. Ibid., pp. 216-217.

55. Ibid., p. 193.

56. *Northern Ireland: A Report on the Conflict,* p. 198.

57. Ibid., p. 204.

58. MacStiofain, *Memoirs of a Revolutionary,* p. 157.

59. Rose, *Time of Choice,* p. 26.

60. McGuire, *To Take Arms,* pp. 104-107. For opposing view see MacStiofain, *Memoirs of a Revolutionary,* pp. 288-300.

61. See ibid., pp. 238-244, 296-300, for MacStiofain's defense of the IRA's use of car bombs.

62. Although it must be remembered that the SDLP boycotted the plebiscite, it is interesting to note that the number of votes cast in favor of unification represented less than 1% of the total electorate.

63. The published constitutional proposals were as follows: (1) that Northern Ireland should remain in the United Kingdom; (2) that a Northern Ireland assembly should be created having eighty members to be elected by propor- tional representation and serving 4-year terms; (3) that an executive office should be created which could *not* be filled by the representative of any party union which drew its support exclusively from one sector of the pop- ulation (that is, religion); and (4) that the assembly be debarred from pass- ing any discriminatory bill.

64. For an analysis of the various reactions to British initiatives in Ulster during this period, see Gary MacEdin, *Northern Ireland: Captive of History* (New York: Holt, Rinehart and Winston, 1974), pp. 269-280.

65. Rose, *Time of Choice,* pp. 29-31.

66. Ibid., pp. 132-138.

67. Ibid., pp. 29-30, 37-43.

68. Bob Purdy, *Ireland Unfree,* Red Pamphlets-2, pp. 29-38.

69. The official IRA program can be found in a booklet titled, *Eire Nua,* Ehnair, 1971.

70. Recently, there have been attempts to intimidate Fitt through violent demonstrations and threats. It is not clear whether the Provos or one of the other IRA factions initiated the violence.

71. For a Provo assessment of the Lynch government, see MacStiofain, *Memoirs of a Revolutionary,* pp. 325-341.

72. O'Brien, *States of Ireland,* pp. 197-201.

73. The former technique consisted of shooting off the kneecaps, thus permanently crippling the victim. In hooding, individuals were kidnapped, a hood was placed over the victim's head, and then the victim was shot in the head.

74. *Facts on File,* November 22, 1975, p. 865.

75. See MacStiofain, *Memoirs of a Revolutionary,* p. 259.

76. "Catholic Moderate is Belfast Target," *Washington Post,* August 16, 1976.

77. "The Violence in Ulster Never Ends," *New York Times,* July 25, 1976.

78. MacStiofain, *Memoirs of a Revolutionary,* pp. 21, 37-38, 48, 93-94.

79. Ibid., pp. 37-38, 258.

80. Ibid., pp. ix, 341.

81. Ibid., pp. 238, 244, 296-300.

82. MacStiofain is particularly vocal on this point. He seems to feel that, without "British exploitation" (that is, British participation in the Irish economy in any form), a united Irish republic could erect a viable economy. Economic facts of life would seem to dictate otherwise. See O'Brien, *States of Ireland,* pp. 197-201.

83. Bell, *The Secret Army,* p. 394.

84. For a description of the goals, tactics, and mentality of the nineteenth-century German student movement and the scope and organization of the Burschenschaft, see Kurt F. Reinhardt, *Germany: Two Thousand Years,* vol. 2 (New York: Ungar, 1962), pp. 464-467. A central figure during this period was Ludwig Jahn, who led the movement for a unique German identity based on Prussian freedom and superiority. Jahn was central in the rise of the ideology that served as a basis of the major forces of German unifica-

tion. "The Glorification of Prussia's Natural Superiority in one of Jahn's
early programmatic works with the significant title, *Deutsches Volkstum,*
laid the groundwork for the evolution of a German-Volkisch theory on
which three movements of major ideological, social, and political impact
. . . the Free Corps of the Napoleonic Wars . . . the formation of the Gymnastic Groups (Turnvereine), whose ideas of nationhood and patriotic-
military training survived ideology in the later gymnastic societies . . . the
nationalistic fervor of the student corporations of 1815." Karl Dietrich
Bracher, *The German Dictatorship* (New York: Praeger, 1970), p. 25. Also,
see Reinhardt, pp. 442-443. Peter Gay argues that this mentality survived
intact in German youth into the Weimar period in the form of a cult of
past greatness. Gay, *Weimar Culture* (New York: Harper Torchbooks,
1968), pp. 86-87.

85.   Reinhardt, *Germany,* pp. 432-444.

86.   Ibid., p. 459. Bracher made the argument that disillusionment with liberal-
       ism after Napoleon's defeat was not only characteristic of the German
       monarch, but also of the middle classes in the form of "anti-Western" ide-
       ology. See Bracher, *The German Dictatorship,* pp. 18, 23-28. He argues
       that "Unlike France, some of the eighteenth-century German states tended
       toward a moderate form of enlightened absolutism which seemed to allow
       for the organic transition to a modern state without a revolutionary rup-
       ture. But, under the impact of the terror and the aggressive expansionism
       of the French Revolution and Napoleon, the initial enthusiasm for the prin-
       ciples of the Revolution gave way to profound disillusionment. . . . typical
       of this development is the rapid transition from a European, humanistic,
       cosmopolitan orientation to a national idea of the German cultural mission,
       as propounded by Fichte in particular. . ." (p. 17). Also see Hans Kohn,
       The Mind of Germany: The Education of a Nation (New York: Scribner,
       1960), pp. 81-98.

87.   The notion of a clear and distinct dichotomy between German middle
       classes and elites along a dimension of "liberalism" is problematic (see note
       3) due to the transfiguration of the notion of liberalism that took place.
       Bracher asserts that "the failure of 1848 also was more than simply the
       result of a series of unhappy circumstances. It was brought on by the am-
       bivalence of German liberalism, which found itself squeezed between an
       unfulfilled desire for a national state and authoritarian government struc-
       tures. . . . Even among the majority of liberals, the idea of freedom was
       overwhelmed by the idea of the state as a force above society assuring unity
       and efficiency, power and protection, and standing above the parties. . . .
       This concept of the state . . . which ultimately benefited defensive, conser-
       vative forces, came to dominate the legal and political thinking of the peo-
       ple. . . ." *The German Dictatorship,* p. 18. Ralf Dahrendorf takes this line
       of thinking even further in asserting that the German middle class never
       successfully separated itself from the aspirations and culture of the nobility,
       leading to what he refers to as a "false middle class" (that is, the bureau-

cracy) void of an economic, and hence political, basis—those who made their "fortunes" quickly adopted the manner and orientation of the nobility. In this sense the notion of a German "middle class" should not imply the same connotation as, for instance, the English "middle classes." Dahrendorf, *Society and Democracy in Germany* (New York: Anchor Books, 1969), pp. 49-50, 93-94.

88. Reinhardt, *Germany*, p. 465.

89. Lewis S. Feuer, *The Conflict of Generations* (New York: Basic Books, 1969), p. 59.

90. Ibid., p. 61.

91. Ibid., p. 63.

92. Ibid., pp. 64-65. Reinhardt, *Germany*, p. 467.

93. Reinhardt, *Germany*, p. 463.

94. Ibid., p. 469.

95. Feuer, *The Conflict of Generations*, pp. 67-68.

96. Ibid., pp. 68-71, and Reinhardt, *Germany*, pp. 526-527.

97. Reinhardt, *Germany*, p. 529.

98. Ibid., p. 467.

99. See note 4; also see Dahrendorf, *Democracy in Germany*, pp. 31-59.

100. For an analysis of the political configuration during this period see Friedrich Meinecke, "Unfortunate Collapse—A Liberal View," *The Creation of the Weimar Republic: Stillborn Democracy?* ed. Richard W. Hunt (Lexington, Mass.: Lexington Books, 1969), pp. 1-15.

101. Peter Gay, *Weimar Culture*, pp. 8-13, 147-155, and Arthur Rosenberg, "Social Revolution to Guarantee Democracy," in *The Creation of the Weimar Republic*, ed. Hunt, pp. 50-55.

102. The rise of the "Free Corps" after the war and their participation in the suppression of the workers "Soviets" that sprang up throughout Germany after the war raises the question of whether they represented "order" or "reaction." The following works give excellent analyses of the role of the army in the revolutionary situation following World War I: Bracher, *The German Dictatorship*, pp. 80-88, and Richard Grunberger, *Germany: 1918-1945* (London: B. T. Basford, 1964), pp. 51-60. What must be kept in mind is that during this period the openly reactionary "Free Corps" were often wrapped within the cloak of legitimacy of the Reichswehr, thereby creating confusion concerning the role of the "army" during this revolutionary period.

103. Bracher, *The German Dictatorship*, pp. 102-104, 169-173; Reinhardt, *Germany*, pp. 656-676.

104. For an account of Hitler's attempted "Beer Hall Putsch," see Deitrich Orlow, *The History of the Nazi Party: 1919-1933* (Pittsburgh: University

of Pittsburgh Press, 1969), pp. 44-45, Grunberger, *Germany,* pp. 61-65; Bracher, *The German Dictatorship,* pp. 115-118.

105. Hannah Arendt, *The Origins of Totalitarianism,* new ed. (New York: Harcourt Brace World, 1966), chaps. 11, 13.

106. Feuer, *The Conflict of Generations,* pp. 290-31.

107. See Derek W. Urwin, "Germany: Continuity and Change in Electoral Politics," in *Electoral Behavior,* ed. Richard Rose (Glencoe, Ill.: Free Press, 1974), pp. 118-127.

108. Arnold J. Heidenheimer and Donald P. Kommers, *The Governments of Germany,* 4th ed. (New York: Crowell, 1975), pp. 78-80.

109. Heidenheimer and Kommers, *The Governments of Germany,* p. 42, and Dahrendorf, *Society and Democracy in Germany,* pp. 110-111.

110. Heidenheimer and Kommers, *The Governments of Germany,* pp. 96-98.

111. Ibid., pp. 69-80.

112. Ibid., pp. 73-80.

113. Ibid., pp. 213-218.

114. Ibid., pp. 95-96.

115. Ibid., pp. 180-182.

116. Ibid., pp. 90-91. It must be remembered however that the move toward a more broad-based appeal of the Social Democrats did not go unopposed. The rise of the "Jusos" represented a rejection of such policies and the attempt to reimpose "Marxist purity." This tension is recognized by Heidenheimer (pp. 91-92). Dahrendorf, on the other hand, interprets the Bad Goedesberg Program as another example of the German refusal to accept fundamental conflict. See Dahrendorf, *Society and Democracy in Germany,* pp. 183-187. See also Otto Kirchheimer, "Germany: The Vanishing Opposition," in *Political Oppositions in Western Democracies,* ed. Robert A. Dahl (New Haven, Conn.: Yale University Press, 1966), pp. 244-245.

117. There is debate as to whether the Grand Coalition represented cooperation or collusion between the two major parties (see note 32). See Heidenheimer and Kommers, *The Governments of Germany,* pp. 83, 182, 188, Dahrendorf, *Society and Democracy in Germany,* pp. 195-196, and Kirchheimer, "Germany," pp. 246-259.

118. Heidenheimer and Kommers, *The Governments of Germany,* p. 91.

119. The relationship between the bureaucracy and the rise of the Third Reich is not clear, yet few disputed the assertion that the bureaucracy viewed the multiparty system of Weimar Germany with disdain. In turn, many members and supporters of the Center and Left political parties distrusted the bureaucrats. Although these sentiments persist to some extent in the Bonn government, most observers such as Ralf Dahrendorf agree that the Bonn bureaucrats cannot be characterized as completely antipluralist. In fact, a

major recent survey of West German bureaucrats revealed that "top-level civil servants in Germany in 1970 displayed great sensitivity to, and support for, the imperatives of politics in a democracy. By all (survey) measures now available, they are hardly less egalitarian, hardly less liberal, hardly less politically responsive or programatic in outlook than their British or Swedish counterparts." Robert D. Putnam, "The Political Attitudes of Senior Civil Servants in Britain, Germany, and Italy," *British Journal of Political Science* (July 1973), pp. 257-290. See also Dahrendorf, *Society and Democracy in Germany,* pp. 234-235, 238-241. Also see Dahrendorf "The Evolution of Ruling Groups in Europe," in *European Politics: A Reader,* ed. Mattei Dogan and Richard Rose (Boston: Little, Brown, 1971), pp. 382-389.

120. Sidney Verba, "The Remaking of the German Political Culture," in *European Politics,* ed. Dogan and Rose, pp. 66-72.

121. Ibid., p. 68, and Seymour M. Lipset, *Political Man* (New York: Doubleday, 1960), chap. 2.

122. Verba, "The Remaking of the German Political Culture," p. 68.

123. See Urwin, "Germany," pp. 118-119. See also Barrington Moore, Jr., *Social Origins of Dictatorship and Democracy* (Boston: Beacon, 1966), pp. 435-442.

124. Ibid., pp. 113-138.

125. Ibid., pp. 127-135. Also, see Dahrendorf, *Society and Democracy in Germany,* pp. 381-396.

126. Urwin, "Germany," p. 159.

127. Karl W. Deutsch, *Politics and Government* (Boston: Houghton Mifflin, 1974), pp. 136-141.

128. Kurt L. Shell, "Extraparliamentary Opposition in Postwar Germany," in *European Political Processes,* ed. Henry S. Albinski and Lawrence K. Pettit (Boston: Allyn and Bacon, 1974), p. 495.

129. Günter Bartsch, *Anarchismus in Deutschland,* vols. 2 and 3 (Hannover: Fackeltrager-Verlag, 1965, 1973).

130. For a discussion of the "Frankfurt School," see Shell, "Extraparliamentary Opposition," pp. 490-493.

131. For a discussion of the Humboldt university system, see Reinhardt, *Germany,* pp. 439-443.

132. Frank Pinner, "Western European Student Movements Through Changing Times," in *Students in Revolt,* ed. Seymour M. Lipset and Phillip G. Albach (Boston: Houghton Mifflin, 1969), pp. 78-79.

133. Joseph Califano, *The Student Revolution* (New York: Norton, 1970), p. 48.

134. Ibid., p. 49.

135. Pinner, "Western European Student Movements," p. 83.

136. Dietrich Goldschmidt, "Psychological Stress: A German Case Study," in *Student Power,* ed. Julian Nagel (London: Merlin Press, 1969), p. 65.

137. Marjorie Hope, *Youth Against the World* (Boston: Little, Brown, 1970), p. 250.

138. Barstch, *Anarchismus in Deutschland,* p. 28.

139. Shell, "Extraparliamentary Opposition," p. 503.

140. Hope, *Youth Against the World,* p. 241.

141. Hope, *Youth Against the World,* p. 242.

142. Barstch, *Anarchismus in Deutschland,* pp. 43-53.

143. Henry Regnery, "The Malaise of the German University," *Modern Age,* vol. 18, pp. 121-132, and *Time,* January 26, 1970, p. 55.

144. *Der Baader-Meinhof Report,* Aus Akten des Bundeskriminalamtes, der "Sonderkommission Bonn" und des Bundesamts für Verfassungssckutz (v. Hase and Koehler Verlag Mainz, 1972), p. 20.

145. *Time,* February 7, 1972.

146. *Baader-Meinhof Report,* p. 159.

147. Another faction called themselves the "2nd of June movement." They restricted themselves to terrorism in West Berlin and concentrated their struggle on gaining support in working class areas.

148. See Goldschmidt "Psychological Stress," pp. 59-70, and Robert Moss *Urban Guerrillas* (London: IISS, 1972), pp. 17-30.

149. Goldschmidt, "Psychological Stress," p. 70.

150. Stanley Rothman, *European Society and Politics* (Indianapolis: Bobb-Merrill, 1970), pp. 282-284.

151. Goldschmidt, "Psychological Stress," p. 60.

152. Ibid., p. 60.

153. *Baader-Meinhof Report,* p. 15.

154. Ibid., p. 69.

155. Neal Acherson, "The Urban Guerrillas of West Germany," *New Society,* April 10, 1975, p. 68.

156. *Baader-Meinhof Report,* p. 97.

157. *Society,* April 4, 1975, p. 190.

158. See *New York Times,* November 14, 1976.

159. See Ralf Dahrendorf, "The Evolution of Ruling Groups in Europe," in *European Politics,* ed. Dogan and Rose, pp. 382-388.

160. See Urwin, "Germany," pp. 121-122, 131, 133, 145-150.

161. *Society,* April 4, 1975, p. 190.

162. Ronald Inglehart, "The Silent Revolution in Europe: Intergenerational Change in Post-Industrial Societies," *American Political Science Review* 65 (December 1971): 1017.

7

Terrorism in Sub-Sahara Africa

Mary B. Welfling*
Department of Political Science
Yale University
New Haven, Connecticut

Images of savagery and violence long have constituted the Western stereotype of sub-Sahara Africa, and events such as postindependence conflict in the Congo (now Zaire), the Nigerian civil war, and the fighting among rival organizations in Angola merely serve to reinforce such images. Africa, then, probably strikes most Westerners as a fertile field for the study of terrorism, but the reality of violence and terror in Africa may be removed somewhat from our myths. E. V. Walter has warned us not to accept

> the old prejudice that still insinuates in subtle ways that rule by violence and fear is alien to the Western political tradition but natural to people who, according to some moral or technical standard of comparison, may be called "barbarians." Inspection of the evidence reveals that such an attitude has no rational ground. [1969, p. 10]

Moreover, at the level of national systems, we have reason to believe that terrorism may be less pervasive than in many Western societies.[1] On the one hand, Africanists recognize that national political systems are very limited in scope

*Present Affiliation: Minnesota Crime Control Planning Board, St. Paul, Minnesota.

(for example, Zolberg, 1966, chap. 5). Lacking material and human resources, political leaders are incapable of affecting the daily lives of most citizens. Power holders may inflict a "regime of terror"[2] on a few but certainly not on the entire society. On the other hand, national populations that are largely unaffected by national political institutions develop little political interest and, hence, are not likely to become politically involved. A "seige of terror," or actions against the existing system of authority, becomes less likely. Gurr, in Chapter 1 in this volume, provides additional support for these assertions. His empirical evidence indicates that terrorist activity in the 1960s was more common in European and Latin American countries than in Afro-Asian ones; more common in democratic states than in autocratic or Third World ones; and more common in richer countries than in poorer ones. He argues that these findings seem reasonable because terrorism is easier to carry out in open societies, in complex societies where organizational bases exist, and in areas where means are readily available and media attention assured. Terrorism on the part of officials and citizens cannot be discounted in Africa, but we must recognize from the outset that it may be far more limited than in more technologically developed societies where citizen and government are much more interdependent.

African states provide a variety of contexts within which terrorism has occurred and continues to occur. Although the continent now is decolonized, the bulk of sub-Sahara countries remained colonies of European powers until the early 1960s. Thus, terrorism at the national level was manifested first in the colonial context.[3] The majority of sub-Sahara countries are now independent nation-states ruled by indigenous blacks. This second context is the forum for most contemporary terrorism. Although events at the time of writing portend future change, a third situation currently exists in Rhodesia and South Africa, where minority whites of European origin (though generally not birth) rule the majority black populations.

Investigations of terrorism in these diverse contexts will reveal that, in spite of the diversity, portions of the population reject with terror the right of existing power holders to rule, and that those who control institutions of power use terror to maintain their power. We shall not attempt to disentangle the "chicken and egg" problem of who used terror first, for terrorism is recognized as an interactive process involving violence on both sides, reactions on both sides, and social effects for all.

Before introducing the African context and outlining the organization of the chapter, we need to clarify the use of the term terrorism in this chapter. Terrorism involves violent acts designed to induce fear, which are indiscriminate, unpredictable, arbitrary, and destructive. (Walter, 1969, chap. 1; Wilkinson, 1974, chap. 1). The concern here is with political terrorism; that is, violent acts employed for political objectives. Finally, terrorism is carried out by organized groups, not by isolated individuals. Although this view of terrorism is conventional, two differences in the use of the term may emerge in comparison to other chapters. First, violent acts on the part of officials as well as violent acts against the state are considered terrorism. The second possible difference relates to the distinction of political terrorism from other forms of violence. In this volume, for example, Gurr separates terrorism from other forms of violence such as guerrilla activity, civil war, and so forth, where activity is more continuous and where practitioners frequently control some territory. He considers terrorism to be a strategy or tactic, however, and as such it can be a part of more widespread guerrilla campaigns or revolutionary movements. In this chapter we shall be working with a definition similar to Gurr's, but in examining the African cases we will not exclude terrorist activity that is a part of other violent movements as Gurr chooses to do in his data collection. The reasons for this choice are largely practical. First, the infrequency of political terrorism in Africa limits the relevant material. Including terrorism related to other violent movements expands this relevant material and permits more interesting examples. Second, the problem of accurate journalistic reporting of events in Africa makes distinctions between terrorism and other violence difficult and arbitrary at best.

Introduction

Although African historians have tended to slight the precolonial periods of the continent and our knowledge of these eras has been biased by the colonial belief that history did not begin until the European intrusion, it is true that contemporary Africa has been unalterably affected by the European presence. Major kingdoms such as Ghana, Mali, Kongo, and Songai saw their days of glory in the tenth through sixteenth centuries. Other kingdoms as well as a variety of other social and political units developed throughout the continent, but by the nineteenth century nothing equivalent to the European nation-state existed. It was the Europeans who created states in Africa and who introduced these states as members of the international system.

The Portuguese began their maritime explorations of Africa in the fifteenth century. Subsequent centuries saw other European powers enter the competition for the trade in slaves and commodities that Africa offered. Increasingly indigenous systems were affected by outside powers, but it was not until European balance-of-power rivalries prompted the "scramble for Africa" in the 1870s and 1880s that real efforts were made by Europeans to claim, settle, and administer Africa. The Berlin Conference of 1884 set the ground rules for claiming territory and gaining recognition. By 1900 Africa had been carved up by the European powers. During this period major decisions on boundaries were made in Europe by Europeans with little knowledge of the territories they were creating.[4]

Once Africa was claimed, the initial colonial phase was relatively uneventful. Europeans had to cope with significant pockets of local resistance, but in general the European powers did little with the colonies and provided for only small administrations. It was not until after World War I that they developed a sense of moral obligation toward the colonies, attempted to articulate more coherent colonial policies, and paid considerable attention to exploiting the resources of their African possessions.

This post-World War I era will be the first context in which we shall investigate terrorism in Africa. What were the political, social, and economic policies of the European powers toward their colonies? What forms of antagonism and resistance did colonial policy engender? It will be argued later in this chapter that colonialism itself in part created the opposition (some of it constituting terror) that would bring its sudden termination in most areas by the early 1960s.

The termination of colonialism ushered in the independence era in which former colonies acquired the international status of independent nation-states. Although technically independent, these new states remained colonial creations— borders of states had been determined by Europeans and not by ethnic realities, political systems were modeled on the West, education and social standards were the result of colonial policy, and economic conditions were dependent upon the ties developed between the primary-product economies of Africa and the industrial economies of Europe. This context presents a second situation in which to study terrorism in Africa.

How have new African political leaders coped with the conditions of independence and to what extent has terror been an element of their rule? Has terrorism been involved in citizens' responses to their new political units and leaders?

Although the Portuguese failed to follow the British, French, and Belgian examples of granting independence to their African colonies, the 1974 military coup in Lisbon brought a change in political leadership and policy that led to the rapid decolonization of the last European empire. However, two notable exceptions remained in sub-Sahara Africa. The Republic of South Africa achieved independence from Great Britain as early as 1910. The result of that early decolonization was the development of a minority white regime where the population of British and Dutch descent developed the system of apartheid whereby political, social, and economic privileges are retained for the white minority. Although the origins of the regime and particular policies differ from those of South Africa, Rhodesia too rejected the general trend toward independent, black majority rule. Here the white minority, fearful that Britain would grant independence to a black majority, unilaterally declared independence in 1965 and prevented meaningful African participation. This third context of white minority rule will be treated briefly as an extension of colonial conditions.

The following analyses of terror in colonial and independent Africa will point to major differences in the two periods. Yet in spite of the marked differences an effort will be made to emphasize similarities and parallels. Within each context we shall first examine the nature of the established systems and focus on aspects that might be viewed as elements of state terror, as well as other elements that might foster responses of terrorism. This examination will involve a description of the political system and of the distribution of social and economic rewards. The description of political arrangements needs to reveal the openness of the political system; that is, who can participate and how meaningful are existing channels of participation? The other side of the coin, of course, is a description of official repression and coercion, because systems that exclude certain groups generally need to repress desired political expression. The extent of openness and adaptability, on the one hand, and of repression and coercion, on the other, is of interest in assessing the extent of official terrorism. It also gives us a clue to sources of antigovernment terror. Gurr has argued, for example:

> Regimes can minimize support for dissidents and channel political discontent to constructive, or at least nondestructive, purposes insofar as they offer stable, effective institutional alternatives to violent dissent. But if regimes rely primarily on force, dissidents can increase the scope of their support and their effectiveness by creating the rewarding patterns of action that regimes fail to provide. [1970, p. 274]

The importance of institutional channels for political expression is supported by a number of scholars. Huntington (1968), for example, argues that the cause of violence lies in weak institutions, particularly when participation in a society expands beyond the capacity of institutions to absorb it. Strong, stable, adaptive institutions are the best insurance for avoiding violence. Moreover, Huntington suggests that the existence of institutions such as political parties (that is, those that are open and encourage participation) are more likely to promote peaceful political processes than are organizations such as militaries and bureaucracies. In addition, investigations of the legitimacy of political systems suggest that more legitimate systems are less likely to experience violence (for example, Gurr, 1970, chap. 6). An important source of legitimacy is believed to be the ability of major segments of the population to participate in the system and, hence, to feel they have a stake in it. But in his chapter in this volume in which he focuses specifically on terrorism, rather than on broader phenomena of conflict, violence, or rebellion, Gurr claims that terrorism flourishes in more open societies.[5] We shall want to probe, then, whether repressive systems in Africa seem to foster or limit political terrorism. The colonial and minority white-ruled political systems may appear very different on the surface from the independent black-ruled states, but we may find underlying similarities across systems if we find that in each case certain groups remain excluded from meaningful political expression, that these groups are the object of official terror, and that such suppression may be a source of (or perhaps a brake to) terrorist responses on the part of these groups.

Established systems distribute social and economic benefits as well as political rights differentially. Some who take a broad view of violence might argue that unequal life chances in terms of social and economic values constitute official terror. Galtung (1969, p. 168) proposes that "violence is present when human beings are being influenced so that their actual somatic and mental realizations are below their actual." Because we are viewing terrorism as violent *acts* designed to induce fear, the importance of social and economic inequality in this chapter is as a source of reactive terrorism rather than an element of regime terror. Inequality and resulting perceptions of deprivation are recognized widely as sources of antisystem violence.[6] Such perceptions can develop in a variety of circumstances. Awareness that one possesses less of a certain value than one did previously, less than does some reference group, or less than one does some other value (for example, one might be economically equal but not be permitted political expression or vice versa) can lead to resentments against the system and to the belief that violence must be used to correct the perceived injustice.

The second element described in each of the three contexts will be terror used against the established systems. What forms of terror have been used against the three types of systems? To what degree can we attribute this terrorism to official terrorism? Will it be possible to conclude that those systems with the most official terror also have the most antisystem terror? Finally, how successful has terrorism been? Has the use of terror by certain groups contributed to the achievement of group goals, or has it merely encouraged more official terrorism?

Colonial Africa

The first context in which to analyze terrorism is the colonial situation from World War I to approximately 1960. During this period African territories were considered possessions of or integral parts of the European mother country. Hence Africans were considered subjects of, or citizens of, a European country. It was a European system of authority to which Africans were subject and European policies that affected the lives of Africans.

The description in the following sections of political arrangements and the distribution of social and economic rewards under colonialism will include an investigation of the separate colonial powers. Britain, France, Belgium, and Portugal[7] had different guiding philosophies and implemented different types of policies in their respective territories. Colonialism necessitated an element of terrorism, although its extent varied according to mother country. The second part of this section includes a discussion of the types of opposition that developed under various colonial powers, emphasizing the degree to which terrorism was involved and proposing under which colonial conditions terrorism seemed most likely to develop.

The Nature of Colonial Rule

Political relationships in colonial Africa inevitably were ones of inequality. In no case did Africans receive political rights comparable to Europeans; in no case prior to the transition to independence were Africans permitted to hold major political offices or to wield significant influence. Colonialism, after all, is defined as a form of political domination. Moreover, the racial attitudes and sense of cultural superiority prevalent among European colonizers reinforced the inequality that characterized European-African political relationships.

Hodgkin (1957) has labeled French policy "Cartesianism" because of its coherence and intelligibility. Even though the French wavered on their conception of the role of the African, at any period of time France implemented a unified policy and treated her African possessions in similar ways. During the first part of the twentieth century France espoused a policy of paternalism under which Africans were treated as subjects rather than citizens. When she adopted a policy of identity (that is, Africans became "citizens") after World War II, Africans began to gain political representation. Under both positions, however, the African territories were considered an integral part of the French empire. Only in the late 1950s were self-government or independence considered.

Political arrangements prior to World War II treated Africans separately and unequally. According to Hodgkin:

> Paternalism meant, in effect, a special regime for the mass of Africans who were subjects, not citizens. They were subject to customary law—not the French legal code—administered by the French *commandant du Cercle* or *Subdivision*; their lives were governed by the system known as the *Indigenat,* which virtually deprived them of the liberties of criticism, association, and movement, and gave to the French administrator power to inflict penalties, without trial, for a wide range of minor offences; and they were liable to compulsory labour, *travail force,* for public, and sometimes, private purposes. [1957, p. 35]

The change to a policy of identity, however, led to increased political rights. Africans received representative positions at three levels—(1) the territory, (2) the federation (eight territories constituted the West African Federation and four constituted the Federation of Equatorial Africa), and (3) the French Republic—and after World War II Africans had frequent opportunity to go to the polls.

Representatives at the territorial level were directly elected, and the franchise was gradually extended and became universal by 1956. Three factors, however, reduce the meaningfulness of these political reforms. First, the African remained unequally represented. In the French national assembly, for instance, Hodgkin estimates that the principle of equality would dictate African representation of 390 deputies instead of the 29 sitting at that time (1957, p. 39). Second, the African was treated separately from white French citizens. Until 1956 French citizens voted on a separate roll for their own representatives; Africans selected their own. Moreover, the minority white population received disproportionate numerical representation to the majority African population, so that the "dual college" electoral system reinforced political inequality as well as separateness. Third, elected positions were reserved for legislative, advisory positions and did not extend to executive power, which until self-government in the late 1950s remained in French hands.

Africans under French colonial rule experienced increased political rights after World War II. In comparison to earlier periods and to other European colonies, the "French" African increasingly saw considerable freedom of political organization and expression. In practice the Africans' political influence remained limited, and contradictions between the avowed French policy of equality for Africans and the reality of second-class citizenship remained.

British political arrangements are more difficult to summarize because Britain had a more pragmatic approach and tended to treat each territory separately and according to local circumstances, an orientation that Hodgkin labels "empiricism." Britain did not offer the pretense that Africans were citizens, but in some cases she permitted considerable political freedom. In West Africa (for example, Nigeria and Ghana), where the white settler population was negligible, freedom of the press and organization led to the development of a vigorous press and numerous political organizations before World War II. Representative bodies existed early and after World War II evolved in the direction of elected parliaments. To an unusual degree in colonial Africa, the British recognized the principle of equality. A government report on the Gold Coast in 1948 was quite critical of colonial conditions and proposed:

> The constitution and Government of the country must be so reshaped as to give every African of ability an opportunity to help govern the country, so as not only to gain political experience but also to experience political power. [quoted in Hodgkin, 1957, p. 41]

In East and Central Africa (for example, Kenya and Rhodesia), however, where many more Europeans settled, Africans received much less equal treatment and were subject to political restrictions. Africans did not vote for African representatives until the 1950s, nor was universal suffrage granted until just before independence. Representation was not based on equality but instead on a communal principle. Africans, Europeans, and, where relevant, Asians voted on separate rolls for their own representatives. The communal principle was a mechanism to ensure European control, because it permitted their numerical overrepresentation. British policy in West Africa was perhaps the most open of all the colonial powers and moved furthest in the direction of principles of equality and early self-government. On the other hand, the East and Central African experience favored the white minorities. Policies seemed less open than the French and more akin to the Belgian and Portuguese.

Belgian colonial policy was guided by a sense of paternalism and a civilizing mission. It was based on a principle of assimilation whereby Africans acquiring a European education and certain European standards could be considered Belgians and hence could acquire the political and social rights of Belgians. In practice very few ever acquired such status. The political position of the African was one of restricted expression and virtually no representation. Belgians and Africans were subject to separate legal systems, in a pattern similar to the pre-World War II French system mentioned earlier. Because territorial elections were not held in the colonies until just prior to independence, political organizations were late in forming. Hodgkin mentions that perhaps Belgian subjects experienced fairly advanced social services, but "their lives have probably been subjected to more thorough-going regulation and supervision by Europeans . . . than any other people in colonial Africa" (1957, p. 52).

The principles of Portuguese policy were quite similar to those of Belgium. The Portuguese also offered the notion of assimilation, but in practice it affected only a small number of Africans. Here too Africans and Europeans were subject to different legal codes and administrative codes, although in 1961 the distinctions were dropped (at least on paper). A number of reforms throughout the 1960s expanded the suffrage and the number of elected positions. With an authoritarian regime in Portugal until 1974, however, the empire remained highly centralized and administrative. While the rest of Africa was decolonizing, official Portuguese policy retained the myths of colonialism and refused to accept principles of equality and self-government.

Colonialism involves social and economic inequality as well as political inequality. The previous discussion should be sufficient to point to basic differences in colonial outlooks, and here we need only mention general aspects of colonial social and economic relations. It is probably a fair generalization to state that economic and social policies parallel political ones—systems that most clearly demarcated separate and unequal political status for Africans (for example, Belgium) tended to have more blatant social separation; systems providing more political rights (for example, British West Africa) tended to provide Africans with more social and economic opportunities as well.[8]

Although unequal relationships between the mother country and the colonies are frequently documented, systematic analyses of unequal relationships within the colonies are more difficult to come by. A classic interpretation of colonialism is that of Frantz Fanon, who was born in French Antilles, trained in France in psychiatry, and practiced in Algeria during the anticolonial war. He is unusually capable of depicting the colonial world from the perspective of the colonized:

> The colonial world is a world divided into compartments. . . . The zone where the natives live is not complementary to the zone inhabited by the settlers. . . . they both follow the principle of reciprocal exclusivity. . . . The settlers' town is a strongly built town, all made of stone and steel. It is a brightly lit town. . . . The settlers' town is a well-fed town, an easygoing town; its belly is always full of good things. The settlers' town is a town of white people, of foreigners. The town belonging to the colonized people . . . is a place of ill fame, peopled by men of evil repute. They are born there, it matters little where or how; they die there, it matters not where or how. It is a world without spaciousness. . . . The native town is a hungry town, starved of bread, or meat, of shoes, of coal, of light. . . . This world divided into compartments, this world cut in two is inhabited by two different species. [1968, pp. 37-40]

Eduardo Mondlane, the former leader of the liberation movement in Mozambique, provides a more detailed account of colonial relationships, at least in that former Portuguese colony. In addition to political restrictions mentioned earlier, Mondlane argues that Africans experienced economic and social discrimination as well. Data on wages support his contention of inequality (see Table 1). He contends that "the law provides for inequality, while actual practice goes far beyond this, to keep the African in the role of a second class being whose whole function is to serve the Portuguese minority. It is only expected that social relations should reflect this" (1969, p. 47).

The nature of a colonial system is based on domination—political, social, economic. A central issue for this chapter is the degree to which terrorism is a part of such a system. To what degree do officials engage in fear-producing acts of violence? E. V. Walter (1969, pp. 12-16) leads us to believe that terrorism would be central, because he considers it to be violence in the service of power, violence with an aim of control. Moreover, he suggests that terrorism is a more likely instrument of power where resistance is likely or at least anticipated. Colonial domination is not a relationship likely to appeal to the dominated; therefore, the dominator would be likely to have terror at hand, if not in constant use. Fanon supports this contention and perceives force as a major weapon sustaining colonialism:

Table 1   Wage Differentials in Mozambique in the 1950s

Race	Annual agricultural wage, in escudos	Daily industrial wage, in escudos
White	47,723.00	100.00
Colored	23,269.10	70.00
Assimilated Africans	5,478.00	30.00
Unassimilated Africans	1,404.00	5.00

Source: Eduardo Mondlane, *The Struggle for Mozambique* (Baltimore: Penguin, 1969), pp. 43–44.

> In the colonial countries . . . the policeman and the soldier, by their immediate presence and their frequent and direct action maintain contact with the native and advise him by means of rifle butts and napalm not to budge. It is obvious here that the agents of government speak the language of pure force. The intermediary does not lighten the oppression, nor seek to hide the domination; he shows them up and puts them into practice with the clear conscience of an upholder of the peace; yet he is the bringer of violence into the home and into the mind of the native. [1968, p. 38]

The arbitrary and unregulated nature of the violence to which Africans were subject suggests further the importance of terrorism as an element of colonial rule. The practice of putting subjects under legal codes that were different from those that applied to European citizens deprived Africans of the security of certain legal protections against unwarranted arrest, detention, and punishemnt. The more a colonial power utilized separate legal codes, thus providing less equal protection for Africans, the more we would anticipate official terrorism to have existed, because colonial actions could be more arbitrary and less predictable.[9] This reasoning would argue that Belgium, Portugal, and pre-World War II France utilized the most official terrorism.

The previous discussion leads to the impression that colonialism in British West Africa and in the French territories after World War II was the least repressive and involved the least terrorism, whereas colonialism in Belgian, Portuguese and British East and Central African territories involved the most repression and terrorism. Further evidence for this impression is provided in the center column of Table 2 where information on government sanctions from the *World Handbook of Political and Social Indicators* is provided. A government sanction is defined as "an action taken by authorities to neutralize, suppress, or eliminate a perceived threat to the security of the government, the regime, or the state itself" and includes three types of actions—censorship; restrictions of political participation

Table 2 Terrorism in Colonial Africa[a]

	Official terror (number of government sanctions)	Anti colonial terror (number of armed attacks)	
British East and Central Africa			
Kenya	243	367	(16)[b]
Malawi	88	33	(16)
Rhodesia	227	98	(18)
Uganda	55	440	(15)
Zambia	61	140	(17)
Group mean	135	136	
Belgian colonies			
Congo (Zaire)	88	109	(13)
Portuguese colonies			
Angola	40	363	(20)
Mozambique	31	91	(20)
Group mean	35	127	
British West Africa			
Gambia	0	0	(17)
Ghana	11	3	(9)
Nigeria	11	8	(13)
Sierra Leone	0	6	(12)
Group mean	5	4	
French colonies			
Central African Republic	1	0	(13)
Chad	1	1	(13)
Congo, Brazzaville	9	1	(13)
Dahomey	0	1	(13)
Gabon	0	0	(13)
Guinea	0	0	(11)
Ivory Coast	1	0	(13)
Mali	4	0	(13)
Mauritania	7	0	(13)
Niger	1	0	(13)
Senegal	1	0	(13)
Upper Volta	0	0	(13)
Group mean	2	0	

[a]Table excludes UN trust territories because colonial policies were affected by international supervision. Events in the year of independence were counted as occurring under colonialism if independence came after mid-year. If perusal of country literature indicated that events clearly occurred prior to or after independence, then the mid-year criterion was dropped.

[b]Number in parentheses is the number of years from 1948, when data collection begins, to independence.

such as bannings, arrests, detentions, and harrassment; and protection against espionage (Taylor and Hudson, 1972, p. 69). The variable reflects, then, both the
closed nature of a political system as well as some of its official terrorist actions.
One sees from the table that in fact French territories and British West Africa experienced the least government sanctions. Although Nigeria and Ghana demonstrate the most sanctions in this group, considering the early and vigorous nationalist opposition (see next section) colonial policy remains surprisingly open. The
Belgian Congo, the Portuguese territories, and particularly British East and Central Africa exhibit considerably more official repression. Kenya and Rhodesia,
where white-settler influence was considerable, inflicted the most sanctions. Belgium's sanctions in the Congo were concentrated in 1959 and 1960. Had opposition developed earlier, or had Belgium not decided abruptly to grant independence, the number of sanctions would no doubt be closer to the totals for Kenya
and Rhodesia. The number of sanctions in Angola and Mozambique (most of
which occur after 1960) actually seems surprisingly low. One possible explanation is that Portuguese repression became based on military force and, therefore,
is not reflected adequately in this variable.

The terrorism of colonial domination should not be exaggerated, however.
Two factors would limit its extent. First, much of the African population remained relatively untouched by the colonial authorities. Factors such as limited
communication and transportation, which reduce the scope of the independent
political systems, would have affected the colonial powers as well. Many administrations remained fairly small, located prodominantly in urban areas. Relatively
untouched, Africans had less incentive to resist; without resistance, authorities
had less need of terrorism, a situation that we shall argue is essentially the same
in independent, black-ruled states. Africans were probably most touched by
colonial power and terrorism where larger white populations existed and had
large colonial administrations to back them up. It would be in such contexts,
then, that one would expect the most state terror. Information in the center
column of Table 2 lends support to this conjecture.

Second we must realize that not all Africans resented colonial domination.
In fact, some most touched by colonialism could see in it a source of advancement and a means to a better life, rather than a domination to be resisted. Colonialism created new African classes and instilled in some a desire to acquire European standards. Although some of these new groups agitated for independence,
others could be seen as props of the colonial system. But this issue borders on
the question we want to investigate next—which colonial conditions fostered the
most resistance and how much terrorism was involved?

In summary, colonial systems were characterized by domination and by
political, social, and economic inequality. However, European countries varied
in the specifics of their policies and the degree of domination and inequality that
they instituted. Terrorism served as a prop of colonial power relations. It was

probably most important in systems that provided for more separate treatment of Africans, and in systems where the European population and administration were most pervasive and obvious to Africans.

The Nationalist Response

The nationalist movements that developed in opposition to colonial domination in Africa involved surprisingly little terrorism, and the transition to independence was generally a peaceful one. Terrorism was the exception rather than the rule. In analyzing the anticolonial response, we need to distinguish two separate questions: (1) what prompted nationalism and (2) under what conditions was terrorism involved? The sources of more violent nationalism seem to be the opposite of the conditions that fostered the growth of nationalism. Relatively open systems experienced the earliest and most peaceful resistance. Although more closed and repressive systems experienced more retarded resistance, it was more likely to be violent and to involve more terror.

The growth of nationalism was the inevitable result of colonial policies. The economic growth, urbanization, and expanded Western education that colonialism stimulated created new groups that acquired some Western standards and values. These groups became aware of Western liberal and Christian values of equality, liberty, and freedom that so obviously contradicted the basic principles of colonialism. Where political policies permitted the formation of some political opposition (for example, British West Africa), members of these new groups formed organizations to lobby for improved conditions and expanded rights. These organizations generally worked through the representative institutions that the colonial powers provided. Riots in the Gold Coast in 1946 surprised British authorities and led to reforms. Other forms of violent incidents occurred prior to independence, but in general violence was rare and there is no evidence of terrorist campaigns against colonialism in these more open contexts. Britain recognized the right to self-government for her West African territories as early as the 1940s; hence, nationalism was directed toward speeding up the process and working out the details, rather than fighting the foundations of colonial domination.

Nationalist movements developed later in other parts of sub-Sahara Africa where economic and social development were slower. When colonial authorities refused African opposition the right to express itself, nationalism was further retarded. The suppression of anticolonialism, however, appears to have made later resistance more violent and thus to have magnified the opposition rather than eliminate it. James Coleman, an early student of African nationalism, notes the effect of colonial recognition of African rights to self-government:

> The possibility of a total fulfillment of nationalist objectives (i.e. *African self-government*) has been a powerful psychological factor which partly

explains the confident and buoyant expectancy of West Coast nationalists.
. . . the tendencies toward accommodation or terrorism in the white settler
areas is a reflection of the absence of such moderating expectancy. [Cole-
man quoted in Hanna, 1964, p. 218]

Lewis Coser (1956), a major writer on social conflict, argues that if conflict is
suppressed, it is likely to erupt later in more violent and destructive ways. The
African pattern of nationalism supports this theoretical argument. In addition,
later expressions of nationalism were likely to be more intense because decolonization was already underway and the deprivations of those remaining under colonial rule appeared less defensible and more humiliating with the model of fellow
Africans experiencing self-government or independence. For instance, Ghana
was granted independence from Britain in 1957, and Guinea voted for independence from France in 1958, but nationalist opposition was still in a formative
stage at that time in Belgian and Portuguese territories and in portions of British
East and Central Africa.

If nationalism was most violent in colonies that refused to recognize principles of African participation and ultimately self-rule or independence, it would
be in Belgian and Portuguese territories and in British East and Central Africa
that violent opposition would be most likely. The more "legitimate" tactics of
British West Africans have been mentioned. Although France was slower to recognize the right to independence, she did permit considerable African participation after World War II and did grant self-rule in the late 1950s. Moreover, British decolonization and the humiliating defeats in Indochina and Algeria quickly
led France to grant independence to the bulk of her African empire in 1960, so
that little resistance was needed to further the process.

In the Belgian Congo colonial paternalism excluded thoughts of independence and retarded the development of nationalist organizations. Small nationalist parties developed for local elections in the late 1950s and were the vehicle
for some protest. Then widespread and unanticipated riots occurred in 1959.
These were directed against colonial targets but were apparently largely spontaneous and unorganized, as was the urban and rural radicalism that was to reap-
pear later. Herbert Weiss (1967) who has studied the Congo of this period interprets the violence as mass radicalism directed against whites but perceives relatively little organized terrorism. The lack of organizational bases in the Congo
meant that terrorism would be slower to develop. Then Belgium's sudden rever-
sal of policy and decision to grant independence in 1960 undercut the perceived
need for anticolonial terrorism. Terrorism was not absent, but conditions in the
Congo favored violence in the form of turmoil instead.

The Portuguese colonies and the British colonies of East and Central Africa
with European settler populations provide the two conditions mentioned above
that are likely to promote terrorism: (1) refusal of colonial authorities to grant

independence, while (2) the remainder of Africa was decolonizing and providing examples of what could be attained. Britain recognized the right to independence and ultimate majority rule but delayed the transfer of power because of strong pressures from settler populations. Portugal, on the other hand, retained the myth of empire until 1974 and refused to recognize the possibility of independence. It was in these territories that we find the only examples of well-organized liberation movements in sub-Sahara Africa that fought sustained guerrilla and terrorist campaigns against colonial domination.

The literature on the preindependence period in sub-Sahara Africa lends impressionistic support to our contentions that terrorism was prevalent in those colonial systems most reluctant to accept African rights. Further evidence is obtained by inspection of data reported in the *World Handbook*. One of the variables there, armed attacks, is very close to the concept of political terrorism[10] and is reported in the right-hand column of Table 2. This table provides evidence that political terrorism (that is, armed attacks) was negligible in French and British West African territories, where Africans experienced relative freedom and were subject to less official terror. The data for Belgian, Portuguese, and British East and Central African countries are as we would predict—many more armed attacks occur in the more closed colonial systems and those least adaptive to ideas of majority rule. By colonial grouping there is a very close relationship between extent of official terrorism (government sanctions) and extent of anticolonial terrorism (armed attacks).

In this first African context, then, we can conclude with some certainty that state terror and antisystem terror are associated. Both seem to be responses to the other, although the data we have employed provide no indication that one form tends to precede or cause the other.[11] Terrorism on the part of opponents may have temporarily stimulated more official repression in some systems, such as the Portuguese and British East and Central Africa, but in the long run it is hard to deny that the goals of opponents, independence, have in large part been achieved. Although a number of factors converged to encourage colonial powers to relinquish their empires, including forms of opposition other than terrorism, the threat of terror and violence contributed to an assessment of the costs of colonial domination. Whether anticolonial terrorism was "successful" in ushering in new political arrangements freer of official repression, however, requires an examination of the majority black-ruled context. Before turning to black-ruled Africa, a few comments will be made on two countries that have followed a different pattern, ones in which a minority white population continued to control the political system after European colonial domination ended.

A Note on the Minority White-Ruled System

With the independence of Guinea-Bissau, Mozambique, and Angola from Portugal, South Africa and Rhodesia stand alone as the last two cases of white rule in sub-Sahara Africa. The international community has refused to recognize the "independence" of Rhodesia, but both Rhodesia and South Africa have been firmly controlled by indigenous white minorities. In many ways, however, these two countries can be viewed as extensions, and extreme ones at that, of colonial conditions. Relationships of domination and control are underlined by the sense of racial and cultural superiority on the part of the white minority. Attitudes reinforcing colonial inequality remain relevant in these two cases.

Both countries have developed elaborate mechanisms to ensure white political domination. South Africa's system is based on apartheid. Each individual is categorized by race—white (about 19 percent of the population), colored (about 10 percent), Asian (about 3 percent), and African (about 68 percent). In theory each race is to live separately and govern its own affairs. The status of coloreds and Asians is least clear, but the system of apartheid is most developed in regard to Africans. Nine homelands have been designated, and Africans are citizens of a homeland on the basis of ethnicity. Homelands are to become self-governing and independent. The Transkei, which achieved independence in October 1976, serves as the model for this process. The system in reality has meant unequal possibilities for Africans and restricted participation. White political institutions have determined the territory of the homelands; 13 percent of the land is designated for the 68 percent African population, and their geographic location surrounded by white territory and often without access to the sea raises questions about the independent viability of the homelands. Whites determine to which homeland an African belongs, and African political participation is restricted to the institutions of one's homeland. Important decisions are made by the white minority, which alone can participate in white institutions. Africans, in other words, cannot participate in the system that ultimately controls them.

Great Britain had always permitted white Rhodesians control of the political system, but after the white minority unilaterally declared independence (UDI) in 1965, a new constitution was written that ensured white domination. The white regime finally succumbed to pressure in the fall of 1976 and has accepted, "in principle," majority rule. Although independent, majority rule might be feasible in the near future, the following description of white domination holds for the period 1965-1977. Moreover, the ability of the white regime to maintain effective control with some form of majority rule (for example, perhaps granting power to the chiefs rather than the nationalists) remains a possibility.

The 1969 constitution provided for a House of Assembly with fifty white representatives and sixteen Africans (eight elected, and eight selected by chiefs). Theoretically Africans could achieve "parity" (fifty representatives) when they contributed more to the national revenue, but in reality parity has been an impossibility since political advance depends on social advance, which has been controlled by whites. The major vehicle for African political expression has been the chiefs, but the ability of chiefs to represent Africans is dubious because they have been appointed by the government and have a stake in the existing system (for example, salaries, land allocation powers, and so forth).

The social and economic position of the African reflects his political subordination. Land is divided equally between the races, so that the white 5 percent of the population has as much land as the African majority. A series of legislative acts, much of it enacted prior to UDI, limits opportunities for Africans and leaves them in low-paying, servile positions. Although Rhodesia has not enacted a system of apartheid, trends since UDI have been in the direction of more formal separation of the races.

Official repression and terrorism have been an important element of white minority rule in both systems. South African legislation throughout the 1950s and 1960s limited African rights to organize, and police were granted wide powers for search, arrest, and detention. The *World Handbook* information on governmental sanctions (used above as a partial indication of official terrorism) ranks South Africa sixth of 136 countries in the number of sanctions imposed from 1948 through 1967. Rhodesia also has enacted an array of security acts to prevent assembly, organization, and criticism of government. Africans are subject to arbitrary arrest, detention, restrictions, and various forms of administrative harassment. Whole segments of the population, not simply nationalist politicians, have been subject to arbitrary removal and resettlement for security reasons.

If the two minority white regimes parallel an extreme form of colonial inequality and repression, we would expect, if previous conclusions are accurate, that violent opposition would develop and some terrorism would be involved. We have here, at least until 1977, the extreme case of (1) refusal of whites to recognize the principle of African equality and rights to self-government, with (2) the remainder of Africa providing the example of independent, black rule. In fact, the data in Gurr's appendix indicate that South Africa and Rhodesia rank among the countries having the highest rates of terrorist activity from 1961 to 1970.

Although South African political opposition was initially influenced by Gandhi and tactics of nonviolence, the banning of the two major African opposition groups (ANC and PAC) in 1960 led to a reassessment of tactics. Both groups went into exile, where they plan ultimately for guerrilla war against the white minority. Both retained internal groups (Spear of the Nation and Poqo, respectively), which carried out acts of sabotage into the 1960s. The effectiveness of South African suppression and the geographical protection of South Africa by the buffer of white-dominated systems until the mid-1970s made difficult both internal terrorism and guerrilla war from exile.

The response in Rhodesia also has been one of increasing violence. A number of African opposition organizations attempted to operate in Rhodesia, but each was banned successively. As a result, major opposition groups (ZAPU,

ZANU, ANC) have gone into exile, where they have launched guerrilla campaigns in which terrorist tactics have been central. The guerrilla war officially began in December 1972. Strikes at white Rhodesians continued through the 1970s. The independence of the Portuguese territories with a new base for operations and a new example of African rule has stimulated a pick-up of guerrilla activity in 1976, particularly from new sanctuaries in Mozambique. This activity has continued in spite of the first efforts in late 1976 to negotiate a transfer to majority rule.

Rhodesia and South Africa may be unrepresentative in their unique forms of white domination, but they lend support to conclusions made earlier. Official terrorism supports the systems of white domination (probably to a greater degree than in colonial Africa), and organized campaigns of terror have developed in response.[12]

Independent Black Africa

On the surface, the change from colonial, foreign, white domination to independence and black-majority rule is one of major proportions, but the changes should not be exaggerated. Even excluding the arguments of neocolonism, which purport that informal domination remains after formal political control has been relinquished, we shall see that certain characteristics of established systems remain similar, as do aspects of popular protest. The major continuity that should be stressed is that terrorism remains in black Africa the exception rather than the rule. The organization of this section parallels that of the previous one, containing first a discussion of the nature of majority, black-ruled regimes; and second, a description of the types of violent responses that have characterized black Africa and the degree to which terrorism has been involved. The section will conclude with a discussion of three countries (Chad, Cameroon, Ghana) that have exhibited relatively high levels of terrorism. It will attempt to highlight the conditions that seem most conducive to terrorism in the African context and, at the same time, indicate why most states have been relatively free of the phenomenon.

Black-Ruled Political Systems

The black-ruled states of sub-Sahara Africa constitute a set of diverse political systems, yet there are certain general patterns that have emerged since independence. Every new state adopted a political system modeled on a Western one, and all initially provided for competitive party systems. The trend in the first decade of independence, however, was toward reduced competition either in the form of military rule or single-party states. The feasibility of competition in these contexts should not be ruled out nor should political openness be equated with Western political forms, but the suppression of opposition that in most cases has accompanied the single-party and military trends suggests that the decline of competitive party systems usually means the decline of channels for political expression (with noteworthy exceptions such as Tanzania). In general, then, independence has not meant the development of more markedly open political systems.

Table 3 reports regime type as of mid-1976. The bulk of African states fit the single-party or military pattern. Only two countries continue to have opposition parties represented, but these are minor parties that pose no threat of replacing the governing group. Elections in the 1970s gave the opposition only five of twenty-seven seats in both Botswana and Gambia. Table 3 also reports numbers of arrests and bans of parties, additional indicators of the extent of political suppression. Some single-party regimes have evolved through relatively voluntary mergers, for instance, and would not necessarily indicate repression (for example, Tanzania). All but two countries report some political arrests as of 1969 and only nine of the thirty-two countries report less than a hundred arrests. The information on bans actually underestimates the extent of political curbs because important parties were banned in some countries prior to or after the 1957-1969 time period, and other mechanisms have been used in addition to outright proscriptions. The single-list electoral law (the party that obtains the most votes wins all of the seats), which is used in the majority of countries that still hold elections quickly discourages participation of minor parties. In addition, ruling groups that face genuine competitive threats have resorted to the postponement or invalidation of elections (for example, the former in Uganda, the latter in Lesotho).

In the colonial context social and economic inequality tended to parallel political restrictions. In independent African states the same relationship is probably true, though the extent of inequality is difficult to assess accurately. One can view social inequality on two levels, which may partially overlap—the extent to which ethnic (or other) groups receive disproportionate shares of goods, and the gap that exists between elites and masses.

Ethnic inequality in independent African states is a problem inherited from colonialism. It was the European powers that drew boundaries that incorporated different ethnic groups into a single nation. Moreover, colonial powers related differently to various ethnic groups, resulting in differential distribution of advantages. Certain ethnic groups may have been more open to adapting Western education and social standards, but often the European development of a certain part of the colony benefited particular groups. Nelson Kasfir notes the importance of this fact for the position of the Baganda ethnic group in Uganda, who were located near the administrative center of the colony (Kampala):

The schools and hospitals built by missionaries were thus disporportion-
ately available to the Baganda. Today the best equipped hospitals in the
country are in Kampala. . . . in 1960 the Baganda had slightly less than
twice as many school places in comparison to their share of the country's
population. . . . Baganda over-representation at Makerere University College . . . has been far more striking. [1972, pp. 76–77]

Kasfir proceeds to document favoritism to Baganda in economic development,
consumption patterns, and employment opportunities. Parallels can be found
with the Kikuyu in Kenya (located in the highlands where white settlement was
located), the Bemba in Zambia (located in the copper belt), and in many more
cases.

    The differential modernity of ethnic groups meant that at independence
more educated groups were more likely to dominate the political system while
previously less favored groups would be excluded. The general effects of the differential colonial opportunities on political representativeness at independence
can be inferred partially from information in Table 4, where countries are ranked
by the ethnic representativeness of their independence cabinets. The data in
Table 4 indicate that at least one-third of the African countries began the independence period with highly unequal ethnic representation. *At least* in these
systems issues of ethnic discrimination would be likely to be important. Moreover, case studies of countries with seemingly representative cabinets demonstrate the salience of even relatively minor ethnic imbalances (for Zambia, for
example, see Dresang, 1974). This question will be probed further in the case
studies to be discussed shortly. One should note now, however, that the effects
of this inequality could take different forms, with different implications for
terrorist activity. Either previously favored minorities would seek to retain their
dominance with the less favored group protesting; or where less economically
favored groups were able to rule, they would seek to redress imbalances with previously favored groups seeking to maintain their privileges.

    The second form of inequality is the gap between elites and masses, rulers
and ruled. The distance between elites and the general populace became readily
apparent after independence. The first rulers were the "Western educated elite,"
those who had acquired not only Western education but often Western styles and
values as well. Their Westernization set them apart from the populace. Moreover,
the conspicuous consumption and sudden acquisition of wealth of this first generation of political leaders became quickly noticeable. It has been suggested that
the roots of this ostentation lie both in African traditions and in the colonial experience, the latter supposedly having created a desire for certain material possessions as well as the racial humiliation that can lead to "flamboyant self-asser-

Table 3 Independent African Regime Characteristics[a]

Country	Regime type, mid-1976	Political arrests, independence–1969[b]	Illegal parties, 1957–1969[c]
Botswana	Competitive	0	0
Burundi	Military	1,295	4
Cameroon	Single party	263	3
Central African Republic	Military	20	4
Chad	Military	135	1
Congo, Brazzaville	Military	287	4
Dahomey	Military	301	7
Ethiopia	Military	1,146	0
Gabon	Single party	75	0
Gambia	Competitive	0	0
Ghana	Military	1,773	2
Guinea	Single party	649	0
Ivory Coast	Single party	952	0
Kenya	Single party	396	1
Lesotho	No party, civilian	33	0
Liberia	Single party	166	0
Malawi	Single party	503	1
Mali	Military	318	1
Mauritania	Single party	166	4
Niger	Military	132	1

Country	Regime	Political arrests[b]	Illegal parties[c]
Nigeria	Military	33,022	14
Rwanda	Military	62	0
Senegal	Single party	603	2
Sierra Leone	Single party	497	4
Somali	Military	43	no data
Sudan	Military	1,902	9
Tanzania	Single party	50	1
Togo	Military	131	5
Uganda	Military	2,819	4
Upper Volta	Military	50	2
Zaire (Congo, Kinshasha)	Military	3,048	13
Zambia	Single party	637	1

[a]Information on political arrests and illegal parties is based on a shorter time period than the regime description and therefore does not necessarily reflect the extent of curbs of the regimes characterized as of 1976. Chad, for example, is now military, but the arrests and bans reflect actions of the single-party regime that existed until 1975.

[b]Political arrests are from the *Black Africa* file but are not reported in Morrison et al. (1972).

[c] Illegal parties are the number of parties banned or proscribed (Morrison et al., 1972, p. 102).

Table 4 Cabinet Ethnic Representativeness at Independence[a]

Country	Score
Liberia	0.84
Chad	0.79
Ghana	0.77
Central African Republic	0.72
Cameroon	0.58
Gambia	0.55
Sierra Leone	0.54
Gabon	0.51
Burundi	0.37
Tanzania	0.25
Ivory Coast	0.17
Ethiopia	0.17
Niger	0.16
Zambia	0.11
Rwanda	0.09
Uganda	0.08
Congo, Brazzaville	0.08
Malawi	0.08
Sudan	0.08
Mali	0.08
Togo	0.06
Senegal	0.06
Zaire	0.05
Mauritania	0.05
Kenya	0.05
Nigeria	0.03
Upper Volta	0.03
Guinea	0.03
Dahomey	0.03
Somalia	0.03
Botswana	0.00
Lesotho	0.00

[a]Data are from Morrison et al. (1972). The score measures the degree to which ethnic proportions in the cabinet deviate from national ethnic population distributions. See Morrison et al. (1972, p. 89) for the formula.

tion." Mazrui argues that "there are forms of deprivation which, when relieved, give rise to excessive indulgence" (1970, p. 23).

The gap between elites and masses is itself an important source of inequality, but it takes on added importance when it accompanies the ethnic inequalities and the repressive nature of regimes mentioned earlier. We have evidence that political leaders in most African systems have suppressed considerable political expression, that these leaders tend to acquire advantages that set them apart from the populace, and that in many systems these leaders disproportionately represent particular ethnic groups. We would expect that regimes characterized by repression and inequality would rely on some official terrorism to support the system, as was argued in the colonial context. Western journalists have depicted to us the terror of Idi Amin in Uganda, where political opponents mysteriously disappear, and of General Bokassa in the Central African Republic, who has been accused of whipping and mutilating opponents. Such sensationalism focuses on extreme cases rather than typical ones, although to deny any terrorism would be equally misleading. The information in Table 3 on arrests and bans partially reflects the extent of arbitrary force. We would expect those systems with most political arrests to rely substantially on terror. The case studies that follow will attempt to probe further the existence of official terror.

Political Opposition in Black Africa—The Rarity of Terrorism

The nature of a colonial system appeared oppressive, and one would expect it to have been conducive to violent opposition. In Africa, however, we saw that both the scope of colonialism, as well as violent responses, were relatively limited. Similarly, most Africanists have not painted benign pictures of the independence political systems, but in spite of apparent closure and some oppression, the response again has been largely nonviolent. The extent of terrorism has been minimal, and where violence has occurred, it has generally taken other forms. The argument presented at the beginning of this chapter and mentioned for the colonial context is that governments of limited scope affect a relatively small proportion of the population; hence, large numbers are not likely to be mobilized for or against a regime. Observers of Africa perceived considerable political ferment at the time of independence, but later assessments perceive more apathy than involvement. Nelson Kasfir (1975), for example, argues that a major trend in the postindependence era has in fact been the reduction of political participation.

Although the general level of political mobilization in Africa may be low, the question remains as to what types of political behavior characterize the participation that does exist. Typical "legitimate" forms of behavior such as electoral participation do occur, but given the large number of systems with few channels for political expression, one would expect political behaviors of less

Table 5 Conflict Behavior in Africa, Independence-1969

Turmoil[a]		Communal instability[b]		Elite instability[c]	
Nigeria	42	Sudan	38	Dahomey	26
Dahomey	25	Ethiopia	30	Sudan	22
Sudan	20	Zaire	27	Zaire	20
Senegal	18	Nigeria	27	Togo	20
Zaire	17	Chad	17	Congo, Brazzaville	17
Zambia	13	Rwanda	15	Burundi	16
Ethiopia	12	Kenya	14	Ghana	13
Kenya	9	Uganda	12	Nigeria	12
Ghana	9	Mali	6	Sierra Leone	11
Congo, Brazzaville	8	Burundi	5	Central African Republic	8
Liberia	7	Ghana	5	Somalia	8
Mauritania	7	Ivory Coast	5	Uganda	8
Sierra Leone	7	Congo, Brazzaville	4	Mali	7
Chad	4	Somalia	3	Upper Volta	7
Ivory Coast	4	Zambia	3	Liberia	6
Upper Volta	4	Mauritania	2	Senegal	6
Guinea	3	Cameroon	1	Chad	5
Tanzania	3	Dahomey	1	Ethiopia	4
Uganda	3	Sierra Leone	1	Guinea	4
Botswana	2	Botswana	0	Gabon	3
Burundi	2	Central African Republic	0	Ivory Coast	2

Gabon	2	Gabon	0	Cameroon	1
Malawi	2	Gambia	0	Kenya	1
Mali	2	Guinea	0	Lesotho	1
Somali	2	Lesotho	0	Malawi	1
Lesotho	1	Liberia	0	Niger	1
Togo	1	Malawi	0	Botswana	0
Cameroon	0	Niger	0	Gambia	0
Central African Republic	0	Senegal	0	Mauritania	0
Gambia	0	Tanzania	0	Rwanda	0
Niger	0	Togo	0	Tanzania	0
Rwanda	0	Upper Volta	0	Zambia	0

[a]The turmoil score is derived from the *Black Africa* file and is the sum of riots, strikes, and demonstrations. It differs from the score reported in Morrison et al. (1972, p. 130), which includes terrorism (argued in the text to be more appropriately considered elite activity) and declarations of emergency (which reflects instead government behavior). Note that this score differs from the next two columns, which report weighted scores.

[b]"Definition: A numerical weight was given to civil wars (5), rebellions (4), irredentism (3), and ethnic violence (1). The index here was computed by multiplying the score for each event by the number of years in which it was reported in any country, and by summing the resultant scores" (Morrison et al., 1972, p. 129).

[c]"Definition: A numerical weight was given to coups d'etat (5), attempted coups (3), and plots (1). The index here is a sum of the scores for all such events . . ." (Morrison et al., 1972, p. 128).

legitimate forms (at least by Western standards). A variety of such modes of participation have occurred in Africa, as information in Table 5 indicates.

Countries are ranked in terms of three forms of conflict behavior in this table. Turmoil (riots, strikes, and demonstrations) is relatively unorganized, often spontaneous political expression. Although turmoil occurred in the independence-to-1969 period in all but five countries, it has been frequent in at most one-third of the countries. Communal instability is another form of mass conflict but involves ethnic groups. Again, this form of conflict has been important in some countries, particularly the top several where open civil wars have occurred, but data in the table indicate that most countries have been relatively free of this violence and in fact one-third experienced none at all. On the other hand, there is evidence of elite activity outside normal political channels. The right-hand column in Table 5 indicates that six countries experienced no coups, attempted coups, or plots from independence through 1969, the majority experienced a moderate level of elite instability, while approximately the top one-third of the countries experienced pervasive elite conflict. Although the bulk of African citizens may not be politically mobilized, some states have experienced significant levels of political expression outside "normal channels." In several states mass, communal violence has been important, but much instability has been on the part of small, elite groups, and some consists of turmoil that may involve large numbers but probably does not reflect mass mobilization. Where, then, does terrorism fit in this general picture of political violence?

Terrorism should be considered an elite form of participation, given its small, organized base. But terrorism remains one of many types of strategies and apparently a minor one. Table 6 ranks countries according to the number of terrorist events from independence to 1969.[13] These data reflect only antigovernment terrorism and would exclude terrorism that might be carried out between rival groups or by the state. Still, we cannot conclude that terrorism is significant in any but a small number of African countries.

If we can assume from the prior discussion of African political systems that all or most countries contain sufficient political restrictions and inequalities to stimulate violent opposition of some group, we can wonder, then, why terrorism is not more pervasive. The following propositions, based in part on the conflict literature and on previous analyses of African conflict,[14] are suggested to explain patterns of violence in Africa and, particularly, the minimal role of terrorism:

I. The greater the ethnic (or other) inequality, the greater the elite-mass gap, and the more coercive and repressive the political regime, the greater the likelihood of conflict (when all three conditions overlap, conflict is likely to be greatest).

   A. The more politically mobilized the population, the more likely conflict will take the form of communal instability and possibly turmoil.

Table 6 Terrorism in Africa, Independence-1969[a]

Country	Number of events
Chad	11
Cameroon	10
Ghana	7
Dahomey	4
Niger	4
Ethiopia	3
Lesotho	3
Senegal	3
Togo	3
Zambia	3
Zaire	2
Liberia	2
Mauritania	2
Somali	2
Botswana	1
Burundi	1
Congo, Brazzaville	1
Guinea	1
Ivory Coast	1
Kenya	1
Malawi	1
Rwanda	1
Uganda	1
Central African Republic	0
Gabon	0
Gambia	0
Mali	0
Nigeria	0
Sierra Leone	0
Sudan	0
Tanzania	0
Upper Volta	0

[a]Data are from the *Black Africa* file but are not reported in Morrison et al. (1972). For definition and discussion of the variable see note 13.

    B. The less politically mobilized the population, the more likely con-
        flict will be of an elite form.

        1. The following conditions in Africa favor elite conflict in the
            form of coups rather than terrorism:

            a. Militaries have the necessary arms and organization.

            b. African regimes are generally weak and hence vulnerable to
                actual seizure.

        2. Terrorism is likely to occur only when the following conditions
            exist:

            a. Where political opposition has an organizational base that
                is an alternative resource to the organization of the military.

            b. Where the opposition perceives the regime to be invulnerable
                to more common tactics of seizure by coup.

The investigation of terrorism in the case studies that follow will have to
document the following in order to lend support to these propositions: (1) some
degree of ethnic inequality, elite-mass gap, and/or political coercion sufficient to
stimulate opposition; (2) inability of the opposition to mobilize the population
to the point of civil war; (3) organizational base of the opposition; and (4) perceived invulnerability of the regime. Although the first and second conditions
are widespread in Africa, the general absence of the third and fourth conditions
may help to explain the relative absence of terrorism in independent Africa.

Case Studies of Terrorism in Black Africa

In Table 6 Chad ranks the highest in number of terrorist events reported from independence through 1969. In Chad terrorism is not an isolated strategy of a
small group but rather a tactic of several movements now waging guerrilla war in
the north.

    A number of ethnic groups exist in Chad, but the primary division is be-
tween the Arab, Muslim population of the north and the non-Muslims of the
south. Potential antagonisms between the two areas have roots in previous eras
when Muslims invaded the south and engaged in slave raids. The southern part
of the country, where France promoted cotton cultivation, however, became the
most advanced area. The result of these precolonial and colonial developments
is that

> The legacy of this slavery can still be seen in the bitter hostility felt by
> Negro Tchadians toward their former Arab masters. It is also evident in
> the contempt tinged with jealousy shown by the Arabs toward their former

slaves, who have now become more prosperous and better educated than they and who today form the elite of the towns and farmlands of the south. [Thompson and Adolff, 1960, p. 427]

At the time of independence the Parti Progressiste Tchadien (PPT) of Francoise Tombalbaye was dominant, although parties representing primarily Muslim segments of the population were represented. The opposition combined into the Parti National Africain (PNA) in 1960, formed a brief national union with the southern-based PPT in 1961, but soon broke with the majority party. Tombalbaye moved quickly to consolidate his position. PNA leaders were arrested in 1961, the opposition was banned in 1962, more arrests followed in 1963, and finally a single party was declared in 1963. The PPT attempted to incorporate elements of the opposition into its ranks, but the Muslim population of the north now had no separate vehicle for political representation. Tombalbaye began to shift from his policy of suppression and initiated a new policy of national reconciliation in 1971. He freed some political prisoners (important ones had died in jail, however), filled half his cabinet with Muslims, and made gestures toward ending some of the blatant inequalities between north and south by demoting some technocrats who had favored southern development (*Africa Contemporary Record*, 1972-1973). Moreover, he initiated a policy of friendship with Libya who then cut off aid to the rebels in the north. The military coup in 1975 ushered in a new southern-based government that continued to adhere verbally to the policy of national reconciliation, but as of 1976 the government remains one of southerners, and the south remains the advantaged section of the country.

Terrorist activity in response to southern domination began in 1965. The major organization representing the opposition, the Tchadian National Liberation Front (FROLINAT), launched its campaign in 1966. Rebels struck at targets such as government outposts, but the conflict intensified through the 1960s and involved more direct clashes between rebel bands and government forces supported by French troops. By 1968 the conflict was considered to be a civil war with rebels claiming to have 2000 troops (Morrison et al., 1972, p. 208). Outside involvement intensified the struggle. The French have supported the government side while Sudan and Libya have aided the rebels. Foreign involvement has lessened in the 1970s, and the policy of national reconciliation has managed to co-opt a number of rebels. Direct confrontations between the two sides may have declined somewhat, but the rebels have continued their tactics of kidnappings, raids, and so forth, into the 1970s.

Ethnic and regional inequality are apparent in Chad, with political domination reinforcing this inequality. The form of conflict that has resulted wavers between terrorism on the part of a few, and more widespread communal violence. The battles between government forces and rebels constitute war rather than terrorism, but the conflict in Chad has never reached the degree of violence experienced in other civil wars, such as that in Nigeria. The ethnic disparities provide a broad base for mobilization (more so than we find in Cameroon, for example), but the sparse population and poor communication and transportation of northern Chad work against widespread mobilization of the northern population. Terrorist tactics, then, have remained an important element of the Chadian rebellion.

The opposition has been able to maintain organization both within and outside Chad. The continuity between the organization and leadership of the banned parties with the new rebel movements is unclear, but because support comes from similar segments some continuity probably exists. Although the government likes to blame terrorism on "armed bandits," some political organization is behind much of the violence in the north. As of 1976 three separate groups existed. A group known as the Toubou rebels (part of FROLINAT until 1968) control much of the north and has been responsible for the much-publicized kidnapping of the French anthropologist Francoise Claustre. The Chad Liberation Front (FLT) operates in the far east while FROLINAT claims the northwest. It is the latter group, led by Sidick who is based in Algiers, that seems to be the major opposition organization (*Africa Research Bulletin,* September 1975, pp. 3757-3758; October 1975, p. 3792). Although the organized opposition in Cameroon and Niger, mentioned below, was forced into exile, the isolated and sparsely populated north favors clandestine operations, no doubt accounting for the ability of the groups to engage in conventional guerrilla war as well as terrorist tactics.

Although Chadian rebels have the advantage of organization and some control of territory, they continue to operate from a position of weakness. They technically represent the 50 percent Muslim population, but even prior to their suppression in the independence period, the legal Muslim parties never obtained a majority. The government remains located in the Bantu south, and so if Muslims were to seize power they would be operating in hostile territory. Moreover, the ability to seize power has been undercut by Muslim underrepresentation in the military, which has been dominated by southerners. The 1975 coup merely brought different southerners to power. The weapons and organization of the military are not advantages available to northerners.

In summary, Chad seems to support the propositions listed earlier. Inequality reinforced by political repression has stimulated opposition; the conflict borders on civil war, but the low level of mobilization has limited the scale of violence so that terrorism remains important; the opposition has an organizational base; and the organizations are working from a position of weakness.

The bulk of antigovernment terrorism in Cameroon has been attributed to the former nationalist party, the Union des Populations du Cameroun (UPC). An understanding of its position in independent Cameroon requires first a review of its existence under colonial rule. Cameroon had been a German colony, but after German defeat in World War I, the colony was divided, with the western section put under British administration and the eastern portion under French. The UPC was formed in French Cameroun in 1948 by Ruben Um Nyobe, Felix Moumie, and several trade unionists and government employees. It was the first and best organized nationalist party. Its goal was complete independence and the reunification of the Camerouns. In the face of French hostility and the lack of a broad base of support (other parties sprang up and gained popularity), the UPC turned to more violent tactics in 1955 and was subsequently banned. The UPC then split into two groups—one faction, led by Um Nyobe and Matip, was based in British Cameroun; the other, led by Moumie, Ouandie, and Kingue, settled in Accra and then Conakry in exile. For the remainder of the colonial period the UPC continued its attempt to foster rebellion in Cameroun, but independence was granted in 1960 with Ahidjo and his Union Camerounaise (UC) controlling the government. In 1961 the two Camerouns united with a coalition of UC and the western KNDP ruling the country. At this point the UPC wing led by Matip (Um Nyobe had been killed) in Cameroon was legalized, but the Moumie group remained in exile and was committed to violent opposition.

The sources of UPC opposition lie more in political exclusion than in ethnic resentments. UPC strength was centered in Bamileke and Basa areas to the south so that ethnic considerations are not irrelevant, but the UPC was founded on ideological principles and initially banned for those reasons. In the independence era the Fulani minority of the north has dominated politics. However, the ethnic imbalance is not the primary basis for continued UPC opposition.

On the other hand, political repression can be seen as a source of continued opposition. Cameroon is a typical example of the African trend toward a single-party system. By 1962 the UC had consolidated its position in the east and in 1966 its merger with the dominant party in the west into the UNC made Cameroon a one-party state. The UC was able to co-opt opposition members, and where co-optation failed, stronger tactics of arrest were employed. The internal "legal" wing of the UPC met the same fate of other opposition parties—the inability to remain a separate, viable opposition:

> The first indication that the government intended to employ more forceful means to create national unity was the dissolution of the UPC congress in Yaounde on January 22, 1962, at bayonet point. The UPC's parliamentary group had already been reduced by the arrest and trial of Deputy Owono Mimbo Simon in 1961 and by the expulsion of another UPC deputy; the elections to fill these seats resulted in victories for UC candidates. It has been claimed that the UPC candidates actually won these by-elections . . . but that the UC candidates were declared elected. [LeVine, 1971, p. 107]

In mid-1962 major opposition leaders joined a united front in opposition to the single-party but were subsequently arrested under a new antisubversion law. By the 1970s the government retained such a large number of political prisoners (most associated with the UPC rebellion) that Amnesty International made official pleas on their behalf (*Africa Contemporary Record,* 1974-1975).

The UPC in exile remained the only active opposition to UC dominance. It refused reconciliation and launched a number of terrorist attacks within Cameroon through the 1960s. The choice of terrorist tactics in the face of UPC inability to operate in the country seems explicable in terms of its limited popular base, the strength of the regime, and its own organizational strength.

Although the UPC might have had the potential for being a majority party, it lacked broad popular support during its legal existence. When it failed to gain support prior to independence, the UPC turned to more violent tactics; and after its banning, its attempts to spark widespread popular rebellion failed. In the independence era, its strength was further cut by the co-optation of the internal wing and by the achievement of its original goals—independence and reunification. Its popular support was probably further eroded by the lack of clear-cut ethnic bases of party competition, which might have stimulated the mobilization of ethnic animosities and provided the group with a new cause. The UPC, then, turned to terrorism as a tactic of the weak. It lacked a strong popular base and was impotent in the face of the UC's and then UNC's ability to co-opt and suppress opposition.

Further, terrorism was probably a tactic for the UPC given its continuing organization and ability partially to control guerrilla and maquis activity within Cameroon.[15] It began as the strongest and most organized party in West Cameroun and then retained an organization and top leadership in exile. Much African opposition has lacked this necessary resource for political terrorism. As the leadership of the UPC is killed or dies, however, this asset is diminishing. One of the last leaders, Ouandie, was captured and along with two others summarily was executed in January 1971. Similarly, terrorist activity has declined, and LeVine states that this "may well mark one of the last gasps of the 15-year-old rebellion" (1971, p. 129).

It is interesting to note as an aside that in Niger, another country with a relatively high incidence of terrorism, conditions are strikingly similar to those in Cameroon. Here the militantly nationalist Sawaba Party of Djibo Bakary was banned by French authorities, went into exile, and after independence launched terrorist attacks against the more moderate government of Hamani Diori, who, like Ahidjo in Cameroon, co-opted and suppressed political opposition. As in Cameroon, the source of conflict was ideological, although with clear ethnic overtones; the group was excluded from political participation; it was a minority party when legal and was weak vis-à-vis the ruling party; yet it retained the one resource of exile organization that enabled terrorist opposition.

The final example, Ghana, appears similar to these others, at least if the alleged source of terrorist activity is accurate. Nkrumah and his Convention People's Party (CPP) took control at independence in 1957. The CPP was a militantly nationalist party and attempted to build support throughout the nation. By independence, however, significant opposition to Nkrumah remained, consisting of some of the older middle-class nationalists (for example, Danquah, Busia, Gbedemah) and groups representing ethnic interests. In fact the opposition parties were largely ethnic ones (for example, the National Liberation Movement represented the interests of Ashanti; the Northern Peoples Party represented the Muslim north) and as such had difficulty uniting in opposition to the CPP. However, shortly after independence Nkrumah banned all regional and ethnic parties, forcing the diverse opposition to form the United Party (UP). The opposition initially held about one-third of the legislative seats, but this representation quickly diminished in the face of political repression. Large numbers of UP members were arrested every year from 1958 through 1964, Nkrumah officially declared a single-party state in 1965, and with that security finally held the election that he had postponed since 1961. All major opposition leaders were arrested, detained, or in exile. Nkrumah thus relied heavily on repression and force. The arbitrary nature of his suppression suggests that official terrorism remained a prop of his regime. In the face of the bombing incidents discussed in the following paragraph, the CPP legislature passed a law prescribing (retroactively) the death sentence for carrying explosives; when the chief justice acquitted two politicians implicated in an assassination attempt, Nkrumah dismissed him and ordered a retrial. The impression we are given of Nkrumah's Ghana is one in which continual plots (whether genuine or imagined) led to the indiscriminate arrest and detention of politicians.

In this context of repression and force, the opposition briefly engaged in terrorist activity. In August 1962 a bomb was thrown at Nkrumah; the leader escaped but four others were killed. More bombs exploded in Accra in September 1962 prior to the president's birthday celebrations; another went off in the midst of a crowd cheering Nkrumah in January 1963; and again in January 1964 another bomb was aimed at, though again missed, Nkrumah. The politicians implicated in these blasts included former UP leaders (one former member of parliament was sentenced to death, and Busia, Gbedemah, and exiles in Togo were implicated) as well as some CPP leaders (*Africa Recorder,* 1962, 1963, 1964).

Although particular official accusations may be open to doubt, the timing and location of the blasts and assassination attempts indicate that they must represent political opposition to Nkrumah and his regime. What then explains the choice of these tactics? First, political opposition appears to be centered among politicians; conflict represents political rivalries at the top. Political opposition had some ethnic basis, but conflict did not involve primarily the mobilization of ethnic animosities (with the exception of Ewe irredentism, but that was apparently unrelated to the terrorism). Opposition politicians had been excluded from the regime and had few resources available to them; Nkrumah's system no doubt seemed invulnerable. If we can believe the allegations of the involvement of the UP exiles in Togo and their role in smuggling the explosives into Ghana, then the primary asset of the opposition was its exile organization and leadership.

Much to everyone's surprise, Nkrumah's regime was toppled by a military coup in 1966. Although Western observers might exaggerate the loss of his support, considerable discontent had developed and, most important, had spread to a major prop of the regime, the military. Opposition was based not only on an exile group of excluded politicians but became more widespread and involved the one organization capable of ending the regime. As a result, opposition tactics could move from terrorism to coup.

Terrorism, though rare, has occurred in Africa and in several contexts has been an important tactic of the opposition. Its success, however, is difficult to assess. The case studies suggest the self-reinforcing nature of terrorism. Political repression seems to have stimulated the terrorist tactics of such groups as the Chadian rebels, the UPC in Cameroon, and the Ghanaian opposition; yet the choice of violent tactics reinforced official repression. Leaders in Cameroon have been unrelenting in their harsh treatment of rebels, as the prompt execution of Ouandie after his conviction in 1971 demonstrates; Nkrumah's response to the bomb incidents in Ghana consisted of more arrests and detentions; and the Chadian opposition leaders spent years in jail, often subject to torture, even though some of their arrests preceded the armed rebellion.

From another perspective, one could argue that terrorist tactics have not been in vain. The hard-core opposition remains subject to repression, but its activities have prompted some adaptive behaviors on the part of officials. The Chadian policy of national reconciliation has led to the integration of some rebels and to gestures toward ending some of the north-south inequalities, although the success of this policy is difficult to assess now. The UPC's program was adopted in Cameroon by 1961 (independence and reunification), while the opposition willing to accept Ahidjo's single-party system was incorporated into the ruling group. The Ghanaian coup of 1966 was a victory for groups discontent with Nkrumah. It is not possible to relate the coup directly to prior terrorism, however, and the coup altered the situation, making conjectures of the success of terrorism moot. The irony of the fate of the terrorist groups such as the exile organizations in Cameroon and Niger is that they remain groups without a cause; where a clear cause remains, as in Chad, the government has been forced to make concessions.

Conclusions

The investigations of terrorism in colonial (and white minority) and independent Africa reveal its limited degree. Two questions, then, have been central: (1) why has terrorism been minimal, and (2) why has it occurred where it has? The rarity of terrorism in the African context can be attributed to factors that Gurr suggests in Chapter 1, as well as to the limited scope of colonial and independent political regimes as elaborated in this chapter.

A number of factors have been discussed as explanations for the terrorism that has developed. The primary theme in the colonial and white-minority context is that official terrorism helps to support systems that discriminate against certain groups and exclude them from meaningful political expression, and that such systems foster responses of terrorism. Investigations of independent Africa support this contention, but they suggest that political exclusion rather than social disadvantage is the primary source of terrorism. The case studies of Cameroon (with the parallel of Niger) and Ghana point to the primacy of political repression, and only in Chad are ethnic and regional disparities clearly related to violent opposition.

These findings deserve comment because they initially appear to contradict others. First, the general arguments linking inequality and deprivation to violence need to be elaborated for terrorism. Social disparities (for example, ethnic, regional, or religious ones) may lead to violence, but such conditions are likely to mobilize relatively large numbers and hence promote more broadly based violence such as civil wars or guerrilla wars rather than terrorism, which has a limited base. In fact in Chad, the one case where ethnic inequality is significant, the response has been guerrilla warfare as well as terrorist tactics.[16]

Second, the primacy of political repression as a source of terrorism contradicts Gurr's thesis that it flourishes in more open societies. But the repression of regimes in Africa needs to be assessed in light of the weakness of most regimes, which limits the efficiency of suppression. Modern totalitarian and authoritarian systems may experience less terrorism because they can successfully suppress it, but African regimes may stimulate opposition by their closure while lacking the ability to control the violent opposition likely to develop. In those systems that have gained in strength, terrorists have experienced greater difficulties in operating (for example, in South Africa and possibly Cameroon).

The study of terrorism in the independence context proposed additional explanations. Groups turning to terrorism were operating from a position of weakness and working against a regime they were incapable of seizing through legitimate (for example, elections) or nonlegitimate (for example, coups) means. The vulnerability of most African regimes to military coups may help to explain the general absence of terrorism in independent Africa. This condition would also be true in colonial Africa, where the more closed systems denied nationalists access to both legitimate and nonlegitimate tactics. The condition of an organizational base was found to exist in all cases of terrorism in the independence context. Similarly in colonial and white-ruled Africa, the major examples of terrorism have occurred where guerrilla organizations have developed in opposition.

Finally, a continuity that emerges from this study is that a major strength of terrorists is an exile base for operations. Exiled political parties were the source of terrorism in Cameroon, Niger, and Ghana; the rebel movements in Chad have more internal strength but also have the advantages of exile organization and sanctuaries in neighboring countries. Similarly, the organizations that developed in opposition to Portuguese colonial rule and to South African and Rhodesian white rule have had the advantage of exile organization and/or sanctuary in newly independent black-ruled states. A disadvantage of the South African opposition until the 1970s was the buffer of white-dominated states that protected the republic from rebel sanctuaries. As this buffer erodes, the South African opposition will benefit from the advantage that other movements opposed to white domination had—rebel sanctuary. Terrorism in the African context, then, underlines the importance of international factors in the study of terrorism.

Notes

1. The intent in this chapter is to analyze terrorism in several contexts in nations in sub-Sahara Africa. However, nation-states in Africa are superimposed on a variety of tribal or ethnic social and political systems, which could be more salient to some individuals than the national unit. Power and authority relationships in an ethnic unit could be more meaningful than national ones. Because points made in the chapter exclude terrorism in these subnational systems of authority, a more complete picture of terrorism in Africa would require an investigation of these subnational or ethnic units. E. V. Walter's *Terrorism and Resistance* (1969) includes studies of African tribal systems and would provide a useful supplement to the national-level material presented in this chapter.

2. The terms "regime of terror" and "seige of terror" are from E. V. Walter (1969).

3. Colonies are not nation-states, but contemporary states correspond to the territory of the European colonies, and colonial political activity was oriented to the same units that are today's nation-states.

4. A survey of the precolonial periods can be found in Paul Bohannan and Philip Curtin (1971).

5. What appear on the surface to be contradictory hypotheses on the relationship between repression and terrorism (violence) may not be contradictory. The conclusions will address this point.

6. These arguments are summarized well in Gurr's discussions of relative deprivation (1970).

7. Discussions will exclude Spain, because her colonies were minimal, and Germany, because she lost her colonies after World War I, and they were put under the administration of other colonial powers.

8. In some cases, such as Angola, whites shared lower status positions, but even here Africans continued not to share higher status positions with Europeans.

9. This statement will remain an untested assumption or hypothesis to be explored in another context. The fact that our information on this period depends on colonial records, which are not likely to reflect accurately the extent of official terrorism, makes a systematic investigation of this assumption very difficult and beyond the scope of this chapter. Assessing the degree of separate treatment of Africans is also difficult, because similar legal provisions were often applied differently in different locations.

10. It is difficult to find appropriate indicators of terrorism for the colonial period. The variable "government sanctions" taps more than official terrorism, but it probably adequately reflects differences among colonies in the extent of official terrorism employed. The variable "armed attacks" is more problematic as an indicator of antigovernment terror. Acts of terrorism would be included in armed attacks but so are other events that do not necessarily reflect the concept as used in this chapter. Taylor and Hudson define the variable in this way:

> An *armed attack* is an act of violent political conflict carried out by (or on behalf of) an organized group with the object of weakening or destroying the power exercised by another organized group. It is characterized by bloodshed, physical struggle, or the destruction of property. . . . The target of an armed attack typically is a regime, government, or political leader, or its (his) ideology, policy, or actions; it may also be a religious, ethnic, racial, linguistic, or special interest minority. . . . When an insurgency situation reaches such proportions that the government can no longer control it by normal punitive measures (such as those coded below as governmental sanctions), the government actions as well as those of the insurgents fall within the definition of armed attacks. [1972, pp. 67-68]

The first part of their definition seems appropriate for our conception of anticolonial terror. The latter portions raise problems. First, events with social groups as targets probably involve terrorism but do not fit in with our two-sided conception of government and antigovernment terror. Second, inclusion of government actions stronger than government sanctions begins to confuse the two phenomena we have been trying to separate. Thus, anticolonial terror may be inflated in Table 2 by inclusion of some acts carried out by colonial officials. The first problem might inflate scores for Uganda, Zambia, Congo, and Angola; while the second problem may inflate scores for Kenya, Rhodesia, Congo, Angola, and Mozambique. In other words, the gap between British East and Central Africa, Belgian colonies, and Portuguese colonies, on the one hand, and British West Africa and French colonies, on the other hand, may be explained partially by their larger number of interethnic and government terrorist events and hence may exaggerate the difference in the extent of anticolonial terrorism. In spite of this problem, this variable probably reflects fairly accurately differences among the colonies, although it exaggerates the *extent* of differences.

11.   There is a tendency for government sanctions and armed attacks to occur within the same year, so data aggregated by year do not enable one to probe which actions tend to occur first.

12.   An excellent treatment of developments in Rhodesia since UDI is Bowman (1973). An analysis of the cycle of repression and violence in South Africa can be found in Horrell (1963).

13.   Morrison et al. define terrorism

> as events involving relatively highly organized and planned activity on the part of small but cohesive groups, in which the aim of the activity is to damage, injure, or eliminate government property or personnel. These activities include bomb plants, sabotage of electrical and transportation facilities, assassinations (attempted and successful), and isolated guerrilla activities. [1972, p. 130]

This variable probably reflects more accurately the concept of antigovernment terror than does the *World Handbook's* "armed attacks." In excluding events associated with interethnic conflict and some associated with communal instability, it is probably underestimating the extent of terror in a system. The actual extent of terrorism probably lies somewhere between that indicated by armed attacks and that indicated by *Black Africa's* terrorist events.

14.   See, for example, Gurr (1970), Gurr and Duvall (1973), Duvall and Welfling (1973), Morrison and Stevenson (1972), and Welfling (1975). The conditions of turmoil are difficult to assess because data on turmoil are considered least reliable, and hence past analyses open to more question. Also problems surround the conceptualization of turmoil (Morrison et al., 1972, p. 124).

15.   Some terrorist activity in Cameroon is apparently carried out by nonpolitical bandits.

16.   Ethiopia is a close parallel to Chad. Here guerrilla organizations in Eritrea have engaged in terrorist activity, but with a strong ethnic and regional basis to the conflict, the situation borders on civil war.

References

Africa Contemporary Record: Annual Survey and Documents (annual). New York: Africana Publishing Corporation.

Africa Recorder (fortnightly). New Delhi, India: Recorder Press.

Africa Research Bulletin (monthly). Exeter, England: Africa Research Ltd.

Bohanan, Paul, and Curtin, Philip. 1971. *Africa and Africans.* New York: Natural History Press.

Bowman, Larry. 1973. *Politics in Rhodesia: White Power in an African State.* Cambridge, Mass.: Harvard University Press.

Coleman, James S. 1964. "Nationalism in Tropical Africa." In *Independent Black Africa: The Politics of Freedom,* ed. William John Hanna. Chicago: Rand McNally, pp. 208-234.

Coser, Lewis. 1956. *The Functions of Social Conflict.* New York: Free Press.

Dresang, Dennis. 1974. "Ethnic Politics, Representative Bureaucracy and Development Administration: The Zambian Case." *American Political Science Review* 68 (December): 1605-1617.

Duvall, Raymond, and Welfling, Mary. 1973. "Social Mobilization, Political Institutionalization, and Conflict in Black Africa: a Simple Dynamic Model." *Journal of Conflict Resolution* 17 (December): 673-702.

Fanon, Frantz. 1968. *The Wretched of the Earth.* New York: Grove Press.

Galtung, Johan. 1969. "Violence, Peace, and Peace Research." *Journal of Peace Research* 6, no. 3: 169-191.

Gurr, Ted Robert. 1970. *Why Men Rebel.* Princeton, N.J.: Princeton University Press.

Gurr, Ted R., and Duvall, Raymond. 1973. "Civil Conflict in the 1960s: A Reciprocal Theoretical System with Parameter Estimates." *Comparative Political Studies* 6 (July): 135-169.

Hodgkin, Thomas. 1957. *Nationalism in Colonial Africa.* New York: New York University Press.

Horrell, Muriel. 1963. *Action, Reaction, and Counteraction.* Johannesburg: South African Institute of Race Relations.

Huntington, Samuel P. 1968. *Political Order in Changing Societies.* New Haven, Conn.: Yale University Press.

Kasfir, Nelson. 1972. "Uganda." In *The Politics of Cultural Sub-Nationalism in Africa,* ed. Victor A. Olorunsola. Garden City, N.Y.: Doubleday Anchor, pp. 47-148.

Kasfir, Nelson. 1975. *The Shrinking Political Arena: Participation and Ethnicity in African Politics with a Case Study of Uganda.* Berkeley: University of California Press.

LeVine, Victor T. 1971. *The Cameroon Federal Republic.* Ithaca: Cornell University Press.

Mazrui, Ali. 1970. "The Monarchical Tendency in African Political Culture." In *Governing in Black Africa: Perspectives on New States,* ed. Marion E. Doro and Newell M. Stults, pp. 18-33. Englewood Cliffs, N.J.: Prentice-Hall.

Mondlane, Eduardo. 1969. *The Struggle for Mozambique.* Baltimore: Penguin.

Morrison, Donald, Mitchell, Robert, Paden, John, and Stevenson, Hugh Michael. 1972. *Black Africa: A Comparative Handbook.* New York: Free Press.

Morrison, Donald, and Stevenson, Hugh Michael. 1972. "Integration and Instability: Patterns of African Political Development." *American Political Science Review* 66 (September): 902-927.

Taylor, Charles L., and Hudson, Michael C. 1972. *World Handbook of Political and Social Indicators.* New Haven, Conn.: Yale University Press.

Thompson, Virginia, and Adloff, Richard. 1960. *The Emerging States of French Equatorial Africa.* Stanford, Calif.: Stanford University Press.

Walter, E. V. 1969. *Terror and Resistance: A Study of Political Violence.* New York: Oxford University Press.

Weiss, Herbert. 1967. *Political Protest in the Congo.* Princeton, N.J.: Princeton University Press.

Welfling, Mary B. 1975. "Models, Measurement and Sources of Error: Civil Conflict in Black Africa." *American Political Science Review* 69 (September): 871-888.

Wilkinson, Paul. 1974. *Political Terrorism.* New York: John Wiley.

Zolberg, Aristide. 1966. *Creating Political Order: The Party States of West Africa.* Chicago: Rand McNally.

8

Political Terrorism in Latin America:
A Critical Analysis

John W. Sloan
Department of Political Science
University of Houston
Houston, Texas

.

Introduction

There are basically two forms of political terrorism, and both exist in Latin America. One may be labeled "*enforcement terror* to describe terror . . . launched by those in power," and the other "*agitational terror* to describe terroristic acts by those aspiring to power." The difference is between terror perpetuated by incumbents in power as an extreme means of enforcing their authority . . . and by insurgents out of power with a view to provoking certain reactions from the incumbents or an otherwise apathetic population."[1] The terrorist, whether he represents the state or the insurgents, is involved in a sustained and conscious policy that is willing "to sacrifice all moral and humanitarian considerations for the sake of some political end."[2] For the humanist, therefore, the subject of political terrorism is not pleasant. Understanding of this subject requires a skeptical analysis that can delve beneath pious governmental lies and self-serving revolutionary rhetoric.

Unfortunately, the realities of Latin American societies "encourage" terrorism. Their authoritarian political systems lack legitimacy, and their paternalistic leaders have never accepted the concept of the "loyal opposition." They are generally characterized by inequitable distributions of income and land, a condition made even more explosive by the rapid population increases. Their cultural traditions such as *machismo* (male virility) glorify violence and inhibit the development of compromise (a feminine value). Their inefficient and corrupt bureaucracies, which include the police system, confront an idealistic and expanding university population that agitates for utopian solutions to extremely complex national problems.

The purpose of this essay is to describe generally the two forms of political terrorism in Latin America and then deal specifically with the problem of terrorism in Argentina, Uruguay, and Brazil. My conclusions are, first, that the fragmentation and isolation (from the masses) of the leftist revolutionaries means that they are incapable of overthrowing any Latin American government within the foreseeable future. Second, that agitational terrorism has not brought the socialist revolution closer; instead, it has provoked the Latin American governments to develop their enforcement terror capabilities. Third, the fragmentation of the government security forces and the socioeconomic conditions in Latin America ensure that the revolutionaries cannot be annihilated and will be able steadily to recruit a small stream of members, especially from the universities.

Agitational Terrorism

The problem for Latin American revolutionaries is to make successful revolutions. According to their Marxist analyses of objective conditions—the disparity between the few rich and the many poor, the unemployment and underemployment, the exploitation of the peasant, and the economic and political dominance of the United States—each of the Latin American states is ripe for revolution. The dilemma is in creating the subjective conditions for fomenting revolution. Most young revolutionaries have lost faith in the orthodox Latin American Communist parties, who are accused of waiting for the Godot of a progressive national bourgeoisie that will fulfill its historic mission of industrializing Latin America so that a proletarian revolution can take place. The revolutionaries want the revolution now.

There are two broad streams of revolutionary thought in Latin America, one urging that the revolution should be initiated in the countryside, the other that the principal battleground should be in the cities. Both rural and urban guerrillas agree that the principal enemies of the revolution are U.S. imperialism, the landowners, and the wealthy bourgeoisie. In the words of a Peruvian revolutionary group, "We realize that the greatest scourge of the peoples of the earth is North American imperialism, and that our country's wealthy bourgeoisie and landowners debase themselves in the slavish pursuit of its interests and are there to exploit the people and to keep them in a state of poverty and backwardness."[3]

Both revolutionary groups recruit mainly from the young, especially the university populations. In Debray's words, "there is a close tie between biology and ideology.... An elderly man ... will not easily adjust himself to the mountains nor—though this is less so—to underground activity in the cities. In addition to the moral factor—conviction—physical fitness is the most basic of all skills needed for waging guerrilla war...."[4] The primary recruiting centers for guerrillas are the university centers of Bogota, Buenos Aires, Lima, Mexico City, and Montevideo. With the exception of Bolivian tin miners, the exploited groups of peasants and workers have generally not been attracted to participate in the guerrilla cause.

Both revolutionary groups also agree that fundamental social change can be brought about only by armed revolution. There cannot be any alliances with the progressive bourgeoisie, as advocated by the Communist parties, because there is no progressive bourgeoisie. They believe that the bourgeoisie is aligned with the traditional oligarchy because of its fear of socialism. The perspective of the revolutionaries is a stark dichotomy: either death (physical or spiritual) under the enforcement terror of colonial fascism or life under a liberating socialist revolution. A Venezuelan revolutionary explains:

> To create a world where the peasants, workers, students and the people in general can share in material benefits and advantages, requires war. This is not because the revolutionaries have so decreed it, but because the reactionaries, the rich, and those who are bolstered by North American imperialism force the people and the revolutionary armies to wage this war and induce the people to take up arms.[5]

Similarly, a Guatemalan revolutionary writes, "They [the Guatemalan Communist party] do not see that armed struggle is the highest form of political struggle, and that our motto of 'to conquer or die for Guatemala' is not a juvenile or leftist boast."[6]

The rhetoric, morality, and behavior of the terrorists suggest that they share certain traits of what Daly calls the revolutionary personality. According to Daly, "The distinctive characteristic of the revolutionary is that he apparently combines extreme dogmatism with extreme cynicism and extreme populism with extreme elitism—that he appears to be a genuine combination of zealot saint and power-hungry butcher."[7]

The agitational terrorist is continually trying to justify (for others and possibly himself) the use of antihumanistic means to attain humanistic ends. In the revolutionary's world view,

> the guerrilla band concentrates within itself the most idealistic, clear-minded and determined elements of the nation and symbolizes the qualities of the

"people"; the power [which is] to be destroyed and superseded becomes an out-and-out enemy, utterly alien to the society it dominates. To strengthen this impression, propaganda will stress the government's dependence on a foreign power.[8]

Because the revolutionaries' goals are "just" and their enemies, the Latin American governments, are "evil," they feel morally justified in initiating agitational terror so that revolutionary conditions can be induced.

The major supporter of rural guerrilla warfare in Latin America was Che Guevara. Guevara's theory, derived from the Cuban experience, was based on four premises: (1) popular forces, initially consisting of thirty to fifty men, could eventually defeat professional armies; (2) the objective, socioeconomic conditions in Latin America made each Latin American country ready for revolution; (3) the creation of a rural guerrilla base (the *foco*) would create the necessary subjective conditions to bring about a revolution; and (4) revolutionaries could succeed only if they concentrated on organizing the peasants in the rural areas. Regis Debray formalized the thought of Guevara and Castro and challenged the orthodoxy of the Communist parties by stressing the Cuban Revolution's decisive contribution to revolutionary experience. The Cuban Revolution "proved" that non-Communists could lead a revolution by shedding their bourgeois skins in the countryside and becoming proletarianized into the leaders of *the* authentic Communist party. In Debray's words, "Under certain conditions, the political and military are not separate, but form one organic whole, consisting of the people's army, whose nucleus is the guerrilla army. The vanguard party can exist in the form of the guerrilla *foco* itself. The guerrilla force is the party in embryo."[9]

The issue of terrorism concerned both Guevara and Debray. Guevara stressed that the ill-conceived use of terrorism might inhibit the guerrilla from being able to demonstrate his moral superiority over the state security forces. Guevara's ambivalence toward the use of terrorism is revealed in his own writings. On the one hand he wrote, "We sincerely believe that terrorism is of negative value, that it by no means produces the desired effects, that it can turn a people against a revolutionary movement, and that it can bring a loss of lives to its agents out of proportion to what it produces." On the other, Guevara asserted that "terrorism should be considered a valuable tactic when it is used to put to death some noted leader of the oppressing forces well known for his cruelty, his efficiency in repression, or other quality that makes his elimination useful."[10] Debray claims that "city terrorism cannot assume any decisive role. . . . But if it is subordinate to the fundamental struggle (of the countryside), it has, from the military point of view, a strategic value; it immobilizes thousands of enemy soldiers in unrewarding tasks of protection."[11] Guevara and Debray apparently agreed that political terrorism is self-defeating as an end in itself; it is valuable only insofar as it promotes revolution.

Guerrilla *focos* were defeated in Argentina (1959, 1964, 1968), Brazil (1962, 1967, 1969, 1970), Bolivia (1967, 1970), Colombia (1961), the Dominican Republic (1960, 1973), Ecuador (1962), Paraguay (1959, 1962), and Peru (1963, 1965).[12] In attempting to apply his Cuban experiences to Bolivia, Che and his guerrillas were defeated by perhaps the most inefficient army in all of Latin America. The rural guerrillas were simply not able to attain the support of the peasants; the enforcement terror of the government proved more effective than their agitational terror. Without the active support of peasants, the guerrillas were isolated and eventually destroyed by armies that had been given counterinsurgency training.

The disasters in the countryside caused the revolutionaries to shift their efforts to the cities in the late 1960s despite Castro's admonition that "the city is a cemetary of revolutionaries and resources."[13] The chief urban revolutionary theoretician was a Brazilian, Carlos Marighela. The son of a black Brazilian woman and an Italian immigrant, Marighela joined the Communist party in 1928 at the age of 16. Inspired by Fidel Castro's Organization for Latin American Solidarity conference in 1967 and its call for revolution, Marighela broke with the Brazilian Communist party in 1967 and launched the Action for National Liberation (ALN). Urban guerrilla warfare was initiated in 1968 with plans to extend the operations into the countryside in late 1969. However, on November 4, 1969, Marighela was killed by a police ambush in São Paulo.

Marighela's major contribution to Latin American revolutionary thought was to transfer Guevara's idea of the *foco* from the countryside to the city. He believed that guerrillas could have a greater impact in the ever-expanding and potentially explosive cities of Latin America rather than getting lost in rural areas. As a Communist, Marighela had been hunted unsuccessfully by the police in São Paulo several times, and so he also believed that revolutionaries would be safer in the city than in the countryside. The impact Marighela desired—to raise political consciousness—was to be achieved not through political explanations, but through acts of political terrorism. These acts would prove that the government sought only to protect the interests of the oligarchy and imperialists rather than "the people." Marighela specifically contrasts the morality of governmental and revolutionary terrorism by emphasizing that

> the Brazilian military dictatorship uses means of repressing the people which are brutal and callous and designed to protect the interests of wealthy capitalists, *latifundiarios* [large landowners], and North American imperialists. On the other hand, the methods used by the revolutionaries against the dictators are legitimate and inspired by a spirit of patriotism. No honorable man can accept the shameful and monstrous regime set up by the military in Brazil.[14]

Because the state was not bound by law, neither were the terrorists.

Marighela advocated that the urban guerrillas be organized in a pyramidal structure with four to six persons to each cell. For security reasons, only one person from each cell would be in regular contact with a leader from a higher cell. Some guerrillas would appear to live ordinary lives and would engage in terrorist acts only occasionally; others would be full-time terrorists living underground.

Obviously, under this system, security concerns interfere with organizational efforts. In the words of one Brazilian revolutionary, "armed action, which means living in small, clandestine cells, reduces the possibility of contact with the population. We must rely on the repercussions of our actions."[15] This isolation from the very people the guerrillas must eventually organize in order to overthrow the government may be insoluble. In brief, security precautions may condemn the urban guerrillas to remain terrorists rather than becoming revolutionary leaders.

In his writings, Marighela is much more explicit about the need for political terrorism than is Guevara or Debray. Marighela stresses that "the urban guerrilla's armed struggle is directed to two objectives: (1) the physical liquidation of the high and low ranking officers of both the armed forces and the police; (2) the expropriation of arms or goods belonging to the government, the large capitalists, the *latifundiarios,* and the imperialists."[16] Marighela urges the recruitment of young men and women who have consciously and without hesitation chosen to pursue a career of violence. In his words, "Since our way is through violence, radicalism and terrorism (the only effective weapons against the dictator's violence), anyone joining our organization will not be deluded as to its real nature and will join because he has himself chosen violence."[17]

The goal of terrorism is, in Marighela's words, "to unleash, in urban and rural areas, a volume of revolutionary activity which will oblige the enemy to transform the country's political situation into a military one. Then discontent will spread to all social groups, and the military will be held exclusively responsible for failures."[18] In brief, the strategy is to make conditions worse in order to raise the population's consciousness to a level where they can be organized against the colonial fascist regime. The Tupamaros in Uruguay reflect a similar belief when they state, "If there is no fatherland for all, there will be none for anyone."[19] The guerrillas are apparently so self-assured concerning their own virtue and good intentions that it never occurs to them that significant portions of the population may hold them responsible for the worsening conditions. It is conceivable that the guerrillas' *macho* commitment to violence helps to maintain the uneasy alliance between the military and the bourgeoisie. The middle class is likely to believe that guerrillas who use terror to attain power will use terror against them to maintain themselves in power.

In any case, Marighela did help popularize the notion of urban terrorism throughout Latin America. Because the guerrillas do not want to antagonize the workers or even the middle class, they have generally not engaged in the destruction of property (for example, by setting off bombs in department stores). Gerald West points out that

> the characteristic that distinguishes terrorist activities in Latin America from such activities in other parts of the world is the predilection to seize hostages for ransom. . . . Between 1968 and 1975 Latin American countries accounted for fully 42 percent of the world's terrorist incidents involving the seizure of hostages. . . . Moreover, the individuals who have been chosen as targets for kidnap/ransom or assassination have usually been selected for symbolic reasons—foreign diplomats, "local agents of North American imperialism" or prominent members of indigenous elite groups.[20]

These activities have been used to attain the release of political prisoners, to obtain ransom money, to embarrass officials, and to strain relations among Latin American governments and Great Britain, West Germany, Japan, and especially the United States. West concludes that "as a low risk, high multiple return activity, the effectiveness of kidnap/ransom has been firmly established in the minds of most terrorist groups in the region."[21]

But after almost a decade of these activities, no urban revolutionary group is close to revolutionary success. Their continued acts of urban political terrorism reveal that, although the security forces cannot stamp them out despite the use of the most brutal methods, neither can the guerrillas move on to a higher level of revolutionary activity. The guerrillas have succeeded in making things worse in a number of countries but with few prospects for making conditions better in the near future.

Enforcement Terror

Although both the Latin American governments and the guerrillas have been brutalized by the nature of their conflict, the former have displayed a contempt for human rights that can only be called barbarous. The torture of political prisoners has always been a characteristic of *caudillo* rule, but today, despite the fact that respect for human rights is written into the constitutions of every nation in Latin America, there is evidence that the problem has become epidemic and more technologically advanced.

For good reasons, most of the world's attention concerning enforcement terror has been centered on such right-wing countries as Argentina, Brazil, Chile, and Uruguay. However, we should not overlook the fact that violations of human rights occur throughout Latin America, including Cuba and Mexico. In 1975,

Amnesty International estimated that Cuba had at least 4000 political prisoners; the U.S. State Department estimates the total at 20,000. The crucial point is that, unlike some of the most notorious Latin American regimes, Castro has not allowed international observers to view conditions among political prisoners. And, we should not forget that the Mexican military was used in October 1968 to shoot and kill at least 300 protesting students. Evelyn Stevens, who studied this incident among several others, concluded:

> The data do not reveal a political system oriented toward the formulation and modification of goals through pluralistic participation in the decision-making process. Instead, we see repression of authentic interest groups and encouragement of spurious groups that can be relied on not to speak out of turn. The regime deals with *bona fide* groups almost as though they were enemy nations.[22]

Recent support for Stevens's thesis is provided by the government-instigated ouster of the editor and senior staff of the Mexican newspaper *Excelsior* for criticizing President Echeverria's policies.[23]

Given the authoritarian political culture in Latin America, almost all of the regimes engage in acts of enforcement terror. Many of these acts are carried out by the military, the police, or quasi-official vigilante groups. The training of these security forces prompts them to apply the concept of "war" to many situations of civil conflict. In their minds, the treachery of guerrillas more than justifies their own use of terror. And because they have the resources of the state at their disposal, they are capable of engaging in greater levels of terrorism than the guerrillas. Many of them appear to be ideologically opposed to the guerrillas, but there are some who are simply sadistic. Sadistic and quasi-criminal elements are especially attracted to the vigilante groups that have sprung up in Mexico, Guatemala, Brazil, and Argentina.

The enforcement terror activities of many of the Latin American governments are frequently aimed at preventing the independent mobilization of interest groups. Most governments are particularly sensitive about the mobilization of peasants; potentially "dangerous" peasant leaders are regularly intimidated by security forces. If this fails to deter them, the military, the police, or local vigilante groups will use stronger measures. In 1962, a Mexican peasant leader, Ruben Jaramillo, was assassinated.[24] In 1975, the Inter-American Commission on Human Rights was investigating the beheading of a Colombian peasant leader. Enforcement terror of this kind is used in much of the rural areas of Latin America to intimidate anyone—priests, teachers, lawyers, students, and peasants—who might help organize the peasants.

In the urban areas, enforcement terror is directed at members of political parties, trade unions, and youth movements, and at professors, priests, lawyers, and journalists. In the cities, "The cycle of arrest and torture is the foundation of counterguerrilla operations."[25]

The demobilization efforts of right-wing regimes that replace left-wing governments are particularly frightening. In Bolivia, more than 2000 people have been arrested for political reasons without being formally charged since General Hugo Banzer Suarez took power through a military coup in August 1971. In Chile, an estimated 60,000 persons were arrested and detained for at least 24 hours between the September 1973 coup that overthrew Allende and March 1974. In 1976 there were still an estimated 10,000 political prisoners in Chile. The Chilean military, under the leadership of General Pinochet, was deeply concerned about how close Allende had come to leading Chile toward socialism. They were determined to remove all those of leftist leanings from positions of authority and to prevent leftist terrorism, which was now prevalent in neighboring Argentina and Uruguay, from spreading to Chile. Consequently, they launched an unprecedented reign of enforcement terror. In this Kafkaesque world, rival intelligence units of the army, navy, air force, and civil police competed with one another in rounding up, interrogating, torturing, executing, and releasing prisoners. Some prisoners who were arrested and eventually cleared and released by one arresting agency found themselves caught in the net again when they were arrested by another agency. Relatives of the political prisoners found themselves frustrated victims of bureaucratic runarounds when each agency denied it had arrested or knew the whereabouts of their husbands or sons. Because the Allende regime had been legally elected, some were arrested for doing what had been legal; others engaged in the same activities were not arrested. Many were tortured; others were not. Some were arrested and released; others were never heard from again. For Chileans, who had prided themselves in their democratic traditions, the whole system was terrifyingly capricious. The Amnesty International report summarizes the Chilean reign of enforcement terror in these words:

> When people are arrested they are usually taken first to a military barracks or a police station or to one of the special interrogation centres established by the intelligence services. They may be held there for weeks or even months. "Pressure," often amounting to severe physical or psychological torture, is frequently applied during this period of interrogation. . . . Methods of torture employed have included electric shock, blows, beatings, burning with acid or cigarettes, prolonged standing, prolonged hooding and isolation in solitary confinement, extraction of nails, crushing of testicles, sexual assaults, immersion in water, hanging, simulated executions . . . and compelling attendance at the torture of others. A number of people have died under torture and others have suffered permanent mental and nervous disabilities.[26]

The situation in Guatemala has steadily declined since leftist President Arbenz was overthrown in 1954 by Castillo Armas with the aid of the CIA. By the middle of the 1960s, there were several guerrilla groups operating in different parts of the nation. To counteract the guerrillas, more than twenty right-wing vigilante groups engaged in terrorist activities armed with weapons supplied to the Guatemalan army by the United States. These paramilitary terrorist groups—with such names as the White Hand, the Purple Rose, and the New Anti-Communist Organization—were composed of military men, police officers, landowners, and occasionally former left-wing terrorists who had been apprehended and had shifted sides. Even though these vigilantes were engaged in illegal activities, they were never interfered with by the security forces of the state. Indeed, there is no question that they functioned as a quasi-official agency of the state under the direction of such prominent officials as Mario Sandoval Alarcon.

Because they believed that threats of death would not deter the guerrillas, the vigilantes resorted to the threat of torture and mutilation to intimidate their adversaries. Norman Gall reports that the vigilantes "first circulated leaflets carrying the names and sometimes the photographs of their announced victims, whose corpses—and those of many others—were later found grotesquely mutilated: dead men with their eyes gouged out, their testicles in their mouths, without hands or tongues, and female cadavers with their breasts cut off."[27]

During the state of siege in effect between November 1970 and November 1971, more than 1000 people were killed, as right-wing and left-wing terrorist organizations engaged in an orgy of violence. Given the greater resources of the right-wing terrorists, they were able to kill about fifteen times as many victims as the guerrillas. A right-wing terrorist group went so far as to machine-gun a partially paralyzed Guatemalan congressman as he was being helped into his car. President Arana's 1970 election campaign warning that "if it is necessary to turn the country into a cemetary in order to pacify it, I will not hesitate to do so"[28] seemed to be coming true.

Perhaps the best way to convey the impact of the terrorist state in Guatemala is to draw an analogous picture of what the same level of violence would mean in the United States.

> It is as if . . . the CIA and FBI, in response to accelerated terrorist activities by the Weathermen and the Black Panthers, were secretly to enlist and equip the Klan and the John Birch Society, fill out their ranks with Green Berets and crack police units, and loose them on the country, leaving 41,000 corpses in 12 weeks. Among the dead from both sides over a two year period would be George Meany and Cesar Chavez, J. Edgar Hoover and Richard Helms, James Reston, Richard Rovere, Ralph Nader, John Kenneth Galbraith and Herbert Marcuse, Ronald Reagan, Averell Harriman, Generals Westmoreland and Wheeler, Roy Wilkins, Senators Fulbright and

Stennis, Abbie Hoffman and Tom Hayden and 3,000 to 4,000 other prominent citizens from the whole spectrum of U.S. public life. . . . Stretch the
analogy back to 1966 and the equivalent would be 240,000 U.S. citizens
murdered and a quarter of a million more in prison or enforced exile.[29]

In brief, throughout the 1960s and 1970s, the security forces of the Latin
American states and their quasi-official helpers have been able to conduct more
effective enforcement terror than the agitational terror activities of the guerrillas.
The result of all this is that many Latin American states are more repressive now
and less close to revolution than they were in 1960. To validate these points, let
us examine the parallel terrorist activities of the security forces and the guerrillas
in Argentina, Uruguay, and Brazil.

Argentina

Of all the countries in the third world, Argentina appears to be the most fortunate. She is not plagued by a whole set of problems that supposedly cause violence and political instability in other countries. Argentina has plenty of fertile
land, a good climate, and an educated population (a 91 percent literacy rate);
she does not have a population explosion, a population suffering from protein
deficiency, nor an Indian problem. The population of Argentina has essentially
a European background. Argentina has not had to confront the problem of integrating a large Indian population into their national culture as is true in Mexico,
Ecuador, Guatemala, Peru, and Bolivia. The problems in Argentina are not socioeconomic in origin; they are political. Their basic political problem was— and is—
Juan Peron and his followers. Peron was an amalgam of characteristics that defy
ideological labeling. He was part fascist, part socialist; part charismatic leader,
part gangster; part nationalist, part opportunist. He introduced some of the most
necessary reforms in Argentine history, such as providing decent wages for the
working class and integrating them into the political system, but he did this in
such a tainted manner that he corrupted the whole political process rather than
stabilizing it. A U.S. reader might understand this point by speculatively answering this question: What would have happened in the United States if a Huey
Long or a Jimmy Hoffa had introduced the New Deal reforms rather than Franklin Roosevelt?

General Peron began his rise to power in 1944 and was overthrown by a
military coup in 1955. During his 18-year exile, Peron supported guerrilla warfare as one of the means designed to enable him to make a triumphant return to
Argentina. Peron's charismatic leadership allowed him to exercise control over
a variety of Peronista labor unions, youth groups, guerrillas, and women's associations. Potential leaders of these groups who threatened to become too indepen-

dent from Peron were often intimidated and occasionally assassinated. A situation was created where rival leaders violently competed among themselves on the basis of who was the most loyal to Peron. In Kenneth Johnson's words, "Viewing Peronism as an emotional relationship goes a long way toward explaining its potential for generating internal conflict. It is like a fight among brothers and sisters for control of a family legacy and/or inheritance. . . . It is possible to worship Peron and hate others who adore him as well."[30] As Johnson wryly notes, "Peronistas . . . could be either Fascists or Marxists, but not both at once. That feat only Peron himself could perform."[31]

Peron orchestrated a motley array of unions, fascists, socialists, and guerrilla groups that finally brought about his return to Argentina in June 1973. The major Peronista guerrilla group was the Montoneros, who had formed as a result of the riots in Cordoba against the Ongania dictatorship. In May 1970 the Montoneros endeared themselves to Peron by kidnapping and executing former President Aramburu, a general who had conspired against Peron in 1955. But each of the Peronista unions also believed that their loyalty to Peron should be rewarded. Most of the Peronista labor syndicates maintained their own paramilitary squads (*grupos de choque*). This volatile combination (plus several million Argentines) was brought together on June 20, 1973, at the Ezliza Airport outside Buenos Aires to welcome Peron back to Argentina. The ideological contradictions of Peronism become obvious when the events of this occasion are reviewed: the contending factions could not agree on where each would sit in the grandstand to hear Peron's arrival speech. Because physical proximity to Peron was considered to be of great symbolic significance among competing Peronists, rival paramilitary groups started shooting each other, and several hundred people were killed.

The violence and terrorism that had plagued Argentina since 1969 continued after Peron took power in 1973 and increased after his death under the inept rule of his wife, Isabel Peron. Acts of agitational terrorism were committed by the Montoneros and the People's Revolutionary Army (ERP), a non-Peronist urban guerrilla group. They have specialized in the assassination of military personnel, police, and right-wing labor officials, and in the kidnapping of foreign businessmen. The latter has been a major source of income for these guerrillas, providing them with over $20 million in 1973.[32] In 1976, they were able to plant bombs under the bed of General Cesario Cardozo, a federal police chief, killing Cardozo and seriously wounding his wife, and in a crowded dining room of the intelligence department of the Argentine Federal Police, killing eighteen policemen and wounding forty others.

The response of the Argentine government, in terms of enforcement terror, has been furious. A novelist, V. S. Naipaul, stresses that "the guerrillas have simplified the problems of Argentina. Like the campus and salon revolutionaries of the north, they have identified the enemy, the police. . . . And the police reply to terror with terror. They too kidnap and kill; they torture, concentrating on the genitals."[33]

The use of right-wing terrorist groups is particularly brutal. In Argentina there is evidence that the most prominent of these vigilante organizations, the Anti-Communist Alliance (the Triple A), was initiated by Jose Lopez Rega, a practicing astrologer and minister of social welfare under Isabel Peron. Lopez Rega used state funds to buy weapons and to recruit members of the federal and provincial police forces. Within a 10-month period between 1974 and 1975, they assassinated over 200 people and intimidated many more.[34] The madness of this period is revealed in the events of December 1974 when the ERP assassinated an army officer and accidentally killed his 3-year-old daughter, and the Triple A retaliated by dragging the mother of one of the guerrilla suspects from her home and murdering her. In August 1976, the Triple A killed forty-six suspected guerrillas in two mass executions.

After the overthrow of Isabel Peron in 1976, the government, led by General Jorge Rafael Videla, condemned right-wing terrorism. It has claimed that left-wing terrorism can be effectively countered only by "a high concentration of centralized violence" initiated by the state. But one cannot be sure whether this statement is honestly made, and, even if it is, there is no guarantee that the government could control the different security agencies and vigilante groups. As is true throughout Latin America, right-wing terrorist groups are hardly ever interfered with in Argentina. No Latin American president can be believed on this issue until right-wing terrorist leaders are arrested and prosecuted.

In any case, the legacy of Peron, and the interaction of agitational and enforcement terrorism, has left Argentina in a frightful condition. In 1974 there were about 250 major political assassinations; in the first half of 1976, more than 600 people were killed in political violence.[35] With no end in sight, Argentines have watched in horror as army officers, police officials, union members, foreign businessmen, newspapermen, lawyers, priests, mothers, daughters, and students have been killed. The sickness is revealed in that both right-wing and left-wing publications have been filled with morbidly detailed reports exulting in the deaths of their rivals. I agree with Johnson's thesis that

> charisma, zealotry, mysticism, the occult, mental syndromes of arrogance and *machismo,* all have coalesced in Argentina to bring about guerrilla warfare and what we . . . term the politics of violent plunder. . . . At issue here is not only the question of whether rule by violence (government by terror) leads inevitably to a cycle of dictatorship-anarchy-dictatorship, but also whether the *ad infinitum* unleashing of such a dialectic will not ultimately destroy the society.[36]

Uruguay

In the early 1900s Uruguay was violently divided by the Colorado (liberal) and Blanco (conservative) political parties. A Colorado leader, Jose Batlle, visited Switzerland and was so impressed that, upon becoming president, he began the process of instituting reforms to make Uruguay the Switzerland of Latin America. Under the influence of Batlle, Uruguay accepted a plural executive, the nationalization of several major industries, a series of welfare programs, and, of course, the inevitable growth of the state bureaucracy. By the 1950s one-third of the population was either working for the state or receiving some kind of state pension. Given Uruguay's small size and its lack of resources and industry, the foundation of the economy remained agriculture. Under Batlle and his successors' urban-oriented policies, agricultural production stagnated. The urban population ate well, but Uruguay was exporting less meat and wool in the 1950s than in the 1920s. The results of this economic stagnation were growing corruption among members of the bloated bureaucracy, inflation (over 1000 percent since 1968), unemployment, and the growing radicalization of a segment of university students who no longer had a bright economic future. Some students and professional people responded to the decay of the economy by joining the Tupamaros, the most successful urban guerrilla group in the history of Latin America.

"Tupamaro" is a contraction of Tupac Amaru, the name of an Inca chief who opposed the Spanish in colonial Peru in the late eighteenth century. One of the principal founders of the Tupamaros was Raul Sendic. Born in 1925, Sendic quit law school to join the Socialist party in the late 1950s. After losing two elections for Congress, he retired from the party and tried to organize the impoverished sugar workers, leading them in strikes in 1960 and 1961. In 1963, Sendic began a series of expropriation raids, seizing arms and robbing banks to finance the development of what became an expertly trained and disciplined urban guerrilla organization. The Tupamaros focused their efforts on Montevideo because the capital has about 1.3 million people, nearly half the country's population. The Tupamaros believed that they could use the houses, streets, and especially the tunnels of Montevideo as advantageously as the Vietcong were using the countryside of Vietnam. One should also stress that the predominantly flat, open countryside of Uruguay is not conducive to guerrilla warfare.

By 1970 the Tupamaros probably had 1000 members grouped in clandestine five-to-seven-man cells, headed by a core of fifty to a hundred members. They also had several thousand active sympathizers. The Tupamaros believe that "the people want change and must choose between the improbable and remote change which some offer through proclamations, manifestos or parliamentary action, and the direct road incarnated by the armed group and its revolutionary action."[37] As is typical of Latin American revolutionaries, they also perceive that "the ruling class of Uruguay is no more than a docile instrument of the U.S. ruling class. Therefore, the Uruguayan ruling class cannot help but to serve U.S. interests."[38] The difference between the voluntarist position of the Tupamaros and the determinist position of the Uruguayan Communist party is summarized by a Tupamaro spokesperson:

> Tupamaros and Communists are in accord on one point: until all the conditions are given, it is not possible to take power; but while the latter wait for them to be given, the former fight to cause them. That is to say, . . . if a wave of terrorism begins, the conditions of the "repressive state" are caused to surface in a much shorter time than if one waits for the slow development of the contradictions. Actions are the process which accelerates revolutionary conditions.[39]

The early actions of the Tupamaros produced widespread publicity and some favorable reactions, but did not create revolutionary conditions. Although the Tupamaros claimed that "any method that is employed to gain justice for the people is a correct method regardless of its individual style . . . ,"[40] most of their early escapades were bloodless operations aimed at embarrassing the Uruguayan governments of, first, President Pacheco and, after 1971, President Bordaberry. The early Tupamaro operations were characterized by split-second timing, discipline, coordination, and even a sense of humor. They kidnapped two close friends of President Pacheco, seized and disclosed records implicating public officials in corruption, and robbed a number of banks and gambling casinos. Their most spectacular feat in humiliating the government was the escape from a government prison of 165 Tupamaro prisoners. The fact that the Tupamaros could retrieve their personnel from government prisons, but the government could not retrieve kidnapped friends of the president or foreign diplomats suggested that the former might be better equipped to run the state than the present elite.

By 1971 the Tupamaros had kidnapped the director of the state phone company (twice), a banker, a Brazilian consul, an American agronomist, the British ambassador, a state prosecutor, a former cabinet minister, and Dan Mitrione, an AID official. Mitrione, the father of nine children, was officially in Uruguay to help train the police; the Tupamaros and Costa-Gavras's film, "State of Seige," claimed that he was a CIA agent and was in part responsible for the barbaric methods of interrogation being employed by the police. When the Pacheco government refused to release any political prisoners, the Tupamaros assassinated Mitrione. Both sides were now seriously engaged in war.

After the 1971 elections in which Bordaberry was elected president, the Tupamaros felt compelled to increase the scope and intensity of their acts of terrorism in order to regain the attention of the Uruguayan people. In one of their discussion papers, they complained about the "people's indifference toward our actions" even though "we've unmasked the real nature of the regime in various ways. . . ."[41] In 1972 the new objective of the Tupamaros was to "harass directly and systematically the repressive forces as our most important method of action."[42] This form of terrorism was to be extended into the countryside through the *tatucera* (a *tatu* is a local species of armadillo; a *tatucera* is the animal's burrow) program in which rural Tupamaros would operate from underground base camps.

The Tupamaros viewed the 12,000 men in the military and the 22,000 in the police as one of the weakest repressive forces in Latin America. Indeed, some of the Tupamaros felt the defeat of these forces would occur quickly; they were more worried about the possible intervention of Brazil or the United States. But the Uruguayan forces proved more capable and ruthless than the Tupamaros had believed possible. In April 1972, the legislature, at President Bordaberry's urging, declared a "state of internal war" under which the armed forces could arrest and confine suspects under military law, make searches without a warrant, censor the press and radio, and command the police. By June 1974, Congress itself was dissolved, the largest labor federation was disbanded, and the political parties were declared inactive. The military, now expanded to 25,000, ruled with Bordaberry until they removed him in June 1976.

Until Chile grabbed the dubious distinction in September 1973, Uruguay was the most repressive state in Latin America. Amnesty International estimates that since 1972, one in every fifty persons has been subjected to interrogation, arrest, imprisonment, or torture. Uruguay now has 6000 political prisoners.[43] The government claims that 2000 Tupamaros have been captured, including Raul Sendic, who, along with other top leaders, is being held in a maximum security cell at a military base. In 1976 Uruguay appeared more repressive than ever before in its history and no closer to a socialist revolution.

Brazil

In April 1964 the Brazilian military launched a coup and created a right-wing authoritarian political system. The Brazilian left, which had seldom been unified before the coup, was now even less so. Before the revolt, the left had been busily mobilizing peasants, workers, and students, but now the new military government made it clear that these groups would either be demobilized or brought under control through corporatist arrangements. The leftist leaders of these groups were removed from positions of authority. Surprisingly, the suddenness of these changes caught the leftists unaware, and it took them several years to respond. The Brazilian Communist party (PCB) advocated organizational work among the working class and marginal classes, who had borne the brunt of the government's early austerity program and who were *not* sharing in the benefits of Brazil's economic miracle, which began in 1968. However, inspired by Castro and the Tricontinental and OLAS conferences, a number of dissident groups believed that only violence could be effective against an efficient authoritarian regime, and they "broke from the PCB like splinters of broken glass."[44] The most influential of these splinters was Carlos Marighela, a leader of the PCB in São Paulo. Marighela emphasized that

> The overwhelming defect of the Brazilian revolutionary movement is the disunited state of the revolutionary organizations and their disagreement over attitudes and objectives. Within this disagreement there is an intense struggle for leadership going on. Each organization is tacitly claiming the leadership of the revolution itself, and this makes it difficult to discover a common denominator among those who are prepared to fight against our common enemy.[45]

Marighela urged all revolutionary groups to launch acts of terrorism without waiting for unity. He hoped that the very disunity of the revolutionary left could be turned to tactical advantage because these guerrilla groups would operate in different places employing a variety of methods. Success would emerge, not out of theoretical arguments in meetings, but out of revolutionary action against the Brazilian government. Consequently, Marighela did not attempt to gain control of the twelve to sixteen guerrilla groups composed of about 500 militants and several thousand sympathizers that emerged in the late 1960s. Marighela simply stressed that "to be an assailant or a terrorist is a quality that ennobles any honorable man because it is an act worthy of a revolutionary engaged in armed struggle against the shameful military dictatorship and its monstrosities."[46]

Political terrorism was launched in 1968. Between 1968 and 1970, Marighela's ALN and the other groups robbed more than a hundred Brazilian banks, which allowed the terrorists to be independent of outside support (especially from Cuba). In October 1968, U.S. Army Captain Charles Chandler was assassinated in São Paulo in front of his wife and 9-year-old son because of his alleged war crimes in Vietnam. In September 1969, U.S. Ambassador C. Burke Elbrick was kidnapped in Rio de Janeiro and exchanged for fifteen political prisoners who were flown to Mexico. The guerrillas achieved a propaganda victory in January 1969 when Carlos Lamarca, an infantry captain who had been widely publicized by the government for teaching bank clerks how to shoot in order to deter terrorist bank robberies, deserted his regiment and joined a guerrilla group, the Popular Revolutionary Vanguard (PRV). Lamarca achieved even greater notoriety and embarrassment for the government when he organized the biggest robbery in Brazil's history by stealing $2.4 million from the mistress of the late governor of the state of São Paulo, Ademar de Barros.[47]

These terrorist activities achieved some successes, but they did not succeed in enlarging the revolutionaries' base. The tiny number of recruits continued to come from among students, professional people, dissidents from the military, and ex-Communists. They were not able to bolster their ranks from the ever-expanding marginal classes who lived in the slums of such cities as Rio de Janeiro and São Paulo. As one revolutionary explained, "We will reach our next phase when we are able to recruit enough men under arms so that we can deploy groups in every region of Brazil. Our class analysis is based on the expected growth of the marginal class, those who are outside the system and can expect nothing from it and are its natural enemies."[48] This stage has never been reached partly because the marginal class has so far proved to be less revolutionary than expected.[49]

However, the rise in agitational terror did succeed in increasing the level of enforcement terror because it strengthened the position of the hard-line faction in the military against the moderates.[50] On December 13, 1968, the Costa e Silva government issued Institutional Act No. 5 which granted the president authority to (1) recess legislative bodies, (2) intervene in the states without limitations, (3) cancel elective mandates, (4) suspend political rights, (5) suspend constitutional guarantees with respect to civil service tenure and habeas corpus, and (6) suspend judicial review of actions taken under this act. In addition, "Operation Bandeirantes" was created in 1969 in São Paulo by the commander of the Second Army as a pilot project to coordinate military and police efforts to combat terrorist activities. Included in this program were representatives of the local army, air force and navy intelligence sections and of the local, state, and federal police organizations. The program was successful in São Paulo, and it was then extended to other major Brazilian cities in the form of Internal Defense Operation Centers under the coordination of the local army intelligence representative.

The reorganization of Brazil's security apparatus and the increased use of torture proved very effective in squelching both student demonstrations and rural and urban guerrillas. In April 1969 the police captured two members of the Revolutionary Movement of the Eighth of October (MR-8), a guerrilla group that had been formed from PCB dissidents in Rio Grande do Sul and Parana and students from the Federal University of Niteroi. The two militants were tortured, which then allowed a São Paulo policeman and alleged leader of a Death Squad, Sergio Parahhos Fleury, to set up the ambush that killed Marighela on November 4, 1969. Marighela's successor in the ALN, Joaquim Camara Ferreira, was killed in October 1970, and Captain Lamarca of the PRV was killed in September 1971.

However strongly one may condemn the use of torture on humanistic grounds, from the military point of view many of these events supported the utility of torture as an effective method of combating terrorism. One high-ranking

Brazilian intelligence officer explained that "in our view there are two basic things to remember when considering the question of torture. The first is that we are at war—a war of subversion—and these people are the enemy. If they get to power, it won't be torture and prison terms for us, but death. . . . The other thing to remember is that a person with an ideology doesn't give information as a gift."[51] Rosenbaum and Tyler add that "in some cases the rumors and assorted horror stories are of benefit to the government, in that repulsion and terror generated have helped to bring compliance on the part of many who might otherwise have resisted the regime. Thus, torture and Death Squad operations . . . have served to help bring about the depoliticization characteristic of an authoritarian regime."[52]

Tyson stresses that "political dissent, if coupled with any clandestine or mobilizational characteristics, has become the instant object of police brutality. . . ."[53] He estimates that since 1964 over 21,000 people have been arrested; there were probably 12,000 political prisoners in 1970, but now there are probably no more than 1000; 3000 petty criminals have been killed by the Death Squads; and the use of torture accelerated after 1968 but began to diminish in 1972 because of the defeat of the guerrillas and international pressures. Tyson's conclusion on Brazil is also mine: "President Medici summed up the situation of human rights and economic growth in Brazil succinctly when he said in 1970: 'Brazil is doing very well, but the people are doing poorly.' "[54]

Conclusion

In Latin America, fragmented security forces confront fragmentary revolutionary groups. But the greater resources of the Latin American governments allow them to engage in levels of enforcement terror that have so far overwhelmed the practitioners of agitational terrorism. Terrorist organizations in the countryside can be isolated and have proved to be no match for Latin American armies who, unlike Batista's corrupt and unprofessional Cuban forces, have received counter-insurgency training. Terrorist organizations in the cities are isolated from the groups they wish to mobilize, are excessively vulnerable to police infiltration, and, when captured, their members inevitably talk when subjected to torture. Believers in the strategy of agitational terrorism in Latin America should pause and consider that the principal theoreticians and practitioners of terrorism are either dead or in jail and that two of the weakest armies in the Western Hemisphere, the Bolivian and the Uruguayan, were able to defeat Che Guevara and the Tupamaros.

The lack of social justice and the slow, uneven pace of development in Latin America probably means that the terrorists will be able to recruit a tiny select stream of students, military deserters, professional people, and dissident splinters from the Communist and socialist parties; but their fragmentation and isolation suggest that they will not be able to overthrow any existing government in the foreseeable future. If agitational terrorism fails to create revolutionary conditions, it becomes just another factor in the power struggle in Latin America. Without the reasonable expectation of creating revolutionary conditions, terrorism becomes "a kind of vengeance activity to satisfy internal psychological needs. . . ."[55] Under these circumstances, it is difficult to demonstrate the superior morality of the guerrillas over the state security forces—a point that Guevara considered essential. In brief, terrorists that cannot move beyond terrorism cannot become revolutionaries.

Furthermore, agitational terror provokes the Latin American governments to expand enormously the already significant levels of enforcement terror these authoritarian regimes are accustomed to using. A Brazilian guerrilla once said, "You must realize that in an underdeveloped country the repression, too, is underdeveloped. The police are underpaid and undermotivated."[56] The guerrillas understood that their activities would cause the repressive characteristics of the state to become more manifest, but they believed this exposure would raise the revolutionary consciousness of the masses. Instead, the repressive capabilities of the state have improved without any visible signs that this has raised the consciousness of the people or hastened the socialist revolution. It appears that agitational terrorism in Latin America has been overwhelmingly counterproductive. The Latin Americans are now stuck with security agencies who will try to justify their existence and possibly their expansion and with vigilante groups who take sadistic pleasure in torturing and executing alleged subversives and petty criminals. In short, enforcement terror now prevails in Latin America.

Notes

1. Thomas P. Thornton, "Terror as a Weapon of Political Agitation," in *Internal War,* ed. Harry Eckstein (New York: Free Press, 1964), p. 72.

2. Paul Wilkinson, *Political Terrorism* (New York: John Wiley, 1974), p. 17.

3. Luis Mercier Vega, *Guerrillas in Latin America: The Technique of the Counter-State* (London: Praeger, 1969), p. 23.

4. Regis Debray, *Revolution in the Revolution? Armed Struggle and Political Struggle in Latin America* (New York: Monthly Review Press, 1967), p. 102.

5. Vega, *Guerrillas in Latin America,* p. 218.

6. J. de Valle, "Guatemala bajo el signo de la guerra," *Pensamiento Critico* 15 (April 1968): 41.

7. William T. Daly, *The Revolutionary: A Review and Synthesis* (Beverly Hills: Sage Publications, 1972), p. 8.

8. Vega, *Guerrillas in Latin America*, p. 4.

9. Debray, *Revolution in the Revolution?* p. 106.

10. Che Guevara, *Guerrilla Warfare* (New York: Vintage Books, 1968), pp. 15, 93.

11. Debray, *Revolution in the Revolution?* p. 74.

12. James Kohl and John Litt, ed., *Urban Guerrilla Warfare in Latin America* (Cambridge, Mass.: M.I.T. Press, 1974), pp. 6-7.

13. Debray, *Revolution in the Revolution?* p. 69.

14. Carlos Marighela, *For the Liberation of Brazil,* trans. by John Butt and Rosemary Sheed (Baltimore: Penguin, 1971), p. 121.

15. Sanche de Gramont, "How a Pleasant, Scholarly Young Man from Brazil Became a Kidnapping, Gun-Toting, Bombing Revolutionary," *New York Times Magazine,* November 15, 1970, p. 136.

16. Marighela, *For the Liberation of Brazil,* p. 66.

17. Ibid., p. 34.

18. Ibid., p. 46.

19. *New York Times,* September 27, 1970.

20. Gerald T. West, "Political Violence and Terrorism in Latin America" (paper delivered in April 1976 at Glassboro, N.J.), p. 10.

21. Ibid., p. 14.

22. Evelyn P. Stevens, *Protest and Response in Mexico* (Cambridge, Mass.: M.I.T. Press, 1974), p. 259.

23. *New York Times,* July 29, 1976.

24. L. Vincent Padgett, *The Mexican Political System,* 2nd ed. (Boston: Houghton Mifflin, 1976), p. 111.

25. Kohl and Litt, *Urban Guerrilla Warfare in Latin America,* p. 21.

26. Amnesty International, *Final Report of Mission to Chile,* April 1974, p. 12.

27. Norman Gall, "Slaughter in Guatemala," *The New York Review of Books,* May 20, 1971, p. 12.

28. *Latin America,* June 30, 1972.

29. Victor Perera, "Guatemala: Always La Violencia," *New York Times Magazine,* June 30, 1971, p. 57.

30. Kenneth Johnson, "A War of Eponyms: Exploring the Psychology of Argentina's Guerrilla Politics" (paper delivered at the Southwest Social Science Convention, San Antonio, March 1975), p. 10.

31. Ibid., p. 11.

32. *New York Times,* December 2, 1973.

33. V. S. Naipaul, "The Corpse at the Iron Gate," *The New York Review,* August 10, 1972, p. 23.

34. *New York Times,* July 28, 1975.

35. *New York Times,* July 6, 1976.

36. Johnson, "A War of Eponyms," pp. 4, 1.

37. Major Carlos Wilson, *The Tupamaros: The Unmentionables* (Boston: Branden Press, 1974), p. 128.

38. Ibid., p. 72.

39. Ibid., p. 88.

40. Ibid., p. 166.

41. Ibid., p. 157.

42. Ibid., p. 159.

43. *New York Times,* March 10, 1976.

44. Joao Quartim, *Dictatorship and Armed Struggle in Brazil* (New York: Monthly Review Press, 1971), p. 159.

45. Marighela, *For the Liberation of Brazil,* p. 42.

46. Jay Mallin, ed., *Terror and Urban Guerrillas* (Coral Gables, Fla.: University of Miami Press, 1971), p. 71.

47. *New York Times,* June 29, 1970.

48. de Gramont, "How a Pleasant, Scholarly Young Man," p. 140.

49. For evidence concerning how unrevolutionary the marginal classes are throughout Latin America see the excellent essay by Alejandro Portes, "Urbanization and Politics in Latin America," *Social Science Quarterly* 52 (December 1971): 697-720.

50. Ronald Schneider, *The Political System of Brazil* (New York: Columbia University Press, 1971), p. 294.

51. Neal Pearson, "Guerrilla Warfare in Brazil" (paper delivered at the Midwest Association of Latin American Studies, Carbondale, Illinois, October 1972), p. 37.

52. H. Jon Rosenbaum and Peter C. Sederberg, "Vigilantism: An Analysis of Establishment Violence," *Comparative Politics* 6 (July 1974): 566.

53. Brady Tyson, "Economic Growth and Human Rights in Brazil: The First Nine Years of Military Tutelage," *American Journal of International Law* 67 (November 1973): 209-210.

54. Ibid., p. 213.

55. Johnson, "A War of Eponyms," p. 2.

56. de Gramont, "How a Pleasant, Scholarly Young Man," p. 148.

9

The Role of Political Terrorism in the Palestinian Resistance Movement: June 1967-October 1973

Vaughn F. Bishop
Department of Political Science
Emory University
Atlanta, Georgia

The period between the June 1967 and the October 1973 wars in the Middle East is often characterized as one in which the use of international terrorism as a political tactic greatly increased. Much of the recent attention devoted to the study of terrorism stems directly from the Middle East conflict and more specifically from the use of terror by sections of the Palestinian community. The emotional responses generated by acts of terrorism and the tendency to lump all acts of terrorism together have blurred many important distinctions. While the frequency of aerial hijackings, letter bombings, acts of sabotage, and isolated attacks on individuals, groups, and nations has increased, the goals, motivations, and attitudes toward the use of terrorism have not remained constant.

The focus of the international community and national governments on the prevention and control of terroristic acts, while crucial and understandable, has often restricted and narrowed the discussion and understanding of the use of terror as a political tactic. The following discussion seeks to assess the role and describe the use of international terror and terrorism in the Middle East between the June 1967 war and the October 1973 war. More specifically, attention is focused on terror as a political tactic, and its use by certain segments of the Palestinian movement and community. The resort to terror in the Middle East is not new, nor is it limited to one of the contending parties. In the past, it has included not only individual and group actions, but also governmental actions—some sanctioned, others not. It has included widely differing types of attacks on widely differing victims and targets and has expressed widely differing goals and motivations.

By limiting the time period and the participants involved, a more detailed analysis of the perspectives of the participants, their long-term and short-term goals, the relationship of terror to other tactics, and the response and counterresponse of those most affected is possible. Although the focus is on an analysis of terror as a political tactic, it is argued that terror can best be understood within the wider context of the Arab-Israeli, Palestinian-Israeli conflict. It is also suggested that, in its broadest form, the use of terror as a political tactic varies with the changing goals and motivations and capabilities of the movement and participants involved, and with changing external political factors. Central, then, is the relationship over time between changing objectives and capabilities. A more inclusive study of terrorism in the Middle East would require more detailed event data, as well as a discussion of the use of terrorism by all participants.[1] An initial, descriptive survey, however, will allow the formulation of several generalizations based on initial empirical evidence concerning the nature and role of international terrorism as a political tactic in the Middle East.

In order to assess this role, several definitions and distinctions concerning terrorism and terror are first raised. These definitions and distinctions are then generalized in a framework that is applied to the Palestinian case. Using this framework, various types of terrorism that occurred from 1967 to 1973 are described. Included in this analysis are not only the different types of acts and their consequences, but also the objectives and motivations of those centrally involved. Finally, several conclusions are drawn concerning both the period under study and the use of terrorism as a political tactic.

Terror, Terrorism, and the Palestinian Case

Definitions of terror, terrorism, and the process of terror vary greatly. During crises, when terrorism appears to be on the increase, government's attention focuses on prevention and control. For activists the prime concern is with the "effectiveness" of terror as a political tactic. Less frequently, the causes of terrorism are the central concern. However, most broad generalizations about terror concur with Moss's statement that it is, in part, "the systematic use of intimidation for political ends."[2] Crozier suggests that terrorism is " the threat or use of violence for political ends,"[3] whereas the Mallisons define terror as "the systematic use of extreme violence and threats of violence in order to achieve public or political objectives."[4] These definitions have several points in common. All distinguish between actions and threats, all stress the idea of the systematic use of violence, and all stress the political nature of certain acts of terror and terrorism. There is also general agreement that terror introduces into the political process, in varying degrees, elements of fear, anxiety, disorientation, and disorganization. Walter, for example, defines the process of terror—as distinct from terror itself—as "the acts or threat of violence; the emotional reaction; and the social effects."[5]

In order to test the applicability of these generalizations to the Palestinian case, more stringent distinctions are needed. Several are current: one of the most common is the distinction between governmental and nongovernmental terror. Hutchinson defines "revolutionary terrorism" (nongovernmental) as "a part of insurgency strategy in the context of internal warfare or revolution: the attempt to seize political power from the extablished regime of a state, if successful causing fundamental political and social change."[6] Wilkinson distinguishes between forms of *revolutionary terrorism,* which are "the systematic tactics of terroristic violence with the objective of bringing about political revolution," *subrevolutionary terrorism,* which is "employed for political motives other than revolution or governmental repression," and *repressive terrorism,* which is the "systematic use of terroristic acts of violence for purposes of suppressing, putting down, quelling or restraining certain groups, individuals or forms of behavior deemed to be undesirable by the repressor."[7] Clearly, most attention, at least recently, has focused on nongovernmental terror. Although interpretations may differ, the Palestinian case generally falls into the classification of either revolutionary terrorism or subrevolutionary terrorism.

A second distinction, and one central to the Palestinian case, is between internal (within nations) and international terror. Although this distinction is an important one, it is often difficult to determine boundaries. The Mallisons point to the difficulty of defining terrorism in international law, suggesting, in part, that it relates to an emphasis on the prevention rather than the causes of terrorism.[8] The problem of boundary definition is made more difficult when there are not internationally or mutually accepted boundaries. Questions arise not only on boundary disputes (the status of the West Bank and Gaza, for example) but also on the relationship of host countries, sanctuaries, and the nature of responses to terrorist attacks. One of the central difficulties in the Palestinian case has been providing a mutually accepted definition of the status of the Palestinian community. Suggesting that at some time most states have given sanction to acts that may be broadly defined as terrorist, Falk argues that "the politics of terror and the use of exile sanctuaries to disrupt 'the enemy' society enjoys an ambiguous status in recent international experience."[9] The primary concern in the following discussion is with what is broadly termed international terrorism rather than national terrorism. This excludes those acts that occurred throughout the 1967-1973 period within the borders of Israel or the occupied territory.

Just as perceptions of boundaries between the international and the national vary, so do perceptions of the legitimacy or illegitimacy of the use of terror as a tactic. Although the general conception that terror and the resort to terrorism are illegitimate political tools is commonly postulated, it is not universally accepted. Wilkinson points out that most of those who resort to terrorism defend or justify their actions in terms of what he refers to as "the morality of just vengeance," "the theory of the lesser evil," that no "other means were available to their movement or group," and that "terrorism has proved to be tactically 'successful' in similar conditions to one's own."[10] The acceptance of terrorism as a "legitimate" political tactic to achieve political goals, then, depends in part not only on the acceptance of the goals of the movement engaged in terror, but also on an evaluation of terror tactics vis-à-vis other potential tactics.

Most actions are justified either in terms of some long-term goal or short-term objective. This excludes those acts of terrorism that have no political content or purpose (for example, the hijacking of an airplane for purposes of extorting money). A distinction may be drawn between the general acceptance of the goals of a movement and a rejection of specific tactics; this rejection may be based on moral valuation or on the effectiveness of the use of a certain tactic for achieving goals and objectives. If this is the case, attention focuses on the clear distinction between victim and target. Hutchinson suggests that one of the characteristics of terrorism is that "there is a consistent pattern of symbolic or representative selection of victims or objects of acts of terrorism."[11] Thornton draws the distinction between "apparent indiscrimination" and "actual discrimination," arguing that the goal of the terrorist or the terroristic act is to appear indiscriminate but actually be discriminate.[12] Terrorism, a fear- and anxiety-producing phenomenon, must create situations and acts that are directed toward a larger audience (specific or general), which is the target. This is done by selecting a victim that serves as a symbol to the target.

It appears then that an individual or a group may have at its command a large arsenal of potential weapons and tactics, among which is terrorism, to achieve a political goal. The evaluation of terrorism as a tactic then requires answers to several crucial questions. The first, centers on the nature of the terrorist. Who are the terrorists? Is there a general set of characteristics that distinguish the terrorist or those willing to resort to terrorism from others? Those concerned primarily with the prevention of terrorism have centered part of their study on the "personality" of the potential terrorist. Walter states that a terror organization requires a "directorate" that is responsible for planning and justifying acts and "agents of violence" who actually carry out the attacks.[13] Serge and Adler suggest that "modern terrorists derive their high behavioural unpredictability largely from three factors: their multiple targets, their limited numbers and (above all) from the variety of their cultural roots.[14] Although this suggests that terrorism may grow out of cultural and political conditions and depends on the specific characteristics and capabilities of the involved movements, studies that focus on personality or the development of personality profiles may tend to obscure the fact that terrorism rarely has a life of its own and is normally viewed as a tactic for achieving a goal.

A second question centers on the acts themselves. What are the criteria of inclusion or exclusion? Airplane hijackings, the use of letter bombs, general bombings, the attacking of civilians are often cited as the most common forms of terrorism. Related to definitions of what is or is not a terroristic attack is the relationship between the type of act selected and the political objective or motive. Certain types of acts may be viewed as more effective or appropriate than others under certain circumstances.

A third concern, and one with much political significance, revolves around the choice of victims and intended targets. Walter identifies three actors in the process of terror, "a source of violence, a victim, and a target."[15] As defined throughout the following discussion, victims are those individuals or groups at which a specific action is directed. Victims provide the symbol for the terrorist. This would include hostages held in airplane hijackings, those killed or wounded in bombings, recipients of letter bombings, and so forth. The target, on the other hand, is the individual, group, or nation whom the action is intended to influence. The target is, in one sense, the recipient of the "message" of the "act" itself. Obviously, in certain cases, an individual or group may be both a victim and a target. Any analysis of the process of terrorism must include not only the identification of the victim but also the target of the stated action.

The victim-target relationship raises the question of the goals and objectives of those considering the use of terror as a political tactic. If terrorist acts are not random, motiveless acts of violence, the target should, from the perspective of the terrorist, relate to both the victim and the goals and objectives of the movement. These objectives and goals fall into several rather broad categories. The first general category includes those acts that are designed to persuade the population, or perhaps more likely a government, to change its values and attitudes concerning a specific situation or issues, or to change a specific policy. Thornton refers to these acts as "negative" acts that are designed to induce "fright," "anxiety," or "despair."[16] The goals of the terrorist may, for example, seek to add a new variable into the political decision-making process by stressing the vulnerability of either a group or nation. Terror may also be used to create dissension among allies or potential allies. Differences on means of prevention and control of terrorism and differing responses to acts of terrorism may weaken the cohesion and unity not only of nations but of groups of nations. This is certainly the case, for example, with differing attitudes toward the question of whether to negotiate with terrorists and meet their demands or to resist demands by force.

Terrorism directed at external targets and victims in general, then, seeks to create fear, anxiety, disorientation, and the appearance of disorganization (the inability of the system to counter acts of terrorism), which in turn creates a climate for change.

However, terror may also be directed internally. Crozier for example suggests that terror may be used to "eliminate traitors" within a movement (citing the Algerian example).[17] A more "positive" role of terrorism within a movement would be the creation of "enthusiasm among the adherents of the insurgent movement."[18] Terrorism may provide the movement with a sense of "effectiveness" or the sense of an ability to influence or control a situation. It may serve to mobilize a targeted group to take a specific action, to create a solidarity and identity with the movement, or to ensure that a group will remain neutral or not actively hostile to a movement.

Any analysis of the role of international terrorism in the Palestinian case must then focus not only on the actors, victims, and targets, but also on the motivations, justifications, objectives, and goals of the participants. What is suggested here is that the acts of terrorism committed by certain sections of the Palestinian community between the June 1967 war and the October 1973 war can be analyzed in terms of (1) the participants involved, (2) the acts themselves, (3) the victims of the acts, (4) the targets of the acts, (5) the motivations, objectives, and goals of the participants, and (6) the consequences of the act. The key factor becomes the relationships between initiators, victims, targets, objectives, and goals. The central question is not only the description of the differing types of actions, but whether trends emerged during this period. Are, for example, specific victims and targets more clearly associated with differing types of motivations and objectives? Are certain types of actions more likely under a certain set of circumstances than others? As indicated in Table 1, the key to an understanding of political terrorism as a political act rests with the linkages between the variables.

The history of the development of the Palestinian community and resistance is beyond the scope of the present discussion. However, it is important to isolate certain important events and trends that are crucial to an understanding of the role of terrorism. Included here, in addition to specific events, are the general development of the Palestinian resistance, the relationship of the Palestinian movement to Israel and to other Arab states, the splits and divisions within the movement itself, and, finally, the relationship of the Palestinian movement and community to the larger international community. The key concern is not with chronology, but with the relationship between the various participants, their differing objectives and goals, and the relationship of these goals to the use of terrorism as a political tactic.

Following the creation of Israel in 1948 the Palestinian population appeared dormant. Attention was focused primarily on the relationship between Israel and neighboring Arab states. Discussions concerning the Palestinians centered on the

Table 1 Possible Factors Influencing the Resort to Terrorism by the Palestinian Resistance Movement, Potential Targets and Victims, and Potential Terroristic Acts

Actors	Movement characteristics		Potential victims and targets	Potential terroristic acts
	Capabilities and resources	Motivations		
Leaders and planners	Size of movement	Long-term goals	Israel and Israelis	Airplane hijackings
Initiators and agents	Unity and cohesion of movement	Short-term objectives	Palestinians in occupied territories and Israeli Arabs	Attacks on air terminals
	Military capabilities of movement		Arab states perceived to be opposed to Israel	Letter bombings
	Freedom of movement; relationship with host nations		Arab states perceived to be positive or neutral to Israel	Attacks on governmental officials and embassies
			Great powers perceived to be opposed to Israel[a]	Attacks on nongovernmental individuals, groups, or concerns
			Great powers perceived to be positive or neutral to Israel	
			Other nations perceived to be positive or neutral to Israel	

[a]Great powers include the United States, the Soviet Union, France, and Great Britain.

problems of refugees and on the collapse of Palestinian social, political, and economic institutions. Hudson describes this early period, approximately 1948-1964, as a prestage to the development of the resistance. Although acts of resistance did occur, the organization and the infrastructure generally considered necessary for effective political action did not yet exist.[19]

However, the conditions were generally favorable for the development of, if not a resistance movement, then a reassertion of a Palestinian sense of community. The period from 1964 to 1967 was essentially a period of gestation and initial growth. It was during this period that Al-Fatah, formed after the Suez war of 1956, first began military operations in Israel (January 1, 1965). It was also during this period that the Arab states encouraged and supported the establishment of the Palestine Liberation Organization (PLO) under the direction of Ahmed Shukairy. Although the PLO represented in many respects a bureaucratic, rather than an effective revolutionary, organization, and although it operated under the supervision of other Arab states, it did (as evidenced by the 1964 Arab summit conference) lend a certain legitimacy to the Palestinian movement and the conception of a Palestinian community.

Along with an increasing consciousness and organization, however, came splits and divisions in the growing movement. The first, and during this period perhaps the most clear-cut, was between the PLO led by Shukairy and Fatah under the direction of Yasir Arafat. The questions centered not only on the ultimate control of the movement but also on the tactics and the goals of the movement itself. Conflicts developed over whether conventional or guerrilla warfare was the more effective strategy, the length or duration of the conflict, and the long-run relationship between the Palestinians and their Arab sponsors and supporters. This last conflict became even sharper in the interwar period following the occupation of the West Bank and Gaza. Thus, although there was general agreement on the broad outlines of long-term goals, there was little agreement on (1) the best methods for achieving these goals and (2) short-term objectives. Splits developed not only between the participant Arab states and the Palestinians but also within the Palestinian movement itself.

The defeat of the Arab states in the June 1967 war forced not only a military reevaluation but also a political reevaluation of the strategic realities of the area. The occupation of the West Bank and Gaza affected the organization of the movement, at least temporarily, by limiting the scope of their action. At the same time, however, it opened two potential new fronts. In the 1965-1967 period Fatah activities varied with the support given by other Arab states and with changes in the internal political situation of those states. Thus, for example, the highest number of operations reported by Al-Asifah (the military wing of Fatah) was in September 1965 following support given by the Syrian Ba'th party. The second highest figure reported occurred in April 1966 following the reascendancy of the Ba'th in Syria. Low periods occurred in February and March 1966, in July and August 1966, and in November and December 1966 when internal power struggles were occurring in Syria, when Syria attempted to limit and control the activities of Fatah, and when Egypt and Syria reached a mutual defense agreement.[20] Following the 1967 war, attention shifted from attacks within the pre-1967 Israeli borders to attacks and actions in the occupied West Bank and Gaza.

As the conflict began to escalate following the 1967 war, many of the distinctions that had begun to develop in the initial stages of the conflict began to sharpen. The distinction between short-term objectives and long-term goals became clearer. The Palestinian leadership, in diaspora, aimed at the ultimate transformation of Israel. They remained, however, dependent on other Arab states not only for material supplies and training but also for bases of operation. As the "effectiveness" and "level" of activity increased, it provoked responses and counterresponses from Israel, which in turn forced Arab host states (primarily Jordan, Lebanon, and Syria) to reevaluate their position vis-à-vis the Palestinians. This, in part, accounts for the almost cyclical nature of the resistance during this early period. The situation was made more complex with occupation in 1967. The situation revolved around a stateless people (Palestinians), claiming a state (Israel), operating from sympathetic, but vulnerable neighboring states (Lebanon, Syria, Jordan, and Egypt). The legitimacy or the illegitimacy of the claims from any of the participants did little to alter the perceptions of the contestants or the realities of the conflict.

Just as the Arab states and Israel were forced to reevaluate their positions following the 1967 defeat, so did the Palestinian movement. The defeat served to discredit both Ahmed Shukairy and the general organization of the PLO. Questions were raised not only about the effectiveness of the PLO and its leadership, but also about who it actually served—the Palestinians or other Arab states. The debate within the Palestinian community centered on the most effective and appropriate strategy and tactics in confronting Israel, given the new situation. In the broadest outlines of the debate there were two major schools. The first, generally argued by Fatah, was that the Palestinian case was paramount. The overriding philosophy was Palestinian nationalism. Although there was intense and detailed discussion about the future of a Palestinian state and its characteristics, most action, discussion, and policy formulation was directed toward the liberation of Israel. Because the paramount goal was the "liberation" of Israel, most action should be directed specifically at Israel and the occupied territories rather than at other states. From approximately 1964 to 1969, Fatah argued for as little interference in the internal politics of Arab states as possible. What Fatah wanted and needed were bases of operation and material support. This, from their perspective, was best achieved through accommodation rather than confrontation.

Countering this position, and emerging partly as a result of the defeat of the Arab states, was a more "radical" ideological position that argued not only for the liberation of Palestine but also for revolutionary change in what were termed the more "reactionary" Arab states. Again, although the general or long-term goal remained fairly constant, this faction argued for the creation of a revolutionary struggle rather than a strictly nationalistic one. Only as a result of radical change in the Arab states could effective action against Israel be taken. Based on this position, involvement in the affairs of other states became not only permissible but necessary. This position is most associated with the Popular Front for the Liberation of Palestine (PFLP) and George Habash.[21]

From these two conflicting positions, attitudes toward tactics and specifically the use of terrorism emerge. For Fatah, from the Palestinian perspective, action should be directed primarily at Israel, within Israel. For the PFLP, action should be directed not only at Israel but also at those Arab states that do not actively support the Palestinian movement and at other individuals, groups, or nations that actively support (or are neutral to) Israel. The inclusion of the latter group widens not only the level of the conflict but also its scope, moving the conflict far beyond a Palestinian/Israeli one. The attitudes of Fatah and the PFLP on the use of terror as a legitimate tactic differ in part because of their differing perceptions of the situation. Quant states that

> the irony of the PFLP-PDFLP viewpoint is that in some ways it is more realistic concerning the balance of forces than Fatah's and yet the conclusions drawn are far beyond the capabilities of the relatively small and poorly financed radical fedayeen groups. Indeed, their militancy ensures that these groups will remain small, since no existing Arab regime can fully agree with their objectives. By contrast, Fatah, with much greater resources and capabilities, is more modest in its goals, and yet less self-critical, and more apologetic in its propaganda than either the PFLP or the PDFLP. Like many radical movements, the PFLP and the PDFLP may count less for their armed strength than for the few well-argued and courageous ideas that they have managed to introduce into the political arena.[22]

The statement is instructive from several perspectives. If, as Crozier suggests, "terrorism is a weapon of the weak,"[23] and strong, well-organized resistance or revolutionary movements generally do not rely on terror as a tactic, then acts of terrorism should be expected in periods of weakness or crisis. These crises may be either internal or external to the movement. The resort to terrorism is then at least in part determined by a realistic assessment of the capabilities of the organization. What characterizes the period between the 1967 and the 1973 wars, in addition to the resort to terrorism as a political tactic, is also a changing perspective among all of the Palestinian movements concerning its use, applicability, and effectiveness. Quite simply, as conditions changed, as the environment for political action changed, so did the objectives of the various movements. Because terror is only one tactic among many available, it is logical to expect that as the situation changed throughout the period so did attitudes toward terrorism and the relationship of terrorism to other tactics. While terrorism may appear, once begun, to be a never-ending, ever-increasing phenomenon, it is extremely complex and, in the Palestinian case, is directly related to the Palestinians' perception of the general and overriding causes of the conflict.

Wilkinson, discussing attitudes toward terrorism, states that

> to understand why large numbers of Palestinians, for example, openly re-joice in each new terrorist "success" is to understand the roots of their feelings of anger and bitter humiliation. They believe they were robbed of their homeland by a new Jewish state which most of them still refuse to recognize as legitimate, and which many of them are deeply committed to destroying. Set in its proper historical context, therefore, much of the re-cent wave of international terrorism can be best understood not as the es-tablishment of a permanent pattern of violence but as a violent and desper-ate aftermath of the Arab defeat in the 1967 war.[24]

The emerging Palestinian movement following the 1967 defeat faced several problems, each requiring a decision that in turn affected attitudes toward terrorism. First, the effective support of the Arab states was thrown into question. It was not clear precisely what role the Arab states might or would be able to play. Throughout the period, the changing relationship between the Arab states and Israel and between the Arab states and the great powers directly affected the Palestinian movement. The clearest example of this influence was the discussion of the Rogers peace plan of 1970. The Palestinian movement during this period attempted to increase its independence as a political force in the Middle East and to ensure that, in any resolution or management of the conflict, Palestinian interests would both be protected and represented, ideally by Palestinians.

A second problem was the introduction of a new boundary variable. The occupation of the West Bank and Gaza by Israel forced the Palestinian resistance to rely more heavily on states neighboring Israel as bases of operation and host countries. In Jordan, the increasing tension between the Palestinian resistance movements and the monarchy culminated in the 1970-1971 Jordanian/Palestinian war. The trend throughout this period was that as the commando raids in both the occupied territories and Israel increased, the response and counterresponse of the Israelis escalated. Many of these responses were directed not only at the Palestinians but at the host country held responsible. This, in turn, often led to an attempt by the host government to control and restrict the operations and actions of the Palestinians.

Finally, throughout this period, the splits within the Palestinian movement continued and grew more severe. Much of this debate centered on tactics and strategy, on the effectiveness of various tactics, on the scope and nature of the conflict, and on the relationship between tactics and goals. Although the split between Fatah and the PFLP was one of the most severe, there also emerged during this period a number of small, splinter groups. It is in this setting that the issue of terrorism moved center stage.

Acts of Terrorism—June 1967 to October 1973

In the following sections specific types of international terrorism are examined and described based on the criteria established earlier. It is admitted and realized that there is a good deal of controversy over what acts should be included as terroristic and which fall under the category of military actions and military situations.[25] In the following discussion, acts between, for example, Palestinian commandos and Israeli military forces have been excluded. One of the largest categories of actions throughout the period involved border infiltration into the occupied territories. Although many of these acts certainly involved aspects of terrorism (fear inducing, anxiety producing), it is argued here that they more properly fall under classifications of guerrilla warfare. Also, because our discussion is concerned primarily with the Palestinian use of terror, we have excluded those acts by Israel that may be considered to be terroristic. A more detailed analysis, involving a larger, more comprehensive and more comparative data set, is required to sort the complex nature of the response-counterresponse issue. Three major groups of international terroristic attacks are discussed. The first, and one of the most visible, includes air hijackings and attacks at air terminals. The second category includes letter and package bombs sent through the post. The third is attacks on individual and property, both governmental and nongovernmental. Where appropriate, distinctions are drawn within these broad classifications; acts of political assassination, political murder, sabotage (which does not involve the loss or wounding of human life) have been excluded. The key factors used in determining inclusion or exclusion of specific acts are, first, the distinction between victims and targets and, second, whether the actions have been directed at people rather than simply at property. This has been done primarily because terrorism, as discussed earlier, involves measuring not only the physical or material effects of an act, but also the psychological responses of both victims and targets.

Each of these three categories is discussed in terms of a fivefold typology. First, each is discussed in terms of its duration and scope in the interwar period. For example, was a particular act limited to a specific subperiod or did it span the entire period? Second, a determination of the initiators is made. This includes both those who carry out the act and those who claim credit. The third category is an analysis of the victims and targets and, more specifically, whether certain victims and targets are more closely associated with specific types of terrorism than with others. Fourth, the motives and objectives of those committing the act are described. Are specific acts or types of terrorism more closely associated with certain objectives and goals than with others? Finally, each of the acts is measured against the response it provokes. A distinction is drawn between intended and unintended responses; although based on available data, this distinction remains at least partially speculative.

Air Hijackings and Attacks on Air Terminals

The general frequency of airplane hijackings has steadily increased. Figures indicate that in the period 1948-1958, for example, there were approximately two hijackings per year. In the 1958-1963 period there were three per year; in the 1963-1968 period, seven per year; and in the 1969-1970 period, approximately fifty per year.[26] Although airplane hijackings were not unique to the Middle East in the 1967-1973 period, much of the international and national attention focused on several acts carried out mainly by the Popular Front for the Liberation of Palestine (PFLP). This section analyzes and describes the general nature of these attacks during the interwar period.

Attacks on air terminals and airplane hijackings are among the most highly visible terroristic acts. Aerial terrorism tends to focus on highly dramatic acts, whose impact goes far beyond the act itself. Mazrui suggests that

> the purpose of aerial terrorism is to manipulate fear as a mechanism of combat. The grand design is to undermine morale, not only among the soldiers but also among the citizen body. An atmosphere of general insecurity, promoted by spectacular acts of destruction, or specially dramatized acts of brutality, is contrived in order to drive the enemy into a desperate readiness to seek a settlement.[27]

These acts fit the general criteria enumerated above. They tend to instill fear, they present a threat to those not directly involved, and (with certain exceptions) are directed at what are perceived to be political targets and victims with political objectives and goals.

There are three classifications of victims of aerial terrorism as practiced by sections of the Palestinian resistance. The first includes Israeli citizens flying on Israeli aircraft (El Al). During the 1968-1969 period, the PFLP directed most of its attacks specifically at El Al planes (see Table 2). The justification for these attacks centered on the holding of hostages to secure the release of Palestinians

Table 2 Aerial Hijackings and Air Terminal Attacks, 1967-1973[a],[b]

Date	Group claiming credit	Victim-target relationship and location of attack	Victims killed	Victims wounded	Initiators killed	Initiators wounded	Destination of hijacked plane
1967	–	–	–	–	–	–	–
7/23/68	PFLP	El Al–Israel in Rome	0	0	0	0	Algiers
12/28/68	PFLP	El Al–Israel in Athens	1	1	0	0	Ground attack
2/18/69	PFLP	El Al–Israel in Zurich	1	5	1	0	Ground attack
8/29/69	PFLP	TWA–Israel in Athens	0	4	0	0	Damascus
2/10/70	PFLP	Transit passengers in Munich–Israel	1	11	0	0	Ground attack
2/21/70	PFLP, Popular Com.	Explosion of Swiss plane, Zurich to London	47 (all)	0	0	0	Explosion
7/22/70	Popular Struggle Front	Greek Olympic Air–Greek Government in Athens	0	0	0	0	Ground attack
9/6/70	PFLP	TWA, Pan Am, Swiss Air–Israel, Great Britain, Switzerland, West Germany from Frankfurt, Zurich, and Amsterdam	0	0	1	1	Jordan
11/9/70	Criminals expelled from Dubai	Iranian Air–Dubai in Dubai	0	0	0	0	Iran
11/10/70	Unidentified gunman	Saudi Arabian Air–unclear in Saudi Arabia	0	0	0	0	Damascus

			—	—	—	—	—
1971	—		0	0	0	0	—
2/21/72	Organization for Victims of Zionist Occupation	Lufthansa—West Germany from New Delhi	0	0	0	0	South Yemen
5/8/72	Black September	Sabena Belgian plane—Israel in Tel Aviv	1	4	2	1	Ground attack
5/30/72	Japanese Red Army	Attack on Lod Air Terminal—Israel in Tel Aviv	25	75	2	0	Ground attack
8/16/72	unclear	El Al plane—Israel, bomb found on plane	0	4	0	0	Bomb attempt
10/6/72	unclear	Royal Jordan Air—Jordan, bomb explodes in suitcase in Beirut	0	0	0	0	Bomb attempt
7/20/73	Japanese Red Army, several splinter groups	Japanese Air—Japan, Israel from Amsterdam to Tokyo	0	1	1	0	Dubai
8/5/73	Black September	TWA—Israel, attack on Athens to New York plane	4	55	0	0	Ground attack
8/10/73	Israel air force	Iraqi—Palestinian, Beirut to Baghdad plane	0	0	0	0	Tel Aviv
8/16/73	Individual (Libyan)	Middle East Airline—unclear, Libya to Lebanon flight	0	0	0	0	Tel Aviv
12/17/73	PFLP (unclear)	Pan Am and Lufthansa—United States and Greece, one attacked (U.S.), another hijacked (Lufthansa)	31	0	0	0	Kuwait

a All data are from *Facts on File*.
b Does not include unsuccessful attempts (those never carried out) or plots and reported plots.

held in Israeli detention and on the assertion that El Al was not a civilian airlines
but an airlines serving a military purpose. The 1968 hijackers of an El Al plane
enroute from Rome to Tel Aviv and the August 1969 hijackers of a TWA plane
(with Israeli passengers) enroute from Rome to Athens to Tel Aviv demanded the
release of Palestinians and Arab prisoners currently held in Israeli prisons.[28] After
the December 26, 1968, attack on an El Al plane in Athens, the PFLP stated that
El Al was not "an airline undertaking innocent civilian transport" but was engaged "in secret flights under supervision of the Israeli Defense Ministry" and that
they were using "air force pilots trained in flying Phantom jets in preparation for
a surprise attack and new aggression against the Arab states."[29]

A second form of aerial terrorism directed specifically at Israel and Israelis
was attacks on air terminals. The most costly in terms of human life, and the
most spectacular, was the May 30, 1972 attack on Lod Airport. This attack,
which resulted in the death of twenty-five and the wounding of approximately
seventy-five, has been attributed to both the PFLP and the Japanese "Army of
the Red Star." Unlike airplane hijackings, this attack—according to its initiators
—was not designed to take hostages, but as a reprisal and a warning. The PFLP,
claiming "complete responsibility," indicated that the attack was designed as a
reprisal for the killing of two Arabs after an earlier attempted (but abortive) attack at Lod in May 1970. It is unclear whether they actually attacked their intended victims (sixteen of the dead were Puerto Ricans visiting the Christian holy
sites). PFLP spokesman in Beirut, Bassam Zayid, stated that "we were sure that
90%-95% of the people in the airport at the time the operation was due to take
place would be Israelis or people of direct loyalty to Israel. Our purpose was to
kill as many people as possible at the airport, Israelis, of course, but anyone else
who was there."[30] Clearly an additional motivation for both airplane hijackings
and terminal attacks is to dissuade potential immigrants and tourists from either
flying on Israeli-owned airliners or immigrating to or visiting Israel itself. By increasing the "cost" (psychological, material, and physical) to those contemplating
flying Israeli carriers or going to Israel, the terrorists not only place an economic
hardship on Israel but also call into question the ability of the government to protect both nationals and visitors. The August 1973 raid by Black September on
the Athens airport, for example, was designed "to hit at emigrants to Israel because they kill our wives and children,"[31] while the PFLP, in claiming credit for
the February 1969 hijacking of an El Al plane, stated that it was in retaliation
for attacks on "unarmed and innocent civilians in occupied territory."[32]

A second category of victim during this period was made up of European
and American nationals flying on European or American carriers. In this case,
the motivation again appears to be twofold—the taking of hostages and the issu-
ance of a warning. The hijacking of a Greek Olympic airliner on July 22, 1970,
a Lufthansa airliner on February 21, 1972, and a Pan Am and Lufthansa airliner
on December 17, 1973, resulted in the demand for the release of Palestinians and

Arabs held in Athens, Rome, and Cologne prisons.[33] Many of the Palestinians and Arabs held in European custody were, in fact, those convicted of previous hijackings or hijack attempts. The cyclical nature of hijacking was such that an attempt during which the hijackers were captured often resulted in a subsequent hijacking designed to free those captured in the initial attempt. The spectacular hijacking of three planes by the PLFP in September 1970 (planes flown to Jordan) was carried out to secure the release of prisoners in Israel, Great Britain, Switzerland, and West Germany, to "give the Americans a lesson after they supported Israel all of these years," and as an indication of the Palestinian response to U.S. peace initiatives in the Middle East.[34]

A third type of general victim was dissident or opposing factions within the movement itself or in other Arab states. Because most of the factions do not control or direct their own airlines, the use of air hijacking in this case becomes rather problematic. However, there were three reported hijackings of carriers belonging to other Arab states, and although it is unclear as to who the exact participants were or whether their motivations were political or apolitical, two merit mention. The first reported incident (November 1970) involved the hijacking of a Saudi Arabian plane to Damascus.[35] The second was the explosion of a bomb intended for a Royal Jordan airplane in Beirut.[36] Although there have been relatively few attacks on carriers of Arab states, it is clear that, for example, the September 1970 hijacking to Jordan did have Jordan as at least a secondary target. As indicated earlier, by September 1970, the relationship between the Palestinians and the Jordanians had reached a low ebb. By the same token, the relationship between various commando organizations (Fatah and PFLP, Arafat and Habash, for example) was also severely strained. The selection by the PFLP of Jordan as the landing site for the hijacked planes placed increased pressure not only on King Hussein to make a decision but also on the Central Committee of the PLO to respond. In one sense, they were forcing the contending factions to take action.

In terms of the frequency of incidents reported, the years 1970 and 1972 show the greatest number of hijackings. Although five events are reported in 1973, one was the hijacking of an Iraqi plane by the Israeli air force (George Habash was thought to be on the plane) and the other apparently a nonpolitical act (August 16, 1973). The marked decline in the number of hijackings in the latter part of 1970 and throughout 1971 is attributable to the shift in strategy within the Palestinian movement, to the internal struggles in the movement, and, perhaps most importantly, to the Jordanian/Palestinian war that began in September 1970 and continued throughout 1971. From the perspective of the Palestinian movement, center stage shifted from the external targets of Israel and her allies to the internal dilemma facing the resistance movement.

The group most closely associated with the use of air hijacking as a tactic is the PFLP under the direction of George Habash. Also involved are various splinter groups and factions that have broken from the major Palestinian resistance groups. These include the Action Organization for the Liberation of Palestine, the Popular Front for the Liberation of Palestine-Popular Command, the Popular Struggle Front, the Organization for Victims of Zionist Occupation (reportedly based in Gaza), and the Organization of Sons of Occupied Territories. In addition, Black September, the splinter group formed from a Fatah nucleus following the Jordanian/Palestinian war, claimed credit for two attacks during 1972-1973.[37] Depending upon the source, Black September has been reported to be independent of Fatah or directly controlled by it.[38] In general, however, those groups that have resorted to, and have advocated the use of, airplane hijackings and air terminal attacks are those groups that also favor the expansion of the scope of the conflict beyond the Middle East. The nature of the victims and the targets, as well as the location of the attacks themselves, indicate that in addition to placing pressure on Israel, they are also designed to place pressure on those who either support Israel or are considering changing a particular policy (see below). Throughout this period, while air hijacking was almost universally condemned by the international community, it served certain sectors of the Palestinian community as a tactic not only for securing short-term objectives (release of prisoners, discouraging international travel to Israel, and so on), but also for ensuring that the "Palestinian question" remained articulated and in public view. It appears that although the PFLP and related groups were aware that acts such as those just described would not win general international favor, they felt them necessary at a specific time and given specific situations and considered the "benefits" to outweigh the "costs."

Although there is a tendency to view the Palestinian movement as being monolithic, the use of this tactic was not universally approved or sanctioned. Sections of the Palestinian movement and various Arab governments expressed contrasting and often conflicting sentiments throughout the period. In general, however, it appears that from the initial hijacking in the period (July 23, 1968) until the September 6, 1970 hijacking, reaction remained generally favorable. The exception to this was the explosion of a Swiss Air plane in February 1970, which resulted in the death of all forty-seven passengers and crew. In this case the General Command broadcast by Fatah stated that "the Revolution strongly condemns such barbaric action," arguing that "no commando contingent would have carried out such an action."[39] Arafat later stated that "the unified command of the commando organizations is now seriously reviewing the entire question of attacks on international airlines" and that "the Palestine Revolution's policy is against endangering all civilians, wherever they are."[40] As Table 2 indicates, with the exception of the Swiss explosion, loss of life due to hijackings during this period remained low. The hijacking of three planes in September 1970, however, appears to signal a sharp break and shift in policy among both the Arab states and the more "moderate" sections of the Palestinian resistance. *Al Ahram* (September 8), arguing against the use of the tactic, stated: "One of the main goals of the battle is to gain world public opinion on the side of the Palestinian struggle and not to lose it. It is evident that the attack on international civil aviation does not encourage world feeling of solidarity with the Palestinian cause."[41] *Al Akhbar* (September 9) reacted in a similar vein stating that the international reaction "reflects the denunciation and disgust of people against those who carry out such acts."[42] Following the destruction of the planes, the PLO Central Committee suspended the PFLP on September 12 for not following committee guidelines and stated:

> (1) The Central Committee . . . declares that it washes its hands of this issue. (2) It suspends the PFLP's membership of the Central Committee because the PFLP has . . . violated the Central Committee's decisions of September 10. (3) It dissociates itself from the PFLP's actions and will not cooperate with it. . . . (4) It will adopt a firm stand against any PFLP command actions prejudicial to the safety and security of the revolution.
> . . [43]

As stated earlier, immediately following this action the Jordanian/Palestinian dispute reached a crisis stage (partly in response to the act itself), and the focus of the conflict changed. Following the resolution, or at least lessening, of the conflict between the two parties, the scope and the focus of acts of aerial terrorism appeared more blurred (see 1972-1973 in Table 2). With the exception of attacks such as those by the PFLP and the Japanese Red Army at Lod in May 1972 and the attack and hijacking of Pan Am and Lufthansa planes in December 1973, the victim-target relationship, as well as the motivations and objectives of the actors, is less precise and less clearly stated. By the same token, the response of the Arab states and other factions of the Palestinian movement continued to be against the use of air hijacking as a political tactic. Speaking of the attack in December 1973 that resulted in the killing of thirty-one persons, Arafat stated that it was "work of hands that do not belong to the Palestinian people" and that it was an act "of sabotage and crime aimed against the Palestinian revolution" rather than for it.[44]

Throughout the interwar period, the attitudes toward the legitimacy or illegitimacy of the use of aerial terrorism as well as the resort to aerial terrorism varied. These differences were due in part to the resource capabilities of those involved, to the internal splits and divisions within the movement itself, to the relationship between the Palestinian resistance movement and other states (specifically Jordan and Lebanon), and to the response of the affected parties (mainly Israel, Western Europe, and the United States). Although aerial terrorism has never been generally accepted as a legitimate political tool, the trend during this period suggests that following the September 1970 incident, the use of aerial terrorism became largely counterproductive for those who practiced it. Increases in security precautions, among other factors, as well as changing attitudes and situations, appear to have minimized the effectiveness of the tactic. Initial evidence suggests that aerial terrorism was a tactic designed to meet a specific situation with limited goals. Mazrui speaking of the hijacking situation in 1970 states:

> But does aerial terrorism succeed only in alienating world opinion? Questions of this kind miss the whole point. In a propaganda campaign to win sympathy in the more influential parts of the world, the Arabs would be no match for the Jews. . . . The Palestinian purpose of aerial terrorism in 1970 was not, therefore, a quest for sympathetic publicity, but an attempt to arouse popular anxiety.[45]

In addition, it focused public attention (whether that attention was favorable or unfavorable is beside the point) on the Palestinian issue and indicated to various targets, through attacks on a variety of victims, that the Palestinian resistance was central, not peripheral, to the larger Middle East conflict. The goal was the creation of a specific situation (Palestinian recognition) by the use of a specific political tactic (aerial terrorism). When that tactic no longer proved effective or in most cases began to be counterproductive, the strategy was changed and new political tactics evolved.

Terrorism by Post—Letter Bombs and Packages

Several fundamental differences become readily apparent when aerial terrorism and terrorism by post are compared. The first is that acts of aerial terrorism are reported throughout most years of the interwar period (with the exception of 1967 and 1971), whereas letter and package bombings are generally restricted to 1972. As a tactic, it had a relatively short life. The intense focus on means of detection and defusing letter bombs and increased protection for potential victims led in the latter part of 1972 to a sharp decrease in the number of bombs that were actually detonated. Although data are much more scarce concerning letter bombs, several generalizations are possible.

Points of origin for letter and package bombs during this period were primarily European cities (Amsterdam, Athens, Vienna), Malaysia, or India. Most were addressed either to locations in Israel or to Israeli embassies and businesses abroad. One of the most extensive of these mailings occurred on September 19, 1972, when letter or package bombs were sent to Israeli offices in at least nine cities. Letters and packages postmarked from Amsterdam were sent to Paris, New York, Montreal, Ottawa, Brussels, and Jerusalem among others. The actions resulted in one death (an Israeli official in the London embassy) and one wounded.[46] Another mailing two days later, September 21, again postmarked from Amsterdam, sent packages and letters to Israeli embassies in Kinshassa, Zaire, in Buenos Aires and to the Jerusalem post office. All of these were defused.[47] During this same period (on September 23) Jordan also reported that it had intercepted four letter bombs addressed to Jordanian officials (also with an Amsterdam postmark).[48] Other acts have included the sending of parcels directly to Israel, mailings to Jewish officials in various Zionist movements in the United States (October 14, 1972), a series of packages addressed to President Nixon, Secretary of State Rogers, and PLO officials in Lebanon, Libya, Algeria, and Egypt (many postmarked from Belgrade, Yugoslavia).[49] Another series included mailings from Malaysia and India to a rather disparate group in late October and early November 1972. Victims and potential victims included Jewish groups in London, Rome, and the United States, the Egyptian embassy in London, a British technical school with ties to Haifa University, and various Jewish individuals in London and Geneva.[50] Finally, there were three reported letter bombings in January 1973, including a letter bomb sent from Israel to Kiryat Gat in Israel, an intercepted letter from Turkey to Israel, and a letter sent from Athens to the honorary Israeli consul in Santiago, Chile.[51]

As indicated from this description of victims, they comprise a rather diverse group. Although there is some evidence to suggest that Black September was responsible for at least some of the mailings,[52] it is difficult to assess responsibility. Unlike the case of aerial terrorism, those responsible for the actions generally did not claim either credit or responsibility. Casualties from letter bombs remain relatively low throughout the period. In many cases, those most severely wounded were bomb-disposal experts injured as they attempted to defuse various letter bombs.

Whereas aerial hijackings and attacks on air terminals tended to have both multiple targets and multiple goals, letter bombs appear to have a much more restricted focus. In some cases the letters and packages were addressed to specific individuals, while in others they were simply sent to a given address. In either case, as security and the ability to defuse these bombs increased, and as it became easier to predict when bombs would be sent and then intercept them, their use decreased.

Commando Raids, Attacks, and Bombings—
Governmental and Nongovernmental

The final descriptive category of acts of international terrorism includes a variety of different types of attacks against individuals and groups. This category includes not only those attacks on governmental officials and institutions (mainly embassies), but also attacks on nongovernmental individuals, groups, and concerns. The types of violence and terror used generally were either bombings or commando-style raids. Victims and targets included Israelis and Arabs, as well as Europeans and Americans.

The most severe attacks on governmental officials and institutions occurred in 1972-1973. One of the earliest attacks reported, however, was the explosion of a bomb (one wounded) in the British consulate in Jerusalem in February 1969. Claiming credit, the PFLP stated that it was in response to a report that Britain planned to sell tanks to Israel.[53] In December 1972 four members of Black September seized the Israeli embassy in Thailand and demanded the release of thirty-six prisoners held in Israeli prisons. The six hostages were held for 19 hours, after which the four commandos were flown to Cairo. Their demands were not met, and there were no reports of loss of life or serious injury.[54] Al Icab, a relatively obscure and little known organization, raided the Saudi Arabian embassy in Paris in September 1973; initially the five attackers took thirteen hostages (including nationals from Saudi Arabia, France, Tunisia, Egypt, Sudan, and Yugoslavia) and demanded that Jordan release the Palestinian resistance leader Abu Daoud, then being held in a Jordanian prison. Later the attackers released all but four Saudi Arabian hostages, dropped their demand for the release of Daoud, and requested safe passage. On September 8, having been condemned by the PLO and having had difficulty finding a safe haven, the five released their hostages and were arrested in Kuwait. Two of the victims were reported to have been wounded.[55]

The most spectacular and violent attack on an embassy occurred in March 1973. Approximately ten members of Black September attacked the Saudi Arabian embassy in Khartoum, Sudan, and held it for 3 days. The attack occurred during a farewell reception for the U.S. ambassador, and the hostages included a wide range of representatives from the diplomatic community. The demands included the release of prisoners held in Jordan (mainly Fatah prisoners and again including Abu Daoud), the release of women held in Israeli detention, the release of members of the Baader-Meinhof Group in West Germany, and reportedly the release of Sirhan Sirhan in the United States. The demands against Israel, West Germany, and the United States were later dropped. The action resulted in the killing of U.S. Ambassador Cleo Noel, U.S. diplomat George C. Moore, and the Belgian Charge d'Affaires, Guy Eid (reportedly because of a plan to build an Israeli-Belgian-American missile plant in Belgium). After prolonged negotiations the terrorists surrendered to Sudanese authorities.[56]

This attack is indicative of several general trends. The first was that the attack was directed at the embassy of an at least nominally sympathetic country (Saudi Arabia) within the borders of another nominally sympathetic country (Sudan). Second, the primary target was another Arab state, in this case Jordan.

The use of this tactic appears to be directly related to the Jordanian/Palestinian war of 1970-1971. Although there were secondary targets, the primary goal appears to have been the release of prisoners taken during the 1970-1971 dispute. The carrying out of the attacks by members of Black September, which grew out of the Jordanian/Palestinian dispute, further supports this contention. Finally the tactic itself provoked a response that generally led to the disuse of the tactic. The killing of the diplomats, coupled with Sudan's refusal to negotiate, resulted in the eventual collapse of the attack; and it has been reported that sections of the Palestinian movement aided in the negotiations that led to the eventual surrender when it became clear that there was no alternative.

A second classification of commando-style attacks and bombings are those directed at nongovernmental institutions and officials. These acts generally fall into two broad types: The first includes bombings and general attacks of sabotage; the second includes attacks carried out by commando units.

In November 1969 the PFLP carried out a series of coordinated attacks on Israeli-staffed offices. These included the El Al office in Brussels and the Israeli embassies in Bonn and the Netherlands. The bombing of the El Al office in Brussels resulted in the injuring of three El Al employees and one bystander. The stated reason for the attack was that the PFLP intended to attack Israeli interests that were involved in bringing people to Israel and the embassies that "are the centers of espionage and collection points for mercenaries and immigrants to our occupied Palestine." This coordinated attack followed an earlier August 25, 1969 bomb blast at the Zim office in London.

It was reported that Bonn and the Netherlands were chosen because both countries were involved in the training of Israeli pilots.[57] In November 1969 the Palestine Popular Struggle Front (based in Amman) claimed credit for a hand-grenade attack on the El Al office in Athens that killed one bystander and wounded fourteen others. No official reason was stated for the attack.[58] A July 1973 attack, also at the El Al office, was foiled by a guard. There were no reported fatalities and the attackers (after holding seventeen hostages in a nearby hotel for 5 hours) were flown to Kuwait.[59] A somewhat different type of attack occurred in March 1970. Claiming credit, the PFLP launched rocket attacks on U.S. property in Beirut and southern Lebanon. In a statement the PFLP suggested that the attacks were in retaliation for "plans of the U.S. embassy in Beirut to foment religious strife and create civil massacres in Lebanon aimed at paralyzing the Palestinian resistance movement." Little damage and no fatalities or injuries were reported.[60]

Several other attacks during this period are worthy of note. One incident involved an attack in Nicosia, Cyprus, on the apartment building in which the Israeli ambassador lived and was combined with a related attack on an El Al plane before takeoff. This double attack, carried out by an unnamed group in

April 1973, resulted in the death of one victim and the wounding of two others.[61]
In September 1973 the Eagles of the Palestinian Revolution, reportedly a splinter
group from Al-Fatah, captured three Jewish hostages on a Moscow-Vienna train.
The stated reason for the action was "because we feel that the immigration of
Soviet Union Jews is a great danger to our cause." Part of the eventual goal of
the action was the closing of the Austrian transit facilities for Soviet Jews immigrating to Israel. There were no reported fatalities.[62]

    Clearly, the most spectacular act of terrorism throughout the entire 1967-
1973 period was the attack, in September 1972, on the Israeli Olympic team in
Munich. The attack on the Olympic village and the subsequent battle at the airport resulted in the death of eleven Israeli athletes. This attack carried out for
the stated purpose of securing the release of Palestinians held in Israeli prisons,
is significant, in part, because it illustrates the interrelatedness of terrorist activity
during this period. For example, many subsequent incidents of terrorism and
counterterrorism are related directly to the Munich attack in 1972. The attack
resulted not only in strong retaliatory action by Israel against guerrilla bases in
Lebanon and Syria (on September 8, 1972, for example), but also in new acts
by sections of the Palestinian movement that were directly related to the Munich
attack. The action/counteraction cycle for example resulted in the placing of
curbs on guerrilla activity in Lebanon, which in turn led to a further straining of
the Lebanese-Palestinian relationship. The Munich action also led to renewed
activity within the United Nations on the question of terrorism and its control.
The almost universal condemnation of the act forced on several sections of the
Palestinian resistance a reevaluation of the use of the tactic. The action in Germany also led to a restriction on both Palestinian and Arab individuals and organizations within Germany and to an investigation of the relationship between
the terrorists responsible for the attack and other radical organizations (the
Baader-Meinhof Group, for example). As suggested earlier, it was also during
this period that a series of letter bombings and political murders occurred throughout Europe. Finally, the Munich attack also led directly to the hijacking of a West
German plane on October 29, 1972 (see Table 2). The plane, enroute from Beirut
to Ankara, was hijacked in order to secure the release of two of the Arab commandos held for the Munich attack. This "successful" operation, in turn, resulted
in new retaliatory raids by Israel against Palestinian bases in Lebanon and Syria.[63]

Conclusions

From the perspective of certain segments of the Palestinian resistance, the resort
to international terrorism and the selection of specific acts of terrorism (aerial
terrorism, letter bombs, commando attacks, and so forth) are based on an assess-

ment of a set of specific criteria. These criteria include—in addition to the supposed "effectiveness" of specific acts—the objectives and goals of the movement,
the victim-target relationship, the degree of cohesion or disunity within the movement, the definition of the scope of the conflict, and the resources and capabilities
of the movement. In terms of the Palestinian movement, these factors and variables were in a constant state of change in the period under study. As they
changed, so did attitudes toward the use of international terrorism as a political
tactic.

The nascent Palestinian resistance movement in this period was characterized by the need to achieve some degree of group cohesion and ideological consensus, to develop an effective institutional organization, and to ensure that in
any settlement reached concerning the Arab-Israeli impasse, Palestinian interests
would be protected and represented. Factors that aided or hindered this growth
were the general defeat of the Arab states in 1967, the occupation of the West
Bank and Gaza, the factionalization of the movement itself, the Jordanian/
Palestinian war of 1970-1971, and the response of Israel to both acts of terrorism and guerrilla-style warfare. Any understanding of the role terrorism has
played in the development of the Palestinian consciousness and resistance is best
understood from the interaction of these factors. For certain segments of the
Palestinian resistance, the use of international terrorism was one tactic, among
many, which was designed to secure the achievement of certain political goals.

A more complete and comprehensive treatment of the role of international
terrorism in both the development of the Palestinian movement and the general
Middle East conflict requires a more detailed analysis of the relationship between
terror as a political tactic and other tactics available to resistance movements.
This chapter has attempted to describe the acts of terrorism that were committed
during a specific period and to provide a base for further study of the role of
terrorism both as a general tactic and in the Middle Eastern context. It briefly
suggests that acts of terrorism are related to a series of variables and factors that
will influence both the types of acts that are initiated and their frequency and
duration. Further, it suggests that acts of terrorism committed during this period
are best understood within the wider context of both the development of the
Palestinian movement and the larger Middle East conflict. More empirically comprehensive and theoretically detailed studies should then concentrate not only on
terror and terrorism but also on the relationship of terror and terrorism to both
national and international violence. What is needed is a larger body of empirical
data on terror and terrorism that, while not condoning or accepting its use as a
legitimate political tactic, can lead to an understanding of its causes, its myriad
forms, and its control.

The tendency in periods of crisis and stress is to predict and expect that
terrorism and the use of terror will be with us always and will continually in-

crease. This, in fact, may be one of terrorism's goals. Initial empirical evidence suggests otherwise, however. From 1967 to 1973 in the Middle East, the use of terrorism varied in terms of types of acts committed, their frequency, their intensity, and their objectives. This suggests that terrorism will not either automatically increase or decrease, but rather that it will vary according to the relationship between a series of complex, often contradictory, political, economic, and social variables.

Notes

1. The initial event data for this paper are drawn from *Facts on File* for the years 1967-1973. Although multiple sources are preferable, the intention at this stage was to isolate trends in the data. One of the difficulties in the study of terrorism (besides definitional problems) is collecting complete data. In addition to the distinctions drawn in the text, only those acts that were actually carried out are included. This, for example, excludes aborted attempts or plots. Where relevant, the event data are cited first by the year edition of *Facts on File* and then the appropriate page numbers.

2. Robert Moss, "Urban Guerrilla Warfare," *Adelphi Papers,* no. 79, August 1971, p. 1.

3. Brian Crozier, *The Rebels, A Study of Post-War Insurrections* (Boston: Beacon Press, 1960), p. 159.

4. W. T. Mallison and S. V. Mallison, "The Concept of Public Purpose Terror in International Law," *Journal of Palestine Studies* 4, no. 2, p. 36.

5. Eugene V. Walter, *Terror and Resistance* (New York: Oxford, 1969), p. 5.

6. M. Hutchinson, "The Concept of Revolutionary Terrorism," *Journal of Conflict Resolution* 16, no. 3 (1972): 384.

7. Paul Wilkinson, *Political Terrorism* (New York: John Wiley, 1974), pp. 36-40.

8. Mallison and Mallison, "The Concept of Public Purpose Terror in International Law."

9. Richard A. Falk, "The Beirut Raid and the International Law of Retaliation," in *The Arab-Israeli Conflict,* vol. 2, *Readings,* ed. John N. Moore (Princeton, N.J.: Princeton University Press, 1974), p. 230.

10. Wilkinson, *Political Terrorism,* pp. 24-25.

11. Hutchinson, "The Concept of Revolutionary Terrorism," p. 385.

12. Thomas P. Thorton, "Terror as a Weapon of Political Agitation," in *Internal War,* ed. Harry Eckstein (New York: Free Press, 1964), pp. 81-82.

13. Walter, *Terror and Resistance,* p. 9.

14. D. V. Serge and J. H. Adler, "The Ecology of Terrorism," *Encounter* 40, no. 2 (February 1973): 14.

15. Walter, *Terror and Resistance,* p. 9.

16. Thorton, "Terror as a Weapon of Political Agitation," pp. 80-81.

17. Crozier, *The Rebels,* p. 160.

18. Thornton, "Terror as a Weapon of Political Agitation," p. 80.

19. In particular see: Michael Hudson, "The Palestinian Arab Resistance Movement," *Middle East Journal* 23, no. 3 (Summer 1969): 291-307; and Hisham Sharabi, "Palestinian Guerrillas: Their Credibility and Effectiveness," *Supplementary Papers* (Washington, D.C.: Georgetown University Center for Strategic and Internal Studies, 1970).

20. William Quant, Fuad Jabber, and Ann Mosley Lesch, *The Politics of Palestinian Nationalism* (Berkeley and Los Angeles: University of California Press, 1973), p. 172.

21. For a more detailed discussion of the positions of various factions within the movement see: Hudson, "The Palestinian Arab Resistance Movement"; Hisham Sharabi, "Palestine Guerrillas"; Y. Harkabi, "Fedayeen Action and Arab Strategy, *Adelphi Papers,* no. 53, 1968; John Cooley, *Green March, Black September: The Story of the Palestinian Arabs* (London: Frank Cass, 1973); and Quant, Jabber, and Lesch, *The Politics of Palestinian Nationalism.*

22. Quant, Jabber, and Lesch, *The Politics of Palestinian Nationalism,* p. 100.

23. Crozier, *The Rebels,* p. 159.

24. Wilkinson, *Political Terrorism,* p. 146.

25. See in particular, W. T. Mallison and S. V. Mallison, "The Juridical Characteristics of the Palestinian Resistance: An Appraisal in International Law," *The Journal of Palestine Studies* 2, no. 2, pp. 64-78.

26. Cited by Wilkinson, *Political Terrorism,* p. 123, from the *Journal of Air Law and Commerce* 37 (Spring 1971): 229-233.

27. Ali A. Mazrui, "The Contemporary Case for Violence," *Adelphi Papers,* no. 82, December 1971, p. 27.

28. *Facts on File* (New York: Facts on File, Inc., 1968), p. 298; *Facts on File,* 1969, pp. 554-555.

29. *Facts on File,* 1968, p. 568.

30. *Facts on File,* 1972, pp. 399-400.

31. *Facts on File,* 1973, p. 614.

32. *Facts on File,* 1969, p. 77.

33. *Facts on File,* 1970, pp. 546-547, 588; 1972, pp. 120, 141; and 1973, pp. 1050, 1070-1071.

34. *Facts on File,* 1970, p. 638.

35. *Facts on File,* 1970, p. 826.

36. *Facts on File,* 1972, p. 831.

37. One of the problems with collecting empirical data on acts of terrorism is determining if those who claim credit for certain acts actually carried them out. In these cases we have accepted that those who claimed credit were in fact responsible.

38. The Jordanian government claimed that Black September was actually a segment of the overall Fatah organization and that it was created in July 1971 following the Jordanian/Palestinian war. Acts attributed to Black September include the assassination of Jordanian Premier Wasfi Tell in November 1971, the May 9, 1972 attack on a Belgian airliner in Tel Aviv, and the Munich Olympic massacre in 1972. See *Facts on File,* 1972, p. 694.

39. *Facts on File,* 1970, p. 101.

40. *Facts on File,* 1970, p. 120.

41. *Facts on File,* 1970, p. 638.

42. Ibid.

43. *Facts on File,* 1970, p. 654.

44. *Facts on File,* 1973, p. 1070.

45. Mazrui, "The Contemporary Case for Violence," p. 21.

46. *Facts on File,* 1972, pp. 733-734.

47. *Facts on File,* 1972, p. 756.

48. Ibid.

49. *Facts on File,* 1972, pp. 15, 820, 861.

50. *Facts on File,* 1972, pp. 907-908.

51. *Facts on File,* 1973, pp. 89, 98.

52. *Facts on File,* 1972, pp. 733-734, 820.

53. *Facts on File,* 1969, p. 113.

54. *Facts on File,* 1972, p. 1037.

55. *Facts on File,* 1973, pp. 738, 779.

56. *Facts on File,* 1973, pp. 177-178, 204, 267, 508-509.

57. *Facts on File,* 1969, pp. 591, 620.

58. *Facts on File,* 1969, p. 770.

59. *Facts on File,* 1973, p. 614.

60. *Facts on File,* 1970, p. 235.

61. *Facts on File,* 1973, p. 285.

62. *Facts on File,* 1973, p. 815.

63. *Facts on File,* 1972, pp. 693-696, 709-711, 733-734, 755-756, 798-799, 819-820, 860-861.

10

Political Violence and Terrorism in Bengal

Richard C. Hula

Department of Political Science
The University of Texas at Dallas
Richardson, Texas

The propensity of Bengal to erupt in spasms of political violence and social disorder has been recognized firsthand by numerous would-be elites as they have attempted to impose a measure of political order in the region. Scholars have noted that of the numerous distinct cultural areas that comprise the Indian subcontinent, Bengal is often late to fall to a conqueror and is often a leader in challenges to an entrenched power. Such challenges have been raised against the Mughals and the British and may yet be repeated in the modern state of India.[1] For example, Bengal's resistance to British rule in the twentieth century debunks the myth that the Gandhi model of peaceful resistance to authority provided the paradigm for the Bengali independence movement.[2] Common features of the political landscape throughout this period were frequent political assassinations and other forms of terrorism. In the postindependence period, politics remained extremist, with numerous outbreaks of violence. For a time West Bengal was governed by a communist-dominated coalition that supported civil disorder. The state has also seen the outbreak of terrorist guerrilla movements, both in the countryside and in the major metropolitan area of Calcutta.

A great deal of energy has been given to the study of social disorder in Bengal. However, much of this literature has centered on elites, particularly the concerns, strategies, and general ideological preferences of political leaders.[3] In this chapter we shall consider a somewhat different set of issues. Our first goal will be a general overview of the role of political violence and terrorism in the politics of Bengal over the last 200 years.[4] In particular we hope to explore the changing structure of such violence in terms of frequency, actors, and motivations. Given the extraordinary levels of such violence, Bengal also provides an interesting case in which to consider more policy-relevant questions. One example is the range of strategies available to a governing elite for the control of political violence and possible impacts of these strategies. We also hope to assess the overall utility of terrorism as a form of political demand.

Changing Patterns of Political Terrorism in Bengal

In viewing Bengal history, we can discern two broad types of political violence that differ in several fundamental respects, including (1) the role of ideology and (2) the source of leadership and participation. We shall label these two categories of violence traditional and modern because they are most common in particular time periods. However, these terms do not imply any evolutionary or developmental sequence.

One feature of traditional political violence that occurred in the eighteenth and nineteenth centuries was the tendency of such violence to be a reaction to specific grievances. The most frequent cause of political and social unrest was the tension between those who held formal title to the land and were charged with collecting taxes and those who actually worked the land. A number of small-scale revolts followed attempts to extract some extra revenue from peasants. For the most part such uprisings were aimed at redressing particular problems and had neither justifying ideology or sustaining organization. In the twentieth century, political violence became more ideologically complete; often violence was tied to a more systematic desire to restructure society. Of course, this difference ought not be overstated. In particular, we want to be careful not to overestimate the ideological sophistication of those involved in more recent political violence.

A second critical difference between modern and traditional forms of political violence in Bengal is that of participation and leadership. Traditional unrest was centered in peasant movements. Often the leaders of these movements were themselves of lower-class origins. In the twentieth century, nationalist violence was often directed and carried out by the Hindu bhadralok.[5] The bhadralok are a Hindu elite, although often their economic status is far from secure. One important element within the bhadralok was the strong aversion to manual labor even if such an aversion meant a severe reduction in one's standard of living. Thus it was the bhadralok who flocked to Calcutta to serve in the lower levels of the British administrative machinery in the late nineteenth century. It was also

the bhadralok who felt the greatest loss in the British reluctance to grant constitutional advances to India. The polite concern expressed by bhadralok spokes-
persons in the late nineteenth century would evolve to revolutionary violence in
the twentieth.

The transition from peasant violence to bhadralok violence implies another
difference between traditional and modern violence in Bengal. Traditional violence was foremost a rural phenomena. Calcutta stood as a fortress of British
culture and political power within the much less secure area of rural Bengal. In
the twentieth century, this changed dramatically, with Calcutta emerging as a
center of radical thought and violent actions. Even violence that occurred in
rural areas was often in response to events within the city. Indeed the violence
was often organized by persons whose roots were in Calcutta. Violence in its
modern form, then, has become an increasingly urban phenomenon.

A final difference between traditional and modern political violence in
Bengal is the increased centrality of religious animosities in precipitating mass
collective disorder. To be sure, the trend could be easily overestimated. Relations between major religious communities, particularly Hindus and Muslims,
have always been far from cordial. In fact, some early peasant uprisings had
strong religious overtones. Nevertheless, the twentieth century witnessed a vast
escalation of these tensions. For example, the fury of intercommunal conflict
in Calcutta has at times been great enough to require the active intervention of
the Indian military to return the city to some minimum level of order.

Traditional Political Violence in Bengal: 1750-1900

Kathleen Gough has reviewed the history of seventy-seven separate peasant uprisings in India over the last 200 years.[6] Gough argues that most of these uprisings were "prepolitical" in the sense that they occurred outside the context of
national politics. Rather than being nationalist uprisings, these agitations most
often centered on protesting some increase in taxes or some form of increased
burden on peasants. Generally these peasant "revolts" can be more accurately
described as small-scale terrorist actions by only loosely organized mobs. The
offending landlord or official was often threatened, sometimes murdered. The
tax and/or loan records of the landlord were another favorite target of such
movements.

Although the Gough article dealt with all of India, it shows that Bengal
represented a center of peasant unrest. This impression is reinforced in a study
by Stephen Fuches, which argues that in the latter decades of the eighteenth
century large areas in Bengal were in a state of virtual insurrection.[7] A number
of these uprisings were particularly important in that they managed to sustain

themselves over a fairly long period of time. Perhaps most notable was the
Sanyasis and Fakirs revolt.[8] Initially, the Sanyasis and Fakirs were Hindu and
Muslim ascetics who were largely able to support themselves through begging. In
the 1760s there is some evidence of bands of Sanyasis and Fakirs attacking several factories of the East India Company and killing at least one company employee.[9] The ranks of the Sanyasis and the Fakirs were swelled by the economic
dislocation of the 1770 famine in Bengal.[10] The same famine, of course, made
it difficult to secure a living through begging. As a response, the Sanyasis and
Fakirs increasingly organized themselves in militarylike groups to acquire food
and other goods forcibly. These attacks received a measure of popular support
in that they were often directed against very unpopular figures like landlords and
grain speculators. Popular support was further increased as at least some of the
spoils were distributed to a starving peasantry.

In 1771 the British authorities took notice of the disorders and dispatched
a sepoy regiment to quell the rebellion. The troops engaged the Sanyasis and
Fakirs between Rangpur and Dacca. The result was a total defeat for the sepoy
force, including the death of the regiment's British officer. After this encounter
the power of the movement increased sharply. Soon much of Bengal and Eastern
Bihar was subject to periodic raids by bands of 5000-7000 men. In Borga and
Mymensingh a shadow government was established. In 1773 a second British
attack was mounted with much the same results as the first. About the turn of
the century the revolt of the Sanyasis and Fakirs finally collapsed from internal
weakness. However, the remnants of the movement joined the Marathas to continue their war against the British.

The first half of the nineteenth century continued to have examples of
peasant violence.[11] In 1825 in the district of Mymensingh, several landlords
were murdered in response to an effort to increase taxes in the area. Unrest did
not die out until the 1830s. A more serious peasant movement developed in
Faridpur. The Faraizis combined attacks on landlords with Islamic proselytizing.
The Faraizis movement was broken only with the arrest and death of its leader,
Dudu Miyan. In the 1830s, Titu Miyan led a Muslim revival movement, calling
for a wave of terror for all nonbelievers. The movement had its roots in the area
near Calcutta, but by 1831 managed to control much of Nadia, Faridpur, and
24-Parganas. Once again, non-British governments were established for a short
time. The initial attempt to suppress the movement with the armed force of the
Calcutta militia resulted in another sound defeat. In this case, however, superior
force would in time provide the British with a military victory.

The Sepoy Mutiny struck India in 1857.[12] However, there was little direct
violence in Bengal related to the mutiny. For example, the sepoy regiment in
Calcutta was quickly and peacefully disarmed. The mutiny did have a strong
symbolic effect, however. The most dramatic impact was a sharp increase in

anti-Indian feeling among Europeans, particularly those in Calcutta. There is evidence that a number of Indian neighborhoods within the city were subjected to rough treatment at the hands of hastily assembled European "defense squads."[13] With the anxieties raised by the mutiny still high, Europeans faced another set of disturbances in rural Bengal during the 1860s. These were the famous indigo revolts in which peasants throughout Bengal resisted the forced planting of indigo.[14] The indigo agitations had two important impacts. First, the movement was successful in that most of the indigo industry was forced from Bengal. A second and perhaps more significant impact was the popular Indian support the agitations generated in Calcutta. Blair Kling argues that Calcutta intellectuals created a post hoc ideology for the disturbances.[15] Thus the indigo agitations provided early support for the notion that there might be some convergence of interest across Indian social classes. It also provided a lesson that suggested that violence could be a useful political weapon. Certainly this latter lesson would not be forgotten.

Nationalist Violence: 1900-1947

The twentieth century saw the emergence of a very different sort of political violence throughout Bengal. Increasingly, violence would be aimed directly at the British rulers by an urban elite seeking political power. Although it is not possible to outline a social history of the Bengali bhadralok, several very general points need to be made. First, the bhadralok intellectual community had been in a state of ferment since the middle of the nineteenth century.[16] One outgrowth of the ferment was an increasing questioning of the obvious discrimination against native Indians, particularly in the governmental service. Potential for advancement for an Indian seemed low. This intellectual concern was reinforced by a very real economic instability. At the turn of the century advancement opportunities for the bhadralok seemed to actually be decreasing. The positions available to Indians and long dominated by the bhadralok were increasingly open and even reserved for other social communities. This was particularly true in provinces outside Bengal where the bhadralok were viewed as outsiders by both the British and native Indians. Competition was also increasing as English education became more readily available to other groups. Finally, sharp increases in population and the constant division of landholdings had contributed to a decline in the economic fortunes of bhadralok generally.

The level of the bhadralok's dissatisfaction with British policy did in fact lead to the emergence of some political protest even in the nineteenth century.[17] For the most part, however, this protest was peaceful. Often it was not even public, but rather took the form of personal pleading by well-placed Bengalis. To the extent that such protests were public, they took the form of petitions and polite newspaper editorials. However, in 1903 the government of Bengal announced that it was preparing to partition the province into two separate and "more manageable" provinces. The response of the bhadralok community was shock and outrage. The resulting agitations would set the stage for a pattern of political violence and terrorism that would rock Bengal for the next 60 years.

The Partition of Bengal

The partition of Bengal was announced as a purely administrative decision, and viewed from a narrow administrative perspective it made a good deal of sense. Bengal was an enormously large administrative area that included not only Bengal proper but also Bihar, Chota Nagpur, and Orissa. The proposed division would create two smaller provinces of almost equal size. However, it was simply not possible to ignore some nonadministrative implications of the partition. First, it would create in East Bengal a province that would have a Muslim majority and thus might be expected to be dominated by Muslims. Obviously such a development would be against the interests of the bhadralok who until the partition had dominated the governmental apparatus then open to Indians. Even in the west, partition seemed to have little to offer the bhadralok. Although there would be a Hindu majority, that majority would be composed of Beharis and Oriyas with whom the Bengali bhadralok shared a common religion but little else. Thus, the political and social impact of the partition would be to isolate the bhadralok. It was an implication well understood by the Bengal government, which had grown increasingly weary of trying to deal with the demands of the bhadralok. Such implications were also clear to the bhadralok themselves.

Broomfield describes four phases of the agitation that developed once it was clear the Bengal government was committed to the implementation of the partition decision.[18] The first phase, which began in late 1903, involved the use of the traditional tools of persuasion that had been used in the past: public meetings, critical press articles, and private consultations. As it became increasingly clear that these traditional forms of protest were having little impact, emphasis shifted to a public boycott of British goods. The boycott was begun in 1905 to "force" the British to renounce the partition. In 1906, large numbers of men were organized in samitis (unions) and akhras (gymnasiums) to help enforce the boycott and provide a mechanism for more general participation in the antipartition movement. Such organizations were established throughout the province, although they were most common in urban areas such as Calcutta, Dacca, Bakarganj, Faridipur, Mymensingh, Dinajpur, Chittagong and Chock Bihar. Particularly important were the Dacca Anusilan Samiti, founded in 1905; the Calcutta Samiti, founded in 1907; and the Manicktola Garden House Secret Society, also founded in 1907. By 1912, the Dacca Anusilan Samiti had established some 500 chapters over various portions of Bengal.[19]

By 1907, the rhetoric of the antipartition movement began to escalate with the frustration within the movement. Support for violence began to appear in the media. A commission created by the British to study revolutionary violence in India cites the following example:

> Will the Bengali worshippers of Shaki shrink from the shedding of blood? The number of Englishmen in this country is not above one and a half lakh! (150,000) and what is the number of English officials in each district? If you are firm in your resolution you can in a single day bring English rule to an end. Lay down your life, but first take a life. The worship of the goddess will not be consummated if you sacrifice your lives at the shrine of independence without shedding blood.[20]

It appears that even before 1907 some of the samiti were collecting arms and explosives.[21] However, it was not until that year that a real terrorist campaign against the British began.

In 1907 there was a sharp increase in the violence directed toward British officials.[22] There were a number of reported assassinations, assassination attempts, bombings, and political dacoities (gang-style robberies involving five or more persons). Several attempts were made on the life of Bengal's lieutenant-governor. One of these attempts did manage to derail the governor's train, although he was uninjured. In 1908 a bomb that was apparently meant for a Mr. Kingsford, a judge at Muzaffarpur, went astray and killed two women nearby. As a result one of the assassins was hanged, the other committed suicide. Kingsford was later the target of a "book bomb." In what was to be a common pattern, the subinspector of police who had captured the bomb thrower was later gunned down in the streets of Calcutta. Such was to be the fate of a number of individuals who had been involved with the capture and prosecution of terrorists. This was particularly true of Indian informers. Several such informers were killed within British jails. For example, in 1908 the British raided a number of Calcutta homes for guns and explosives based on information supplied by Narendra Goasin. Shortly after the raids Goasin was killed while being held by the British. The men who murdered Goasin were later hanged, and, in retaliation, the prosecutor in that case was murdered in February 1910.

The campaign against the partition, particularly in its more violent aspects, had an impact far beyond that of producing the short-run British response. Perhaps the most important was the tension the movement generated between Muslims and Hindus.[23] Although the bhadralok leadership attempted to speak for all Bengalis, theirs was a movement largely defined by bhadralok interests. Furthermore, the movement was based largely on Hindu ideology and symbolism. Indeed the partition was very popular with many Muslims who saw it as a chance to escape the domination of a bhadralok elite. As the antipartition movement became more vocal, so did Muslim attempts to organize support for the division. In 1906, for example, the newly formed Muslim League held a series of public meetings which drew 20,000 to 30,000 people in Dacca and nearly 20,000 in Calcutta.

Muslim concerns that the Hindu leadership was firmly committed to a policy opposed to Muslim interests received strong support in 1906 with the forced retirement of East Bengal's governor, Bampfylde Fuller. Fuller was widely known for his sympathies for the Muslim community, and it was widely believed that his dismissal was an attempt to appease angry Hindus. As the Muslims continued to step up their support for the partition the British made what turned out to be a fateful policy decision. Seeing the Muslim as a source of countervailing power to the increasingly hard to manage bhadralok, the British made a conscious effort to support the development of separate Muslim political organizations. In several instances, the British allowed Muslim violence against Hindus to go unchecked so that the Hindus might "be taught a lesson." It was a dangerous strategy, one that ultimately the British would not be able to control.

A series of Muslim-Hindu clashes were set off in 1907 as the Muslim League attempted to expand its support for the partition. The initial incident occurred in the East Bengal town of Comilla. The Nawab of Dacca had come to assist personally in the formation of a local chapter of the Muslim League with the hope that the league could counteract the effect of the local boycott organization. While in Camilla, the Nawab's secretary was shot by a Hindu. John McLane has described the result:

> The local administration was slow to act against the Muslim violence and gave the impression that they wanted to teach the Hindu agitators a lesson. The evidence was considerable and well publicized. . . .
>
> When the Nawab of Dacca arrived in Comilla he was permitted to go through the town in a procession, although when the delegates to the Tippera District Conventions nine days earlier had attempted to accompany their president, Abdul Rasul, in procession the police prevented them on the grounds that they did not have a permit. On the other hand after two days of communal trouble on the occasion of the Nawab's visit, the police did not stop an unlicensed Muslim procession from marching through the Hindu section of town. The District Magistrate refused the call of Hindus under attack.[24]

As tensions rose between the Muslims and Hindus, the character of many of the samiti organizations also changed. Once viewed as organs to enforce the boycott, they often became "defense squads" to guard against Muslim attacks. Although there were to be several attempts to create intercommunal cooperation in Bengal, the tension and mistrust between the communities would remain high throughout the preindependence period.

The response of the British to this rapid escalation of violence, both toward its own officials and between Hindus and Muslims, was the rapid implementation of a set of severe laws to control the disorder. Broomfield has described the British strategy:

> In 1907 and 1908 the British imposed a strict censureship on the press; they extended the activities of the secret police, placing high schools, colleges, and voluntary organizations under political surveillance; they resorted to imprisonment without trial, and the deportation of political offenders and the externment of political suspects.[25]

In the short run, the British response sharply reduced the level of political violence in the province. However, it also served to create an ever higher level of anger and frustration. It would not take long for that anger to assert itself.

One of the direct effects of the British action against the terrorists in 1908 had been to cut off traditional sources of funds to the would-be revolutionaries. In response, terrorist organizations increasingly turned to dacoities to finance their activities. Although it is clear that only a small number of reported dacoities in this period had political implications, some small but significant proportion were undertaken to finance political activity. These attacks were often quite violent, and often the stakes were large. For example, a Calcutta resident in 1916 was relieved of some Rs 11,500. He shortly received a note in the mail acknowledging the "loan" and promising repayment (with interest). The note was signed by the finance secretary to the Bengal branch of the "Independent Kingdom of India."[26]

In addition to strong police action and limited funds, the terrorist movement had been hampered by a lack of weapons and explosives. Prior to 1914 the terrorists had relied primarily on sources of weapons in the French settlement at Chandernagore, the quality and quantity of which was very limited. In 1914 an employee of Rhodda and Company in Calcutta made off with fifty Mauser pistols and 46,000 rounds of ammunition. The distribution of these weapons throughout Bengal served to spur the spread of a renewed terrorist campaign that had begun in 1912. The British government itself was sharply divided on the proper strategy in meeting this new terrorist challenge. Bengal's Governor Carmichael was convinced that the repressive strategy of 1908 was only a short-run solution and in the long term would only lead to greater violence.[27] Carmichael argued that the government had to engage Bengali moderates in the government so that they might be persuaded to help control their own countrymen. This perspective was rejected at the all-India level, which saw Bengal as a center of sedition and violence and in need of "strong action" along the lines of 1908. The two governments argued among themselves as the level of terrorism continued to grow. Finally, the outbreak of World War I provided the pretext of imposing "order"

in the province. In March 1915, the Defense of India Act was implemented in
Bengal. Introduced as an emergency war measure, the act allowed the detention,
without trial, of suspected terrorists. Large-scale arrests followed shortly. Once
again the implementation of strong law had the effect of bringing about a short-
term reduction in political violence. In the year 1919 only one terrorist act had
been reported in Bengal.

In 1916, in part spurred on by a mutual distaste for the terms of the Defense of India Act, national Hindu and Muslim leaders agreed to the terms of the
Lucknow Pact. The Lucknow Pact attempted to unite Hindus and Muslims to
press the British jointly for responsible provincial government and domination
status for India. At the heart of the agreement was the predetermination of communal representation in the provincial legislatures. As an all-India compromise,
the terms of the pact as they applied to Bengal were disliked by both communities.
Although the Lucknow Pact had been thought to be a vehicle to reduce intercommunal conflict, it had precisely the opposite effect in Bengal. In 1918 the city of
Calcutta was racked by a series of communal riots of unprecedented magnitude.
The largest lasted some 3 days and was quelled only with the active intervention
of the British military.

In 1920 Bengal was once again thrown into turmoil in response to national
politics. In that year the national Congress called for a program of "noncooperation." Gandhi argued that if the nationalist movement were to succeed, it would
be necessary for the movement to turn inward, to make society more "worthy."
In an effort to bring about such a transformation, Gandhi called on the members
of the Congress party to withdraw from British institutions and return to the
countryside. Here they were to work with "the people" to establish local cottage
industries. Of particular importance was the spinning of cloth, which was to be
the symbol of the noncooperation movement.

Much of Bengal's leadership was unenthusiastic about the noncooperation
movement, particularly the emphasis on spinning. However, the symbolic value
of the effort was recognized as efforts were made to enforce a boycott of all foreign cloth in Calcutta. Shortly the markets were being patrolled by groups seeking to impose such a boycott. Tensions rose as these groups displayed increasing
aggressiveness in the city's markets. Large-scale violence broke out in the city
when the national Congress Committee allowed the noncooperation movement
to include acts of civil disobedience. Three days after the call for civil disobedience a police sergeant was killed during a riot in Howrah. The riot was broken
up only after police fired on the mob. As the Prince of Wales landed in Bombay
on a long-awaited goodwill tour of India, a total hartal, or general strike, was
called in Calcutta. Broomfield describes the result:

> All shops were closed and no private or public transport was allowed to
> move in the streets. The police lost control to the volunteer brigades, but

they in turn were unable to manage the gang of factory laborers who had been brought into the city from the outlying mills by the Kalafatists. Assisted by Goondas, these gangs looted shops, molested pedestrians, and in South Calcutta fought pitched battles with the police.[28]

It was clear that if order was not restored the visit of the Prince of Wales would have to be canceled. This the British wanted very much to avoid. Following some abortive negotiations, the British moved again to crush the violence through repression. Public meetings were banned, nationalist organizations were declared illegal, and nationalist leaders were thrown in jail. By the end of 1921 much of the violence in Calcutta was under control. The first months of 1922 saw an increase in violence outside the city. Attacks on police and other governmental officials were common; numerous government buildings were attacked and burned. In early 1922 the level of violence generated by the civil disobedience movement had reached such a high level, that Gandhi himself called for a halt to the movement.

Following the formal collapse of the noncooperation movement, moderate Bengali Hindu and Muslim leaders forged the Swaraj party to contest the approaching provincial elections. However, by 1923 Hindu extremists were again waging a terrorist campaign against the British. A favorite target of Calcutta terrorists was the city's police commissioner, Charles Tegart. Although Tegart survived the several attempts on his life, those around him were not always so lucky. Lady Tegart described one such episode:

> The murder took place in the early hours of the morning when it was still pleasantly cool. Day had paused during a morning walk to look in at the window of Hall and Anderson's, a large European shop facing the main thoroughfare of Chowringhee and near the right-angle turn to Kyd Street, in which Tegart's house was situated; he was about the same build as Tegart and was wearing a khaki shirt and shorts; as he was gazing into the windows, his back to the street, a young Bengali suddenly came up behind him and shot him in the back, shooting him again repeatedly after he had fallen to the ground and then running away. The murderer was chased by several people and fired at them as he ran, wounding two of them severely, but he was eventually captured.[29]

In 1924 an organization called "Red Bengal" circulated a pamphlet throughout Calcutta announcing the beginning of a campaign of police assassination. Although it is not clear whether the group was actually involved with any police murders, Griffiths reports that during that year the Calcutta police did uncover several plots to murder police.[30]

Throughout the early 1920s tension between Hindus and Muslims began to increase once again. Although the Swaraj party had enjoyed a solid electoral success in 1924, it was a most tenuous alliance. A continual source of irritation between the coalition partners was the attitude of the Hindu bhadralok to the terrorist movement. Muslim mistrust was increased by the terrorist claim of support from the more moderate Hindu politicians. During a party conference in 1924 a resolution that appeared to endorse the terrorist campaign was adopted over the objection of Muslim members of the party. In response to this resolution the British moved against the party. In October 1924 the British authorities ordered police raids throughout Bengal. Some eighty-five persons were detained, including members of the Bengal Legislative Council and the chief administrative officer of the Calcutta Corporation.

The prospect of cooperation between Hindus and Muslims was further reduced as the British continued to implement their strategy of "divide and conquer." The British not only continued to support Muslim political organization but moved forward with plans to expand the electorate in Bengal. Although this decision was justified by reference to democratic ideology, the intent of the plan was clear—to reduce the power of the Bengali bhadralok with voting power of Muslims. Increasingly, the bhadralok saw the electoral process as threatening their dominance in Bengal. As the prospect of a Muslim government became more and more likely in Bengal, radical Hindus increased their attacks on any form of cooperation with Muslims. Agitators were not lacking from either community, and in 1926 communal violence erupted throughout Bengal. As one would expect, the violence was particularly great in Calcutta. Something like a state of war existed, as the city passed through ever-increasing cycles of violence:

> On the 24th a drunken brawl in Cotten Street in Central Calcutta sparked off another fortnight's bitter civil war. A method of killing in the first round—the imprisonment of victims in buildings which were then fired— gave way to the stabbing of individuals in back alleys by roving bands of the opposite community. Firearms made their appearance for the first time in Indian communal affrays. . . . This time looting was more widespread and there were more deaths—seventy killed, four hundred injured.[31]

With the formation of a Muslim ministry in 1927, the bhadralok political alienation seemed complete. The ensuring retreat from electoral politics brought on yet another wave of terrorist attacks on British officials. In 1928, attempts were made on the life of the Calcutta police commissioner and the superintendent of prisons for Bengal, the latter successful. In addition there were a number of politically motivated strikes, often accompanied by a significant personal violence. A number of these strikes were broken only after police firings.

In 1930 Gandhi called for a new wave of civil disobedience, and Bengal once again responded with violence. Boycotts, demonstrations, attacks on police, and various acts of sabotage occurred throughout Bengal. In the same year the province was electrified when a band of terrorists attacked the British armory just outside Chittagong. After killing the guards, the raiders took control of the armory and declared themselves to be the provisional government of an independent Indian state. Although the British rather quickly drove the raiders from Chittagong, much of the district remained in a state of near civil war. The Chittagong raid not only provided ammunition and weapons but a symbol for the Bengal revolutionaries.

Through the early 1930s attacks on individual British officials were once again accelerated. Four top police and prison officials were murdered. In addition a number of minor officials and nonofficial representatives of the British establishment were attacked. In Midnapore district the Congress established a shadow government including police force and other civil administrators. British administration in the area largely collapsed after three successive district magistrates were assassinated. Some measure of formal control was returned only after a Bengali was named as magistrate. In Calcutta there were a number of attempts on the lives of prominent members of European society in the city. In 1931, Edgar Villar, president of the European Association, was murdered, and Alfred Watson, editor of the British *Statesman,* had two narrow escapes. A number of government buildings were bombed, and the police continued to discover stores of guns and explosives. In what was by now a well-established pattern, the British attempted to suppress the violence through the enforcement of a series of repressive laws. Under the new laws some 10,000 Hindu nationalists had been jailed. By 1934 the civil disobedience movement was in disarray, with most of its leadership in jail.[32]

Throughout the 1930s it became increasingly clear that the British administrative institutions were near the point of collapse. Nevertheless, pressures on the government continued to grow. There was, of course, World War II, which, given the fall of Burma, seemed to offer the prospect of a direct possible Japanese threat to Bengal. In 1942 the Indian Congress called on the British to declare themselves firmly for Indian independence as a price for Congress support in the war effort. If such a declaration was not made, the Congress was prepared to engage in yet another civil disobedience movement. Using emergency war powers, British officials quickly moved against prominent Congress leaders. The effect was to return Bengal to a state of revolutionary turmoil. In the early 1940s, there were reported 301 police firings, 2000 police injuries, and 322 jails and over 2000 government buildings destroyed. In a number of areas within Bengal, British administration completely collapsed.

In 1946 the British government announced that it was sending a Cabinet Commission to India to discuss terms of Indian independence. Communal tension rose as each group attempted to secure favorable treatment. Given the added stress of chronic food shortages, violence seemed inevitable.[33] The explosion that so many feared occurred on October 16, 1946. On that day a public demonstration had been called by the Muslim government of Bengal to support the creation of a Muslim state from British India. The communal riots that were set off in the city are referred to as the "great killing." Although estimates of the number of persons killed vary, it is certain that the riots were the most extensive and deadly in the history of the city.[34] Although some measure of order was returned to Calcutta, outbreaks of communal violence continued until the formal granting of independence.

Political Violence in the Postindependence Period

The coming of independence to India was viewed throughout the country as an occasion for hope and optimism for the future. In Bengal, however, independence was viewed with a distinct ambivalence. There was a general delight taken in the fact that the British had been driven from the country. Yet the terms of independence had been harsh for Bengal. Once again Bengal had been partitioned. What was worse, the present partition created two provinces that were not under the same political administration but rather under two separate and hostile national governments. The economic effect on West Bengal was profound. Calcutta found itself cut off from its major source of raw goods; the entire region found its transportation system severely disrupted.[35] There was also a political component to the unrest in West Bengal after independence, and that was an unhappiness with the makeup of the new political leadership in the state. Much of the radical elements of the Bengali independence movement remained out of power. A common response was to define the new Congress government as simply an extension of the old order and to call for a continued revolution.

Following independence, leadership for continuing turmoil in West Bengal came from the Communist Party of India (CPI). Franda has described the activities of that party:

> The most intense party activity in Bengal took place in an eighteen-month period that extended from October 1948 until March 1950, during which time innumerable trams, busses, trains, and buildings were either bombed or set on fire. Demonstrations by students, mass organizations, and cultural front groups took place at the rate of one or two a week in Calcutta, and deaths from the activities of the revolutionaries were estimated to be in the hundreds.[36]

Acts which were specifically traced to the CPI or related organizations included: an attack on the West Bengal labor minister, an attack on a public meeting held by the same minister, the complete destruction of the Calcutta telephone exchange, an attempt to blow up the Calcutta waterworks, a number of raids on the home of the state Congress party, attacks on a number of Congress officials, an attack on Prime Minister Nehru, and large-scale raids on Dum Dum Airport, in which a number of airline employees were killed. Late in 1950 communal violence in which some units of the CIP were thought to be involved flared in Calcutta.

The new government of West Bengal reacted in what by now could be called a traditional response. The state government moved against the party with a series of laws very similar in content to those that the British had used against the nationalist movement. Leaders of the party were arrested and interned until the end of 1951. Upon their release the party leadership assumed a strategy of seeking power through the electoral process. It is important to note, however, that an electoral strategy in Bengal does not preclude violence. Indeed, violence had proved to be an effective vote-getting technique. Throughout the mid-1950s, the party was involved in numerous public demonstrations that were broken up only after police fired into the crowds.[37] Bayley has argued that throughout the entire decade of the 1950s, public disorder was increasing on an all-India level.[38] Alan Watts has argued that a similar trend has continued for India into the 1960s.[39]

Public disorder reached new levels in the mid-1960s with the coming to power of a United Front government in West Bengal. The United Front was a collection of leftist parties, dominated by the state's two major Communist parties. The coalition's major point of agreement was the desirability of removing Congress from political power in the state. An immediate impact of the United Front government was a sharp increase in labor unrest. The number of strikes rose sharply. Moorhouse reports that in 1967 there were 438 labor disputes reported in West Bengal involving 165,000 workers with a loss of 5 million man-hours. By 1969 this figure had increased to 710 industrial disputes involving 645,000 workers with a loss of 8.5 million man-hours.[40] From the numerous labor agitations a new form of protest emerged—the "gherao," in which a target individual is surrounded for a prolonged period by a group making demands on him. The person facing the gherao can either give in to the demands being made of him or hope for rescue from the police. It is unlikely that he would be able to escape unaided. The use of the gherao increased sharply in the state after the Communist state labor minister announced that police were not to intervene in gheraos without specific instructions from his office. Although this restriction was later removed by the courts, the morale of the police was severely damaged.

The unstable political climate in West Bengal was shaken again in 1967 with the outbreak of peasant agitation in the Naxilbari area of West Bengal. A number of landlords and police were murdered in the area. Finally, the movement was largely brought under control by the police forces of the United Front government.[41] The agitation had a number of more lasting impacts, however. First of all, the movement had a good deal of popular support, which was translated into the formation of a largely covert terrorist organization, the CPML (Communist Party of India-Marxist-Leninist). Once again we find the Calcutta based bhadralok at the center of a major terrorist movement in Bengal. The extremist bhadralok continued to challenge state government with rhetoric and arms in spite of the fact that the government was Communist-dominated. In 1969, the CPML instituted a policy of "annihilation" in selected rural portions of the state. The strategy called for the assassination of landlords, creating a power vacuum that the party would be able to exploit.

Although a number of landlords were killed, and several areas of the state declared "liberated," there is little evidence that the CPML had generated much popular support.[42] By 1970 much of this rural agitation had been brought under control by the police and other paramilitary forces. A second phase of the party's activities was reached in 1970 with the attempt to implement an urban strategy. The annihilation campaign was brought to Calcutta in an attempt to create conditions for a sustaining urban guerrilla movement. Although numerous attacks on police and other officials did occur, once again the Naxalites failed to generate popular support. After the final fall of the United Front government, the government response became increasingly effective. By the end of 1970 most of the party's leadership was either in jail or dead. Finally in late 1970 there was a call for the party to return to the countryside.[43]

Conclusion

The study of political violence and terrorism in Bengal raises several general questions concerning the role of violence within a political system. First, there is the issue of political control; that is, what are the options available to political elites for controlling outbreaks of violence? Such questions have become more important, and implicitly more respectable for academics to discuss, given the recent rash of terrorist attacks against what are generally thought to be democratic governments. For Bengal, there appears to be a consistent pattern of violence followed by periods of repression that dampen the level of violence, only to be followed by fresh outbreaks of violence, often more extreme than the last. Such a finding turns out to be consistent with a good deal of literature, which suggests that if coercion is to be used in controlling violence, it is likely to succeed only if that coercion is extreme.[44] The British government showed a clear reluctance to impose such a regime. For example, following several mass arrests few individuals were interned for long periods of time. The British seemed to adopt a middle-range strategy that had the opposite of its intended effect. In the post-independence period the picture is not so clear. Although there seemed to be a similar trend through the first 20 years of Indian independence, the official response to the Naxalite challenge, particularly with the rumors of police assassin squads, suggests that a sharp increase in the level of coercion has occurred. It is, of course, problematic whether the "critical" level of coercion has been reached. Indeed, there is little evidence to assure us that such a threshold does in fact exist. Perhaps future events in West Bengal will provide a clue.

A very different question might be raised as to the impact of violence itself, rather than the impact of attempts to control it. It is perhaps something of a paradox to note that given the extraordinary level of social and political violence that has occurred in Bengal, there seems to be a surprising stability of political elites. For example, the British were to remain in control through nearly 40 years of violence. Much the same has been true for the postindependence period as well. Although it is true that there has been instability in the makeup of the West Bengal government, there has been little question of West Bengal succeeding or overturning the Indian Union government. To be sure, this stability does not imply any measure of effectiveness. There is general agreement that neither the Union government nor the state government has ever had the will or the resources to begin to deal with the enormous social and economic problems of the area.[45] Yet, when an alternative elite such as the Naxalites has presented itself, the alternative has been rejected. This resistance to fundamental political change is dramatically underscored by the striking similarity in policy outputs of the pre- and postindependence Indian governments. We have, for example, noted the similarity of criminal laws.[46]

It may be that some of the apparent ineffectiveness of violence as a demand for political change can be tied back to the nature of the society itself. Certainly the very high degree of social and political fragmentation in the society creates conditions conducive to widespread social disorder. Yet that same fragmentation would seem to mitigate against the formation of a single interest or group of interests that could effectively challenge the dominant political elite. What we seem to find in Bengal, then, is a sort of perverse political pluralism in which the various "groups" keep each other in check. A highly unpleasant aspect of the balancing process is that it tends to occur in the street. Although the resulting society may not be a very pleasant place to live, there is a measure of political stability.

A further consideration of the role of political violence in Bengali politics brings us to the most basic question of the nature of violence itself. We have assumed that we fully understand the nature of violence and terrorism in a political order. Yet students of comparative politics have long argued caution in assuming that objectively similar events have similar social meanings. Certainly we are familiar with examples in which such equivalence does not hold true, as in the case of elections or political parties. The student of Western politics tends to assume that violence represents extreme and desperate acts. It is further assumed that violence is a relatively inefficient way to make political demands as compared to other possible inputs. Do these examples hold in the case of Indian politics? Perhaps, but there is reason to suggest that they may not. To continue a crude pluralist framework, we may describe Bengali politics as a regulated struggle of competing groups. However, the rules that operate the game are a bit rougher than those familiar to Western social science. The nature of the struggle may in part be defined by the nature of the resources available to the actors. In a resource-poor environment many groups have little short of street action that they can bring to bear on the political process.

The view that at least some violence represents "normal" politics receives a bit of support if one considers the nature of some of the issues that have generated violence in Bengali politics, particularly in the twentieth century. For example, in 1953 a number of leftist parties, led by the Communists, formed a coalition to protest an announced increase in second-class tram fares. After failing to obtain a negotiated rollback of fares, the Tram Fare Resistance Committee called for a hartal. The city came to a virtual halt as only about 10 percent of all shops were open. A general boycott of trams was begun, and those who attempted to ride were likely to find themselves pulled into the streets. Students blocked the streets until driven away by the police. The potential for violence increased as the government attempted to ban all public demonstrations. The result was a series of large and disorderly demonstrations. Shortly the police discovered that the situation was completely out of hand and had to appeal for military intervention. Even after the army responded with troops, several neighborhoods in the city remained under the control of mobs. The violence continued until the tram fare increase was finally rescinded.[47] Other examples of the use of violence to seek specific material or political goals could easily be cited. It is most common in labor disputes.[48] Myron Weiner points to an example of some 400 students attacking a number of examination centers in protest against an exam that the students felt unfair and too difficult. Similar violence broke out later in the city when thousands of persons appeared to fill a few positions in the Calcutta Fire Brigade.[49] While the use of violence in such situations may be "inefficient" by North American standards, there are repeated examples of such violence obtaining some desired policy outcomes.

If there is merit in this notion of violence as "normal politics," we are forced to confront the problem of defining the characteristics of such violence. A major task of future research should be comparing violence that represents a threat to regime stability with violence that does not. It is a task that calls for the development of a useful theoretical context that, it is hoped, can place in some order the massive empirical work presently available to the student of political violence in Asia.

Notes

1. For an overview of the Mughal period see Vincent A. Smith (revised by J. B. Harrison), "The Mughal Period," in *The Oxford History Of India,* ed. Percival Spear (Oxford: Clarendon Press, 1958), pp. 320-445.

2. After the Bengalis lost their leadership role in the nationalist movement to Gandhi, they continued to be a source of opposition. This opposition was lead by C. R. Das in the 1920s and by Subhas Chandra Bose in the 1930s. See Leonard A. Gordon, *Bengal: The Nationalist Movement, 1876-1940* (New York: Columbia University Press, 1974).

3. Perhaps the best example of such work is J. G. Broomfield, *Elite Conflict in a Rural Society* (Berkeley: University of California Press, 1968).

4. We shall restrict our discussion to Bengal proper rather than try to include the much larger administrative jurisdiction under the Bengal provincial government. In addition we shall limit our discussion of the postindependence period to West Bengal. For a discussion of East Bengal (first East Pakistan and now Bangladesh), see Talukder Maniruzzaman, "Radical Politics and the Emergency of Bangladesh," in *Radical Politics in South Asia,* ed. Paul Brass and Marcus Franda (Cambridge, Mass.: M.I.T. Press, 1973), pp. 223-280.

5. There is some disagreement as to whether "bhadralok" refers to a genuine Bengali subculture or is simply a European stereotype. Gordon (*Bengal,* pp. 7-8) has argued this latter position. The counterargument is given in Broomfield, *Elite Conflict in a Rural Society,* pp. 1-41, and Marcus F. Franda, *Radical Politics in West Bengal* (Cambridge, Mass.: M.I.T. Press, 1971), pp. 1-41. On balance the evidence would seem to support the existence of the group.

6. Kathleen Gough, "Indian Peasant Uprisings," *Economic and Political Weekly,* August 1974.

7. Stephen Fuches, *Rebellious Prophets: A Study of Messianic Movements in Indian Religions* (New York: Asia Publishing House, 1965), pp. 108-124.

8. See Fuches, *Rebellious Prophets,* and Gough, "Indian Peasant Uprisings."

9. See J. C. Chatterji, *Indian Revolutionaries in Conference* (Calcutta: Firma K. L. Mukhopadhyay), pp. 2-3.

10. The problem of recurring famines has been treated in a number of sources. See, for example, Bengal Publicity Board, *Famines in India* (Calcutta: Indian Association Publicity Company, 1944).

11. These various civil uprisings are discussed in Chatterji, *Indian Revolutionaries in Conference,* Fuches, *Rebellious Prophets,* and Gough, "Indian Peasant Uprisings." See also Binod S. Das, *Civil Rebellion in the Frontier Bengal (1760-1805)* (Calcutta: Punthi Putak, 1973).

12. See Vincent A. Smith (revised by Percival Spear), "India in the British Period," in *The Oxford History of India,* ed. Spear.

13. The strong reaction of the European community in Calcutta to news of the mutiny is described in Geoffrey Moorhouse, *Calcutta* (New York: Harcourt Brace Jovanovich, 1971), pp. 62-64.

14. See Gough, "Indian Peasant Uprisings." Also, Blair Bernard Kling, *The Blue Mutiny: The Indigo Disturbances in Bengal 1859-1862* (Philadelphia: University of Pennsylvania Press, 1966).

15. Kling, *The Blue Mutiny.*

16. The role of the bhadralok within the British service and its effect within their community are discussed in Nemai Sudhan Bose, *The Indian Awakening and Bengal* (Calcutta: Firma Mukhopadhyay, 1969). For an overview see Broomfield, *Elite Conflict in a Rural Society,* pp. 1-41.

17. Much of this early protest was in response to efforts by the Viceroy Lord Curzon's attempt to make the governmental apparatus more "efficient" and halt what seemed to be a trend for "Indianization" of the British government in Bengal. Curzon moved first to reduce the authority of the elected members of the Calcutta Corporation. A similar bill was proposed for Calcutta University. However, the greatest bhadralok anger would be generated by Curzon's plan to partition Bengal. See Moorhouse, *Calcutta,* p. 69.

18. Broomfield, *Elite Conflict in a Rural Society,* pp. 29-30.

19. The "official" history of the boycott and subsequent terrorist campaign is given in *Sedition Committee Report, 1918* (Calcutta: Superintendent Government Printing Office, 1918). See also Saleem Oureshi, "Political Violence in South Asia," in *International Terrorism: National, Regional and Global Perspectives,* ed. Yonah Alexander (New York: Praeger, 1976); and John McLane "The Mofussilization of Bengali Politics," in *Urban Bengal,* ed. Richard Park (East Lansing: Asian Studies Center, Michigan State University, 1969). For a general overview of the nationalist movement in the city of Calcutta see Ted Robert Gurr, Peter Grabosky, and Richard Hula, *The Politics of Crime and Conflict: A Comparative History of Four Cities* (Beverly Hills, Calif.: Sage, 1978).

20. Cited by Percival Griffiths, *To Guard My People: The History of the Indian Police* (London: Earnst Benn Limited, 1971), p. 231. The quote is taken from *Jugantar,* a radical Bengali newspaper.

21. McLane, "The Mofussilization of Bengali Politics."

22. The *Sedition Committee Report, 1918,* gives a narrative of the major terrorist events in Bengal in the years 1906-1916. Further information can be obtained from the relevant *Annual Report on Police Administration in the City of Calcutta and Its Suburbs* and *Annual Report on Police Administration in the Lower Provinces.*

23. See John McLane, "The 1905 Partition and New Communalism," in *Bengal: East and West*, ed. Alexander Lipski (East Lansing: Asian Studies Center, Michigan State University, 1970).

24. Ibid.

25. Broomfield, *Elite Conflict in a Rural Society*, p. 34.

26. *Sedition Committee Report, 1918*, p. 36.

27. With the nullification of the partition in 1912, Surendranath Banerjea and other leading Bengali moderates showed a new willingness to work within British institutions. It was with this group that Carmichael placed his hope for future peace in Bengal. See Broomfield, *Elite Conflict in a Rural Society*, pp. 43-81.

28. Ibid., p. 222.

29. Cited in Griffiths, *To Guard My People*, p. 259.

30. Ibid., p. 261.

31. Broomfield, *Elite Conflict in Rural Society*, p. 277. See also Moorhouse, *Calcutta*, p. 203.

32. One lasting impact of the mass jailings of the 1930s was the large-scale conversion of suspected terrorists to Marxism. This has been discussed at some length by Marcus Franda in *Radical Politics in West Bengal*, pp. 1-41.

33. Bengal had but recently (1943) passed through what was probably the worst famine in its history. Another source of concern was the large number of firearms available in the city. British authorities were particularly concerned that many of the firearms were obtained as a result of lax procedures used by the American military to dispose of surplus firearms.

34. For a discussion of the great Calcutta "killing," see Griffiths, *To Guard My People*, and Francis Tuker, *While Memory Serves* (London: Cassell, 1950).

35. For a brief discussion of the economic impact of partition on Bengal see Marcus Franda, "West Bengal," in *State Politics in India*, ed. Myron Weiner (Princeton, N.J.: Princeton University Press, 1968). For a more general comment on the economy of the area see Richard Meier, *Observations upon the Developmental Character of Great Cities* (Berkeley: Institute of Urban Planning, University of California, 1969).

36. Franda, *Radical Politics in West Bengal*, p. 48.

37. For a more detailed account of these disorders see Gurr et al., *The Politics of Crime and Conflict*.

38. David H. Bayley, "Violent Protests in India: 1900-1960," *The Indian Journal of Political Science* (July-December 1963).

39. Alan Watts "Violent Protest in India Since 1960," *Indian Journal of Political Science*.

40. Moorhouse, *Calcutta*, p. 323.

41.   See Gough, "Indian Peasant Uprisings," p. 1405.

42.   Changing Naxalite strategies have been discussed by Mohan Ram, "Shift in Naxalite Tactics," *Economic and Political Weekly,* August 21, 1971.

43.   The main exponent of the "annihilation" strategy was the party's chairman, Charu Mazumdar. With his death in 1972 the strategy was rejected by most of the remnants of the party leadership.

44.   A curvilinear relationship between regime coercion and political violence has been noted in Ted Robert Gurr, *Why Men Rebel* (Princeton, N.J.: Princeton University Press, 1970). Gurr cites empirical support for such a relationship.

45.   The general ineffectiveness of government in Bengal was noted with some outrage by Moorhouse in *Calcutta.* For a more systematic discussion on the role of government in Bengal, particularly for Calcutta, see the series of reports written by Richard Meier, including *Observations upon the Developmental Character of Great Cities* (Berkeley: Institute of Urban Planning, University of California, 1969) and *Developmental Features of Great Cities of Asia II: Japanese, Chinese and Indian* (Berkeley: Institute of Urban Planning, University of California, 1970).

46.   For more detail see Gurr et al., *The Politics of Crime and Conflict.*

47.   See Moorhouse, *Calcutta,* and the *Calcutta Police Report, 1953.*

48.   An overview of violent labor disputes is given in Gurr et al., *The Politics of Crime and Conflict.*

49.   Myron Weiner, "Violence and Politics in Calcutta," *Journal of Asian Studies* 20 (May 1961): 275-281.

11

Terror in the United States:
Three Perspectives

Frederic D. Homer

Department of Political Science
University of Wyoming
Laramie, Wyoming

Introduction

Happily, there are many excellent summaries and analyses of violence and terror in the United States.[1] Those who now explore the subject are at liberty to interpret terror in the American experience without necessarily analyzing every historical and contemporary event that falls under the rubric of terror. This chapter will be limited to the presentation of three perspectives that will help organize the reader's present knowledge of terror as well as integrate future events into his or her own experience. The perspectives will highlight several viewpoints concerning the role of terror in America, each embodying propositions about the relationship of terror to social change and exploring ideas about the appropriateness of terror to bring about change. Each embodies its own definition of terror.

In an attempt to understand the role of terror in the United States, the propriety of terror as a strategy or tactic of either the government or its opposition will be questioned. Does the justification of terror depend upon the form of government? Is it to be condoned in a democratic society, in a society that espouses only democratic goals, or in any human situation? How does the justification of terror depend upon the type of terrorist act performed? It is also important for an understanding of both the present and the future to determine the empirical consequences of terrorist activity. Does terror accomplish reform or revolutionary goals? How successful is it as a tool of government to quell reform, revolution, or other "undesirable" activities? In short, concern here will be with both normative and empirical consequences of political terror in the United States.

Terror in a Democratic Society

Many individuals believe that the United States is an open, democratic society where grievances can be heard and where alternatives are presented (both candidates and policies) and, after open deliberation, decided upon by the people. Few believe democracy in this country functions ideally, but proponents of this perspective feel that despite delay, obstruction, and even corruption, groups and individuals can peaceably air their views and, if acceptable to the majority, get these views forged into law.[2] Therefore, with an operable democratic society that allows for peaceful change, one cannot tolerate terrorism. Irving Howe states this position succinctly: "In a society where reasonable (which is necessarily to say, an imperfect) measure of freedom to speak and organize is available, we must regard it as utterly impermissible to resort to terrorist methods or to give the faintest encouragement to them" (1976, p. 60). Terrorism is intolerable when other modes of expression are available. "And it [terrorism] is wrong because minorities in a democratic society, as long as their freedom to dissent is largely protected, do not have the right to impose their will upon the majority through violence" (1976, p. 60). Howe also reasons that terror is intolerable for pragmatic reasons as well as on moral grounds. "In countries with highly developed and articulate class structures, terrorism has never succeeded, nor is it likely to succeed, in effecting any basic change of power—though it may through an art of sudden blackmail achieve a limited end such as forcing the release of prisoners, etc." (1976, p. 60).

The democratic perspective has often been used to suggest the limits to which a group can go in articulating its grievances even when terrorism is not in the forefront as a tactic. As an example, in the 1960s, many were concerned with the establishment of acceptable limits of nonviolent protest in a democratic society. People argued as to whether nonviolent protest should be carried so far as to provoke a violent response from the opposing side.[3] The democratic perspective can also focus on acts of terror by government officials that might threaten the existence of democratic institutions. Joseph Schumpeter raised this problem when he asked whether in a democracy the people have the right to dissolve a democratic system, or if the government may, by undemocratic means, restore a democratic system (1950, pp. 242-243). For instance, James Burnham believes that a democracy is worth saving even at the cost of counterterror and other activities that may temporarily abridge freedom: "... if terrorism is both serious and long-continued—[it] apparently also requires a certain amount of counterterror. A contemporary anti-terror strategy that did not include many sorts of undercover surveillance, infiltration, enemy and potential enemy lists, secret search and seizure, etc., would be ludicrous" (1974, p. 365).

The perspective of terror in a democratic society is useful for its attempts to establish permissible limits of terror in a system for government and its opposition.[4] Adherents of this perspective, including those like Burnham who advocate strong measures in response to terrorists, seem to agree that terror should be limited as much as possible. Thus, terror as defined by this perspective is a pejorative term: It is something to be avoided in a democratic system if at all possible. To define terror further, we shall examine a typology of acts that Feliks Gross (1970) calls terrorist and shall elaborate upon it. His categories will be analyzed to see if, according to democratic theorists, some acts are more repugnant than others and thus less tolerable in a democratic system. The acts Gross is concerned with involve death to victims, normally thought of as less desirable than threats of violence, unsuccessful attempts at terror, and the destruction of property.

Gross suggests the objective of dynastic assassination is the "elimination of a ruler or a family, as well as a change of ruling elites, and usually a change of political orientations" (1970, p. 533). We are all too familiar in this country with assassinations of our presidents. John F. Kennedy was the eighth presidential victim of a violent attack and the fourth to be killed (Kirkham, Levy, and Crotty, p. xv). This country seems to be victimized by lone assassins for the most part, even though some may have been part of complex conspiracies, as recent speculations on the Kennedy assassination seem to indicate. The assassins' objectives have been elimination of a "bad" leader or covert takeover of the country by elites. There has been no overt show of force in this country after an assassination, although in many other countries dynastic assassinations are preludes to power plays by conspiracies.[5]

Individual assassination is the murder or attempted murder of someone "taken to be crucially representative of autocratic power" (Howe, 1976, p. 60). In this country it is difficult to describe just who this nexus of individuals would be. Is a senator part of the ruling elite or the opposition? Are cabinet members, dissident members of the federal bureaucracy, or Supreme Court justices part of the opposition to government? It depends upon one's definition of such concepts as power, power elite, and opposition.[6] We shall define individual assassination as the murder or attempted murder of someone taken to be crucially representative of autocratic power, whether or not the person holds a formal office. Thus, we can include here Martin Luther King, Jr., Robert Kennedy, Malcolm X,

George Lincoln Rockwell, Joseph A. Yablonski, George Wallace, and James R. Hoffa, all apparent victims of foul play. Prominent individual assassination victims in the past include, for example, Senator Huey Long of Louisiana and Henry C. Frick, head of Carnegie Steel, who was shot by Alexander Berkman in 1892 (see Berkman, 1970). These terrorist acts represented the elimination or attempted elimination of individuals who were of major political influence in this country.[7]

There needs to be a classification of terrorist acts for those acts whose targets are groups, not individuals. Focused random terror is, for example, planting explosives to kill a number of people who are part of the opposition. The example Gross gives is the placing of explosives in cafes where German officers met during World War II (1970, p. 533). Recently in New York City an individual or individuals placed a bomb in historic Fraunces Tavern, killing several people. The victims were most likely to be representatives of wealthy interests in the city.

The placing of a bomb, in 1975, at La Guardia Airport to kill innocent victims is an example of random terror. The threats made by groups in the 1960s to poison or drug the water supply of our cities, if carried out, would have been examples of random terror. Thus, random terror simply involves doing bodily harm to individuals indiscriminately.

Gross's typology may be utilized to establish which acts of terror are least justifiable. Irving Howe indicates that "the closer to random terror we get, the more reprehensible such actions become" (1976, p. 15). The basis for this observation appears to be that acts increase in reprehensibility if the victims have little or no association with, or responsibility for, the conflict that generated the act of terror. Interestingly enough, although in the nineteenth and early twentieth centuries the concept of terror was most closely associated with individual or dynastic assassination, currently it has become almost synonymous with focused random or random terror. For the terrorist, however, no act of terror is defined as random, and, hence, to him or her no terrorist act is fully reprehensible. Just to live in the United States may make one culpable for the crimes of the regime. If everyone, as terrorists imply, is collectively guilty for excesses of the regime, then no terror is random.

The most obvious objections to individual or dynastic assassination is that such acts breach the law of the land. Also, in the case of dynastic assassination, the democratic adherent sees the public's electoral preferences negated by the hands of an assassin. In general, those who adhere to the democratic perspective deny all acts of terror, finding random terror, and perhaps acts of dynastic assassination, most reprehensible.

Terror in a Violent Society

Individuals who believe that the United States is a violent society must reject the democratic perspective on terror. They believe that threats of, as well as actual incidents of, violence and terror, along with the democratic myth, are used to maintain social peace. In such instances, Frantz Fanon argues, violence may be useful for individual as well as societal liberation (1967, p. 103). Some go even further and suggest that the act of killing itself may be enjoyable. One of the most chilling expressions of the intrinsic joys of killing was given by Susan Adkins, a member of the Manson family, when she described how she tasted blood after participating in the murder of Sharon Tate, a movie starlet. "Wow, what a trip!" she told Virginia [her cellmate]. "I thought 'to taste death, and yet give life.' " Had she ever tasted blood? she asked Virginia. "It's warm and sticky and nice" (Bugliosi, 1974, p. 114).

More often, the terrorist will emphasize that it is necessary to use violence to accomplish collective goals. Rather than the ideal of a peaceful society being a poor one, the problem is that leaders utilize the myth to keep potential opposition humble while exploiting violence to their own ends. Walter Laqueur suggests that the terrorist tries to test the "democratic regime." "He [the terrorist] looks for shortcuts, for ways to compel democratic regimes to adopt dictatorial measures and thus reveal their true face!" (1976, p. 29). The Weather Underground, a radical group in the United States in the 1970s, published a statement called "Prairie Fire" expressing these views: "Our intention is to disrupt the empire . . . to incapacitate it, to put pressure on the cracks, to make it hard to carry out its bloody functioning against the people of the world, to join the world struggle, to attack from the inside" (1976, p. 30). The ideal of a peaceful society is merely a tactic of governments to keep people oppressed. "Some on the left dissociate mass struggle from revolutionary violence and condemn any act of public militancy or armed struggle as adventurist. This is the characteristic of oppressor-nation movements where violence is raised to a question of abstract principle and the illusion is fostered that imperialism will decay peacefully" ("Prairie Fire," 1976, p. 31).

Thus, those who believe that violence and terror are endemic to American society usually believe that the ideal of a peaceful society is self-serving and that the only way to change certain concrete conditions is through acts of violence and terror. The justifications for the use of violence or terror may be the liberation from a repressive regime, the individual liberating potential, or intrinsic satisfaction in the commission of violent acts. Of course, one does not necessarily have to go to great lengths to justify violence if one believes one lives in a violent society. Harrison Salisbury suggests that "violence may not be, in the wry expression of Rap Brown, 'as American as cherry pie,' but it has been synonymous with the American experience from the earliest days" (Kirkham, Levy, and Crotty, 1970, p. xix). Salisbury does not use this empirical assessment to justify more violence in the society. Others who *do* hold to the view that America is permeated by violence do not buy the argument that time, legal procedure, and persuasion will bring needed change. Past and present experience shows them the utility of violence in changing social conditions, and they need no more justification for their violent acts than that provided by the government.

To those who hold to this perspective, terror is a strategy or tactic for achieving one's ends, and the normative question of whether terror is good or bad is ignored, transformed as above, or devalued. The normative question is important only insofar as it has tactical or strategic value. Paul Wilkinson suggests that "in attempting to determine whether a specific action (or series of actions) is terroristic or not, the scholar should be aware that he is making a value judgment about the perpetrators of that alleged act . . ." (1973, p. 292). For instance, it is useful for a group using terror tactics to label themselves as liberators and the other side as terrorists. In December 1969, a Chicago newspaper headline read "Panther Chief, Aid, Killed in Gun Battle with Police," and the author of the article went on to interview some of the police who participated in the fray (Arlen, 1974, p. 20). The question was subsequently raised as to whether this was the murder of Fred Hampton and Mark Clark by Chicago policemen, an act of police terror, or the killing by police of Black Panther terrorists. The question of who terrorized whom was subsequently fought in the courts. Edward Hanrahan, United States Attorney of Cook County, and policemen involved in the raid were tried on charges of conspiracy to obstruct justice, but were acquitted by the judge presiding in the case. Nevertheless, the debate as to who terrorized whom did not abate with the judge's decision (Arlen, 1974, p. 20).

The two perspectives, terror in a democratic society and terror in a violent society, are utilized to an unequal extent by participants in social conflict. Those committed to terror, participants on all sides of violent conflict, rarely utilize sophisticated justifications of their actions. Usually those committed to the perspective of terror in a democratic society are committed to dialogue. Except for rare instances, such as in the statement "Prairie Fire," terrorist's normative statements are brief and justify terror as a response to an enemy that has used the same terror tactics, only with a greater number of troops on their side. The only justification needed is to describe oneself as an underdog.

Theories of Change

Both perspectives as stated depict static pictures of society, one of peaceful conflict in a democratic society and the other of violence in a society where democracy is the prevailing myth. Each perspective embodies an empirical theory of change. Those who hold that the United States is a violent society argue that terror and opposition on the part of government leads to counterterror. Eventually, the ascendancy of their group to power will bring the restoration of a higher, peaceful, moral order. *Terror therefore begets terror* until the triumph of a liberation movement. Those who adhere to the image of the United States as a peaceful society hope for the restoration of peaceful civil society as well, but not through the success of dissident groups. They view terrorist activities on the part of dissident groups as the *last gasp* of revolutionary activities. Democracy is restored when revolutionary activity fails.

Terror Begets Terror

The terrorists' strategy is to combat government oppression and terror with terrorist activities of their own. The hope is not to win an all-out war but simply to gain the support of the people for their activities. Groups, by keeping their activities clandestine, can keep from being annihilated and can gain support from the population by their actions. These supporters may contribute in peaceful ways to the cause or contribute to armed insurrection. In "Prairie Fire," the Weather Underground proclaims: "From the very beginning of guerrilla action, mass armed capability develops. Its spontaneity will be slowly transformed into the energy of a popular armed force" (1976, p. 33).

The desired dynamic is that as violence continues to escalate, there is a marked tendency for one side to imitate another's tactics. For instance, Phillip Agee in *CIA Diary* demonstrates how the CIA responds in kind to enemy maneuvers. When the Soviets develop international labor and student organizations, the CIA tries to disrupt them and develop organizations of their own (Agee, 1975, pp. 68-69). If the police begin to carry weapons with laser sights, there is a good chance that these weapons will soon be in the hands of their adversaries. When a group of blacks were indiscriminately killing whites in San Francisco (the Zebra killings), the police stopped all young blacks having even the slightest resemblance to the killers. This persisted until the police were stopped by court order. Thus, there is a tendency for one side to adopt the other's tactics.

The theory that terror begets terror contains several other interesting hypotheses. First, that those who adhere to the democratic perspective will abandon this perspective completely in responding to terror. When they do, the frailties of their ideology will be exposed. Second, the terrorists' own annihilation will not come before additional moral and armed support is forthcoming. Third, their terrorist acts will be perceived by the general public as acts of liberation, and, fourth, once the revolution comes terrorists will be able to restore a just regime (Bienan, 1968, pp. 92-98). Supporting all of these notions is the perspective that the

United States is a violent society, that the population will not condemn terrorist actions, and that the government will not fail to respond violently.

It is the contention here that the terror-begets-terror theory does not always hold. The government does not always respond to terror in kind. It has responded everywhere on the spectrum of action from indifference to counterterror. Also, the annihilation of dissident groups before they gain additional support is a distinct possibility, for the popular support they perceive may not be forthcoming. If the citizens cannot be convinced of the validity of the "terror in a violent society" perspective, revolutionaries might have to fight out the war to the bitter end by themselves. The terror-begets-terror position seems to be the hope and the program of would-be liberators. Empirically, these movements have not been very successful in overthrowing the American system, although they may have achieved limited objectives. Even if revolutionary hopes were fulfilled, the promise of restoration of freedom could not be quickly obtained by the liberators because they have learned, and been reinforced by, the use of violent tactics. Moreover, they would continue to force these same tactics on their opponents if the terror-begets-terror hypothesis is correct.

Some liberals, as well as terrorists, often can foresee no end to the cycle of violence in society. Hence, they become unwitting supporters of would-be liberators. They become fatalists who see conflict as the inevitable consequence of the inequities of society. Until these inequities are corrected, the haves will remain at war with the have-nots. The only remedy is the development of a new economic superstructure and the providing of political opportunity for the unfortunate. Although democratic ideology may have successfully masked the inequities in the past, only material distribution of goods to the dissidents can now restore order (National Commission, 1969, pp. 1-29).

The evidence seems to be in disagreement with both terrorists and others who see violence abating only when the material inequities of society disappear. The United States has suffered periodic violent disruptions, but violence does seem to abate, and before the coming to power of a new regime. Michael Stohl (1976) suggests, for example, that changes in levels of violence may be related to disruptions caused by wars and coercion by dominant segments in the postwar periods. Ted Gurr ties changes in levels of violence to expectations, not the actual level of material goods in a society (1971, pp. 304-305). Also, the government, as was suggested, may respond peaceably; furthermore, the public, even if it comes to view history from the perspective of violence, may not select the liberators as their champions. Terror may beget terror, but it is not yet an endless escalating battle in the American system.

Terror: The Last Gasp of Revolutionary Activity

From the democratic perspective, society is perceived to be generally peaceful, and terrorist activity is often thought of as the last desperate hope of revolutionary groups. However, H. L. Neiburg in *Political Violence* suggests that analysts too often have studied violence as an aberration in society: "It is not only the last resort in the bargaining spectrum, but also a potentiality or a threat which does in fact change the bargaining equation itself" (1969, p. 9). We shall see if terror is the last desperate hope of revolutionaries or merely a transient stage in the life of a revolution.

As proof of the "last-gasp" hypothesis, one can point, by example, to the activities of the Weather Underground, a small component of the once militant, but nonviolent, SDS (Students for Democratic Society). The Panthers seem to be the last militant gasp of the nonviolent black movements; and the Symbionese Liberation Army is a frantic residue of the New Left of the 1960s. None of these movements appear as viable as they did in their nonviolent days.

Empirically it is virtually always true that the individuals in their first contacts with the political system confront it with peaceful means. The child in the patriotic grammar school play precedes the bomb-throwing revolutionary. Groups frustrated in peacefully trying to accomplish their goals may progressively move toward violent activity. Robert Penn Warren in *Night Rider* describes this process as it takes place in an individual who joins a group that inexorably moves toward violent activity. The protagonist finally is led to commit a murder, certainly not his intention when he joined the night riders in previous less violent protest (Warren, 1948 edition). The suicidal acts of some groups, such as the SLA fighting it out with the police to the bitter end, do nothing to discourage the last-gasp theory.

However useful this theory is to describe the individual history of groups, it has certain drawbacks. Because we have had nothing in this country that can be called a successful or full-scale revolution except for the Civil War, we might say, on the basis of past experience, that violence is the death knell of insurrection or a terrorist group's life. In terms of rather significant societal change, however, violence may be intermediary in a protracted struggle. A strike at U.S. Steel in 1919 apparently ended labor unrest. As we know, the changes proposed by the strikers were gained over time.[8] Some groups turn violence on and off depending upon the climate of opinion and are careful not to annihilate themselves. For instance, organized crime goes through periods of terror and peace as have the Klans and labor groups in pursuing their ends. The Panthers changed their tactics when confrontations with police became more costly. In Nieburg's terms, violence and terror need not be bargaining tools of desperation only. Finally, there are people who may never go through a cycle of peaceful to violent in making their claims upon society. Some terrorists are becoming professionalized and can be hired immediately by various groups to commit violent acts. Organized criminals have often contracted with outside "experts" in extortion, arson, and murder to have these experts do their "dirty work."

The hypothesis that terror is the last gasp of protest groups in a democratic society may be descriptive of particular periods in our history, and it describes trends in certain groups, but it not a complete explanation of change in social movements. It may be an excellent description of a particular group's development, but it tells little as to why a group's cause may be taken up either peacefully or violently even after the original group's demise. Nor is it necessarily true that a group turns to terror out of desperation. Terror at a particular historical juncture may be a good working strategy; in Neiburg's terms, "it becomes a part of the bargaining relationship . . ." (1969, p. 77).

Summary of Two Perspectives

The prior perspectives help to clarify the meaning of the concept of terror. The concept appears to have no common usage; each side uses the concept to accuse the other of unacceptable activities. Adherents to the democratic perspective refer to terror today as what we defined as random terror. From the terrorists' point of view, the deaths of business executives in the Fraunces Tavern bombing do not materially change the position of industry in this country but are symbolic of an attack on the industrial system. To democratic adherents they were senseless murders. In the early 1900s, the word "terror" was attached to acts that might materially alter the political system, such as dynastic assassinations or individual assassinations, destroying those who are responsible for social conditions. Many of today's terrorists see the problems as structural and denigrate the idea of an individual villain or hero in history, except when he or she shows up on their side. Therefore, to them individual assassination is not an effective tool to render broad social change.

The prior perspectives also demonstrate the normative justifications of conflict and peace in American society. They are rationalizations on the lips of participants, as well as arguments used to win the American public to their particular side. They constructed from the contemporary ideas of violence and terror the fullest implications of these positions. Now one may be better able to judge the fitness of one's action.

The theories of change introduced some interesting empirical ideas. Why does conflict ebb and flow? Social deterministic models do not fully explain fluctuations in terrorist activities, nor does the notion that terror begets terror. They do force us to look for other reasons, some of which will be speculated upon in ensuing discussion.

The problems with the two perspectives and the attendant theories of change are twofold. First, they assume a unitary structure of society and the opposition, consisting only of those in power and those in opposition. However, in reality there are many levels of government and many types of terrorist groups, each with its own goals. Little attention is paid to these differences, and hence the democratic and violent perspectives may describe the role of terror in a unitary European country but not in the complex, variegated American society. The pluralist perspective will show that although both governmental and nongovernmental terrorists might want to grasp a Manichaean perspective of terror, the actual situations are far more complex.

Second, the outcome of conflict situations may depend on more variables than either prior conflict theory takes into account. A terrorist response by one side or another might lead to a variety of outcomes, such as escalation, annihilation, or stalemate. The winning of the American public to one side or another is also another complex matter, and the prior perspectives make the assumption that terror is sufficient to polarize an indifferent society.

Terror in a Pluralist Society

The pluralist perspective suggests that we look at the social system as a congeries of groups acting and reacting with one another, sometimes in conflict and at other times coalescing. Unlike the democratic perspective, it does not assume that government is unitary in any way. We have, as Robert Dahl suggests, some 90,000 governmental units in this country. That counts the national government as only one unit, but in this study, as in his text, we shall not assume that the national government is a single entity (Dahl, 1967, pp. 171-172). Multiplicity of governmental units and autonomous agencies means that terrorist acts may be made at many levels of government. Thus an attack on one unit may not be construed necessarily as an attack on the whole system of government. Also, people may support the government as a whole while decrying the activities of one of its agencies, such as the CIA, State Department, or FBI.

In the United States in 1975, 2305 actual bombings occurred, killing 22 and injuring 187 persons. The targets, as well as the perpetrators, represent diversity. "A bomber would be someone mad at the system, an ex-employee taking revenge on a company, or even a dissatisfied customer bombing a department store" (Coleman, 1976, p. 65). The tactics used by terrorists, such as kidnappings, hijackings, and extortion attempts, vary as well. These data suggest that terror in the United States does not always translate into a war between those in and those out of power. The government, as we shall see, may be neutral or indifferent in certain struggles.

Terror, for purposes of this perspective, may be political not only because either the target or perpetrator of terror may be government but also because other acts of terrorism, which we shall call "indirect political terror," though not aimed at, or perpetrated by, government, are supposed to be acted upon by government because of statutory or common-law authority. For example, a southern sheriff takes a position of neutrality or bias toward the KKK when the Klan intimidates blacks through the use of terror tactics. The Klan may act directly to keep blacks from the polls, but it is also an indirect political act of terror, for the sheriff is supposed to act, but does not, to protect the public from illegal activities. In a real sense, most acts of terror are at least "indirect political terror," for most often they provoke some type of response by law enforcement authorities against perpetrators or involve a direct decision to stay out of the action. What we tend to become most concerned with, of course, is the terrorist attack that seems a direct threat to the existence of our political system. Yet, the response of our various governmental units to indirect as well as direct political terror is critical in determining the quality of government we shall have.

Terror in this perspective has yet to be fully defined. E. V. Walter in *Terror and Resistance* suggests that "conventionally, the word 'terrorism' means a type of violent action, such as murder, designed to make people afraid" (1969, p. 5). It could mean either the psychic state or the object that makes people afraid. He goes on to speak of the process of terror, "by which I mean a compound with three elements; the act or threat of violence, the emotional reaction, and the social effects" (Walter, 1969, p. 5). His definition assumes that terror is a form of interaction between various groups, and the act or threatened act serves as a form of communication. We shall be interested in the act itself, and the responses to the act, as well as the effects of the act as communication.

It is recognized that the definition does little to distinguish between terror and violence, for every act of violence is accompanied by communication to others. Perhaps the difference is that terror may be a threat as well as an act; in addition, its primary intent is to communicate fear or encourage "respect." Hence, the murder of a loan shark's victim may be an act of violence or terror, depending on whether it was committed as an act of vengeance by the organized criminal or to communicate to others that the loan shark is not to be trifled with. In Ted Gurr's terms, terror will be considered as more expressive than instrumental when compared with violence (Gurr, 1971, pp. 304-305).

From the pluralist perspective we are interested in promulgating as well as studying certain values. First, various government units are concerned with how widely polarization takes place among groups in the system and, hence, how many people are drawn into a conflict. This may vary from a bomb threat in the local junior high school, which is handled by the municipal police, to a civil war or full-fledged revolution. Governmental agencies usually try to contain or diminish the influence of opposition groups, while the opposition tries to broaden the scope of conflict (Schattschneider, 1960, pp. 17-18).

Second, it is useful to understand what the dissident groups want to accomplish and are accomplishing. Are they trying to overthrow the government, gain publicity, change a specific policy, or commit suicide? Is the government involved in vengeful acts, trying to maintain social peace, finding an outlet for professionals, or creating a mythical war?

Terrorist Groups: Categories

Terror is often identified with groups or individuals who are called terrorists. This simply means they have been identified with a response they have made to a particular situation or situations. Most groups and individuals can be separated into three categories: ideational, professional, and cathartic.

The ideational category includes the groups of individuals who believe in a cause and utilize terror to reach their ends. Terror may be utilized in desperation, as merely one tool of the bargaining process, but its primary purpose is to promote collective revolutionary or counterrevolutionary goals.

The professional category includes the groups or individuals who specialize in terrorist acts, usually for hire. In organized crime, you have the hit man, the extortionist, or the arsonist. Often these people are not full-time professionals but work at other tasks. For instance, the group called Murder Incorporated in the 1930s, even though it had a proclivity to violence, was also engaged in gambling, loan-sharking, and other lucrative criminal activities (Turkus and Feder, 1953, pp. 9, 79). The key to being a professional is the importance of the skill as opposed to the cause.

One of the great fears of governments in recent years concerns the professionalization of terror in the world (Steiner, 1976, p. 31). Various groups, regardless of ideology, have begun to share techniques, and even personnel, in the commission of terrorist acts. Ultimately, the fear in the United States is that terrorist skills may not remain a fad of ideational groups but a marketable skill available for various illegal activities and movements. Revolutionary groups may turn to professional terrorists more frequently, for they no longer take the direct risks the perpetrators did in the past.

Professionalization of terror is not new to this country. A look back to those hired by unions and labor alike in early industrial wars reveals the professionalization of violence and terror. Moreover, the army may be the oldest occupation that involves professionalized violence and terror. Many fear that we shall not be able to restrict professionals to the army, to other governmental units, and to groups like organized crime and the KKK, which do not overtly threaten the government.

However, the existence of these skills within the above groups is a more subtle threat to the fiber of a democratic system. Government groups such as the CIA and FBI have become expert professionals in use of methods of terror. Phillip Agee in *CIA Diary* speaks of techniques CIA operatives learn to harass the enemy: "Horrible smelling liquids can be hauled into meeting halls. A fine clear powder can be sprinkled in a meeting-place, becoming invisible after settling, but having the effect of tear-gas when stirred up by the later movement of people. . . . Chemically processed tobacco can be added to cigarettes and cigars to produce respiratory ailments" (Agee, 1975, pp. 68-69). The litany of harassment techniques goes on and on. These professional techniques were originally taught to those who were trained to think in terms of a Manichaean world, communist or capitalist. However, many of these tactics have been used on citizens of this country, the most blatant and publicized example being the burglary of the Watergate complex. Those with the professional skills may hire themselves out, or the agency that trains them may search for a cause. As Abraham Kaplan has suggested, "Give a small boy a hammer and he will find that everything he encounters needs pounding" (Kaplan, 1964, p. 28).

The cathartic category includes groups or individuals who appear to commit violence for the sake of violence. It is done because it makes the perpetrator(s) feel good, is liberating, or is an example of individual freedom. Most frightening is that all citizens may become victims of such terror, because it is often expressed in random form. The motives behind such terrorist acts may be complex, but the public fears its random, apparently uncontrolled use. The mass murderer, the Manson family, or the Zebra killers may fit this category. Killing may have been done for profit, honor, or out of fear, but it appears to be enjoyed and even celebrated by the perpetrators.

Terrorist Groups: Typology

The pluralist perspective recognizes that besides a variety of motivations that characterize terror groups, these groups may also be distinguished as to social origins, scope of goals, and chances for success. A typology will be constructed of terrorist groups, taking into account these qualities as well as suggesting the motivations that characterize these groups.

National terror groups are one type of terrorist group very much in the public view. These groups endeavor to gain concessions for their native land by committing terrorist acts in the United States and on U.S. personnel and possessions abroad. Puerto Rican nationalist groups attempt to disrupt government operations and cause fear in this country, all to support a separation movement for Puerto Rico. A Puerto Rican separatist group attempted to kill President Harry Truman in the 1940s. The president of Panama, General Omar Torrijos, announced that his country may indulge in terrorist acts to secure the Panama Canal for Panama. ("Panama's Torrijos," 1976, p. 30). There have been fears that the PLO and other Middle East terrorist groups might carry their campaign for U.S. support to the United States. U.S. diplomats overseas have fallen victim to nationalist terror groups seeking ransom money for their cause or drawing attention to their plight.

The ideology of nationalist terror groups is most often anticolonial, and the American experience is the paradigm for action. The American Revolution has been used as an example of the successful use of violence and terror. It was utilized against a "foreign intruder," Great Britain, and was ultimately successful in repelling the foreign invader (Brown, 1970, p. 1). The American revolution was an anticolonial movement against a government that had only a modicum of popular support. Chances of victory were greater because England could ultimately withdraw from its possessions. Nationalist terror goals are often anticolonial as in the case of Puerto Rico and Panama and are perhaps more attainable than the more sweeping revolutionary goals of domestic groups.

Nationalist terror groups in this country working against American foreign interests may have degrees of success in bringing the government to the negotiating table, depending on our perception of the U.S. national interest. We may be able to afford to give tangible property or make territorial concessions. Terror in these cases does publicize a conflict between the United States and a foreign power, and even though citizens of this country may not identify with specific acts of terror, they may sympathize with the rebels for demanding what they believe is theirs. These terrorists probably have their best chance of success if they engage in continual acts of destroying only property, not lives, and couple this with diplomatic action. The United States, out of irritation and fear, might be eased into further negotiating the status of the Panama Canal, Puerto Rican statehood or granting concessions to the PLO.

The United States can expect to receive little aid from other nations in curbing terrorism, unless we begin to apply individual diplomatic pressure. William F. Buckley points out that the only real movement in international bodies to do something about terrorism comes when government officials are involved: "Then the happy thought occurred to the General Assembly that, it was perhaps all right to acquiesce in terrorism against ordering species of mankind, but killing diplomats was really quite wrong" (Buckley, 1974, p. 339). "They passed a convention which provided that participating countries are supposed to extradite or punish terrorists who have abused diplomats residing locally" (Buckley, 1974, p. 339). Hence, actions against diplomats usually bring swift retaliation even if the goals of the group are limited.

The acceptability of tactics for dealing with nationalist terror movements may differ from those used to deal with groups that operate purely on the domestic scene. In the past there seemed to be much more tolerance toward "dirty tricks" if performed against foreign nationals operating in other lands than if against U.S. citizens. The American people, acting as private citizens, or their government, may support foreign governments or their opponents, something we will call "foreign intervention." Often the government may be supportive or look the other way if private citizens wish to intervene in foreign conflict. For instance, American citizens, prior to 1948, engaged in a massive operation to supply the Israelis with arms and ammunition to defend against their Arab neighbors. All indications are that the FBI and other domestic agencies were indifferent to these efforts and did little actively to enforce laws being broken by these groups (Slater, 1970, pp. 76-77). Mercenaries, although discouraged by this country, often organize under the nose of government authorities by advertising in newspapers for recruitment purposes. At times, of course, as in the Bay of Pigs fiasco, the government has actively supported the overthrow of foreign governments (Marchetti, 1974, p. 52). Sal Vizzini indicates that he, single-handedly, blew up the chief of a small Southeast Asian kingdom that refused to withdraw from the opium trade. This indicates our willingness to deal on tougher terms with foreigners, as well as illustrating another act of U.S. foreign intervention. These represent clandestine attempts at foreign intervention, and the list grows longer if we include conflict like Vietnam in this category of foreign intervention (Vizzini, 1962, pp. 236-238).

Ethnic groups protesting their plight in this country have generated much terror and violence. This has occurred along with a multiplicity of other tactics, many of them nonviolent. The group ideology may involve a negotiation for a larger share of the social, economic, and political pie, disruption of the system, revolution, or demand for internal sovereignty within the borders of the United States (McCartney, 1973, p. 2). Ethnic violence may be cathartic, an indication of a group's willingness to fight for what it believes, or merely suicidal. Much has been written about recent movements; the unrest among the black community in the 1960s, and the Native Americans and Chicanos in the 1970s.

Terror or violence may lead to some meliorative goals, although it appears that support for a reform revolution by a minority ethnic group succeeds only insofar as majority guilt is a factor in negotiations. If the activities become terrorist and are perceived negatively by the majority community, the results may be less successful. Repression without too much remorse may follow on the heels of the terror of ethnic minorities. A war of attrition does not, as a tactic, make numerical sense as a course a minority group should follow. There is no doubt that struggles utilizing terror and counterterror have gone on frequently in minority-majority confrontations in this country. Blacks and other minorities have tried to indicate, by pointing to instances of government terror, that terror is not their fault but a response to government actions.

"*International* revolutionary movements" have markedly lacked success in this country. Their goals are to overthrow existing governments and establish an international regime; one such revolutionary group is, for example, the Japanese Red Army. The danger these groups pose by their actions is less than the dangers of overreaction to them by the government. The government and private citizens may fear that these groups have the money and support of powers in other countries, and may therefore overestimate their ability to succeed. The monolith of international communism has always raised such a specter from the fear of communists and anarchists in the post-World War I period to the Hoover and McCarthy

fear of communism in the 1950s, to the fear of the Maoists, Castroites, Trotskyites of the 1960s. A government is more likely to be destroyed by overresponse
to groups than by what actions the groups take and the destruction they cause.
These groups utilize terror to augment the guise of power. The danger to a government exists if it is deceived by this appearance.

International movements have often been led by college students in this
country, the progeny of middle-class parents (Dalen, 1975, p. 22). This terror
from middle-class students strikes much fear in this country. Overall, it appears
to reflect a failure of the American dream. Here are Americans who can have all
the education and material goods they want. Given these amenities, the need for
violence, which is viewed as a last gasp in the bargaining process, should be superfluous. These middle-class representatives are dissident; for instance, 60 percent
of the bombings in the United States in 1975 occurred in California, a bastion of
middle-class America (Coleman, 1976, p. 65). Moreover, much of this violence
may be cathartic, not expressing a particular purpose and perhaps reflective of
boredom with contemporary society. These movements when coupled with
foreign ideology raise great fears. Again, hopes of victory for revolutionary goals
lie in overreaction. The following statement by the Weather Underground is
meant to be and is inflammatory: "We are a guerrilla organization. We are communist women and men, underground in the United States for more than four
years. We are deeply affected by the historical events of our time in the struggle
against U.S. imperialism" ("Prairie Fire," 1976, p. 30). Of course the problem
for the would-be revolutionaries is that these very same groups that provoke government terror are widely loathed by the majority of citizens and police alike.
Even though all may agree on some of the ills in the United States, many may
not shed a tear if the spreaders of the bad news are dealt with harshly. Social
class movements, from socialism to the middle-class-oriented movements of the
New Left, have not been as successful in achieving their revolutionary goals here
as elsewhere. More controversial is whether social reforms in this country are
the "direct result" of social class movements.

Intimidating groups, a different form of terror group, and perhaps the most
successful in achieving its goals, are those that attempt to achieve control over
other groups—usually nongovernmental— through violence. The aim here is, not
to wring concessions from government, but the intimidation of other groups. As
an example of these intimidating groups, we can look at the activities of organized criminal groups, the Klans, vigilante movements, and industrialists in the
early labor struggles. These groups try to maintain the neutrality of government
while they pursue their goals or at least hope for only indifferent enforcement
of the law. This form of terror has been persistent and pervasive in our nation
since its inception. In Chicago in the 1920s, gangsters drew extortion money
from a variety of small businessmen, laundry owners, and bar owners, for ex-

ample (Kobler, 1971, p. 51). The famous directive from the film as well as the book, *The Godfather,* "Make him an offer he can't refuse," is not a threat to the system but a way of gaining power over another individual (Puzo, 1969). Tolerance of this type of violence and terror does have indirect consequences for the political system. It generally weakens faith in the ability of government to enforce the law.

Other individuals and groups that have no avowed purpose in dominating or influencing other groups also create terror. These are the murderers, rapists, kidnappers, and armed robbers who commit these crimes for economic gain or nonutilitarian purposes. Concern about these crimes and the safety of the average citizen brings in the political concerns for law enforcement. How do we best deal with these problems? The responses to these crimes may not be within the bounds of legitimate, legal behavior. Innocent citizens have had their homes raided by agents looking for narcotic drugs, and police have mistreated suspects, especially minorities, because of the pressures to do something about crime. Crime and an inappropriate response may indirectly affect strength of a society.

Responses to Terror

The types of individuals and groups that promote terror in our society have been broken down into the following categories: national terror groups, ethnic groups, international movements, social class movements, government agencies, groups that tyrannize private groups, and others who perpetrate violent crimes. Now it is appropriate to concentrate on the responses made by governments to terrorist groups. Their response is integral to the success or failure of the group.

Inaction, or no response at all, may be the most interesting response to terror. It will not necessarily mean the suspension of all apprehension or prevention activities, but merely very little intensification of investigations. This strategy may be utilized if terror in terms of material and human losses is very marginal. People may have their quotient of fear raised, but society suffers comparatively little damage from terrorists. "In 1975, bombings killed 22 persons and injured 87 persons at a cost of $7.25 million to the American public" (Coleman, 1976, p. 65). These damages are not great even when compared with the highway death and damage toll of a sparsely populated state measured only in terms of material cost and loss of life, not public fear. The minimal utilization of resources may give the psychological edge to the governmental unit. They are not responding in kind to terror, and the psychological battle may be won. Inaction in this case simply means not sounding the alarm and publicizing terrorist action, thereby creating a war with terrorists. The goal of terrorists may succeed if people become confused as to who fired the first shot and if the government's response is not measured, but frantic and illegal. This strategy should not be confused with fatalism.

Fatalism usually means a public admission that it is difficult, if not impossible, to stop acts of terror. For instance, reporter Don Tate has said: "The fact is, however, that if the bomber is determined to bomb, is willing to pay the price and has luck, there is no foolproof way to stop him. That's the consensus. 'Impossible' is the word heard most often, even though [FBI Director] Kelley insists 'it has to be possible . . . we have to stop them' " (1976, p. 47). As we shall point out later, there is no need to be this fatalistic about acts of terror, and fatalistic statements create the image the terrorist wants of a helpless giant falling before David's slingshot. The fatalist position has been uttered and reuttered by public officials with respect to assassinations in this country.

Submission takes place when the governmental unit is overwhelmed by terrorist activities, as was the case in wide-open towns of the American West. The best the local government can hope for is private intervention on the side of the law, which usually involves counterterror, or the intercession of a higher unit of government. The coming of statehood, the calling in of the national guard, and the intercession of the Pinkertons in the late 1800s to deal with western and midwestern gangs are all examples of intercession of a higher level of government or arrival of private help.

There is also a problem when a governmental unit is in league with, and co-opted by, outlaw groups. In this case, local units will try to intercede to keep out higher authorities. For instance, the Indiana police can stop people on highways in all parts of the state but have to get permission of local authorities to do something about organized crime in an urban jurisdiction.[9]

Neutrality is used by units of government that may stay relatively "neutral" when terror takes place between warring groups. In the early days of labor-management disputes, governmental units often stayed out of the dispute. Also, enforcement agents may be indifferent to the fate of organized criminals in gang wars. They often sit out the war on the sidelines and take a body count afterward. The side benefit is the annihilation of a significant part of the criminal population. This neutrality may occur because these crimes are hard to solve, but more often because we are indifferent to the criminal's fate. Robert Sherrill in *The Saturday Night Special* indicates that gun control may fail because even though there are many deaths due to handguns, Americans are indifferent or secretly pleased at the victim's demise; especially when they are gangsters or the poor. In street-gang killings, organized-crime slayings, and family wars among the lower class, we have the demise of people the majority of citizens do not care about. In his chapter titled "Department of Good Riddance," Sherrill, describing these categories of demise, feels that few people show real chagrin about such data (Sherrill, 1973, p. 19). The Senate Juvenile Delinquency Subcommittee staff put together a gun-murder profile. Sherrill suggests that "the only surprising thing about such revelations is that our opinion-shapers still pretend to care about

what happens to such people, pretend to argue earnestly that in losing the friends
and family of such men, we are losing something we cannot muddle along with
rather comfortably" (1973, p. 29). He is arguing the empirical position that in
certain events of terror and violence, law enforcement can be indifferent because
the citizenry is also. What does shake the government into action is a touch of
terror that threatens the middle class or that carries with it a hint of foreign influence or intervention.

Inaction, as opposed to fatalism, submission, and neutrality, is successful
at times if one wants to contain conflict. If it means enforcing the law without
resort to extreme actions, it may be an intelligent, morally defensible strategy.
Also, because terror rarely exacts large human and material costs, publicity is the
terrorist's best resource. Indifference on the part of agencies, who handle acts as
routine and not as an emergency, may have its effect on the public. Boredom on
the part of the public may have a great deal of impact on ideational, professional,
or cathartic terrorist groups and lead them to abandon terrorist tactics. The fatalism position is not useful, first, because it promotes the terrorist goals of exposing
impotence and, second, because it is empirically false.

Deterrents, both symbolic and material are important in combating terrorism. President Eisenhower used symbolic deterrence when he issued periodic
press releases describing the effectiveness of the Secret Service. Similarly, television commentators often mentioned the existence of massive security at the
1976 Olympic games in Montreal as the games progressed. Publicity on new preventive measures, security precautions, dogs that can sniff dynamite, new electronic sensors, all are symbolic deterrents. They create the image of invulnerability. Material deterrents are significant weapons in the fight against terrorism.
The assassination of a president may occur, but many attacks can be prevented.
Security checks at doors, presence of Secret Service agents, and bullet-proof lim-
ousines cut down chances of murder while also furnishing symbolic deterrence.
Specific methods to deal with airline hijacking cut down on the number of hijackings when it appeared that nothing could stop them. The use of metal detectors, contingency plans, and open lines of communication made airline hijacking
a high risk for the perpetrator.

Laws are used as a weapon against terror. Existing laws or the drafting of
new ones may be used to catch terrorists even though these laws may infringe on
civil liberties. Alan Dershowitz speaks of Israel's use of an old British law to deal
differentially with individuals who threaten the public safety: "The Israeli law
permits the imprisonment—without limits of time—of 'any person' whose confinement is deemed 'necessary or expedient' for securing the public safety, the
defense of Palestine, the maintenance of public order or the suppression of meeting, rebellion, or riot" (Dershowitz, 1970, p. 67). He goes on to suggest that
Israel does not abuse the law. The strategy demands the suspension of liberties

of a suspected individual. The United States, however, tried this on a mass scale when it moved Japanese Americans to relocation camps during World War II. Senator John McClellan once suggested that merely belonging to an organized criminal group should be made a crime (hearings, Permanent Subcommittee on Investigation, 1963, p. 20). The question for a country is: If you resort to such a law, can you use it on a temporary basis and not indiscriminately? Detaining the whole Japanese population of the United States in internment camps in hopes of containing what might be at the most a few spies is terrible indiscrimination (Haak, 1973, p. 2).

In this country, there has been a lessening of civil liberties for all to catch the few. Many of the laws and court orders approving wiretapping, "no-knock" searches, entrapment, conspiracy, search, and seizure have been designed to catch organized criminals or "national security risks." In speaking of the conspiracy laws that made it illegal to cross state lines and incite riots, Tom Hayden, who was prosecuted under the law, suggests: "The new law was not aimed at preventing violence and disruption per se. It exempted, for example, all union organizing activities that often involve interstate travelers who cause whole industries to be paralyzed" (Hayden, 1970, p. 13). Whenever government begins to declare war on groups, instead of concentrating on activities, the means used to deal with groups may become imitative of those very groups and can erode other civil liberties. One cannot add laws to the books to catch our "worst enemies" and not expect government to utilize them on groups with whom we have sympathies. Experiences in the last years of the Nixon presidency show that one politician's version of who the state's enemies are may not coincide with the views of others. The administration utilized the country's laws and court rulings to deal with their "enemies," the Democrats.

Counterterror may not be ruled out as a tactic for dealing with terrorist activities. Like the suspension of certain liberties, it can be justified only on the basis of saving democracy at a high cost. There is no doubt, one concludes with reluctance, that counterterror may be effective in eliminating threats. Some have described the police dealings with the Black Panthers as a police war. Usually they are highly critical of police and point out that the police seemed to cast restraints to the winds (Lewin, 1970, pp. 14-18). What these same critics fail to point out is that police appear to have succeeded in their aims of erasing the Panthers as a significant militant influence in the black community (Kempton, 1971, pp. 49-52). One finds it difficult, if not impossible, to justify this type of warfare by the government. For instance, Christopher Chandler suggests that "theoretically we believe that any organization (and particularly any political organization) is entitled to win as much popular support as its platform and leadership permit. Surely this is the democratic way. But we make exceptions to that rule, particularly during periodic red scares" (1970, p. 23). Do we know how to keep the police from fighting private wars we do not want fought? Can we allow government lawlessness to deal with dissidents? The answer for most of us is no.

The killings at Jackson State and Kent State seems to have had a sobering effect on protest movements. On the other hand, violence short of death, such as the confrontations during the 1968 Democratic National Convention seemed to escalate conflict, harden participant resolve, and convince many that peaceful solutions to the country's problems were not possible. It seems, then, that death as a part of a strategy of counterterror may be a terror stopper, but other types of combat are not.

Reaction to an action already underway is an additional governmental strategy for dealing with terror. If it is a murder, enforcement is the response needed (capture of the suspects), and some preventive measures must be taken in the future. However, many acts of terror today, as well as the past, involve hostage situations. Terrorists usually demand material concessions, money, safe passage, or freedom for jailed compatriots in exchange for the release of the hostages. There appear to be three governmental responses to this exchange situation; silence, capitulation, and negotiation to buy time.

Silence means to fail to enter negotiation with the antagonists. More than any other strategy, it indicates a governmental unwillingness to reward terrorists for their actions or even acknowledge their existence. The terrorist may still achieve the goal of gaining some modicum of sympathy if the government response is viewed as indifferent to the kidnappers or callous toward the hostages. This strategy, however, does effectively take away many material rewards from kidnappers and is most often the typical response of Israel to PLO terror. "This reporter [Don Tate] once saw Israel's tough defense minister, Moshe Dayan, blanch when a school full of children in Maalot in Northern Israel was seized by Arab gunmen. With a reputation for never giving in to terrorist demands, the Israelis at that point were confused and wavering. Finally, as always, the Israelis charged . . . Dayan didn't give in, even then" (Tate, 1976, p. 47). Silence is likely to be most successful against professional terrorist groups that are likely to repeat their activities and are difficult to catch once given sanctuary.

Capitulation is simply to meet the demands of the terrorist and is most likely to be followed as a strategy when the human costs may be very high, especially when children are involved. If the demands are made of private citizens, capitulation may often be the strategy followed. Randolph Hearst, for example, agreed to give the SLA what they wanted in exchange for the release of his daughter. The pitfalls of capitulation come from the encouragement others may receive to perform the same actions. Also, unless the exchange can be guaranteed by both sides, there is often no guarantee, as in the case of Patty Hearst, that the hostages will be returned.

Negotiation to buy time has as its objective, not the release and sanctuary of kidnappers, but the freedom of the hostages. Perhaps the most dramatic example of this strategy occurred when the Israelis dropped their policy of not negotiating with terrorists by agreeing to negotiate the release of hostages from an airline hijacked and flown to Uganda. The Israelis thus bought time to deploy tactical units that were eventually used to free the hostages. This method is standard operating procedure for the FBI and was exemplified in the film *Dog Day Afternoon*. The bank robbers negotiated for hours until they were given a car to drive to the airport with some hostages. One of the bank robbers was shot and the other was captured by the agents while in the auto. Time is bought for two reasons. One is to be able to separate the hostages from those who took them. This may also be done by escape of the hostages as well as death or capture of the perpetrators. Second, the more time that elapses in negotiations, the greater the chance that the kidnapper's resolve will begin to slip. Especially if they are amateurs, the kidnappers may be talked out of the escapade.

Pluralist Theory of Change

The pluralist perspective has described warring groups in events that involve terror. We have groups that are looking to gain some concession from government, are at full-scale war against some unit of government, or are combating each other. Opposing them often have been government forces at various levels, anything from school authorities to the FBI. The pluralist theory of change will describe how the relationships between opposing forces have altered over the years.

We shall begin with a historical framework, admittedly self-serving, a liberty social scientists often take but do not acknowledge. When the colonies had gained their independence from Britain, the framework of government was a loose coalition of states forged under the Articles of Confederation. There are many explanations as to why the Articles were inadequate: For instance, government under the Articles had no common front in foreign policy and lacked effective sanctions that could be brought against those states that chose not to contribute to public revenues. Also contributing to the insecurities of this fledgling government were internal, domestic conflicts and fears of future conflicts. The need to deal with the Indians on the western frontiers necessitated the development of stronger forces than individual states could muster. Shays' Rebellion in 1786-1787 crystallized the fears that many Americans had of internal insurrection. "A postwar depression, exacerbated by high taxes levied to pay off the Massachusetts Revolutionary War debt as rapidly as possible, hit the states' farmers hard" (Hofstadter and Wallace, 1970, p. 118). The farmers began to organize, and they tried legally to close the courts. Eventually, led by Daniel Shays and Luke Day, the debtors tried to close the courts by force. They were finally defeated, but the memory of the fighting was deep. Secretary of War Henry Knox had to persuade "Congress to authorize the stationing of troops at Springfield arsenal, obstensibly to fight the Indians, actually to suppress the rebellion" (Hofstadter and Wallace, 1970, p. 119). The Continental Congress acted slowly, and over the long haul had much trouble raising funds for the new Republic. One of the consequences of this rebellion was that "the fears aroused by the insurrection lightened the task of those who were trying to form a stronger national government than the Confederation" (Hofstadter and Wallace, 1970, p. 119).

The pattern of violence and counterviolence in this country paralleled these early insurrections. Local governments had to be prepared to deal with internal conflict, often bringing in larger units of government or private forces. One problem was the inability to comprehend the extent of internal conflict expected and worries about the government's ability to manage it. In the early days of the Republic, it was left to the army to put down major insurrections. For instance, in 1791, Congress levied a tax on whiskey that hit frontiersmen hard. "The only way they would make a profit on a grain crop was to distill it into whiskey. The distillers were issued subpoenas and marshalls were prevented from delivering them" (Hofstadter and Wallace, 1970, p. 79). Insurrectionists now began to terrorize excise collectors, rob mails, and suspend trials. When the frontiersmen did not listen to George Washington's call to return to their homes, he called out 12,900 men to put down the insurrection, an army larger than the normal strength of the Continental Army during the Revolution. No fighting ensued, and the insurrectionists returned to their homes (Hofstadter and Wallace, 1970, p. 20).

During the "pacification" of the Indians during the 1800s, the army was often the settlers' only protection. It was the army that was called on during the Civil War to restore order. In post-Civil War years, a private agency, the Pinkertons, was called on by local citizens when their law enforcement officers were forced into submission or co-opted by large outlaw bands. A third method, other than looking to the army or private agencies for help against insurrection, involved direct actions by private citizens against those terrorizing their towns. Richard Maxwell Brown suggests that from 1767 to 1900, "vigilantism was almost a constant factor in American life" (Brown, 1969, p. 144). He defines vigilantism as "organized, extralegal movements which take the law into their own hands" (Brown, 1969, p. 144). "There were 326 known movements and perhaps 500 in total, making vigilantism a significant force for order in our history" (Brown, 1969, p. 144).

Up to 1900, vigilante movements, the army, state militias, and private detective agencies handled most of the domestic terrorists. They usually entered the fray when local units of government were indifferent or overwhelmed or were captive of insurgent or threatening movements. Most significantly, the agencies asked to deal with insurrection had little interest in permanent conflict with the domestic insurgents. A call-up of the militia brought in men anxious to return to their homes. The armies were trained primarily for full-scale warfare and to deal with foreign enemies. Only in the case of the Indian wars was the army's role in "domestic insurrection" institutionalized. Private agencies found putting down insurrection useful and lucrative, and they trained men for these tasks. Their role continued into the twentieth century, and they participated in breaking up labor strikes and demonstrations. However, when a local government or private business concern such as railroads or banks was paying for their services, rarely did they desire to keep a private detective agency on indefinitely. In sum, the early years of our history were marked by transitory groups, both governmental and nongovernmental, whose job it was to put down insurrection and terror.

In the twentieth century, the roles of these forces continue. Vigilante groups are not unknown. For instance, the Jewish Defense League was formed in 1968, and one of its activities was to patrol the streets of Brooklyn to help protect people from street crimes. In these activities, they often tried to work with police (Seedman, 1974, p. 291). The National Guard and Army Reserves were called out and were used frequently in the 1960s to deal with urban unrest. "In April [1968] alone, more National Guard troops were called than in all of 1967 (34,900 to 27,700) and more federal troops as well (23,700 to 4,800)" (Skolnick, 1969, p. 173). When violence abated, the soldiers went back to their homes. However, private agencies have pretty much changed their role. "As public police forces developed, the private security forces shifted their roles increasingly from investigative to guard services" (Kakalik, 1972, p. 18).

The monumental change in our system has been the development of public police agencies to handle violence and terror. At the state level, but more so at the local level, they had a role in dealing with these activities early in our history, but only in the twentieth century did the federal government and many of the states train forces to deal with terrorist activities. It was Alan Pinkerton who warned Lincoln of early assassination attempts on the president's life. Today this is the function of the Secret Service. Today when a group appears to threaten stability and local law enforcement agents ask for help, it is the FBI, IRS, Alcohol and Tax Division of the Treasury Department, federal marshalls, or even the CIA that responds. In other words, we have many agencies who are in the business, at least part time, of quelling domestic conflict. The big change, however, is that these agencies, unlike earlier agencies that responded to terror, are in the prevention business as well. These agencies, or at least for some of their agents, are involved full time in preventing and dealing with internal insurrection. In terms used earlier, they become professionals in combating and using terror tactics.

It is not the existence of a "national police force" that is the problem. We still have multiple police forces on the national level, even though some experts claim that the sharing of data and cooperation between these agencies creates, in effect, a monolithic police force. There is certainly evidence of multiple agencies and ample conflict among them. The problem is not that law enforcement is monolithic but that some agencies are in the counterterror business permanently. The FBI is the prime example of a group that is now permanently involved in the counterterror movement. Its intelligence-gathering activities and infiltration into the Communist party since World War II are well known and have been publicized by the FBI. This has been followed by COINTELPRO, the FBI's counterintelligence program, which has targeted many groups—including the KKK, student groups, and organized crime— for infiltration and even disruption. "It appears that the first FBI disruption program (apart from the CP) was launched in August 1960, against groups advocating independence for Puerto Rico" (Perkus, 1975, p. 12). In October 1961, one such program was launched against the Socialist Worker's party. From 1966 to 1968, the FBI engaged in Operation Hoodwink, designed to ignite a war between organized crime and the Communist party. In the 1960s, much of the FBI's energy was diverted toward student revolutionaries. Much of this information has come to light as a result of suits under the Freedom of Information Act (Perkus, 1975, pp. 9-17).

In sum, there has been a very large-scale change in the way in which terrorist groups have been handled in this country. We have moved from a mixture of vigilante, private agency, and army response to the development of professionalized antiterror forces. The measures in the nineteenth century were temporary, and except for the Indian wars, there were no standing armies. The problems, of course, were that the "troops" used to deal with terror were often ill-trained, as in the case of the vigilantes, and violated the law while responding emotionally to situations; in addition, such "troops" were in few ways subject to strict central controls, either on a tactical or strategic level. Today, the problem is the existence of standing forces to deal with terror. No longer do they merely respond to terror, they also anticipate it. This is the justification for disrupting the activities of groups that have not yet engaged in overt treason.

Permanent antiterror troops may help to create an enemy to fight. If they are an institutionalized force, they need an adversary. It is easy to convince the American public of a conspiracy and then operate against the "conspiracy" in a rough and clandestine fashion. The Panthers, the Ku Klux Klan, and the Weather Underground have been viewed in recent years as conspiracies. In organized crime we have had the Black Hand, Mafia, and Cosa Nostra. One writer even suggests that there is a "national crime syndicate," a society more powerful than the Mafia, that thrives because public attention is riveted on the Mafia while the "national crime syndicate" works silently behind the scenes (Messick, 1971, pp. 7-8). In each case, the groups are viewed as conspiracies, deviants from society, and a threat to American life. Explanations of *their* behavior need not rest on laws that govern *our* behavior. Indeed, they are usually portrayed as organized, efficient, and single-minded. It is true that the conspiracy explanation may tell of the existence of collectivities that do, in fact, operate, but this explanation also fabricates the existence of conspiracies. Even if a conspiracy really exists, adherents to this theory often give an exaggerated view of the group's influence, prowess, and determination to destroy others, which in turn obstructs inquiry into the group's real nature.

As a corollary to conspiracy theories, people are often looking for the behind-the-scenes leader who is making all the decisions. Over the years dozens of candidates have been suggested as "Mr. Big" in organized crime (Homer, 1974, p. 27). It is easier to understand a conspiracy if we can locate the dominant person behind it. Another basis for holding the "conspiracy" view may be the prevalence of ethnic prejudices. It is easy to impute organized crime to one ethnic group. For instance, some infer that organized crime is purely Italian crime; that if Italians were to disappear from the scene, there would be no more organized crime. This is clearly at odds with the realities of organized crime. As sociologist Daniel Bell has suggested, various ethnic groups have participated in organized crime as a means to achieve social and economic advancement (1960, pp. 115-116).

The conspiracy view is useful to public officials because it can mobilize public opinion behind enforcement programs. By pointing to a secret enemy (organized and efficient) government officials can expect to generate more funds than by trying to explain complex interrelationships between groups and individuals in crime. At Attorney General Robert Kennedy's insistence, Joe Valachi appeared before a Senate committee to talk about the inner workings of Cosa Nostra. Kennedy wanted to prod the FBI into investigating organized crime more thoroughly and to get public opinion behind a drive against organized crime (Navasky, 1971, pp. 49-50). Government agencies have also been known to use the notion of a conspiracy to divert public attention away from their failure to prevent crime. Government agencies sometimes pursue certain criminal groups while leaving others alone to carry on their activities unmolested.

Many revolutionary groups seeking to show their own strength, trying to show government's vulnerability or brutality, contribute to the powerful conspiracy myth by inflating estimates of their own strength. Hence, small groups of revolutionaries call themselves the Symbionese Liberation Army, the New World Revolution Front, Continental Revolutionary Army, or the Chicano Liberation Front when they may more resemble an army squad than a large complex organization. The government contributes to this hyperbole. The strength of a group may be inflated if the government gives a conservative estimate of the number of actual members but then claims that many others are influenced by the group to the extent that they are virtual sympathizers or dupes of the group. In speaking about the Black Panther party, a special report to the president in 1970, suggests: "Its [the Panther's] 'hard-core members' were estimated at about 800, but a recent poll indicates that approximately 25 percent of the black population has a great respect for the BPP, including 43 percent of blacks under 21 years of age" (Perkus, 1975, p. 17). Sympathizers may be a long way from being activists. For instance, in a recent showing of *Dog Day Afternoon,* a film about two bank robbers caught inside a bank who were negotiating with the New York City police and later the FBI, the theater patrons, including a policeman, applauded and cheered the bank robbers' actions. This may be a source of discontent to be tapped. But, it is a huge step between giving someone moral support from a theater seat to actually running into the bank and joining them. More important, just because a group gains popular support, yet does nothing illegal, does a governmental unit have the right to use force and intimidation to dissipate support?

The whole issue is complicated, of course, by the fact that there are some conspiracies. Furthermore, it is becoming easier to assemble weapons of destruction. Such sophistication has led to the sending of letter bombs. In the future it could be the poisoning of the water system, nuclear blackmail, or use of chemical or biological warfare. These can always be used to justify a permanent, preventive, antiterror organization.

Armed with these reasons, agencies justify their antiterror tactics. The president will justify their use on the same basis but paradoxically cannot always control these groups (Marchetti, 1975, p. 73). Most important, in making a decision about the merits of such a standing establishment, one must decide where the dangers to this country are to come from: internal revolution or ourselves?

The pluralist perspective views terror as a complex activity involving many groups with diverse purposes, interacting on different levels of government. If one is interested in promulgating or preventing terrorist activity, this approach has much to recommend it, for it allows one to see the interplay between public, government, and interest groups in conflict situations. Out of this struggle, I have chosen to concentrate upon an evolving pattern of interaction between groups and the development of an antiterror establishment. A key feature of this perspective, however, is the ability to see difference, nuance, and change in terrorist activities in this country.[10]

Conclusion

This chapter has elaborated upon three perspectives that help the reader to understand some of the normative and empirical questions about terror in the United States. Each perspective tells us something of what we mean by the concept of terror, whether it is justifiable, and what changes we foresee in terrorist activity in this country in the future. However, there are many other ways of looking at the concept of terror and terrorist activities in the United States. It is hoped that such thoughts will be stimulated by this chapter. Not everyone will agree with basic tenets of the perspectives. There may be literally dozens of different groups that may feel sympathy with the perspective of terror in a violent society, each disagreeing with the nuances of this position. The goal here was not to formulate consensus but to provoke thought and to formulate a starting point for further inquiry into the concept of terror in the United States.

Acknowledgment

The author thanks Kip Homer for his thorough editorial assistance.

Notes

1. Aside from studies cited in following notes, see *National Commission on the Causes and Prevention of Violence: To Establish Justice, To Ensure Domestic Tranquility* (New York: Vintage Books, 1969); Robert H. Connery, ed., *Urban Riots,* (New York: Vintage Books, 1969).

2. For an excellent statement of this position, see Charles S. Hyneman, *Popular Government in America* (New York: Atherton Press, 1968). It is recognized that one cannot encapsulate all the ideas of democratic theory in a sentence or two. Most obviously missing are the institutions and mechanisms in our system that can obviously thwart majorities, and within the rules of the game.

3. The theoretical underpinnings of these debates are found in Joseph Tussman, *Obligation and the Body Politic* (New York: Oxford University Press, 1960); Sidney Hook, *The Paradoxes of Freedom* (Berkeley: University of California Press, 1964), p. 120; and Staughton Lynd, ed., *Non-Violence in America: A Documentary History* (Indianapolis: Bobbs Merrill, 1966).

4. The idea of establishing acceptable limits of terror and violence in society is by no means the special province of democratic theorists. For an interesting discussion of violence and possible limitations see, Albert Camus, *The Rebel* (1956 edition).

5. I am alluding here to inquiries into a possible Cuban connection in the assassination of John F. Kennedy. Even if there is such a connection, it remains true that there has been no overt show of force by the opposition after an assassination or attempt.

6. See for example, C. Wright Mills, *The Power Elite* (New York: Oxford University Press, 1959), or Herbert Marcuse, *One-Dimensional Man: Studies in the Ideology of Advanced Industrial Society* (Boston: Beacon Press, 1964), for debates as to the composition of influentials in this country.

7. Of course, there will be variations as to who is included on the list of influentials. It depends upon the definition of "influential."

8. For an excellent summary of labor violence, see Philip Taft and Philip Ross, "American Labor Violence: Its Causes, Character, and Outcome," in *Violence in America,* ed. Hugh Davis Graham and Ted Robert Gurr (New York: Signet Books, 1969), pp. 270–376.

9. Conversations with individual members of the Indiana State Police in 1971–1972.

10. In this chapter, the literature on pluralism has only been alluded to; I have concentrated on substantive problems of terror. For a much more extended discussion, see Frederic D. Homer, *Analytic Dimensions of Pluralism* (Ph.D. diss., Indiana University, 1970).

References

Agee, Philip. 1975. *Inside the Company: CIA Diary.* New York: Bantam Books.

Arlen, Michael J. 1974. *An American Verdict.* Garden City, N.Y.: Doubleday.

Bell, Daniel. 1960. *The End of Ideology.* Glencoe, Ill.: Free Press.

Berkman, Alexander. 1970. *Prison Memoirs of an Anarchist.* New York: Schocken Books.

Bienan, Henry. 1968. *Violence and Social Change.* Chicago: University of Chicago Press.

Brown, Richard Maxwell. 1969. "The American Vigilante Tradition." In *Violence in America,* ed. Hugh Davis Graham and Ted Robert Gurr. New York: Signet Books.

Brown, Richard Maxwell. 1970. *American Violence.* Englewood Cliffs, N.J.: Prentice-Hall.

Buckley, William F., Jr. 1974. "Dance of the Terrorists." *National Review* 26.

Bugliosi, Vincent. 1964. *Helter Skelter.* New York: Bantam Books.

Burnham, James. 1974. "The Protracted Conflict." *National Review* 26 (March 29).

Camus, Albert. 1956. *The Rebel.* New York: Alfred A. Knopf.

Chandler, Christopher. 1970. "Black Panther Killings in Chicago." *New Republic* 162, no. 2 (January 10).

Coleman, Diane. 1976. "Handling a Touchy Situation." *Emergency Product News* 8, no. 1: 36.

Connery, Robert H. 1969. *Urban Riots.* New York: Vintage Books.

Dahl, Robert A. 1967. *Pluralist Democracy in the United States: Conflict or Consent.* Chicago: Rand McNally.

Dalen, Hendrick van. 1975. "Terror as a Political Weapon." *Military Police Law Enforcement Journal* 2.

Dershowitz, Alan M. 1970. "Terrorism and Preventive Detention: The Case of Israel." *Commentary* 50, no. 6 (December).

Fanon, Frantz. 1967. *Toward the African Revolution (Political Essays).* New York: Grove Press.

Gross, Feliks. 1970. "Political Violence and Terror in 19th Century and 20th Century Russia and Eastern Europe." In *Assassination and Political Violence,* ed. James F. Kirkham, Sheldon G. Levy, and William J. Crotty, New York: Praeger.

Gurr, Ted Robert. 1971. *Why Men Rebel.* Princeton, N.J.: Princeton University Press.

Haak, Ronald O. 1973. *Co-opting the Oppressors: The Case of the Japanese-Americans.* Andover, Mass.: Warner Modular Publications, Reprint 48.

Hayden, Tom. 1970. *The Trial.* New York: Holt, Rinehart & Winston.

Hearings Before the Permanent Subcommittee on Investigation of the Committee on Government Operations (McClellan Committee). 1963. 88th Cong., 1st sess.

Hofstadter, Richard, and Wallace, Michael, eds. 1970. *American Violence: A Documentary History.* New York: Alfred A. Knopf.

Homer, Frederic D. 1974. *Guns and Garlic: Myths and Realities of Organized Crime.* West Lafayette, Ind.: Purdue University Press.

Hook, Sidney. 1964. *The Paradoxes of Freedom.* Berkeley: University of California Press.

Howe, Irving. 1976. "The Ultimate Price of Random Terror." *Skeptic,* no. 2 (January/February).

Hyneman, Charles S. 1968. *Popular Government in America.* New York: Atherton Press.

Kakalik, James S., and Wildhorn, Sorrel. 1972. *Private Police in the United States: Findings and Recommendations.* U.S. Department of Justice, Law Enforcement Assistance Administration.

Kaplan, Abraham. 1964. *The Conduct of Inquiry.* San Francisco: Chandler.

Kempton, Murray. 1971. "Too Late for the Panthers?" In *Government Lawlessness in America,* ed. Theodore L. Becker and Vernon G. Murray. New York: Oxford University Press.

Kirkham, James F., Levy, Sheldon G., and Crotty, William J. 1970. *Assassination and Political Violence.* New York: Praeger.

Kobler, John. 1971. *Capone.* New York: G. P. Putnam's Sons.

Laqueur, Walter. 1976. "Can Terrorism Succeed?" *Skeptic,* no. 2 (January/February).

Lewin, Walter. 1970. "Justice Cops Out." *New Republic* 162, no. 23 (June 6).

Lynd, Staughton, ed. 1966. *Non-Violence in America: A Documentary History.* Indianapolis: Bobbs Merril.

McCartney, John. 1973. *Black Power: Past, Present, and Future.* St. Louis, Mo.: Forum Press.

Marchetti, Victor, and Marks, John D. 1975. *The CIA and the Cult of Intelligence.* New York: Dell.

Marcuse, Herbert. 1964. *One-Dimensional Man: Studies in the Ideology of Advanced Industrial Society.* Boston: Beacon Press.

Messick, Hank. 1971. *Lansky.* New York: G. P. Putnam's Sons.

Mills, C. Wright. 1959. *The Power Elite.* New York: Oxford University Press.

National Commission on the Causes and Prevention of Violence. 1969. *To Establish Justice to Ensure Domestic Tranquility.* New York: Award Books.

Navasky, Victor. 1971. *Kennedy Justice.* New York: Atheneum.

Nieburg, H. L. 1969. *Political Violence: The Behavioral Process.* New York: St. Martin's Press.

"Panama's Torrijos Warns of Violence." 1976. *Rocky Mountain News,* March 8.

Perkus, Cathy. 1975. *CONTELPRO: The FBI's Secret War on Political Freedom.* New York: Monad Press.

"Prairie Fire." 1976. *Skeptic,* no. 2 (January/February).

Puzo, Mario. 1969. *The Godfather.* Greenwich, Conn.: Fawcett Publications.

Report on the National Advisory Commission on Civil Disorders. 1968. New York: New York Times Company.

Schattschneider, E. E. 1960. *The Semi-Sovereign People.* New York: Holt, Rinehart & Winston.

Schumpeter, Joseph A. 1950. *Capitalism, Socialism and Democracy,* 3rd ed. New York: Harper & Row.

Seedman, Albert, and Hellman, Peter. 1974. *Chief!* New York: Avon Books.

Sherrill, Robert. 1973. *The Saturday Night Special.* New York: Penguin Books.

Skolnick, Jerome H. 1969. *The Politics of Protest: A Task Force Report Submitted to the National Commission of the Causes and Prevention of Violence.* New York: Simon & Schuster.

Slater, Leonard, 1970. *The Pledge.* New York: Simon & Schuster.

Steiner, George. 1976. "New Faces of Aggression." *Atlas* 23, no. 1 (January).

Stohl, Michael. 1976. *War and Domestic Political Violence.* Beverly Hills, Calif.: Sage Publications.

Taft, Philip, and Ross, Philip. 1969. "American Labor Violence: Its Causes, Characters and Outcome." In *Violence in America,* ed. Hugh Davis Graham and Ted Robert Gurr. New York: Signet Books.

Tate, Don. 1976. "Law Agencies Braced for Possible Years of Terror." *Rocky Mountain News,* January 25.

Tarkus, Burton B., and Feder, Sid. 1953. *Murder Inc.* London: Victor Gollancz.

Tussman, Joseph. 1960. *Obligation and the Body Politic.* New York: Oxford University Press.

Vizzini, Sal. 1972. *Vizzini.* New York: Pinnacle Books.

Walter, Eugene Victor. 1969. *Terror and Resistance: A Study of Political Violence.* New York: Oxford University Press.

Warren, Robert Penn. 1948. *Night Rider.* New York: Bantam Books.

Wilkinson, Paul. 1973. "Three Questions on Terrorism." *Government and Opposition* 8, no. 3.

Index

A

Action for National Liberation
(ALN), 54, 60, 164, 175,
305
Action Organization for the Liberation of Palestine, 173, 340
Action for the Rebirth of Corsica,
171
Adenauer, Konrad, 231
Adkins, Susan, 377
Africa, sub-Sahara, 259-300
colonial, 262-277
Belgian colonial policy, 267,
269, 273, 274
British colonial policy, 266-
267, 269, 273-274
French colonial policy, 265-
266, 269, 273, 274
minority white-ruled system
in, 274-277
nationalist movements in,
272-274
nature of colonial rule, 265-
272
Portuguese colonial policy, 267,
269, 273-274
terrorism in, 270
effect of European presence in,
261-264
independent black, 277-295
black-ruled political systems,
277-283

[Africa, sub-Sahara]
cabinet ethnic representativeness,
282
case studies of terrorism in, 288-
294
class inequality in, 279-283
conflict behavior in, 284-285
ethnic inequality in, 278-279
political opposition in, 288
regime characteristics, 280-281
terrorism in, 287
Agee, Phillip, 379, 385
Agitational terrorism, 301, 302-307,
320
Aircraft hijackings, 6, 65, 147, 150-152
Al Icab, 344
Al Saiqa, 173
Al-Asifah, 330
Alcohol and Tax Division of the Treasury Department, 397
Alexander III, Czar, 65
Al-Fatah, 173, 178, 330-334, 339, 340
Algeria, 95-110
Ben Bella and, 96-99
bureaucratic arbitrariness, 107-109
depoliticizing the FLN, 101-103
human failures, 104-106
latent and residual terror in, 109-
110
psychological action, 99-100
socialism for the poor, 103-104
Algerian War, 42
Algiers, Battle of, 54